KU-342-979

Praise for SALTFATACIDHEAT

"This beautiful, approachable book not only teaches you how to cook, but captures how it should *feel* to cook: full of exploration, spontaneity, and joy. Samin is one of the great teachers I know, and wins people over to cooking with real food—organic, seasonal, and alive—with her irrepressible enthusiasm and curiosity."

—**Alice Waters**, *New York Times* bestselling author of *The Art of Simple Food*

"Everyone was impressed when Michael Pollan managed to summarise the huge and complex subject of what we should be eating in just seven words: 'Eat food, not too much, mostly plants.' Samin Nosrat has managed to summarise the huge and complex subject of how we should be cooking in just four words: 'salt, fat, acid, heat.' Everyone will be hugely impressed."

—**Yotam Ottolenghi**, *New York Times* bestselling author of *Jerusalem*

"*Salt, Fat, Acid, Heat* is a must for anyone wanting to be a better cook. Samin Nosrat, along with Wendy MacNaughton's fun illustrations, teaches the fundamentals of cooking and dives into the four elements that make food taste great. So do yourself a favour and buy this book. I promise you won't regret it."

—**April Bloomfield**, James Beard Award–winning chef and author of *A Girl and Her Pig*

"Like the amazing meals that come out of Samin Nosrat's kitchen, *Salt, Fat, Acid, Heat* is the perfect mixture of highest-quality ingredients: beautiful storytelling, clear science, an infectious love of food, and Wendy MacNaughton's powerful art. Nosrat's prose combined with MacNaughton's beautiful illustrations are a perfect guide to employing the science of cooking for maximum deliciousness."

—**Rebecca Skloot**, *New York Times* bestselling author of *The Immortal Life of Henrietta Lacks*

"*Salt, Fat, Acid, Heat* is a very important book not because it contains many excellent recipes, although it does, or because it is written by a Chez Panisse alum, although it is. It is important because it gives home cooks a compass with which to navigate their own kitchens, and it places trust in them that they will be able to use that compass. Samin's easygoing, cook-by-feel approach is never condescending or elitist. It is a step towards cooking without recipes and true empowerment (and joy!) in the kitchen."

—**John Becker** and **Megan Scott**, fourth-generation stewards of the *New York Times* bestselling *Joy of Cooking*

"*Salt, Fat, Acid, Heat* is a wildly informative, new-generation culinary resource. Samin Nosrat's wealth of experience comes together here in a pitch-perfect combination of charm, narrative, straight-talk, illustration, and inspiration. Ticking all the boxes for new and seasoned cooks alike, this book meets you wherever you are in the kitchen, in all the right ways."

—**Heidi Swanson**, *New York Times* bestselling author of *Super Natural Cooking*

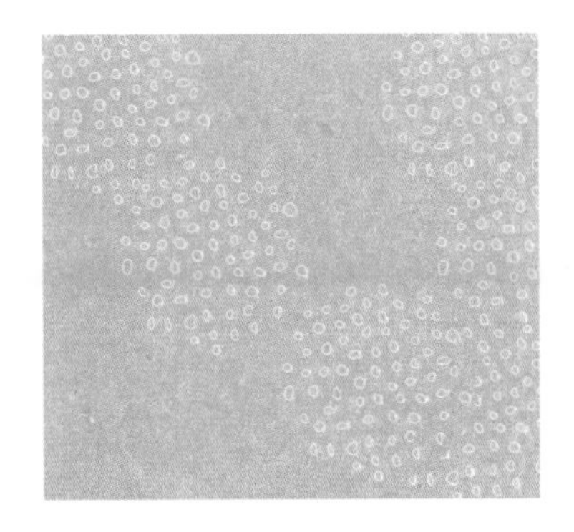
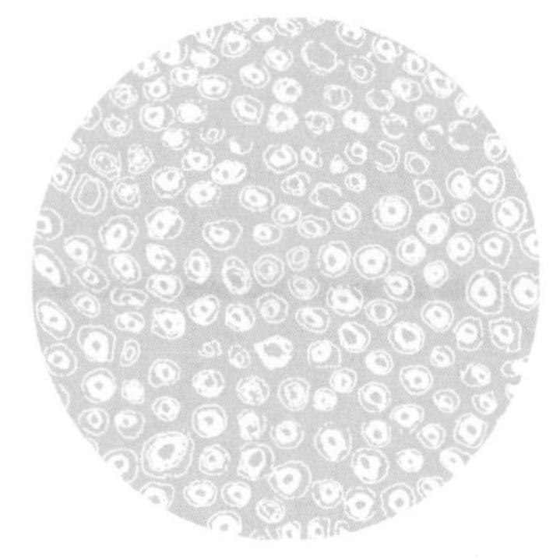

SALT, FAT, ACID, HEAT

Mastering the Elements of Good Cooking

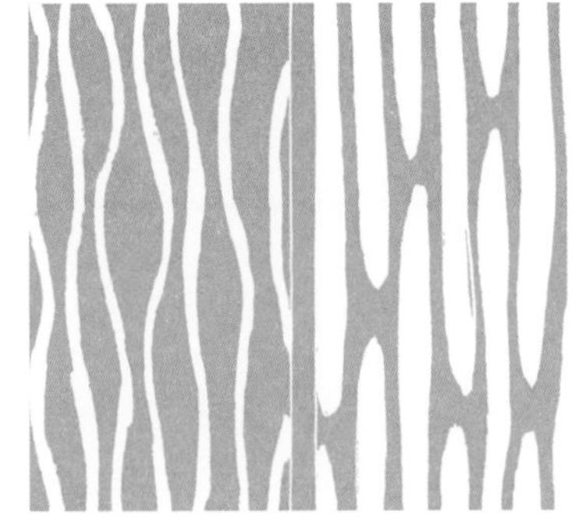

Art by Wendy MacNaughton
Foreword by Michael Pollan

Samin Nosrat

CANONGATE

Published in Great Britain in 2017 by Canongate Books Ltd,
14 High Street, Edinburgh EH1 1TE

canongate.co.uk

10

First published in the USA by Simon & Schuster, 1230 Avenue of the Americas
New York, NY 10020

British Library Cataloguing-in-Publication Data
A catalogue record for this book is available on
request from the British Library

978 1 78211 230 3

Interior design by Alvaro Villanueva

Printed and bound in India by Gopsons Papers Ltd
by arrangement with Associated Agencies Ltd, Oxford

For Alice Waters, who gave me the kitchen,
and for Maman, who gave me the world

Anyone who likes to eat, can soon learn to cook well.

—Jane Grigson

CONTENTS

PART TWO

Recipes and Recommendations

FOREWORD

As I write these words, this book hasn't even been published yet, but already it feels indispensable.

That must sound over-the-top, I know, but I honestly can't remember the last time I read a book on cooking that was this useful or unusual. I suspect that's because reading *Salt, Fat, Acid, Heat* feels less like being in the pages of a cookbook than at a really good cooking school, standing in your apron around the butcher-block island listening as a smart, eloquent, and occasionally hilarious chef demonstrates how to repair a broken mayonnaise. (Add a few drops of water and then "whisk with the urgency of a swimmer escaping a shark.") Now she passes around the bowl of silky, no-longer-broken emulsion so you can dip a tasting spoon and feel it on your tongue. *I get it.*

In *Salt, Fat, Acid, Heat,* Samin Nosrat manages to take us so much deeper and farther into the art of cooking than cookbooks ordinarily do. That's because her book offers so much more than recipes, a literary genre that, while useful, has severe limitations. A well-written and thoroughly tested recipe might tell you how to produce the dish in question, but it won't teach you anything about how to cook, not really. Truth be told, recipes are infantilising: *Just do exactly what I say,* they say, *but don't ask questions or worry your little head about why.* They insist on fidelity and faith, but do nothing to earn or explain it.

Think how much more we learn—and retain!—when a teacher doesn't just enumerate the step-by-step instructions but explains the principles behind them. Armed with reasons, we no longer have to cling to a recipe like a lifeboat; now we can strike out on our own and begin to improvise.

Even though it contains plenty of excellent recipes, this is a book concerned foremost with principles. Samin Nosrat has taken the sprawling, daunting, multicultural subject we call cooking and boldly distilled it to four essential elements—or five, if you count the core principle of tasting along the way. Master these principles, she promises, and you will be able to cook delicious food of any kind, in any tradition, whether a salad dressing or a braise or a galette. Season food with the proper amount of salt at the proper moment;

choose the optimal medium of fat to convey the flavour of your ingredients; balance and animate those ingredients with acid; apply the right type and quantity of heat for the proper amount of time—do all this and you will turn out vibrant and beautiful food, with or without a recipe. It's a big promise, but if you take her course—i.e. read this book—you will find that Samin delivers. Whether you are new to cooking or have decades of experience under your apron, you will understand how to build striking new layers of flavour in whatever you cook.

• • •

Besides being a gifted and deeply experienced cook with years of experience in some of the best kitchens in the Bay Area, Samin is a natural teacher—exacting, inspiring, and eloquent. I happen to know this firsthand, because Samin, who had once been my writing student, became my cooking teacher when I set out to research my book *Cooked*.

We had met a decade earlier, after Samin had written asking if she could audit my graduate class in food journalism at Berkeley. Letting her in was one of the best decisions I've made, not only as a professor of writing but as an eater of food. Samin more than held her own with the journalists in the class, demonstrating the winning voice and surefooted prose now on display in this book, but she really put the rest of us in the shade when it came to snack.

This being a class about food, naturally we ate, taking turns each week bringing in a "storied snack"— some food item or dish that tells a little story, whether about the student's background, project, or passion. We've snacked on baguettes salvaged from a Dumpster; on foraged mushrooms and weeds; and on ethnic foods of every description, but we seldom got to consume more than a bite or two plus the story. Samin served us a whole meal: a sumptuous spinach lasagna made completely from scratch and served on actual plates with linens and silverware, items that had never before crossed the threshold of my classroom. While we ate the best lasagna any of us had ever tasted, Samin told us the story of how she learned to make pasta, mixing the flour and eggs by hand, while in Florence, apprenticed to Benedetta Vitali, one of her most influential teachers. We were all captivated, as much by her storytelling as her cooking.

So years later, when I decided to get serious about cooking, there was no question whom I would ask to teach me. Samin agreed immediately, and so once a month for more than a year, she would come over, usually on a Sunday afternoon, and together we would cook a three-course meal, each one organised around a different theme. Samin would burst into the kitchen with her market bags, apron, and roll of knives, announcing the theme of that day's lesson, which often matched the principles laid out in this book. "Today we're going to learn all about emulsions." (Which she memorably described as "a temporary peace treaty between fat and water.") If meat were on the syllabus, Samin would often stop by or phone the night before, to make sure the roast or chicken was properly seasoned, which is to say early and amply: at least twenty-four hours in advance, with about five times as much salt as your cardiologist would recommend.

The sessions began as one-on-one tutorials, with Samin and me chopping and chatting around the kitchen island, but in time, my wife, Judith, and our son, Isaac, found themselves drawn into the kitchen by the aromas and the laughter emanating from it. It seemed a shame not to share the delicious meals we began turning out more widely, so we began inviting friends to join us for dinner, and in time, our friends began arriving earlier and earlier in the evening and then in the afternoon, so that they might help roll out a piecrust on the kitchen island or turn the crank on the pasta machine as Isaac fed it amber discs of eggy dough.

There is something infectious about Samin's teaching, in the combination of her passion, humour, and patience, but especially in her ability to break the most complex operation down into steps that immediately made sense because she never failed to explain the principle behind them. You salted meat so early to give it time to diffuse into the muscle, where it dissolves strands of proteins into a liquid-retaining gel, thus making for moister meat at the same time it builds flavour from the inside out. Every such step has a little story behind it; and as soon as you know it, the step makes perfect sense and, eventually, it becomes second nature, part of your culinary muscle memory.

Yet as logical and even scientific as Samin can be about the techniques she's imparting, in the end she believes cooking with distinction depends on tasting and smelling—on educating our senses and then learning to trust them. "Taste, taste, and then taste again," she would tell me, even as I did

something as simple and seemingly boring as sautéing an onion. Yet there was an intricate evolution unfolding in that pan as the rectangles of onion went from crisply acidic to clean and sweet to faintly smoky as they caramelised and then bittered slightly as they browned. She showed me how a half dozen distinct flavours could be teased from that single humble ingredient, all depending on how you managed principle number four, heat—and deployed your senses, for each stage in the onion's evolution carried its own distinct and learnable aroma. Now what recipe ever conveyed all that? As Samin likes to say, quoting another of her teachers, "Recipes don't make food taste good. People do."

What I love most about this book is that Samin has somehow found a way (with the help of Wendy MacNaughton's equally inspired and informative illustrations) to bring both her passion for, and intelligence about, cooking to the page. The result is a book that instructs and delights in equal measure (no mean feat in any piece of writing) and one that I predict will soon find its place on the short shelf of books on cooking that you can't imagine living without. You will want to make room for this one.

—Michael Pollan

INTRODUCTION

Anyone can cook anything and make it delicious.

Whether you've never picked up a knife or you're an accomplished chef, there are only four basic factors that determine how good your food will taste: salt, which enhances flavour; fat, which amplifies flavour and makes appealing textures possible; acid, which brightens and balances; and heat, which ultimately determines the texture of food. Salt, Fat, Acid, and Heat are the four cardinal directions of cooking, and this book shows how to use them to find your way in any kitchen.

Have you ever felt lost without a recipe, or envious that some cooks can conjure a meal out of thin air (or an empty refrigerator)? Salt, Fat, Acid, and Heat will guide you as you choose which ingredients to use, how to cook them, and why last-minute adjustments will ensure that food tastes exactly as it should. These four elements are what allow *all* great cooks—whether award-winning chefs or Moroccan grandmothers or masters of molecular gastronomy—to cook consistently delicious food. Commit to mastering them and you will too.

As you discover the secrets of Salt, Fat, Acid, and Heat, you'll find yourself improvising more and more in the kitchen. Liberated from recipes and precise shopping lists, you'll feel comfortable buying what looks best at the farmer's market or butcher's counter, confident in your ability to transform it into a balanced meal. You'll be better equipped to trust your own palate, to make substitutions in recipes, and cook with what's on hand. This book will change the way you *think* about cooking and eating, and help you find your bearings in any kitchen, with any ingredients, while cooking any meal. You'll start using recipes, including the ones in this book, like professional cooks do—for the inspiration, context, and general guidance they offer, rather than by following them to the letter.

I promise this can happen. You can become not only a good cook, but a great one. I know, because it happened to me.

I have spent my entire life in pursuit of flavour.

As a child, I found myself in the kitchen only when Maman enlisted me and my brothers to peel raw broad beans or pick fresh herbs for the traditional Persian meals she served us every night. My parents left Tehran for San Diego on the eve of the Iranian Revolution, shortly before I was born in 1979. I grew up speaking Farsi, celebrating No-Ruz, the Iranian New Year, and attending Persian school to learn how to read and write, but the most delightful aspect of our culture was the food—it brought us together. Rare were the nights when our aunts, uncles, or grandparents didn't join us at the dinner table, which was always filled with plates mounded high with herbs, platters of saffron rice, and fragrant pots of stew. Invariably, I was the one who snagged the darkest, crunchiest pieces of *tahdig*, the golden crust that formed at the bottom of every pot of Persian rice Maman made.

Though I certainly loved to eat, I never imagined I'd become a chef. I graduated from high school with literary ambitions, and moved north to study English literature at UC Berkeley. I remember someone mentioning a famous restaurant in town during my freshman orientation, but the idea of dining there never occurred to me. The only restaurants I'd ever eaten at were the Persian kebab places in Orange County my family trekked to each weekend, the local pizza joint, and fish taco stands at the beach. There were no famous restaurants in San Diego.

Then I fell in love with Johnny, a rosy-cheeked, sparkly-eyed poet who introduced me to the culinary delights of his native San Francisco. He took me to his favourite taqueria, where he taught me how to construct an order for the perfect Mission burrito. Together, we tasted baby coconut and mango ice creams at Mitchell's. We'd sneak up the stairs of Coit Tower late at night to eat our slices of Golden Boy Pizza, watching the city twinkle below. Johnny had always wanted to dine at Chez Panisse but had never had the chance. It turned out that the famous restaurant I'd once heard about was an American institution. We saved up for seven months and navigated a labyrinthine reservation system to secure a table.

When the day finally arrived, we went to the bank and exchanged the shoe box of quarters and dollar bills for two crisp hundred-dollar bills and two twenties, dressed up in our nicest outfits, and zoomed over in his classic convertible VW Beetle, ready to eat.

The meal, of course, was spectacular. We ate *frisée aux lardons*, halibut in broth, and guinea hen with tiny chanterelle mushrooms. I'd never eaten any of those things before.

Dessert was chocolate soufflé. When the server brought it to us, she showed me how to poke a hole in the top with my dessert spoon and then pour in the accompanying raspberry sauce. She watched me take my first bite, and I ecstatically told her it tasted like a warm chocolate cloud. The only thing, in fact, that I could imagine might improve the experience was a glass of cold milk.

What I didn't know, because I was inexperienced in the ways of fancy food, was that for many gourmands the thought of consuming milk after breakfast is childish at best, revolting at worst.

But I was naïve—though I still contend that there's nothing like a glass of cold milk with a warm brownie, at any time of day or night—and in that naïveté, she saw sweetness. The server returned a few minutes later with a glass of cold milk and two glasses of dessert wine, the *refined* accompaniment to our soufflé.

And so began my professional culinary education.

Shortly afterwards, I wrote a letter to Alice Waters, Chez Panisse's legendary owner and chef, detailing our dreamy dinner. Inspired, I asked for a job waiting tables. I'd never considered restaurant work before, but I wanted to be a part of the magic I'd experienced at Chez Panisse that night, even in the smallest way.

When I took the letter to the restaurant along with my résumé, I was led into the office and introduced to the floor manager. We instantly recognised each other: she was the woman who'd brought us the milk and dessert wine. After reading my letter, she hired me on the spot. She asked if I could return the next day for a training shift.

During that shift, I was led through the kitchen into the downstairs dining room, where my first task was to vacuum the floors. The sheer beauty of the kitchen, filled with baskets of ripe figs and lined with gleaming copper walls, mesmerised me. Immediately I fell under the spell of the cooks in spotless white chef's coats, moving with grace and efficiency as they worked.

A few weeks later I was begging the chefs to let me volunteer in the kitchen.

Once I convinced the chefs that my interest in cooking was more than just a dalliance, I was given a kitchen internship and gave up my job as a waitress. I cooked all day and at night I fell asleep reading cookbooks, dreaming of Marcella Hazan's Bolognese sauce and Paula Wolfert's hand-rolled couscous.

Since the menu at Chez Panisse changes daily, each kitchen shift begins with a menu meeting. The cooks sit down with the chef, who details his or her vision for each dish while everyone shells peas or peels garlic. He might talk about his inspiration for the meal—a trip to the coast of Spain, or a story he'd read in the *New Yorker* years ago. She might even detail a few specifics—a particular herb to use, a precise way to slice the carrots, a sketch of the final plate on the back of a scrap of paper—before assigning a dish to each cook.

As an intern, sitting in on menu meetings was inspiring and terror-inducing in equal measure. *Gourmet* magazine had just named Chez Panisse the best restaurant in the country, and I was surrounded by some of the best cooks in the world. Just hearing them *talk* about food was enormously educational. *Daube provençal,* Moroccan *tagine, calçots con romesco, cassoulet toulousain, abbacchio alla romana, maiale al latte*: these were the words of a foreign language. The names of the dishes were enough to send my mind reeling, but the cooks rarely consulted cookbooks. How did they all seem to know how to cook anything the chef could imagine?

I felt like I'd never catch up. I could hardly imagine the day would come when I'd be able to recognise all of the spices in the kitchen's unlabelled jars. I could barely tell cumin and fennel seeds apart, so the thought of getting to a point where I could ever appreciate the nuanced differences between Provençal *bouillabaisse* and Tuscan *cacciucco* (two Mediterranean seafood stews that appeared to be identical) seemed downright impossible.

I asked questions of everyone, every day. I read, cooked, tasted, and also wrote about food, all in an effort to deepen my understanding. I visited farms and farmers' markets and learned my way around their wares. Gradually the chefs gave me more responsibility, from frying tiny, gleaming anchovies for the first course to folding perfect little ravioli for the second to butchering beef for the third. These thrills sustained me as I made innumerable mistakes—some small, such as being sent to retrieve coriander and returning with parsley because I couldn't tell the difference, and some large, like the time I burned the rich beef sauce for a dinner we hosted for the First Lady.

As I improved, I began to detect the nuances that distinguish good food from great. I started to discern individual components in a dish, understanding when the pasta water and not the sauce needed more salt, or when an herb salsa needed more vinegar to balance a rich, sweet lamb stew. I started to see some basic patterns in the seemingly impenetrable maze of daily-changing, seasonal menus. Tough cuts of meat were salted the night before, while delicate fish fillets were seasoned at the time of cooking. Oil for frying had to be hot—otherwise the food would end up soggy—while butter for tart dough had to remain cold, so that the crust would crisp up and become flaky. A squeeze of lemon or splash of vinegar could improve almost every salad, soup, and braise. Certain cuts of meat were always grilled, while others were always braised.

Salt, Fat, Acid, and Heat were the four elements that guided basic decision making in every single dish, no matter what. The rest was just a combination of cultural, seasonal, or technical details, for which we could consult cookbooks and experts, histories, and maps. It was a revelation.

The idea of making consistently great food had seemed like some inscrutable mystery, but now I had a little mental checklist to think about every time I set foot in a kitchen: Salt, Fat, Acid, Heat. I mentioned the theory to one of the chefs. He smiled at me, as if to say, "Duh. Everyone knows that."

But everyone *didn't* know that. I'd never heard or read it anywhere, and certainly no one had ever explicitly related the idea to me. Once I understood it, and once it had been confirmed by a professional chef, it seemed inconceivable that no one had ever framed things in this way for people interested in learning how to cook. I decided then I'd write a book elucidating the revelation for other amateur cooks.

I picked up a legal pad and started writing. That was seventeen years ago. At twenty years old, I'd been cooking for only a year. I quickly realised I still had a lot to learn about both food and writing before I could begin to instruct anyone else. I set the book aside. As I kept reading, writing, and cooking, I filtered everything I learned through my newfound understanding of Salt, Fat, Acid, and Heat into a tidy system of culinary thinking.

Like a scholar in search of primary sources, a desire to experience authentic versions of the dishes I loved so much at Chez Panisse took me to Italy. In Florence, I apprenticed myself to the groundbreaking Tuscan chef Benedetta Vitali at her restaurant, Zibibbo. At first it was a constant challenge to work in an unfamiliar kitchen where I barely spoke the language, where temperatures were measured in Celsius, and where measurements were metric. But my understanding of Salt, Fat, Acid, and Heat quickly gave me my bearings. I might not have known all of the specifics, but the way Benedetta taught me to brown meat for *ragù*, heat olive oil for sautéing, season the pasta water, and use lemon juice as a foil for rich flavours echoed what I had learned back in California.

I spent my days off in the hills of Chianti with Dario Cecchini, an eighth-generation butcher with a huge personality and an even bigger heart. Dario took me under his wing, teaching me about whole-animal butchery and Tuscan food heritage with equal vigour. He took me all over the region to meet farmers, vintners, bakers, and cheese makers. From them, I learned how geography, the seasons, and history have shaped Tuscan cooking philosophy over the course of centuries: fresh, if modest, ingredients, when treated with care, can deliver the deepest flavours.

My pursuit of flavour has continued to lead me around the world. Fuelled by curiosity, I've sampled my way through the oldest pickle shop in China, observed the nuanced regional differences of lentil dishes in Pakistan, experienced the way a complicated political history has diluted flavours in Cuban kitchens by restricting access to ingredients, and compared varieties of heirloom corn in Mexican tortillas. When unable to travel, I have read extensively, interviewed immigrant grandmothers, and tasted their traditional cooking. No matter my circumstances or whereabouts, as reliably as the points on a compass, Salt, Fat, Acid, and Heat have set me on the path to good food every time I cook.

I returned to Berkeley and went to work for Christopher Lee, my mentor at Chez Panisse, who'd recently opened his own Italian restaurant, Eccolo. I quickly took the role of *chef de cuisine*. I made it my job to develop exquisite familiarity with the way an ingredient or a food behaved and then follow the crumb trail of kitchen science to understand *why*. Instead of simply telling the cooks under my watch to "taste everything," I could really teach them *how* to make better decisions. A decade after I first discovered my theory of Salt, Fat, Acid, and Heat, I'd gathered enough information to begin teaching the system to my own young cooks.

Seeing how useful the lessons of Salt, Fat, Acid, and Heat had been for professional cooks, I used them as a rubric when my journalism teacher, Michael Pollan, hired me to teach him how to cook while writing *Cooked*, his book about the natural history of cooking. Michael quickly noticed my obsession with the four elements of good cooking and encouraged me to formalise the curriculum and begin teaching it to others. So I did. I've taught the system in cooking schools, senior centres, middle schools, and community centres. Whether the foods we cooked together were inspired by Mexican, Italian, French, Persian, Indian, or Japanese traditions, without exception, I've seen my students gain confidence, prioritise flavour, and learn to make better decisions in the kitchen, improving the quality of everything they cook.

Fifteen years after arriving at the idea for this book, I began to write in earnest. After first immersing myself in the lessons of Salt, Fat, Acid, and Heat, and then spending years teaching them to others, I've distilled the elements of good cooking into its essence. Learn to navigate Salt, Fat, Acid, and Heat, and you can make anything taste good. Keep reading, and I'll teach you how.

HOW TO USE THIS BOOK

As you can probably tell, this isn't your typical cookbook.

I recommend that you start by reading it through from beginning to end. Pay attention to the techniques, the science, and stories, but don't worry too much about committing it all to memory. Come back again later to revisit the concepts that are relevant to *you*. Readers who are new to the kitchen will quickly catch on to the basics—each element is organised by its flavour and its science, guiding you through both the *whys* and the *hows* of good cooking. More experienced cooks will find *aha!* gems buried throughout and even see cooking tricks you already know with fresh eyes.

Throughout each chapter, I've suggested a handful of kitchen experiments—essentially, recipes that will illustrate some of the major concepts and give you a chance to put theory into practice.

And at the back of the book, I've compiled a canon of recipes to illustrate just how far a grasp of Salt, Fat, Acid, and Heat will take you. Over time, you'll grow comfortable enough to cook *without* recipes on a daily basis. But when learning to cook intuitively, recipes can be necessary and comforting, like training wheels.

To underscore the patterns that guide all good cooking, I've organised the recipe section by type of dish, rather than by the particular course in the meal. With the help of the brilliant and hilarious illustrator, Wendy MacNaughton, I've created a variety of visual guides to help convey concepts where words aren't enough. The choice to embellish this book with illustrations rather than photographs was deliberate. Let it liberate you from feeling that there's only one perfect version of every dish. Let it encourage you to improvise, and judge what good food looks like on your own terms.

If jumping straight into the recipes after reading through the book seems overwhelming, take a look at the **Cooking Lessons**, which will steer you to recipes that will help you hone particular skills and master specific techniques. If you feel unsure of how to put together dishes to create a menu, use the list of **Suggested Menus** as a guide.

Finally, remember to have fun! Don't forget to enjoy the pleasures, both small and large, implicit to cooking and eating with people you love!

PART ONE

THE FOUR ELEMENTS of GOOD COOKING

SALT

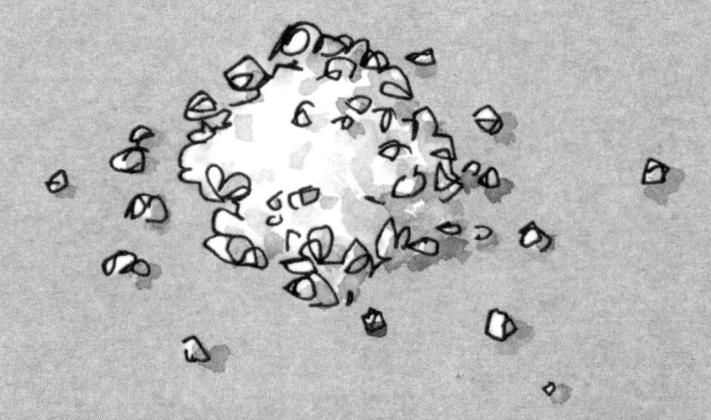

Growing up, I thought salt belonged in a shaker at the table, and nowhere else. I never added it to food, or saw Maman add it to food. When my aunt Ziba, who had a well-documented taste for salt, sprinkled it onto her saffron rice at the table each night, my brothers and I giggled. We thought it was the strangest, funniest thing in the world. "What on earth," I wondered, "can salt do for food?"

I associated salt with the beach, where I spent my childhood seasoned with it. There were the endless hours in the Pacific, swallowing mouthful after mouthful of ocean water when I misjudged the waves. Tidepooling at twilight, my friends and I often fell victim to the saltwater spray while we poked at anemones. And my brothers, chasing me on the sand with giant kelp, would tickle and taunt me with its salty, otherworldly tassels whenever they caught up to me.

Maman always kept our swimsuits in the back of our blue Volvo station wagon, because the beach was always where we wanted to be. She was deft with the umbrella and blankets, setting them up while she shooed the three of us into the sea.

We'd stay in the water until we were starving, scanning the beach for the sun-faded coral-and-white umbrella, the only landmark that would lead us back to Maman. Wiping saltwater from our eyes, we beelined to her.

Somehow, Maman always knew exactly what would taste best when we emerged: Persian cucumbers topped with sheep's milk feta cheese rolled together in lavash bread. We chased the sandwiches with handfuls of ice-cold grapes or wedges of watermelon to quench our thirst.

That snack, eaten while my curls dripped with seawater and salt crust formed on my skin, always tasted *so good*. Without a doubt, the pleasures of the beach added to the magic of the experience, but it wasn't until many years later, working at Chez Panisse, that I understood why those bites had been so perfect from a culinary point of view.

While waiting tables during the first year I worked at Chez Panisse, the closest I usually got to the food was at tasters, when the cooks made each dish for the chef to critique before service. With a menu that changed daily, the chef needed tasters to ensure that his or her vision was realised. Everything had to be just right. The cooks would tinker and adjust until satisfied; then they'd hand over the dishes to the floor staff to taste. On the tiny back porch, a dozen of us would hover over the plates, passing them around until we'd all had a bite of everything. It was there that I first tasted crisp deep-fried quail, tender salmon grilled in a fig leaf, and buttermilk panna cotta with fragrant wild strawberries. Often, the powerful flavours would haunt me throughout my shift.

Once I developed culinary aspirations, Chris Lee, the chef who'd eventually take me under his wing, suggested that I pay less attention to what was happening on the porch during tasters, and more to what was happening in the kitchen. The language the chefs used, how they knew when something was right—these were clues about how to become a better cook. Most often, when a dish fell flat, the answer lay in adjusting the salt. Sometimes it was in the form of salt crystals, but other times it meant a grating of cheese, some pounded anchovies, a few olives, or a sprinkling of capers. I began to see that there is no better guide in the kitchen than thoughtful tasting, and that nothing is more important to taste thoughtfully for than salt.

One day the following year, as a young cook in the prep kitchen, I was tasked with cooking polenta. I'd tasted polenta only once before coming to Chez Panisse, and I wasn't a fan. Precooked and wrapped in plastic like a roll of cookie dough, it was flavourless. But I'd promised myself that I would try everything at the restaurant at least once, and when I tasted polenta for the second time, I couldn't believe that something so creamy and complex could share a name with that flavourless tube of astronaut food. Milled from an heirloom variety of corn, each bite of the polenta at Chez Panisse tasted of sweetness and earth. I couldn't wait to cook some myself.

Once the chef, Cal Peternell, talked me through the steps of making the polenta, I began cooking. Consumed by the fear of scorching and ruining the entire humongous pot—a mistake I had seen other cooks make—I stirred maniacally.

After an hour and a half, I'd added in butter and Parmesan, just as Cal had instructed me. I brought him a spoonful of the creamy porridge to taste. At six foot four, Cal is a gentle giant with sandy-blond hair and the driest of wits. I looked expectantly up at him with equal parts respect and terror. He said, in his signature deadpan, "It needs more salt." Dutifully, I returned to the pot and sprinkled in a few grains of salt, treating them with the preciousness I might afford, say, gold leaf. I thought it tasted pretty good, so I returned to Cal with a spoonful of my newly adjusted polenta.

Again, a moment's consideration was all he needed to know the seasoning was off. But now—to save himself the trouble and time, I imagine—he marched me back to the pot and added not one but three enormous palmfuls of kosher salt.

The perfectionist in me was horrified. I had wanted so badly to do that polenta justice! The degree to which I'd been off was exponential. Three *palmfuls*!

Cal grabbed spoons and together we tasted. Some indescribable transformation had occurred. The corn was somehow sweeter, the butter richer. All of the flavours were more pronounced. I'd been certain Cal had ruined the pot and turned my polenta into a salt lick, but no matter how I tried, the word *salty* did not apply to what I tasted. All I felt was a satisfying *zing!* with each mouthful.

It was as if I'd been struck by lightning. It'd never occurred to me that salt was anything more than pepper's sidekick. But now, having experienced the transformative power of salt for myself, I wanted to learn how to get that *zing!* every time I cooked. I thought about all of the foods I'd loved to eat growing up—and that bite of seaside cucumber and feta, in particular. I realised then why it had tasted so good. It was properly seasoned, with salt.

WHAT IS SALT?

The secret behind that *zing!* can be explained by some basic chemistry. Salt is a mineral: sodium chloride. It's one of several dozen essential nutrients without which we cannot survive. The human body can't store much salt, so we need to consume it regularly in order to be able to carry out basic biological processes, such as maintaining proper blood pressure and water distribution in the body, delivering nutrients to and from cells, nerve transmission, and muscle movement. In fact, we're hardwired to crave salt to ensure we get enough of it. The lucky consequence of this is that salt makes almost everything taste better to us, so it's hardly a chore to add it to our food. In fact, by enhancing flavour, salt increases the pleasure we experience as we eat.

All salt comes from the ocean, be it the Atlantic or a long-forgotten sea like the giant prehistoric Lake Minchin of Bolivia, home of the earth's largest salt flat. Salt that is left behind when seawater evaporates is *sea salt*, whereas *rock salt* is mined from ancient lakes and seas, some of which now lie far underground.

The primary role that salt plays in cooking is to amplify flavour. Though salt also affects texture and helps modify other flavours, nearly every decision you'll make about salt will involve enhancing and deepening flavour.

Does this mean you should simply use *more* salt? No. It means use salt *better*. Add it in the right amount, at the right time, in the right form. A smaller amount of salt applied while cooking will often do more to improve flavour than a larger amount added at the table. And unless you have been specifically told by your doctor to limit your salt consumption, you can relax about your sodium intake from homecooked food. When students balk at the palmfuls of salt I add to pots of water for boiling vegetables, I gently point out that most of the salt will end up going down the drain with the cooking water. In almost every case, anything you cook for yourself at home is more nutritious, and lower in sodium, than processed, prepared, or restaurant food.

SALT AND FLAVOUR

James Beard, the father of modern American cookery, once asked, "Where would we be without salt?" I know the answer: adrift in a sea of blandness. If only one lesson from this book stays with you, let it be this: *Salt has a greater impact on flavour than any other ingredient.* Learn to use it well, and your food will taste good.

Salt's relationship to flavour is multidimensional: it has its *own* particular taste, and it enhances the flavour of *other* ingredients. Used properly, salt minimises bitterness, balances out sweetness, and enhances aromas, heightening our experience of eating. Imagine taking a bite of a rich espresso brownie sprinkled with flaky sea salt. Besides providing the delightful experience of its delicate flakes crunching on the tongue, the salt minimises the espresso's bitterness, intensifies the flavour of the chocolate, and offers a welcome savoury contrast to the sugar's sweetness.

The Flavour of Salt

Salt should taste clean, free of any unpleasant flavours. Start by tasting it all on its own. Dip your finger into your salt cellar and let a few grains dissolve on your tongue. What do they taste like? Hopefully like the summer sea.

Types of Salt

Chefs all have their saline allegiances and will offer lengthy, impassioned arguments about why one variety of salt is superior to another. But honestly, what matters most is that you're familiar with whichever salt *you* use. Is it coarse or fine? How long does it take to dissolve in a pot of boiling water? How much does it take to make a roast chicken taste just right? If you add your salt to a batch of cookie dough, will it melt away or make itself known, announcing its presence with a pleasant crunch?

Though all salt crystals are produced by evaporating water from saltwater brine, the pace of evaporation will determine the shape those crystals take. Rock salts are mined by flooding salt deposits with water and then rapidly evaporating that water from the resulting brine. Refined sea salt is similarly produced through the rapid evaporation of seawater. When formed as a result of rapid evaporation in a closed container, salt crystals become small, dense cubes—granular salt. On the other hand, salt produced slowly through solar methods at the surface of an open container will crystallise into light, hollow flakes. If water splashes into the hollow of the flake before it's scooped off the surface, it will sink into the brine and transform into a large, dense crystal. This is unrefined, or minimally processed, sea salt.

These varying shapes and sizes can make a big difference in your cooking. A tablespoon of fine salt will pack more tightly, and can be two or three times "saltier" than a tablespoon of coarser salt. This is why it makes sense to measure salts by weight rather than by volume. Better yet, learn to salt to taste.

Table Salt

Common table salt, or granular salt, is found in salt shakers everywhere. Shake some out into your palm and its distinct cubic shape—the result of crystallising in a closed vacuum chamber—will be apparent. Table salt is small and dense, making it very salty. Unless otherwise noted, iodine has been added to it.

I don't recommend using iodised salt as it makes everything taste slightly metallic. In 1924, when iodine deficiency was a common health problem, Morton Salt began iodising salt to help prevent goitres, leading to great strides in public health. These days, we can get sufficient amounts of iodine from natural sources. As long as your diet is diverse and full of iodine-rich foods such as seafood and dairy, there's no need to suffer through metallic-tasting food.

Table salt also often contains anticaking agents to prevent clumps from forming, or dextrose, a form of sugar, to stabilise the iodine. Though neither of these additives is harmful, there's no reason to add them to your food. The only thing you should be adding to your food when you're salting it is salt! This is one of the few times I'll insist on anything in this book: if you've got only table salt at home, go get yourself some kosher or sea salt right away.

Several Salt Structures

Kosher Salt

Kosher salt is traditionally used in koshering, the traditional Jewish process by which blood is removed from meat. Since kosher salt contains no additives, it tastes very pure. There are two major producers of kosher salt: Diamond Crystal, which crystallises in an open container of brine, yielding light and hollow flakes; and Morton's, which is made by rolling cubic crystals of vacuum-evaporated salt into thin, dense flakes. The difference in production methods yields two vastly different salts. While Diamond Crystal readily adheres to foods and crumbles easily, Morton's is much denser, and almost twice as salty by volume. When following recipes requiring kosher salt, make sure to use the specified brand because these two salts are not interchangeable! For this book, I tested all the recipes with Diamond Crystal, which comes in a red box and is widely available online but sea salt can be used as an alternative.

Diamond Crystal dissolves about twice as quickly as denser granulated salt, making it ideal for use in food that is cooked quickly. The more quickly salt dissolves, the less likely you are to overseason a dish, thinking it needs more salt when actually the salt just needs more time to dissolve. Because of its increased surface area, Diamond Crystal also sticks to foods better, rather than rebounding or falling off.

Inexpensive and rather forgiving, kosher salt is fantastic for everyday cooking. I prefer Diamond Crystal—even when I've accidentally salted dishes twice with this salt while enjoying a little too much my conversation, the company, or a glass of wine, the food has emerged unscathed.

Sea Salt

Sea salt is what's left behind when seawater evaporates. Natural sea salts such as *fleur de sel*, *sel gris*, and Maldon are the less-refined result of gradual, monitored evaporation that can take up to five years. Taking the shape of delicate, distinctly aromatic flakes, *fleur de sel*—literally, "flower of salt"—is harvested from the surface of special sea salt beds in western France. When it falls below the surface of the water and attracts various sea minerals, including magnesium chloride and calcium sulphate, pure white *fleur de sel* takes on a greyish hue and becomes *sel gris*, or grey salt. Maldon salt crystals, formed much like *fleur de sel*, take on a hollow pyramid shape, and are often referred to as *flaky salt*.

Because natural salts are harvested using low-yield, labour-intensive methods, they tend to be more expensive than refined sea salts. Most of what you're paying for when you buy these salts is their delightful texture, so use them in ways that allow them to stand out. It's a waste to season pasta water with *fleur de sel* or make tomato sauce with Maldon salt. Instead, sprinkle these salts atop delicate garden lettuces, rich caramel sauces, and chocolate chip cookies as they go into the oven so you can enjoy the way they crunch in your mouth.

The refined granular sea salt you might find at the grocery store is a bit different: it was produced by rapidly boiling down ocean water in a closed vacuum. Fine or medium-size crystals of this type are ideal for everyday cooking. Use this type of sea salt to season foods from within—in water for boiling vegetables or pasta, on roasts and stew meats, tossed with vegetables, and in doughs or batters.

Keep two kinds of salt on hand: an inexpensive one such as sea salt or kosher salt for everyday cooking, and a special salt with a pleasant texture, such as Maldon salt or *fleur de sel*, for garnishing food at the last moment. Whichever salts you use, become familiar with them—with how salty they are, and how they taste, feel, and affect the flavour of the foods to which you add them.

Salt's Effect on Flavour

To understand how salt affects flavour, we must first understand what flavour is. Our taste buds can perceive five **tastes**: saltiness, sourness, bitterness, sweetness, and umami, or savouriness. On the other hand, **aroma** involves our noses sensing any of thousands of various chemical compounds. The descriptive words often used to characterise the way a wine smells, such as *earthy*, *fruity*, and *floral*, refer to aroma compounds.

Flavour lies at the intersection of taste, aroma, and sensory elements including texture, sound, appearance, and temperature. Since aroma is a crucial element of flavour, the more aromas you perceive, the more vibrant your eating experience will be. This is why you take less pleasure in eating while you're congested or have a cold.

Remarkably, salt affects both taste *and* flavour. Our taste buds can discern whether or not salt is present, and in what amount. But salt also unlocks many aromatic compounds in foods, making them more readily available as we eat. The simplest way to experience this is to taste an unsalted soup or broth. Try it next time you make **Chicken Stock**. The unseasoned broth will taste flat, but as you add salt, you'll detect new aromas that were previously unavailable. Keep salting, and tasting, and you'll start to sense the salt as well as more complex and delightful flavours: the savouriness of the chicken, the richness of the chicken fat, the earthiness of the celery and the thyme. Keep adding salt, and tasting, until you get that *zing!* This is how you'll learn to salt "to taste." When a recipe says "season to taste," add enough salt until it tastes right to you.

This flavour "unlocking" is also one reason why professional cooks like to season sliced tomatoes a few minutes before serving them—so that, as salt helps the flavour molecules that are bound up within the tomato proteins, each bite will taste more intensely of tomato.

Salt also reduces our perception of bitterness, with the secondary effect of emphasising other flavours present in bitter dishes. Salt enhances sweetness while reducing bitterness in foods that are both bitter *and* sweet, such as bittersweet chocolate, coffee ice cream, or burnt caramels.

Though we typically turn to sugar to balance out bitter flavours in a sauce or soup, it turns out that salt masks bitterness much more effectively than sugar. See for yourself with a little tonic water, Campari, or grapefruit juice, all of which are both bitter *and* sweet. Taste a spoonful, then add a pinch of salt and taste again. You'll be surprised by how much bitterness subsides.

Seasoning

Anything that heightens flavour is a **seasoning**, but the term generally refers to salt since it's the most powerful flavour enhancer and modifier. If food isn't salted properly, no amount of fancy cooking techniques or garnishes will make up for it. Without salt, unpleasant tastes are more perceptible and pleasant ones less so. Though in general the absence of salt in food is deeply regrettable, its overt presence is equally unwelcome: food shouldn't be *salty*, it should be *salted*.

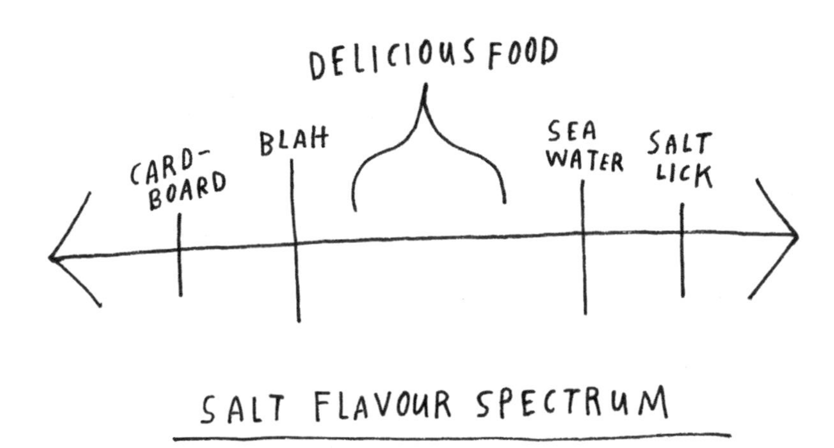

Salting isn't something to do once and then check off your list; be constantly aware of how a dish tastes *as it cooks*, and how you want it to taste at the table. At San Francisco's legendary Zuni Café, chef Judy Rodgers often told her cooks that a dish might need "seven more grains of salt." Sometimes it really is that subtle; just seven grains can mean the difference between satisfactory and sublime. Other times, your polenta might require a handful. The only way to know is to taste and adjust.

Tasting and adjusting—over and over again as you add ingredients and they transform throughout the cooking process—will yield the most flavourful food. Getting the seasoning right is about getting it right at every level—bite, component, dish, and meal. This is **seasoning food from within**.

On the global spectrum of salt use, there's a range, rather than a single point, of proper seasoning. Some cultures use less salt; others use more. Tuscans don't add salt to their bread but more than make up for it with the copious handfuls they add to everything else. The French salt baguettes and *pain au levain* perfectly, in turn seasoning everything else a little more conservatively.

In Japan, steamed rice is left unseasoned to act as the foil for the flavourful fishes, meats, curries, and pickles served alongside it. In India, *biryani*, a flavourful rice dish layered with vegetables, meat, spices, and eggs, is never left unsalted. There is no universal rule other than that salt use must be carefully considered at every point in the cooking process. This is seasoning to taste.

When food tastes flat, the most common culprit is underseasoning. If you're not sure salt will fix the problem, take a spoonful or small bite and sprinkle it with a little salt, then taste again. If something shifts and you sense the *zing!*, then go ahead and add salt to the entire batch. Your palate will become more discerning with this sort of thoughtful cooking and tasting. Like a jazz musician's ear, with use it will grow more sensitive, more refined, and more skilled at improvisation.

HOW SALT WORKS

Cooking is part artistry, part chemistry. Understanding how salt works will allow you to make better decisions about *how* and *when* to use it to improve texture and season food from within. Some ingredients and cooking methods require giving salt enough time to penetrate food and distribute itself within it. In other cases, the key is to create a cooking environment salty enough to allow food to absorb the right amount of salt as it cooks.

The distribution of salt throughout food can be explained by **osmosis** and **diffusion**, two chemical processes powered by nature's tendency to seek equilibrium, or the balanced concentration of solutes such as minerals and sugars on either side of a semipermeable membrane (or holey cell wall). In food, the movement of water across a cell wall from the less salty side to the saltier side is called **osmosis**.

Diffusion, on the other hand, is the often slower process of salt moving from a saltier environment to a less salty one until it's evenly distributed throughout. Sprinkle salt on the surface of a piece of chicken

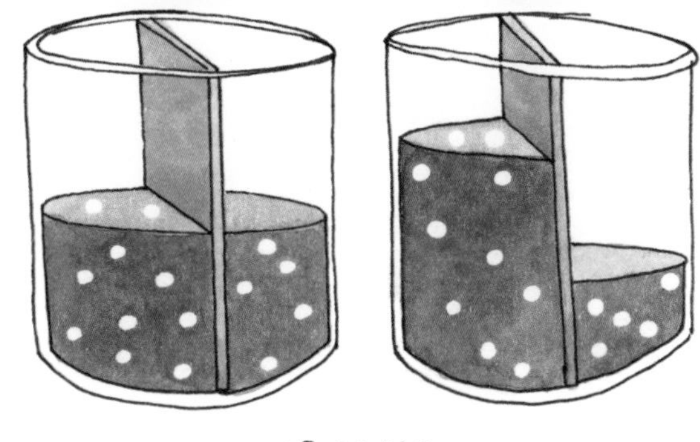

OSMOSIS

THE MOVEMENT of WATER IN and OUT of A CELL WALL

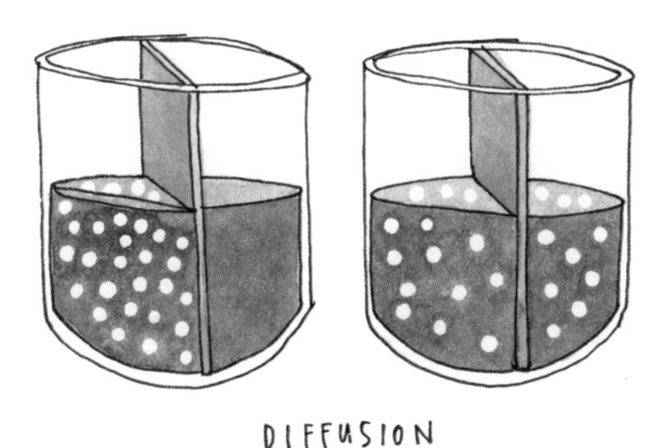

DIFFUSION

THE MOVEMENT of SALT THROUGH A CELL WALL UNTIL IT'S EVENLY DISTRIBUTED and come back twenty minutes later. The distinct grains will no longer be visible: they will have started to dissolve, and the salt will have begun to move inward in an effort to create a chemical balance throughout the piece of meat. We can taste the consequence of this diffusion—though we sprinkle salt on the surface of the meat, with the distribution that occurs over time, eventually the meat will taste evenly seasoned, rather than being salty on the surface and bland within.

Water will also be visible on the surface of the chicken, the result of osmosis. While the salt moves *in*, the water will move *out* with the same goal: achieving chemical balance throughout the entire piece of meat.

Given the chance, salt will always distribute itself evenly to season food from within, but it affects the textures of different foods in different ways.

How Salt Affects . . .

Meat

By the time I arrived at Chez Panisse, the kitchen had already been running like a well-oiled machine for decades. Its success relied on each cook thinking ahead to the following day's menu and beyond. Every day, without fail, we butchered and seasoned meat for the following day. Since this task was a classic example of kitchen efficiency, it didn't occur to me that seasoning the meat in advance had anything to do with flavour. That was only because I didn't yet understand the important work salt was quietly doing overnight.

Since diffusion is a slow process, **seasoning in advance** gives salt plenty of time to diffuse evenly throughout meat. This is how to season meat from within. A small amount of salt applied in advance will make a much bigger difference than a larger amount applied just before serving. In other words, time, not amount, is the crucial variable.

Because salt also initiates osmosis, and visibly draws water out of nearly any ingredient it touches, many people believe that salt dries and toughens food. But with time, salt will dissolve protein strands into a gel, allowing them to absorb and retain water better as they cook. Water is moisture: its presence makes meat tender and juicy.

Think of a protein strand as a loose coil with water molecules bound to its outside surface. When an unseasoned protein is heated, it **denatures**: the coil tightens, squeezing water molecules out of the protein matrix, leaving the meat dry and tough if overcooked. By disrupting protein structure, salt prevents the coil from densely **coagulating**, or clumping, when heated, so more of the water molecules remain bound. The piece of meat remains moister, and you have a greater margin of error for overcooking.

This same chemical process is the secret to brining, the method in which a piece of meat is submerged in a bath of water spiked with salt, sugar, and spices. The salt in this mixture, or **brine**, dissolves some of the proteins, while the sugar and spices offer plenty of aromatic molecules for the meat to absorb. For this reason, brining can be a great strategy for lean meats and poultry, which tend to be dry and even bland. Make **Spicy Brined Turkey Breast**, and you'll see how a night spent in a salty, spicy bath will transform a cut of meat that's often devastatingly dry and flavourless.

I can't remember the first time I tasted—consciously, anyway—meat that had been salted in advance. But now I can tell every time I taste meat that hasn't. I've cooked thousands of chickens—presalted and not—over the years, and while science has yet to confirm my suspicions, I'll speak from experience here: meat that's been salted in advance is not only more flavourful, it's also more tender, than meat that hasn't. The best way to experience the marvels of preseasoned meat for yourself is with a little experiment: the next time you plan to roast a chicken, cut the bird in half, or ask your butcher to do so for you. Season one half with salt a day ahead. Season the other half just before cooking. The effects of early salting will be apparent long before the first bite hits your tongue. The chicken salted in advance will fall off the bone as you begin to butcher it, while the other half, though moist, won't begin to compare in tenderness.

When salting meat for cooking, any time is better than none, and more is better than some. Aim to season meat the day before cooking when possible. Failing that, do it in the morning, or even in the afternoon. Or make it the first thing you do when collecting ingredients for dinner. I like to do it as soon as I get home from the grocery store, so I don't have to think about it again.

The larger, denser, or more sinewy the piece of meat, the earlier you should salt it. Oxtails, shanks, and short ribs can be seasoned a day or two in advance to allow salt time to do its work. A chicken for roasting can be salted the day before cooking, while Thanksgiving turkey should be seasoned two, or even three, days in advance. The colder the meat and surrounding environment are, the longer it will take the salt to do its work, so when time is limited, leave meat on the worktop once you season it (but for no longer than two hours), rather than returning it to the fridge.

Though salting early is a great boon to flavour and texture in meat, there is such a thing as salting *too* early. For thousands of years, salt has been used to preserve meat. In large enough quantities, for long enough periods of time, salt will dehydrate meat and cure it. If dinner plans change at the last minute, a salted chicken or a few pounds of short ribs will happily wait a day or two to be roasted or braised. But wait much longer than that, and they will dry out and develop a leathery texture and a cured, rather than fresh, flavour. If you've salted some meat but realise you won't be able to get to it for several days, freeze it until you're ready to cook it. Tightly wrapped, it'll keep for up to two months. Simply defrost and pick up cooking where you left off.

Seafood

Unlike meat, the delicate proteins of most fish and shellfish will degrade when salted too early, yielding a tough, dry, or chewy result. A brief salting—about fifteen minutes—is plenty to enhance flavour and maintain moisture in flaky fish. 2.5cm -thick steaks of meatier fish, such as tuna and swordfish, can be salted up to thirty minutes ahead. Season all other seafood at the time of cooking to preserve textural integrity.

Fat

Salt requires water to dissolve, so it won't dissolve in pure fat. Luckily, most of the fats we use in the kitchen contain at least a little water—the small amounts of water in butter, lemon juice in a mayonnaise, or vinegar in a vinaigrette allow salt to slowly dissolve. Season these fats early and carefully, waiting for salt to dissolve and tasting before adding more. Or, dissolve salt in water, vinegar, or lemon juice before adding it to fat for even, immediate distribution. Lean meat has a slightly higher water (and protein) content—and thus, greater capacity for salt absorption—than fattier cuts of meat, so cuts with a big fat cap, such as pork loin or rib eye, will not absorb salt evenly. This is illustrated beautifully in a slice of prosciutto: the lean muscle (rosy pink part) has a higher water content, and thus can absorb salt readily as it cures. The fat (pure white part), on the other hand, has a much lower water content, and so it doesn't absorb salt at the same rate. Taste the two parts separately and you'll find the lean muscle unpleasantly salty. The strip of fat will seem almost bland. But taste them together and the synergy of fat and salt will be revealed. Don't let this absorption imbalance affect how you season a fatty cut. Simply taste both fat and lean meat before adding more salt at the table.

Eggs

Eggs absorb salt easily. As they do, it helps their proteins come together at a lower temperature, which decreases cooking time. The more quickly the proteins set, the less of a chance they will have to expel water they contain. The more water the eggs retain as they cook, the more moist and tender their final texture will be. Add a pinch of salt to eggs destined for scrambling, omelettes, custards, or frittatas before cooking. Lightly season water for poaching eggs. Season eggs cooked in the shell or fried in a pan just before serving.

Vegetables, Fruits, and Fungi

Most vegetables and fruit cells contain an undigestible carbohydrate called **pectin**. Soften the pectin through ripening or applying heat, and you will soften the fruit or vegetable, making it more tender, and often more delicious, to eat. Salt assists in weakening pectin.

When in doubt, salt vegetables before you cook them. Toss vegetables with salt and olive oil for roasting. Salt blanching water generously before adding vegetables. Add salt into the pan along with the vegetables for sautéing. Season vegetables with large, watery cells—tomatoes, courgettes, and aubergines, for example—in advance of grilling or roasting to allow salt the time to do its work. During this time, osmosis will also cause some water loss, so pat the vegetables dry before cooking. Because salt will continue to draw water out of vegetables and fruits and eventually make them rubbery, be wary of salting them *too* early—usually 15 minutes before cooking is sufficient.

While mushrooms don't contain pectin, they are about 80 percent water, which they will begin to release when salted. In order to preserve the texture of mushrooms, wait to add salt until they've just begun to brown in the pan.

Legumes and Grains

Tough beans: a kitchen fiasco so common it's become an idiom. If there's one way to permanently turn people off of legumes, it's serving them undercooked, bland beans that are hard to eat. Contrary to popular belief, salt does not toughen dried beans. In fact, by facilitating the weakening of pectins contained in their cell walls, salt affects beans in the same way it affects vegetables: it softens them. In order to flavour dried beans from within, add salt when you soak them or when you begin to cook them, whichever comes first.

Legumes and grains are dried seeds—the parts of a plant that ensure survival from one season to the next. They've evolved tough exterior shells for protection, and require long, gentle cooking in water to absorb enough water to become tender. The most common reason for tough beans and grains, then, is undercooking. The solution for most: keep simmering! (Other variables that can lead to tough beans include using old or improperly stored beans, cooking with hard water, and acidic conditions.) Since a long cooking time gives salt a chance to diffuse evenly throughout, the water for boiling grains such as rice, farro, or quinoa can be salted less aggressively than the water for blanching vegetables. In preparations where all of the cooking water will be absorbed, and hence all of the salt, be particularly careful not to overseason.

Doughs and Batters

The first paid job I had in the kitchen at Chez Panisse was called Pasta/Lettuce. I spent about a year washing lettuces and making every kind of pasta dough imaginable. I'd also start the pizza dough every morning, adding yeast, water, and flour into the bowl of the gigantic stand mixer and tending to it throughout the day. Once the water and flour brought the dormant yeast back to life, I'd add more flour and salt. Then, after kneading and proofing, I'd finish the dough by adding in some olive oil. One day, when it was time to add the flour and salt, I realised the salt bin was empty. I didn't have the time right then to go down to the storage shed to get another bag of salt, so I figured I'd just wait to add the salt at the end, along with the oil. As I kneaded the dough, I noticed that it came together much more quickly than usual, but I didn't really give it a second thought. When I returned a couple of hours later to finish the dough, something unbelievable happened. I turned on the machine and let it deflate and knead the dough, like I always did, and then I added the salt. As it dissolved into the dough, I could actually *see* the machine begin to strain. The salt was making the dough tougher—the difference was remarkable! I had no idea what was happening. I was worried that I'd done something terribly wrong.

It was no big deal. It turns out that the dough tightened immediately because salt aids in strengthening **gluten**, the protein that makes dough chewy and elastic. As soon as I allowed the dough to rest, the gluten relaxed, and the pizzas that night emerged from the oven as delicious as always.

Salt can take a while to dissolve in foods that are low in water, so add it to bread dough early. Leave it out of Italian pasta dough altogether, allowing the salted water to do the work of seasoning as it cooks. Add it early to ramen and udon doughs to strengthen their gluten, as this will result in the desired chewiness. Add salt later to batters and doughs for cakes, pancakes, and delicate pastries to keep them tender, but make sure to whisk these mixes thoroughly so that the salt is evenly distributed before cooking.

Cooking Foods in Salted Water

Properly seasoned cooking water encourages food to retain its nutrients. Imagine that you're cooking green beans in a pot of water. If the water is unseasoned or only lightly seasoned, then its concentration of salt—a mineral—will be lower than the innate mineral concentration in the green beans. In an attempt to establish equilibrium between the internal environment of the green beans and the external environment of the cooking water, the beans will relinquish some of their minerals and natural sugars during the cooking process. This leads to bland, grey, less-nutritious green beans.

On the other hand, if the water is more highly seasoned—and more mineral rich—than the green beans, then the opposite will happen. In an attempt to reach equilibrium, the green beans will absorb some salt from the water as they cook, seasoning themselves from the inside out. They'll also remain more vibrantly coloured because the salt balance will keep magnesium in the beans' chlorophyll molecules from leaching out. The salt will also weaken the pectin and soften the beans' cell walls, allowing them to cook more quickly. As an added bonus, there will be less of an opportunity for the green beans to lose nutrients because they'll spend less total time in the pot.

I can't prescribe precise amounts of salt for blanching water for a few reasons: I don't know what size your pot is, how much water you're using, how much food you're blanching, or what type of salt you're using. All of these variables will dictate how much salt to

A SEASONED BEAN
IS A
HAPPY BEAN

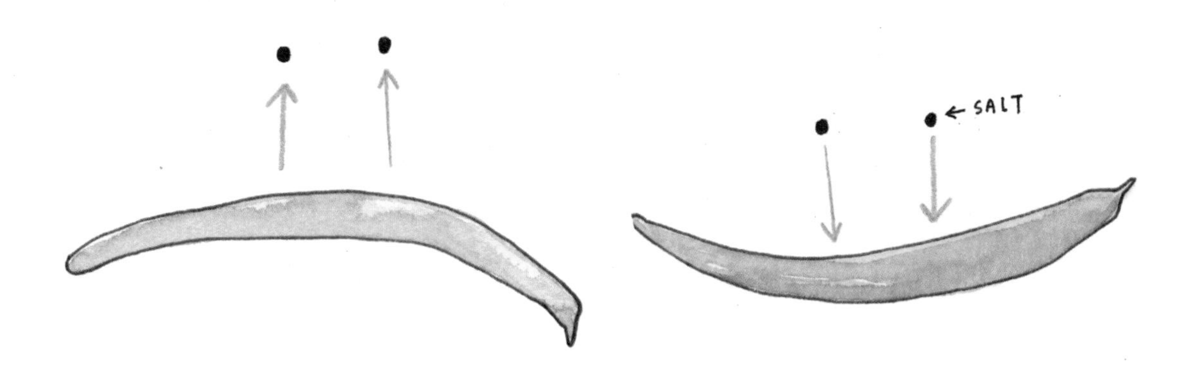

use, and even they may change each time you cook. Instead, season your cooking water until it's as salty as the sea (or more accurately, your *memory* of the sea. At 3.5 percent salinity, seawater is much, much saltier than anyone would ever want to use for cooking). You might flinch upon seeing just how much salt this takes, but remember, most of the salt ends up going down the drain. The goal is to create a salty enough environment to allow the salt to diffuse throughout the ingredient during the time it spends in the water.

It doesn't matter whether you add the salt to the water before or after you set it on the heat, though it'll dissolve, and hence diffuse, faster in hot water. Just make sure to give the salt a chance to dissolve, and taste the water to make sure it's highly seasoned before you add any food. Keep a pot boiling on the stove for too long, though, and water will evaporate. What's left behind will be far too salty for cooking. The cure here is simple: taste your water, and make sure it's right. If not, add some water or salt to balance it out.

Cooking food in salted water is one of the simplest ways to season from within. Taste roasted potatoes that were seasoned with salt as they went into the oven, and you'll taste salt on the surface but not much farther in. But taste potatoes that were simmered in salted water for a little while before being roasted, and you'll be shocked by the difference—salt will have made it all the way into the centre, doing its powerful work of seasoning from within along the way.

Salt pasta water, potato cooking water, and pots of grains and legumes as early as possible to allow salt to dissolve and diffuse evenly into the food. Season the water for vegetables correctly and you won't have to add salt again before serving. Salads made with boiled vegetables—be it potatoes, asparagus, cauliflower, green beans, or anything else—are most delicious when the vegetables are seasoned properly while they're cooking. Salt sprinkled on top of one of these salads at the time of serving won't make as much of a difference in flavour as it will in texture, by adding a pleasant crunch.

Salt meats that are going to be cooked in water, like any meats, in advance, but season the cooking liquids for stews, braises, and poached meats conservatively—keep in mind that you'll be consuming any salt you add here. While some salt may leach from the seasoned meat into the less savoury broth, it will have already done its important tenderising work. Anticipate the flavour exchange that will happen between the seasoned meat and its cooking liquid, and taste and adjust the liquid, along with the meat, before serving.

Read on to learn more about the nuances of **blanching**, **braising**, **simmering**, and **poaching**, in Heat.

How Should I Season my Chicken?

A HANDY GUIDE to SALTING for MAXIMUM ENJOYMENT

ASK YOURSELF: "HOW MUCH TIME UNTIL I EAT?"

OPTION 1. A DAY or MORE

OPTION 1(A)

SEASON THE BIRD, LEAVE IT WHOLE, and BATHE IT in BUTTERMILK for BUTTERMILK-MARINATED ROAST CHICKEN (pg.340), THEN PUT in FRIDGE OVERNIGHT. THE MOST TENDER BIRD YOU'VE EVER TASTED.

OPTION 1(B)

BREAK THE CHICKEN DOWN (SEE pg.318) and SEASON IT. REFRIGERATE IT OVERNIGHT and MAKE CHICKEN with LENTIL RICE (pg.334).

or

OPTION 2. 8-12 HOURS

OPTION 2(A)

REMOVE THE BACKBONE, SEASON BIRD LIBERALLY on BOTH SIDES, and REFRIGERATE. LET IT COME UP to ROOM TEMPERATURE WHILE YOU PREHEAT THE OVEN for CRISPIEST SPATCHCOCKED CHICKEN. (pg.316)

OPTION 2(B)

BREAK THE BIRD DOWN into FOUR PIECES, SEASON, and PLAN to MAKE CHICKEN with VINEGAR (pg.336). SIMMERING THE MEAT in A LITTLE SEASONED WINE WILL HELP THE SALT PENETRATE THE BONE.

or

OPTION 3. ASAP!* (NOW!)

*BREAK IT DOWN - SMALLER THE BETTER!

OPTION 3(A)

MAKE CHICKEN and GARLIC SOUP (pg.332). COOKING THE CHICKEN in A FLAVOURFUL BROTH WILL HELP SEASON THE MEAT.

OPTION 3(B)

REMOVE THE BONES from THE LEGS and THIGHS and MAKE CONVEYOR BELT CHICKEN (pg.325). COOK THE BREASTS THE SAME WAY!

DIFFUSION CALCULUS

The three most valuable tools to encourage salt diffusion are time, temperature, and water. Before setting out to cook—as you choose an ingredient, or a cooking method—ask yourself, "How can I season this from within?" Then, use these variables to plot out how far in advance—and how much—to salt your food or cooking water.

Time

Salt is very slow to diffuse. If you are cooking something big or dense and want to get salt into it, season the ingredient as early as possible to give salt the time to travel to the centre.

Temperature

Heat stimulates salt diffusion. Salt will always diffuse more quickly at room temperature than in the fridge. Use this fact to your advantage when you've forgotten to salt your chicken or steak in advance. Pull the meat out of the fridge when you get home, salt it, and let it sit out while the oven or grill preheats.

Water

Water promotes salt diffusion. Use watery cooking methods to help salt penetrate dense, dry, and tough ingredients, especially if you don't have time to season them in advance.

SALTING CALENDAR

A FRIENDLY REMINDER of WHEN to SALT YOUR FOOD

3 YEARS in ADVANCE

PRO-SCIUTTO & JERKY & RATIONS for THE APOCALYPSE

3 WEEKS in ADVANCE

CORNED BEEF

SALTED COD

5-7 DAYS in ADVANCE

A WHOLE STEER

3 DAYS in ADVANCE

WHOLE PIG for A BDAY LUAU!

WHOLE LAMB OR GOAT for YOUR TYPICAL CEREMONIAL ROAST.

2 DAYS in ADVANCE

THANKSGIVING TURKEY, CHRISTMAS GOOSE & ANY OTHER BIG BIRD for ANY BIG HOLIDAY.

RIB ROAST, LEG of LAMB

1 DAY in ADVANCE

CHICKEN! THICK STEAKS, QUAIL, DUCK, SOAKING A POT of BEANS

TODAY

HOURS BEFORE COOKING

ANYTHING YOU WERE SUPPOSED to SALT EARLIER BUT FORGOT. BECAUSE SOME TIME IS BETTER THAN NO TIME!

15-20 MINUTES BEFORE COOKING

AUBERGINES & COURGETTES (THEN PAT DRY), CABBAGE for SLAW, THICK TUNA, SWORDFISH STEAKS

JUST BEFORE COOKING

FLAKY FISH & DELICATE SHELLFISH, VEGETABLES for ROASTING & GRILLING, SEASON WATER for BOILING, SCRAMBLED EGGS

WHILE COOKING

MUSHROOMS, VEGETABLES YOU'RE COOKING ON THE STOVE, SIMMERING SAUCES

A FEW MINUTES BEFORE SERVING

TOMATOES for SALAD

JUST BEFORE SERVING

SALAD

SERVE

EAT

HOPEFULLY YOU WON'T NEED to SALT WHILE EATING, BUT IF YOU MUST, OK!

USING SALT

The British food writer Elizabeth David once said, "I do not even bother with a salt spoon. I am not able to see what is unmannerly or wrong with putting one's fingers into the salt." I agree. Get rid of the shaker, dump the salt in a bowl, and start using your fingers to season your food. You should be able to fit all five fingers into your salt bowl and easily grab a palmful of salt. This important—but often unsaid—rule of good cooking is so routine for professional cooks that when working in an unfamiliar kitchen, we instinctively hunt for containers to use as salt bowls. When pressed, I've even used coconut shells to hold salt. I once taught a class at the national cooking school in Cuba: the state-run kitchen was so barren that I ended up sawing plastic water bottles in half to use for holding salt and other garnishes. It got the job done.

Measuring Salt

Abandoning precise measurements when using salt requires an initial leap of faith. When I was first learning how to cook, I always wondered how I'd know when I'd added enough. I wondered how I'd avoid using way too much. It was discombobulating. And the only way to know how much salt to use was to add it incrementally and taste with each addition. I had to get to know my salt. With time, I learned that a huge pot of pasta water required three handfuls to start. I figured out that when I seasoned chickens for the spit, it should look like a light snowstorm had fallen over the butchering table. It was only with repetition and practice that I found these landmarks. I also found a few exceptions: certain pastry, brine, and sausage recipes where all of the ingredients are precisely weighed out don't need constant adjusting. But I still salt every other thing I cook to taste.

The next time you're seasoning a pork loin for roasting, pay attention to how much you use, and then take a moment when you take your first bite to consider if you got the seasoning right. If so, commit to memory the way the salt looked on the surface of the meat. If not, make a mental note to increase or decrease the amount of salt next time. You already possess the very best tool for evaluating how much salt to use—a tongue. Conditions in the kitchen are rarely, if ever, identical twice. Since we don't use the same pot every time, or the same amount of water, the same size chicken or number of carrots, measurements can be tricky. Instead, rely on your tongue, and taste at every point along the way. With time, you'll learn to use other senses to gauge how much salt to use—touch, sight, and common sense can be just as important as taste. The late, great Marcella Hazan, who authored the indispensable *Essentials of Classic Italian Cooking*, could tell when a dish needed more salt by simply smelling it!

My general ratios for measuring salt are simple: 1 percent salt by weight for meats, vegetables, and grains, and 2 percent salinity for water for blanching vegetables and pasta. To see what these numbers translate to by volume for various salts, take a look at the chart on the next page. If using the amounts of salt I prescribe terrifies you, try a little experiment: set up two pots of water, and season one as you normally would. Season the other to 2 percent salinity, and note what it feels and looks like to use that much salt. Cook half of your green beans, broccoli, asparagus, or pasta in each pot of water, and compare the flavour when you eat them. I suspect the taste test will be enough to convince you to trust me.

Consider these ratios a starting point. Soon—maybe just after one or two pots of pasta—you'll be able to judge how much salt is enough by trusting the way the grains feel as they fall from your palm and whether or not, upon tasting, you're transported to the sea.

BASIC SALTING GUIDELINES*

TYPE of SALT	WEIGHT per TABLESPOON in GRAMS	AMOUNT per POUND of BONELESS MEAT	AMOUNT per POUND of MEAT ON THE BONE (AKA ROAST CHICKEN)	AMOUNT per POUND of VEGETABLES and GRAINS	AMOUNT per QUART of BLANCHING or PASTA WATER	AMOUNT per CUP of FLOUR for DOUGHS and BATTERS
ACROSS THE BOARD	—	1.25% by WEIGHT	1.5% by WEIGHT	1% by WEIGHT	2% SALINITY	2.5% by WEIGHT

WHICH TRANSLATES to:

FINE SEA	14.6	1⅛ tsp.	1⅓ tsp.	1 scant tsp.	1 Tbl + 1 scant tsp.	¾ tsp.
MALDON	8.4	2 tsp.	2½ tsp.	1⅔ tsp.	2 Tbl + ¾ tsp.	1⅓ tsp.
SEL GRIS	13	1¼ tsp.	1¼ tsp.	1 tsp.	1 Tbl + ⅜ tsp.	1 scant tsp.
TABLE	18.6	⅔ tsp.	1⅛ tsp.	¾ tsp.	1 Tbl	⅔ tsp.
MORTON'S KOSHER	14.75	1⅛ tsp.	1⅓ tsp.	1 scant tsp.	1 Tbl + 1 scant tsp.	¾ tsp.
DIAMOND CRYSTAL KOSHER	9.75	1¾ tsp.	2⅛ tsp.	1⅓ tsp.	2 scant Tbl	1⅛ tsp.

* REMEMBER, YOUR PALATE IS THE ULTIMATE ARBITER. THESE ARE JUST SUGGESTIONS on WHERE to START.

How to Salt

Once you realise how much salt it takes to season something properly, you might start to believe there's no such thing as too much. This happened to me. I remember when a chef I particularly admired walked into the downstairs butchery room where I'd been sent to season pork roasts for the following night's dinner. Having recently come to appreciate the power of salt, I decided that in order to cover the roasts evenly, I'd roll them in a huge bowl of salt to ensure that every surface was adequately coated. As she came down the stairs, her eyebrows shot up. I'd been using enough salt to cure the roasts for three years! They'd be completely inedible the next night. I spent the next twenty minutes rinsing the salt off the meat. Later, the chef showed me the proper hand grasp for distributing salt evenly on large surfaces.

I didn't understand the nuances of the *act* of salting until I began paying attention to the various ways cooks used salt in different situations. There was the way we salted pots of water for blanching vegetables or pasta with near abandon, adding palmful after palmful, only to await its dissolution, lightly skimming a finger across the rolling boil, tasting

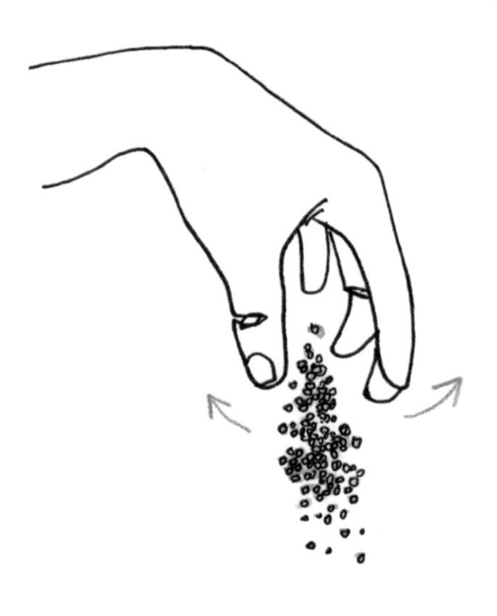

The Palmful

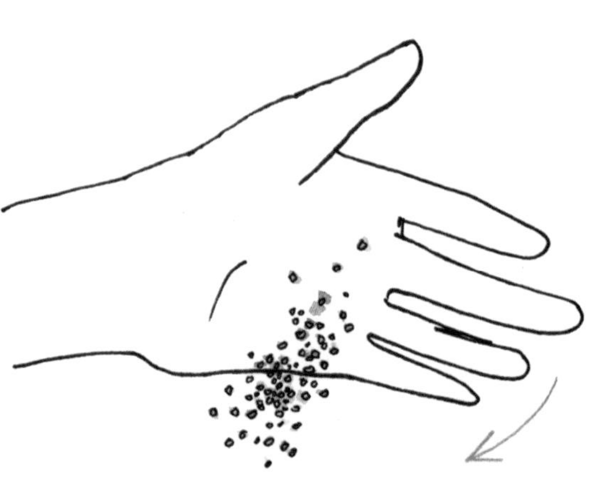

The Wrist Wag

thoughtfully, and more often than not, adding even more.

There was the way we seasoned trays of vegetables, lined up duck legs butchered for confit, even larger cuts of meat, and pans of focaccia ready for the oven. This was done by lightly grasping the salt in your upturned palm, letting it shower down with a wag of the wrist. This grasp—not the hovering pinch I was used to—was the way to distribute salt, flour, or anything else granular, evenly and efficiently over a large surface.

The Pinch

Practise the wrist wag in your own kitchen over a piece of parchment paper or on a baking sheet. Get used to the way the salt falls from your hands; experience the illicit thrill of using so much of something we've all been taught to fear.

First, dry your hands so the salt won't stick to your skin. Grab a palmful of salt and relax. Jerky or robotic hand motions make for uneven salting. See how the salt lands. If it lands unevenly, then it means you're seasoning your food unevenly. Pour the salt back into the bowl, and try again. The more your wrist flows, the more evenly the salt will land.

This isn't to say that you never want to use a pinch of salt, which can be used like a nail-polish-size bottle of touch-up car paint to fix a scratch on a fender. It might not have much potential to repair major damage, but applied precisely and judiciously, it will yield flawless results. Use a pinch when you want to make sure each bite is salted just so: slices of avocado atop a piece of grilled bread, halved hard-boiled eggs, or tiny, perfect caramels. But try to attack a chicken or a tray of butternut squash slices with the pinch, and your wrist will give out long before you're done.

Salt and Pepper

While it's true that where there's pepper there should almost always be salt, the inverse isn't necessarily so. Remember, salt is a mineral and an essential nutrient. When salted, food undergoes a number of chemical reactions that change the texture and flavour of meat from within.

Pepper, on the other hand, is a spice, and proper spice usage is primarily guided by geography and tradition. Consider whether pepper belongs in a dish before you add it. Though French and Italian cooks make abundant use of black pepper, not everyone does. In Morocco, shakers of cumin are commonly set on the table along with salt. In Turkey, it's usually some form of ground chilli powder. In many Middle Eastern countries, including Lebanon and Syria, it's the blend of dried thyme, oregano, and sesame seeds known as *za'atar*. In Thailand, sugar can be found alongside chilli paste, while in Laos, guests are often brought fresh chillies and limes. It doesn't make any more sense to automatically season everything with pepper than it would to add cumin or *za'atar* to every dish you cook. (To learn more about spices used around the world, refer to **The World of Flavour** on page 194.)

When you do use black pepper, look for Tellicherry peppercorns, which ripen on the vine longer than other varieties, and therefore develop more flavour. Grind them at the last moment onto a salad, a toast smeared with creamy *burrata* and drizzled with oil, sliced ripe tomatoes, ***Pasta Cacio e Pepe***, or slices of perfectly cooked steak. Add a few whole peppercorns to a brine, braise, sauce, soup, stock, or pot of beans as you set it on the stove or slip it into the oven. In liquid, an early addition of whole spices initiates a flavour exchange: as the spices absorb liquid, they relinquish some of their volatile aromatic compounds, gently flavouring the liquid in a way that a little sprinkle at the end of cooking could never achieve.

Spices, like coffee, always taste better when ground just before use. Flavour is locked within them in the form of aromatic oils, which are released upon grinding, and again upon

and NEVER

heating. The slow leak of time causes preground spices to relinquish flavour. Purchase whole spices whenever you can, and grind them with a mortar and pestle or spice grinder as you use them, to experience the powerful release of aromatic oils. You'll be astonished by what a huge difference it makes in your cooking.

Salt and Sugar

Don't abandon everything you know about salt when you turn to making dessert. We're taught to think of salt and sugar existing in contrast to, rather than in concert with, one another: food is either sweet or savoury. But remember that the primary effect salt has on food is to enhance flavour, and even sweets benefit from this boost. Just as a little sweetness can amplify flavours in a savoury dish—whether in the form of caramelised onions, balsamic vinaigrette, or a spoonful of applesauce served with pork chops—salt will also improve a sweet dessert. To experience what salt does for sweets, divide your next batch of cookie dough and omit salt from half. Taste cookies from both batches side by side. Because salt will have done its aroma- and taste-enhancing work, you'll be astounded by the notes of nuttiness, caramel, and butter you detect in the salted cookies.

The foundational ingredients of sweets are some of the blandest in the kitchen. Just as you'd never leave flour, butter, eggs, or cream unseasoned in a savoury dish, so should you never leave them unseasoned in a dessert. Usually just a pinch or two of salt whisked into a dough, batter, or base is enough to elevate flavours in pie and cookie doughs, cake batters, tart fillings, and custards alike.

Considering *how* you plan to eat a dessert can help you decide which type, or types, of salt to use. For example, use fine salt that will dissolve evenly in chocolate cookie dough, and then top it with a flakier one such as Maldon for a pleasant crunch.

THE TWAIN SHALL MEET

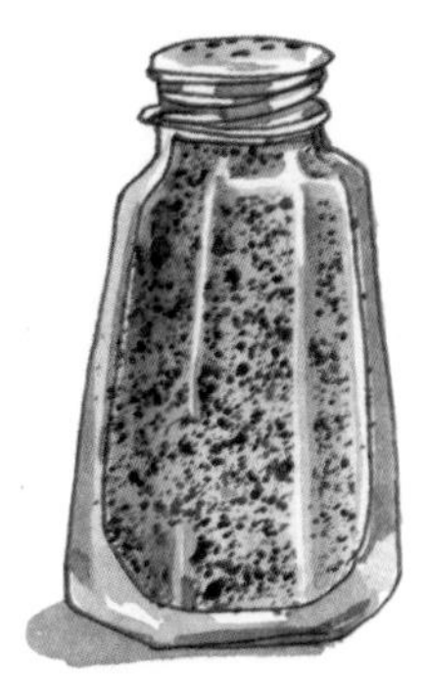

CAESAR SALAD

or, AN EXERCISE in THE ART of LAYERING SALT

1. START by PREPARING ALL YOUR SALTY INGREDIENTS.

PARMESAN
(GRATE)

ANCHOVIES
(POUND)

GARLIC
(POUND with A PINCH of SALT)

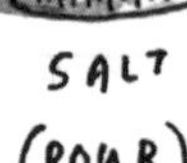

SALT
(POUR)

WORCESTERSHIRE SAUCE
(REMOVE CAP)

2. MAKE A STIFF, UNSALTED MAYO

(SEE HOW to MAKE MAYONNAISE - IT'S A LITTLE LATER in THE BOOK)

3. WORK in EACH SALTY INGREDIENT A LITTLE at A TIME. THEN ADD LEMON and VINEGAR.

THEN **TASTE**

NOW STOP.

NEEDS SALT, RIGHT? BUT WHAT ELSE?

MORE ANCHOVY? MORE PARM? ADD SOME.

NOW **TASTE AGAIN.**

MAYBE ADD A LITTLE MORE WORCESTERSHIRE.

TASTE AGAIN.

KEEP REPEATING THIS TILL IT TASTES JUST RIGHT, ADJUSTING with ACTUAL SALT AS NEEDED

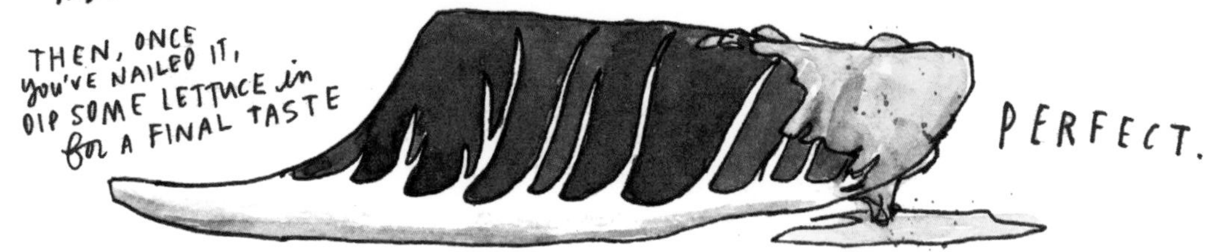

PERFECT.

TOSS with CRISPY LETTUCE and TORN CROUTONS

TOP with PARM & PEPPER to TASTE.

EAT.

Layering Salt

From capers to bacon to miso paste to cheese, there are many sources of salt beyond the crystals we add directly into our food. Working more than one form of salt into a dish is what I call **layering salt**, and it's a terrific way to build flavour.

When layering salt, think about the dish as a whole and consider all of the various forms of salt you hope to add *before* you begin. Neglecting to account for the later addition of a crucial salty ingredient could result in oversalting. Think of layering salt the next time you make **Caesar Dressing**, which has several salty ingredients—anchovies, Parmesan, Worcestershire sauce, and salt. Garlic, which I like to pound with a pinch of salt in a mortar and pestle into a smooth paste, is a fifth source of salt. Since making a delicious, balanced dressing depends on working in the right amounts of each of those—and other, unsalted—ingredients, refrain from adding salt crystals until you're sure that you've added the right amount of everything else.

First, make a stiff, unsalted mayonnaise by whisking oil into egg yolks, drop by drop (find more specific instructions for making mayonnaise by hand on page 86–87). Next, work in initial amounts of pounded anchovies, garlic, grated cheese, and Worcestershire. Then, add vinegar and lemon. Taste. It will need salt. But does it also need more anchovy, cheese, garlic, or Worcestershire? If so, add salt in the form of any of those ingredients. But do it gradually, stopping to taste and adjust with acid as needed. It may take several rounds of tasting and adjusting to get it right. As with any dish with multiple forms of salt, add crystals only after you're satisfied with the balance of all other flavours. And to be sure you've got it right, dip a lettuce leaf or two into the finished dressing to taste, to ensure that the combination delivers the *zing!* you're after.

Even when following a recipe, if you realise that a dish needs more salt, take a moment to think about *where* that salt should come from.

SOURCES OF SALT

1. LITTLE FISH PACKED in SALT (ANCHOVIES, SARDINES, etc.) 2. CAPERS STORED in SALT OR BRINE
3. PICKLED and FERMENTED VEGETABLES, i.e. DILL PICKLES, CORNICHONS, KRAUTS, and KIMCHEES
4. FISH SAUCE 5. SOY SAUCE and MISO PASTE 6. CHEESE 7. MOST CONDIMENTS, SUCH AS MUSTARD, KETCHUP, SALSA, and HOT SAUCES 8. CURED MEATS, i.e. PROSCIUTTO, PANCETTA, BACON, etc.
9. NORI, KOMBU, and OTHER SEAWEEDS 10. OLIVES 11. SALTED BUTTER (OBVS.)

Balancing Salt

No matter how attentive you are while cooking, there will be times you sit down to eat only to discover that you've underseasoned your dinner. Some foods forgive undersalting more readily than others. You can easily adjust a salad at the table with a pinch of salt. Stir a shaving of salty Parmesan into a cup of soup to bump up its seasoning. Other foods don't respond as well: no amount of salty sauce or cheese or meat could ever make up for bland pasta—the tongue will always know the water was nowhere nearly as salty as the sea. Roasted and braised meats cannot pardon the transgression of underseasoning, either.

Ever since witnessing a series of underseasoning disasters at Chez Panisse, I've been obsessed with preventing it. There was the day a cook forgot to add salt to the pizza dough altogether, an accident we didn't notice until the taster, when nothing could be done but remove pizza from the menu. There was the time I braised chicken legs that had been marked "salted" but clearly were not, a mistake that went undiscovered until I pulled the chicken from the oven and tasted it. Since sprinkling the surface of cooked meat will do little to make up for the lack of seasoning within, the only thing we could do was shred the meat, season it, and turn it into a *ragù* to be served with pasta. The instance of underseasoning that made the biggest impression on me, though, was the time a very senior cook undersalted his lasagna, which he had already cut into one hundred pieces for that night's service. Since salting the top would do little to correct a mistake that had been made from within, as the intern I was given the task of gingerly lifting each of the twelve layers on each of the one hundred pieces of lasagna to sneak a few grains of salt into each one. After that, I've never underseasoned a lasagna.

You will also inevitably oversalt. We all do. It might happen soon after you become a member of the newly converted, now awakened to the power of salt. You might grow cavalier, like I did as a young cook with those pork roasts, and start to use so much salt, you render everything inedible for a while. It could happen when you're simply not paying attention. It's not that big a deal. We all make mistakes from time to time. I certainly still do.

There are a handful of fixes for oversalting. But none involves serving something terribly salty alongside something terribly bland. Intentional blandness won't ever cancel out oversalting.

Dilute

Add more unseasoned ingredients to increase the total volume of the dish. More of anything that's unsalted will work to balance out what's salted, but bland, starchy, and rich things are particularly helpful in these circumstances, because just a small amount of them can help balance out a relatively large amount of food. Add bland rice or potatoes to an overseasoned soup, or olive oil to an oversalted mayonnaise. While water evaporates from a boiling soup, stock, or sauce, salt won't, and what's left behind will be overly salty. The solution here is simple: add more water or stock. If you overseason a dish made with many ingredients mixed together, add more of the main ingredient and adjust everything else until it's all balanced again.

Halve

If you've already put the dish together and diluting will yield more food than you'll be able to use, then divide the oversalted amount and correct only half of it. Depending on what it is, you may be able to refrigerate or freeze the rest until you can get around to adjusting and using it. Or, you might have to face the sad reality of throwing it out. But that's better than using thirty dollars' worth of olive oil to correct a batch of mayonnaise, and then only using a quarter of it.

Balance

Sometimes, food that seems salty isn't actually oversalted; it just needs to be balanced with some acid or fat. Doctor up a spoonful of the dish with a few drops of lemon juice or vinegar, a little olive oil, or some of each. If it tastes better, then apply the changes to the whole batch.

Select

Foods cooked in liquid, such as beans or braises, can often be salvaged if the salty cooking liquid is discarded. If beans are too salty, change out the water. Make refried beans or turn the beans, but not their liquid, into soup, adding unseasoned broth and vegetables. If braised meat is just a little too salty, serve it without the liquid and try to balance it with a rich, acidic condiment such as crème fraîche. Serve a lightly seasoned starch or starchy vegetable alongside it to act as a foil.

Transform

Shred an oversalted piece of meat to turn it into a new dish where it's just one ingredient of many—a stew, chilli, a soup, hash, ravioli filling. Add *more* salt to oversalted raw, flaky, white fish and turn it into *baccalà*, or salt cod.

Admit Defeat

Sometimes the best thing you can do is call it a loss and start over. Or order some pizza. It's okay. It's just dinner—you'll get another chance tomorrow.

Never despair. View mistakes of under- or overseasoning as opportunities for learning. Not long after my salt epiphany over polenta with Cal, I was tasked with making some corn custards for the vegetarian guests in the restaurant. It was the first time I was trusted with cooking an entire dish from start to finish. I could hardly believe that paying guests would be eating something I cooked! It was thrilling and terrifying, all at once. I made the custard just as I'd been taught: cooking onions until soft, adding corn I'd stripped from the ears, steeping the cobs in cream to infuse it with sweet corn flavour, making a simple custard base with that cream and eggs, and then combining everything and gently baking it in a water bath until barely set. I was thrilled with how silky the custards had turned out, and towards the end of the night the chef came by and tasted a spoonful. Seeing the hope in my eyes, he graciously told me I'd done a good job, and then gingerly added that next time, I should increase the seasoning. Even though he'd delivered the criticism just about as gently as any chef ever could, I was floored, and completely embarrassed. I'd been following all of the instructions for making the custards so intently that I'd completely forgotten the most important rule in our kitchen—one that I had thought I'd already internalised, but clearly hadn't: taste everything, every step of the way. I'd never tasted the onions, the corn, or the custard mixture. Not once.

After that experience, tasting became reflexive in a whole new way. Within a few months, I was consistently cooking the most delicious food I'd ever made, and it was all because of a single tweak in my approach. I'd learned how to salt.

Develop a sense for salt by tasting everything as you cook, early and often. Adopt the mantra **Stir, taste, adjust**. Make salt the first thing you notice as you taste and the last thing you adjust before serving a dish. When constant tasting becomes instinctive, you can begin to improvise.

Improvising with Salt

Cooking isn't so different from jazz. The best jazz musicians seem to improvise effortlessly, whether by embellishing standards or by stripping them down. Louis Armstrong could take an elaborate melody and distil it down to a single note on his horn, while Ella Fitzgerald could take an utterly simple tune and endlessly elaborate upon it with her extraordinary voice. But in order to be able to improvise flawlessly, they had to learn the basic language of music—the notes—and develop an intimate relationship with the standards. The same is true for cooking; while a great chef can make improvisation look easy, the ability to do so depends on a strong foundation of the basics.

Salt, Fat, Acid, and Heat are the building blocks of that foundation. Use them to develop a repertoire of basic dishes that you can cook any time, anywhere. Eventually, like Louis or Ella, you'll be able to simplify or embellish your cooking at the drop of a porkpie hat. Begin by incorporating everything you've learned about salt into all of your cooking, from the casual frittata to the holiday roast.

The three basic decisions involving salt are: When? How much? In what form? Ask yourself these three questions every time you set out to cook. Their answers will begin to form a road map for improvisation. One day soon, you'll surprise yourself. It might be when, shortly after standing before a near-empty fridge, convinced you don't have the makings for anything worth eating, you discover a wedge of Parmesan. Twenty minutes later, you could be tucking into the most perfectly seasoned bowl of ***Pasta Cacio e Pepe*** you've ever tasted. Or, it might be after an unplanned shopping spree at the farmers' market with friends. Returning home with an abundance of produce, you'll lay it all out on the worktop, pull the chicken you seasoned the night before out from the fridge, and preheat the oven without skipping a beat. Pouring your friends a glass of wine, you'll offer them a snack of a few sliced cucumbers and radishes sprinkled with flaky salt. Without a second thought, you'll add a palmful of salt to the boiling pot of water on the stove, then taste and adjust it before blanching the turnips and their greens. As your friends take their first bites, they'll ask you to share your culinary secrets. Tell them the truth: you've mastered using the most important element of good cooking—salt.

FAT

Just after I began cooking at Chez Panisse, the chefs held a contest to see which employee could come up with the best tomato sauce recipe. There was only one rule: we had to use ingredients readily available in the restaurant's kitchen. The prize was five hundred dollars in cash and an acknowledgement on the menu each time the recipe would be used . . . *forever*.

As a total novice, I was too intimidated to enter, but it seemed like everyone else—from the maître d' to other waiters, porters, and, of course, the cooks—wanted to try.

Dozens of entrants brought in their sauces for a blind tasting by a team of "impartial judges" (i.e., the chefs and Alice). Some sauces were seasoned with dried oregano, others fresh marjoram. Some entrants crushed their canned tomatoes by hand while others painstakingly seeded and diced them. Others added chilli flakes while still others channelled their inner *nonnas* and puréed their sauces, *pomarola*-style. It was tomato mayhem and we were all atwitter, waiting to hear who would be the winner.

At one point, one of the chefs came into the kitchen to get a glass of water. We asked him how it was going. I'll never forget what he said.

"There are a lot of great entries. So many, in fact, that it's hard to narrow them down. But Alice's palate is so sensitive she can't ignore that some of the best versions were made with rancid olive oil."

Alice couldn't understand why everyone hadn't used the high-quality olive oil we cooked with at the restaurant, especially when it was always available to employees to buy at cost.

I was shocked. Never before had it occurred to me that olive oil would have much effect on the flavour of a dish, much less one as piquant as tomato sauce. This was my first glimpse of understanding that as a foundational ingredient, the flavour of olive oil, and indeed any fat we choose to cook with, dramatically alters our perception of the entire dish. Just as an onion cooked in butter tastes different from an onion cooked in olive oil, an onion cooked in good olive oil tastes different—and in this case better—than one cooked in a poorer quality oil.

My friend Mike, another young cook, ended up winning the contest. His recipe was so complicated I can hardly remember it all these years later. But I'll never forget the lesson I learned that day: food can only ever be as delicious as the fat with which it's cooked.

While I was taught to appreciate the flavours of various olive oils at Chez Panisse, it wasn't until I worked in Italy that I saw fat as an important and versatile element of cooking *on its own*, rather than simply a cooking medium.

During the olive harvest, or *raccolta*, I made a pilgrimage to Tenuta di Capezzana, the producer of the most exquisite olive oil I'd ever tasted. Standing in the *frantoio*, I watched rapt as the day's olive harvest was transformed into a yellow-green elixir so bright it seemed to illuminate the dark Tuscan night. The oil's flavour was as astonishing as its colour—peppery, almost acidic, in a way I never imagined a fat could be.

The following autumn I was in Liguria, a coastal province, during the *raccolta*. *Olio nuovo* pressed on the shores of the Mediterranean was wholly different: this oil was buttery, low in acid, and so rich I wanted to swallow spoonfuls of it. I learned that *where* olive oil comes from has a huge effect on how it tastes—oil from hot, dry hilly areas is spicy, while oil from coastal climates with milder weather is correspondingly milder in flavour. After tasting the oils I could see how a peppery oil would overwhelm a delicate preparation such as fish tartare, while the more subtle flavour of a coastal oil might not be able to stand up to the bold flavours of a Tuscan *bistecca* served with bitter greens.

At Zibibbo, Benedetta Vitali's Florentine *trattoria*, we used peppery Tuscan extra-virgin olive oil more liberally than any other ingredient. We used it to make salad dressings. We used it to drench the dough for the focaccia we baked each morning. We used it to brown *soffritto*, the aromatic base of onions, carrots, and celery at the foundation of all of our long-cooked foods. We used it to deep-fry everything from squid to squash blossoms to *bomboloni*, the cream-filled doughnuts I ate with gusto every Saturday morning. Tuscan olive oil defined the flavour of our cooking; our food tasted delicious because our olive oil was delicious.

As I travelled throughout Italy, I saw how fat determines the particular flavours of regional cooking. In the North, where pastures and the dairy cattle they sustain are abundant, cooks use butter, cream, and rich cheeses readily in dishes such as polenta, *tagliatelle Bolognese*, and risotto. In the South and on the coasts, where olive trees flourish, olive oil is used in everything from seafood dishes to pastas and even desserts such as olive oil gelato. Because pigs can be raised in just about any climate, though, one thing unites the diverse regional Italian cuisines: pork fat.

As I immersed myself in the culture and cuisine of Italy, one thing became clear: Italians' remarkable relationship to fat is essential to why their food tastes so good. Fat, then, I realised, is the second element of good cooking.

WHAT IS FAT?

The best way to appreciate the value of fat in the kitchen is to try to imagine cooking *without* it. What would vinaigrette be without olive oil, sausage without pork fat, a baked potato without sour cream, a croissant without butter? Pointless, that's what. Without the flavours and textures that fat makes possible, food would be immeasurably less pleasurable to eat. In other words, fat is essential for achieving the full spectrum of flavours and textures of good cooking.

Besides being one of the four basic elements of good cooking, fat is also one of the four elemental building blocks of all foods, along with water, protein, and carbohydrates. While it's commonly believed that fat, much like salt, is universally unhealthy, both elements are essential to human survival. Fat serves as a crucial backup energy source, a way to store energy for future use, and plays a role in nutrient absorption and essential metabolic functions, such as brain growth. Unless you've been directed by your doctor to strictly reduce your fat consumption, you don't need to worry—there's nothing unhealthy about cooking with moderate amounts of fat (especially if you favour healthy plant- and fish-based fats). As with salt, my aim isn't so much to get you to use more fat as it is to teach you how to make better use of it in your cooking.

In contrast to salt, fat takes on many forms and is derived from many sources (see **Sources of Fat**, page 63). While salt is a mineral, used primarily to enhance flavour, fat plays **three distinct roles** in the kitchen: as a main ingredient, as a cooking medium, and, like salt, as seasoning. The same type of fat can play different roles in your cooking, depending on how it is used. The first step in choosing a fat to use is to identify the primary role it will play in a dish.

Used as a **main ingredient**, fat will significantly affect a dish. Often, it's both a source of rich flavour and of a particular desired texture. For example, fat ground into a burger will render as it cooks, basting the meat from within and contributing to juciness. Butter inhibits the proteins in flour from developing, yielding tender and flaky textures in a pastry. Olive oil contributes both a light, grassy flavour and a rich texture to pesto. The amount of cream and egg yolks in an ice cream determines just how smooth and decadent it'll be (hint: the more cream and eggs, the creamier the result).

The role fat plays as a **cooking medium** is perhaps its most impressive and unique. Cooking fats can be heated to extreme temperatures, allowing the surface temperature of foods cooked in them to climb to astonishing heights as well. In the process, these foods become golden brown and develop the crisp crusts that so please our palates. Any fat you heat to cook food can be described as a medium, whether it's the peanut oil in which you fry chicken, the butter you use to sauté spring vegetables, or the olive oil in which you poach tuna.

Certain fats can also be used as **seasoning** to adjust flavour or enrich the texture of a dish just before serving: a few drops of toasted sesame oil will deepen the flavours in a bowl of rice, a dollop of sour cream will offer silky richness to a cup of soup, a little mayonnaise spread on a BLT will increase its succulence, and a smear of cultured butter on a piece of crusty bread will add untold richness.

To determine which role fat is playing in a dish, ask yourself these questions:

- Will this fat bind various ingredients together? If so, this is a main ingredient.
- Does this fat play a textural role? For **flaky**, **creamy**, and **light** textures, fat plays the role of main ingredient, while for **crisp** textures, it's a cooking medium. For **tender** textures, fat can play either role.
- Will this fat be heated and used to cook the food? If so, this is a cooking medium.
- Does this fat play a flavour role? If it's added at the outset, it's a main ingredient. If it's used to adjust flavour or texture at the end of cooking the dish as a garnish, it's a seasoning.

Once you've identified which role fat will play in a dish, you'll be better equipped to choose which fat to use, and how to cook food that will result in the taste and texture you're after.

SOURCES OF FAT

FATS:

1. BUTTER, CLARIFIED BUTTER, GHEE 2. OILS: OLIVE, SEED, and NUT OILS 3. ANIMAL FAT: PORK, DUCK, CHICKEN

FAT INGREDIENTS:

4. SMOKED and CURED MEATS, i.e. BACON, PROSCIUTTO, PANCETTA, etc. 5. NUTS and COCONUTS 6. CREAM, SOUR CREAM, and CRÈME FRAÎCHE 7. COCOA BUTTER and CHOCOLATE 8. CHEESE 9. WHOLE FAT YOGURT 10. WHOLE EGGS 11. OILY FISH, i.e. SARDINES, SALMON, MACKEREL, and HERRING 12. AVOCADOS

FAT AND FLAVOUR

Fat's Effect on Flavour

Put simply, fat carries flavour. While certain fats have their own distinct flavours, any fat can convey aromas—and enhance flavours—to our palates that would otherwise go unnoticed. Fat coats the tongue, allowing various aromatic compounds to stay in contact with our taste buds for longer periods of time, intensifying and prolonging our experience of various flavours. Peel and slice two cloves of garlic. Gently sizzle one clove in a couple of tablespoons of water, and the other in the same amount of olive oil. Taste a few drops of each liquid. You'll have a much more powerful impression of the garlic flavour in oil. Take advantage of this capability to intensify and circulate flavour by adding aromatics directly into the cooking fat. When baking, add vanilla extract and other flavourings directly into the butter or egg yolks for the same result.

Fat enhances flavour in another extraordinary way. Because cooking fats can withstand temperatures well beyond the boiling point of water (100°C at sea level), they perform a crucial task that water cannot—the facilitation of surface browning, which typically does not begin at temperatures below 110°C. In some foods, browning will introduce entirely new flavours, including nuttiness, sweetness, meatiness, earthiness, and savouriness (umami). Imagine the difference in flavour between a poached chicken breast and one browned on the stove in a little olive oil, and the incalculable value of this attribute will be clear.

The Flavours of Fat

Different fats have different flavours. To select the right fat, get to know how each fat tastes, and in which cuisines it's commonly used.

Olive Oil

Olive oil is a staple in Mediterranean cooking, so make it your default fat when cooking foods inspired by Italian, Spanish, Greek, Turkish, North African, and Middle Eastern cuisines. It shines as a medium for everything from soups and pastas to braises, roasted meats, and vegetables. Use it as a main ingredient in mayonnaise, vinaigrette, and all manner of condiments from **Herb Salsa** to chilli oil. Drizzle it over beef carpaccio or baked ricotta as a seasoning.

Your food will taste good if you start with a good tasting olive oil, but choosing the right one can be daunting. At my local market alone, there are two dozen brands of extra-virgin olive oil on display. Then there are all the virgin, pure, and flavoured oils. Early in my cooking career, as I approached these aisles, I often found myself overwhelmed by choices: virgin or extra-virgin? Italy or France? Organic or not? Is that olive oil on sale any good? Why is one brand £25 for 750 millilitres while another is £7.50 for a litre?

As with wine, taste, not price, is the best guide to choosing an olive oil. This might require an initial leap of faith, but the only way to learn the vocabulary of olive oil is to taste, and pay attention. Descriptors like *fruity*, *pungent*, *spicy*, and *bright* might seem confusing at first, but a good olive oil, like a good wine, is multidimensional. If you taste something expensive but don't like it, then it's not for you. If you find a ten-dollar bottle that's delicious, then you've scored!

While it's a challenge to explain what good olive oil tastes like, it's fairly simple to describe a bad one—bitter, overwhelmingly spicy, dirty, rancid—all deal-breakers.

Colour has little to do with the quality of olive oil, and it offers no clues to whether an olive oil is rancid. Instead, use your nose and palate: does the olive oil smell like a box of crayons, candle wax, or the oil floating on top of an old jar of peanut butter? If so, it's rancid. The sad truth is that most Americans, accustomed to the taste of rancid olive oil, actually prefer it. And so, most of the huge olive oil producers are happy to sell to us what more discerning buyers would reject.

Olive oil is produced seasonally. Look for a production date, typically in November, on the label when you purchase a bottle to ensure you are buying a current pressing. It will go rancid about twelve to fourteen months after it's been pressed, so don't save it for a special occasion, thinking it will improve over time like a fine wine! (In this way, olive oil is *nothing* like wine.)

As with salt, there are various categories of olive oils—everyday oils, finishing oils, and flavoured oils. Use **everyday olive oils** for general cookery and **finishing olive oils** for applications where you really want to let the flavour of the olive oil stand out: in salad dressings, spooned over fish tartare, in herb salsas, or in olive oil cakes. Purchase and use **flavoured olive oils** with caution. Flavourings are often added to mask the taste of low-quality olive oils, so I generally recommend staying away from them. But there is an exception: olive oils marked *agrumato* are made using a traditional technique of milling whole citrus fruit with the olives at the time of the first press. At Bi-Rite Creamery in San Francisco, one of the most popular sundaes features bergamot *agrumato* drizzled over chocolate ice cream. And it is delicious!

It can be difficult to find a good, affordable everyday olive oil. My standbys include the extra-virgin oils from Seka Hills, Katz, and California Olive Ranch. Another good everyday oil is the Kirkland Signature Organic Extra Virgin Oil from Costco, which regularly scores well on independently administered quality analyses. In their absence, look for oils that are produced from 100 percent Californian or Italian olives (as opposed to those with labels that simply read "Made in Italy," "Packed in Italy," or "Bottled in Italy," which imply that the oil is pressed in Italy from olives whose provenance cannot be traced or guaranteed). The production date should always be clearly marked on the label.

If you can't track down a good, affordable everyday olive oil, instead of using a lower-quality one, make your own blend of good olive oil and a neutral-tasting cold-pressed grapeseed or canola oil. Save the pure stuff and use it as a finishing olive oil for salads and condiments.

Once you find an olive oil you love, take good care of it. Constant temperature fluctuations from a nearby stove or daily brushes with the sun's rays will encourage olive oil to go rancid, so store it somewhere reliably cool and dark. If you can't keep it in a dark place, store olive oil in a dark glass bottle or metal can to keep light out.

Butter

Butter is a common cooking fat in regions with climates that support pasture for grazing cows throughout the US and Canada, the UK and Ireland, Scandinavia, Western Europe including northern Italy, and Russia, Morocco, and India.

One of the most versatile fats, butter can be manipulated into several forms and used as either a cooking medium, main ingredient, or seasoning. In its natural state, butter is available **salted** and **unsalted**, and **cultured**. Salted and tangy cultured butters are best as is, spread on warm toast, or served with radishes and sea salt as an hors d'oeuvre. There is no way to know exactly how much salt is in any one particular brand of salted butter, so use unsalted butter when cooking and baking, and add your own salt to taste.

Chilled or at room temperature, unsalted butter can be worked into doughs and batters as a main ingredient to lend its rich dairy flavour to baked goods and produce a variety of luxurious textures, from flaky to tender to light. Unlike oil, butter is not pure fat—it also contains water, milk protein, and whey solids, which provide much of its flavour. Gently heat unsalted butter until those solids brown and you get **brown butter**, which is nutty and sweet. Brown butter is a classic flavour in French and northern Italian cooking—particularly apt for pairing with hazelnuts, winter squash and sage, as I like to do in **Autumn Panzanella**, which is dressed with a **Brown Butter Vinaigrette**.

Melt unsalted butter gently over sustained low heat to clarify it. The whey proteins will rise to the top of the clear, yellow fat, and other milk proteins will fall to the bottom. The water will evaporate, leaving behind 100 percent fat. Skim the whey solids and save them to toss with *fettuccine*—the buttery flavour is an ideal complement to the eggy noodles, especially if you top the dish with grated Parmesan and freshly ground black pepper. Since the proteins can sneak through even the finest cheesecloth, take care to leave them undisturbed at the bottom of the pot. Carefully strain the rest of the butter through cheesecloth to yield **clarified butter**, which is an excellent medium for high-heat cooking. I love using clarified butter for frying potato cakes—with the solids removed, the butter doesn't burn, and the potatoes take on all of that buttery goodness. Indian ghee is simply clarified butter that's been cooked at a higher temperature, allowing the milk solids to brown and lend the finished fat a sweeter flavour. *Smen*, used to fluff Moroccan couscous, is clarified butter that has been buried underground for up to seven years to develop a cheesy taste.

Seed and Nut Oils

Almost every culture relies on a neutral-tasting seed or nut oil, because cooks don't always want fat to flavour a dish. Peanut oil, expeller-pressed canola oil, and grapeseed oil are all good choices as cooking fats precisely because they don't taste like *anything*. Since they have high **smoke points**, these oils can also withstand the high temperatures required to crisp and brown foods.

Spreading a rumour of tropical flavour to any dish where it's used, coconut oil tastes particularly good in granola, or as the cooking fat for roasted root vegetables. Coconut oil is also the rare vegetable oil that's solid at room temperature. Read on to learn how solid fat is a boon for making flaky pastries, and use coconut oil to make a pie crust the next time your lactose-intolerant friend comes over for dinner. (Cook's tip: Both skin and hair readily absorb coconut oil, so it makes for a fantastic luxury treatment whenever you're feeling dry!)

Speciality seed and nut oils with vibrant flavours can be used as seasonings. Fry leftover rice in toasted sesame oil with an egg and kimchee for a Korean-inspired snack. A little toasted hazelnut oil in a vinaigrette will amplify a simple rocket and hazelnut salad with an echo of nuttiness. Garnish pumpkin soup with a **Herb Salsa** pumped up with toasted pumpkin seeds and a drizzle of pumpkin seed oil to incorporate multiple dimensions of a single ingredient.

Animal Fats

All meat-eating cultures make use of animal fats, which can be incorporated into food as a main ingredient, cooking medium, or seasoning depending on its form. Most aromatic molecules are repelled by water, so in meat they're predominantly found in an animal's fat. As a result, any animal's fat will taste much more distinctly of that animal than its lean meat—beef fat tastes beefier than steak, pork fat tastes porkier than pork, chicken fat tastes more chickeny than chicken, and so on.

Beef

When solid, it's called suet. Liquid, it's called tallow. Beef fat is a crucial component in hamburgers and hot dogs, lending beefy flavour and enhancing moistness. Without suet, or another added fat, a hamburger would be dry, crumbly, and tasteless. Tallow is often used for frying french fries and cooking Yorkshire pudding.

Pork

When solid, it's called pork fat. Liquid, it's called lard. Pork fat is an important addition to sausages and terrines, providing both flavour and richness. Use solid pork fat for **barding** and **larding**, two hilariously named terms for supplementing lean meats with solid fat to keep them from drying out. Barding is the term for covering lean meat with slices of pork belly— either smoked and called bacon, cured and called pancetta, or left unadulterated—to protect it from the dry heat of roasting, while larding refers to the act of threading pieces of fat through a lean piece of meat with a long, thick needle. Both processes add richness and flavour.

PORK BELLY

Since it has a high smoke point, lard is a terrific cooking medium and is commonly used in Mexico, the American South, southern Italy, and the northern Philippines. It can also be used as an ingredient in doughs, though it should be used with care, because while it makes for a perfectly flaky empanada dough, its distinctly porky taste may not always be desirable in your blueberry pie!

Chicken, Duck, and Goose

These fats are only used in their liquid forms as cooking media. Schmaltz—or rendered chicken fat—is a traditional ingredient in the Jewish kitchen. I love sizzling rice in it to lend it some chickeny flavour. Save duck or goose fat that renders when roasting a bird, strain it, and use it to fry potatoes or root vegetables. Few things are tastier than potatoes fried in duck fat.

Lamb

Also called suet, it's generally not rendered, but it is an important ingredient in lamb sausages such as *merguez* in countries where pork is not consumed.

In general, fat makes meat taste good. We prize—even grade—steaks based on how marbled, or fatty, they are. There's also the fat that we don't love to eat—the rubbery, chewy lump at the top of a chicken breast, or the bit of brisket fat that always ends up on the edge of the plate. Why do we value some animal fats and eschew others?

When four-legged animals are fattened up with lots of calories, the cuts of meat from the centre of the animal receive the most flavour benefits. Some fat ends up layered between groups of muscles, or directly under their skin, as in the cap of fat on the outside of a pork loin or prime rib. Some fat ends up within a muscle. This is the more prized kind of fat—what we call marbling when we look at a steak. As a well-marbled steak cooks, the fat will melt, making the meat juicier from within. And since fat carries flavour, many of the chemical compounds that make any one kind of meat taste like itself (beef like beef, pork like pork, chicken like chicken) are more concentrated in fat than in lean muscle. That's why, for example, chicken thighs taste more chickeny than the leaner breast meat.

Though lumps of fat might not be so tasty on the plate, you can remove them from the meat and melt them down, then use the rendered fat as a cooking medium. The distinct flavours of animal fats lend themselves well to being used in dishes where the goal is to evoke a certain meatiness: matzoh balls fortified with schmaltz will amplify a chicken soup's chickeniness, and hash browns cooked in bacon fat will lend breakfast a smoky, rich flavour even if no meat makes it onto the plate. A little animal fat will go a long way towards enriching and flavouring even the simplest foods.

How to use the Flavour Maps

Flip this page open. Inside you'll find one of the three flavour maps in this book. Use it to navigate through the flavours of the world. Each level of the wheel contains a layer of information: use the two inner layers to guide you to your cuisine of choice, and then refer to the outermost layer to choose the right fat for cooking foods from that cuisine.

the World of Fat

FAT = FLAVOUR.

USE THIS WHEEL to HELP you CHOOSE WHICH FATS to USE AS you COOK FOODS from AROUND THE WORLD.

Continent	Region	Fats
EUROPE	GREECE & CYPRUS	OLIVE OIL
EUROPE	SCANDINAVIA	BUTTER, NEUTRAL OIL
EUROPE	EASTERN EUROPE	BUTTER, SCHMALTZ, NEUTRAL OIL, OLIVE OIL
EUROPE	GERMANY	BUTTER, CREAM, PORK FAT, NEUTRAL OIL
EUROPE	SPAIN	OLIVE OIL, PORK FAT
EUROPE	ITALY	OLIVE OIL, BUTTER, LARD
EUROPE	FRANCE	BUTTER, OLIVE OIL, LARD, CREAM
EUROPE	UNITED KINGDOM	BUTTER, NEUTRAL OIL, OLIVE OIL
NORTH AMERICA	USA & CANADA	BUTTER, OLIVE OIL, BACON FAT, LARD, NEUTRAL OIL
NORTH AMERICA	MEXICO	NEUTRAL OIL, LARD
NORTH AMERICA	CENTRAL AMERICA	NEUTRAL OIL, LARD
NORTH AMERICA	CARIBBEAN	COCONUT OIL, COCONUT MILK, NEUTRAL OIL
SOUTH AMERICA	ARGENTINA & URUGUAY	OLIVE OIL
SOUTH AMERICA	CHILE, PERU & BOLIVIA	NEUTRAL OIL
SOUTH AMERICA	BRAZIL	PALM OIL, NEUTRAL OIL, OLIVE OIL, LARD
ASIA	MEDITERRANEAN	OLIVE OIL
ASIA	IRAN	NEUTRAL OIL, CLARIFIED BUTTER
ASIA	INDIA	CLARIFIED BUTTER, GRAPESEED OIL, COCONUT OIL
ASIA	VIETNAM	NEUTRAL OIL
ASIA	THAILAND	COCONUT OIL, LARD, NEUTRAL OIL, PALM OIL
ASIA	KOREA	NEUTRAL OIL, SESAME OIL
ASIA	JAPAN	NEUTRAL OIL, SESAME OIL
ASIA	CHINA	NEUTRAL OIL, SPRING ONION OIL, SESAME OIL
AFRICA	HORN of AFRICA	NEUTRAL OIL, SESAME OIL, SMEN
AFRICA	NORTH AFRICA	OLIVE OIL, SMEN (FERMENTED BUTTER)
AFRICA	WEST AFRICA	PALM OIL, COCONUT OIL, SHEA BUTTER, PEANUT OIL, WATERMELON SEED OIL

Fats of the World

Just as I'd discovered in Italy, cuisines are distinguished by their fats. Since fat is the foundation of so many dishes, choose culturally appropriate fats to flavour food from within. Use the wrong fat, and food will never taste right, no matter how carefully you use other seasonings.

Don't use olive oil when cooking Vietnamese food, or smoky bacon fat when making Indian food. Instead, refer to this flavour wheel to guide your decision making as you cook foods from around the world. Sauté **Garlicky Green Beans** in butter to serve with a French-inspired meal, in ghee to serve alongside Indian rice and lentils, or with a splash of sesame oil to serve with **Glazed Five-Spice Chicken**.

HOW FAT WORKS

Which fats we use primarily affect flavour, but *how* we use them will determine texture, which is just as important in good cooking. Varied textures excite our palates. By transforming foods from soft and moist to crisp and crunchy, we introduce new textures and make the experience of eating more amusing, surprising, and delicious. Depending on how we use fats, we can achieve any one of five distinct textures in our food: Crisp, Creamy, Flaky, Tender, and Light.

Pan Surfaces

(A NOT ENTIRELY SCIENTIFIC MAGNIFICATION)

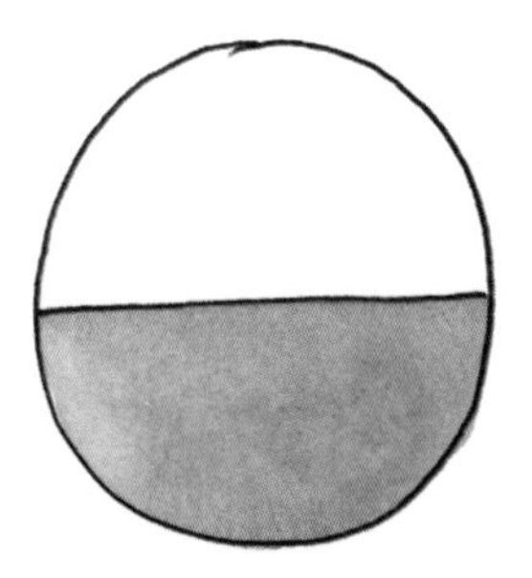

NONSTICK or WELL-SEASONED CAST IRON

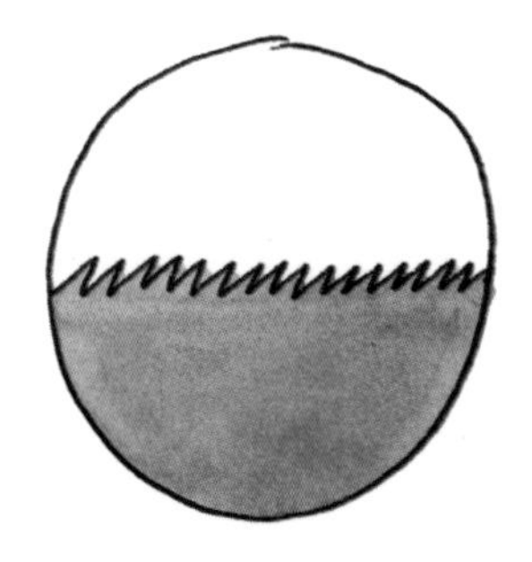

STAINLESS STEEL

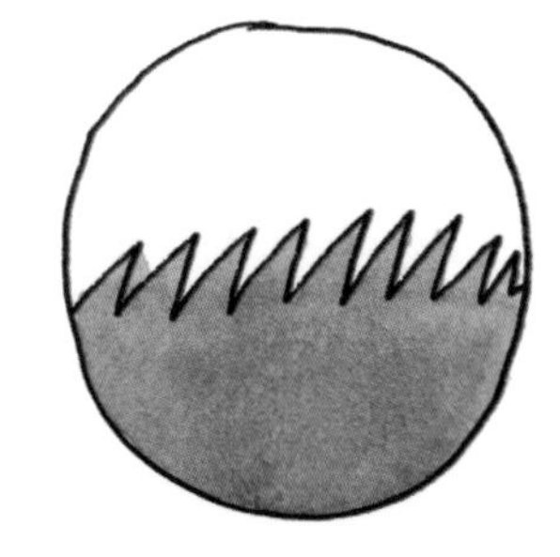

UNSEASONED CAST IRON

Crisp

Humans love crisp and crunchy foods. According to chef Mario Batali, the word *crispy* sells more food than almost any other adjective. Crisp foods stoke our appetites by conjuring up past experiences of foods with pleasing aromas, tastes, and sounds. Just think of fried chicken, a version of which you'll encounter in practically any country around the world. Few moments in a meal can rival that first bite of chicken, fried so expertly that the skin shatters the moment your teeth sink into it. Steam ripe with the mouthwatering aromas of that crisp batter; a loud, attention-grabbing crunch; and the comforting flavours of fried chicken all emerge simultaneously to deliver that universal experience of deliciousness.

For food to become crisp, the water trapped in its cells must evaporate. Water evaporates as it boils, so the surface temperature of the ingredient must climb beyond the boiling point of 100°C.

To achieve this effect on the entire surface of the food, it needs to be in direct, even contact with a heat source, such as a pan at temperatures well beyond water's boiling point. But no food is perfectly smooth, and at the microscopic level, most pans aren't either. In order to get even contact between the food and the pan, we need a **medium**: fat. Cooking fats can be heated to 176°C and beyond before beginning to smoke, so they are ideal mediums for developing the crisp, golden crusts that delight our palates so much. Cooking methods where fat is heated to achieve crispness include searing, sautéing, pan-, shallow-, and deep-frying. (A bonus: using enough fat to create even surface contact will prevent food from sticking to the pan.)

As with salt, I encourage you to abandon any fear of fat, for knowing *how* to use fat properly may lead you to use less of it. The best way to know how much fat to use is to pay attention to certain sensory cues. Some ingredients, such as aubergines and mushrooms, act like sponges, quickly absorbing fat and then cooking dry against the hot metal. Using too little fat in a pan, or letting the fat be absorbed and neglecting to add more, will result in dark, bitter blisters on the surface of the food. Other ingredients, such as pork chops or chicken thighs, will release their own fat as they cook; walk away from a pan of sizzling bacon for a few minutes and you'll return to see the strips practically submerged in their own fat.

Let your eyes, ears, and taste buds guide you in how much fat to use. Recipes can be a useful starting point, but conditions vary from kitchen to kitchen, depending on the tools available to you. Say a recipe asks you to cook two diced onions in two tablespoons of olive oil. In a small pan that might be enough to coat the bottom but in a larger pan with greater surface area it probably isn't. Instead of just following a recipe, use your common sense, too. For example, make sure that the bottom of the pan is coated with fat when sautéing, or that oil comes halfway up the sides of the food when shallow-frying.

Food cooked in too much fat is no more appetising than its inverse. Few things can retroactively ruin a meal like a puddle of grease left on an otherwise empty plate. Drain fried foods—even pan- or shallow-fried foods—with a quick dab on a clean dish towel or paper napkin before serving. And lift sautéed foods out of the pan with a slotted spoon or tongs, rather than tilting them out onto a plate, to leave the excess fat behind.

While you're cooking, if you notice you've used more fat than you'd intended, you can tip the excess out of the pan, taking care to wipe its outer edge where fat may have dripped, to prevent a flare-up. Just do it carefully so you don't burn yourself. If the pan is too heavy or hot, then be smart: take the food out and use tongs to place it on a plate, then tip some of the fat out, replace the food, and continue cooking. It's not worth a burn or a grease spill to avoid washing an extra dish.

Heating Oil Properly

Preheat the pan to reduce the amount of time fat spends in direct contact with the hot metal, minimising opportunity for it to deteriorate. As oil is heated, it breaks down, leading to flavour degradation and the release of toxic chemicals. Food is also more likely to stick to a cold pan—another reason to preheat. But exceptions to the preheating rule exist: butter and garlic. Both will burn if the pan is too hot, so you must heat them gently. In all other cooking, preheat the pan and then add the fat, letting it too heat up before adding any other ingredients.

The pan should be hot enough so that oil immediately ripples and shimmers when added. Various metals conduct heat at different rates, so there's no set amount of time to recommend; instead, test the pan with a drop of water. If it crackles a little bit before evaporating—it doesn't have to be a violent sound—then the pan is ready. A general clue that both the pan and fat are hot enough is the sound of a delicate sizzle upon addition of the food. If you add food too early and don't get that sizzle, just take the food out, let the pan heat up sufficiently, and put it back in to ensure it doesn't stick or overcook before it browns.

Rendering

Intermuscular and subcutaneous fats—the lumpy bits between the muscles and the layer of fat just beneath the skin—can be cut into small pieces, placed in a pan with a minimal amount of water, and **rendered**, or cooked over gentle heat until all the water has evaporated. This process transforms solid fat into a liquid that can be used as a cooking medium. The next time you roast a duck, trim all of its excess fat before cooking and render it. Strain it into a glass jar and store it in the fridge. It'll keep for up to six months. Save it to make **Chicken Confit**.

While fat in meat is a great boon to flavour, it can also prevent meat from crisping. Even when the aim is not to render fat to use as a cooking medium, this technique is crucial for transforming texture. Crisp bacon is the happy result of properly rendered fat. Fry at too high a temperature, and it'll burn on the outside while remaining flabby. The key is to cook it slowly enough to allow the fat to render at the same rate the bacon browns.

Since animal fats begin to burn at around 176°C, try arranging sliced bacon in a single layer on a baking sheet, and then slipping it into an oven set to that temperature. The heat of the oven will be gentler and more even than on the stove, giving the fat an opportunity to render. Or, when cooking bits of bacon or *pancetta* on the stove, start with a little water in the pan to help moderate the temperature and give the fat a chance to render before browning begins.

The skin of a roast chicken or turkey will crisp up on its own as long as the bird cooks long enough for the fat to render. Duck needs a little more help, though, since it has a thicker layer of subcutaneous fat to provide the bird with energy for flying and help keep it warm in the winter months. Using a very sharp needle or metal skewer, prick the skin of the entire bird, focusing particularly on the fattiest parts—the breast and the thighs. The holes will allow the rendering fat to escape and coat the skin as it melts, leaving you with glassy, crisp skin. If roasting a whole duck is beyond your comfort zone right now, start with duck breasts. Before cooking, score the skin on both diagonals with a sharp paring knife, leaving behind a pattern of tiny diamonds. The same rendering will occur on a smaller scale, leaving the breasts with perfectly crisped skin.

I'm a stickler for rendering the fat cap on pork chops and rib steaks. I hate getting a nicely cooked steak with a strip of flabby, barely cooked fat running down the side. So either start or finish the cooking process by laying a chop or steak on its side in the pan or on the grill, allowing the fat to render. This might require a little bit of balancing trickery on your part—hold the meat in place with your tongs, or try to cleverly lean the meat up against a carefully placed wooden spoon, or the edge of the pan itself. Whatever you do, don't skip this step! You won't regret taking the time to turn that strip of fat into something golden, crisp, and delicious.

Smoke Points

The **smoke point** of a fat is the temperature at which it decomposes and transforms into a visible, noxious gas. Have you ever added oil into a hot pan for sautéing vegetables and then been distracted by a ringing phone? If you've returned to an offensive, smoky scene at the stove, then the oil has surpassed its smoke point. Once, while I was trying to demonstrate the importance of preheating the pan to an intern, another cook approached me with an urgent question. By the time I addressed him and turned back to the pan, it was so aggressively hot that the second I added olive oil, it hit the smoke point, turning the pan black and throwing everyone nearby into a coughing fit. In an attempt to save face, I tried to imply that I'd made the mistake on purpose, and it had been a lesson about smoke points from the start. But, blushing hard before the other cooks, I couldn't keep a straight face, and we soon all dissolved into laughter.

The higher a fat's smoke point, the further it can be heated without ruining the flavour of the food cooking in it. Pure, refined vegetable oils such as grapeseed and peanut begin to smoke around 200°C, making them an ideal choice for high-heat applications such as deep- or stir-frying. Impure fats don't do as well at extreme heats; the sediment in unfiltered olive oil and the milk solids in butter will begin to reach their smoke point, or burn, at about 176°C, making them well suited for applications where a very high temperature isn't needed and their flavours can shine, such as oil-poaching, simple vegetable sautés, pan-frying fish or meat. Or, use them for dishes that don't involve any heating, such as mayonnaise and vinaigrettes.

Achieving Crispness

Crispness results from food's contact with hot fat and water evaporating from the surface of food. So do everything in your power to keep the pan and the fat hot when seeking a golden crust. Preheat the pan, then preheat the fat. Avoid putting more than a single layer of food into the pan, which will cause the temperature to drop drastically and steam to condense and make food soggy.

Delicate foods especially suffer in these instances. Cooking in fat that's insufficiently hot will cause food to absorb the oil, resulting, for example, in unappetisingly beige, greasy fish fillets, cooked through but not golden. Steaks and pork chops placed in cold fat will take so long to sear that by the time they *appear* to be perfectly cooked, the meat within will be well-done, rather than medium-rare.

This doesn't mean you should categorically crank the heat. If the fat is too hot, the outer surface of the food will brown and become crisp before the centre has a chance to cook through. Crisp onion rings with crunchy slivers of onion that slip out on first bite and chicken breast with burnt skin and a raw, flabby centre both suffer from having been cooked at temperatures that were too high.

The goal with all cooking is to achieve your desired result on the outside and inside of an ingredient at the same time. In this case, it's a crisp surface and a tender centre. Add foods that take time to cook through, such as aubergine slices or chicken thighs, to hot fat, allowing a crust to form. Then, reduce the heat to prevent burning and allow them to cook all the way through. I'll explain more about how to navigate between different levels of heat in **Using Heat**.

Once you have achieved crispness, do your best to retain it: do not cover or pile up crisp foods while they are still hot. They will continue to release steam. The lid will entrap steam, which will condense and drip back onto the food, making it soggy. Allow hot, crisp foods to cool off in a single layer to prevent this from happening. If you want to keep crisp foods such as fried chicken warm, set them in a warm spot in the kitchen, such as the back of the stove, until ready to serve. Alternatively, cool the chicken on a baking rack and then pop it into a hot oven for a few minutes to reheat it before serving.

Creamy

One of the great alchemical wonders of the kitchen, an **emulsion** happens when two liquids that normally don't like to mix together or dissolve give up and join together. In the kitchen, an emulsion is like a temporary peace treaty between fat and water. The result is tiny droplets of one liquid dispersed in another, resulting in a creamy mixture that's neither one nor the other. Butter, ice cream, mayonnaise, and even chocolate—if it's creamy and rich, chances are it's an emulsion.

Consider a vinaigrette: oil and vinegar. Pour the two liquids together and the oil, being less dense, will float above the vinegar. But *whisk* the two liquids together—breaking them up into billions of tiny droplets of water and oil—and the vinegar will disperse into the oil, creating a homogenous liquid with a new, thicker consistency. This is an emulsion.

EMULSION

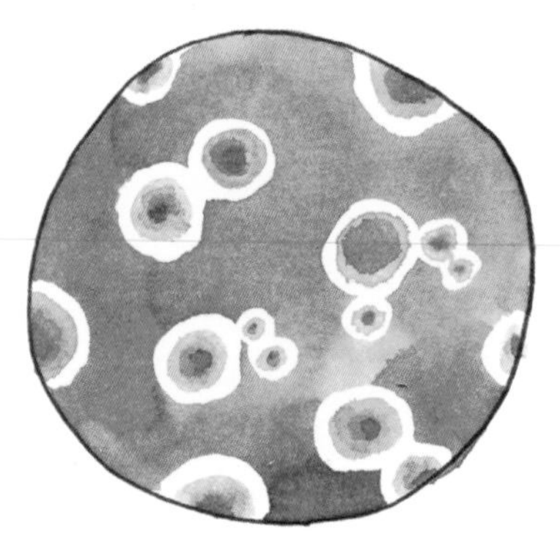

SHAKEN VINAIGRETTE on ITS WAY to BREAKING

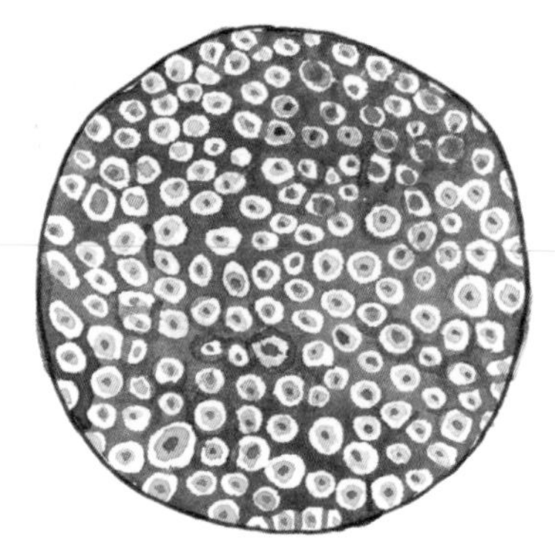

WHISKED MAYONNAISE STABLE AS CAN BE

Yet little more than momentary bewilderment will hold together this simple vinaigrette. Left alone for a few minutes, the oil and vinegar will begin to separate, or **break**. Use this broken vinaigrette to dress lettuce and the oil and vinegar will unevenly coat leaves, tasting too sour in one bite and too oily in the next. In comparison, a well-emulsified vinaigrette will offer balanced flavour in each bite.

When an emulsion breaks, the fat and water molecules begin to coalesce back into their own troops. In order make an emulsion more stable, use an **emulsifier** to coat the oil and allow it to exist contentedly among the vinegar droplets. An emulsifier is like a third link in the chain, a mediator attracting and uniting two formerly hostile parties. Mustard often plays the role of emulsifier in a vinaigrette, while in a mayonnaise, the egg yolk itself has some emulsifying qualities.

Using Emulsions

Emulsions are efficient tools for enriching plain foods: a knob of butter swirled into a pan of pasta at the last moment, a spoonful of mayonnaise added into a dry, crumbly egg salad, a creamy vinaigrette drizzled over otherwise unadorned cucumbers and tomatoes for a simple summer salad.

Some cooking requires you to make an emulsion. Other times you will be handed an existing emulsion and your only job will be to keep it from breaking. Become familiar with common kitchen emulsions so you can protect their delicate bonds of cooperation.

Some familiar emulsions:

- Mayonnaise and hollandaise
- Vinaigrettes (though some are very temporary)
- Butter, cream, and milk
- Peanut butter and tahini (once you stir in the oil)
- Chocolate
- The ephemeral *crema* on top of an espresso

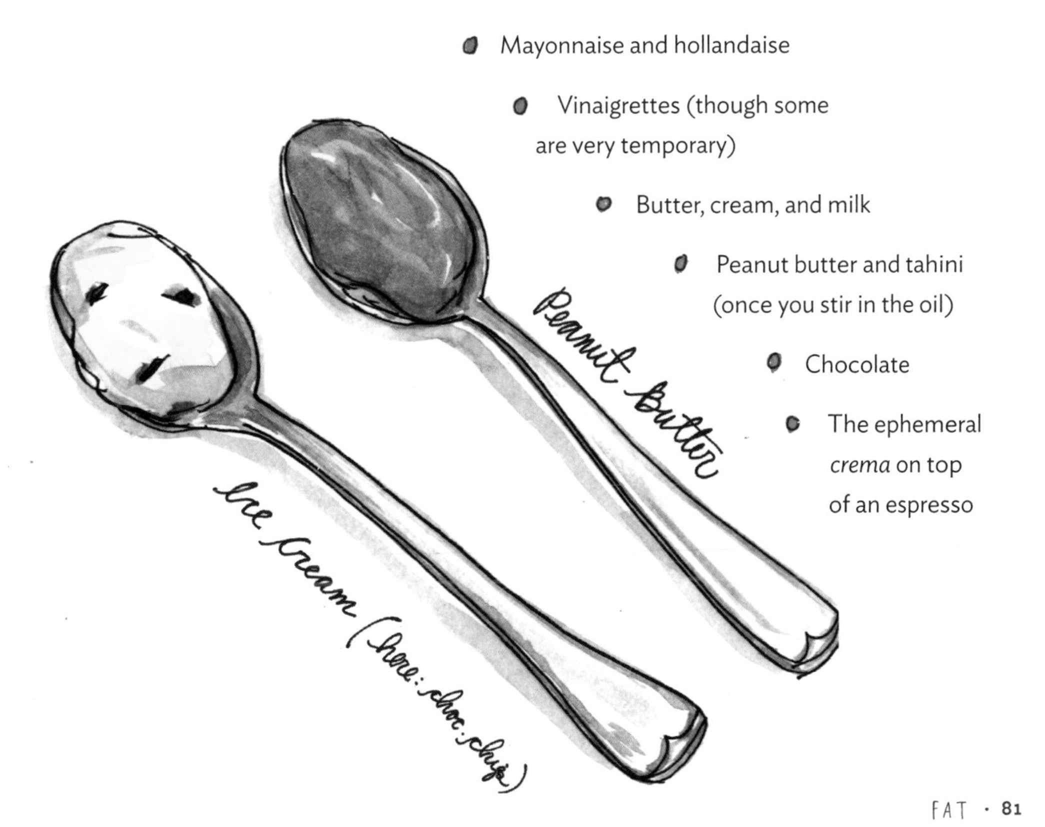

Achieving Creaminess: Mayonnaise

Mayonnaise is an oil-in-water emulsion made by slowly whisking tiny droplets of oil into an egg yolk, which itself is a natural emulsion of fat and water. Fortunately, the yolk offers us a little insurance, as it contains lecithin, an emulsifier with one end that likes fat and another that likes water. With vigorous whisking, lecithin connects the minuscule amount of water innate to a yolk to the oil droplets and surrounds tiny air bubbles. The two distinct ingredients integrate into a rich, unified sauce.

But mayonnaise—and this is true of all emulsions—is always looking for an excuse to **break**, or separate into the hostile groups of oil and water once again.

For a basic mayonnaise, measure out—or at least eyeball—the oil before you start. Choose your oil depending on how you intend to use the mayo—for spreading on a BLT or a Vietnamese *bánh mì* sandwich, use a neutral oil such as grapeseed or canola. For aïoli to serve alongside **Tuna Confit** in a Niçoise salad, use olive oil. Each egg yolk will comfortably hold about three-quarters of a cup of oil in a stable emulsion. Since homemade mayonnaise is best when it's fresh, aim to make the smallest amount possible at a time, though any leftovers will keep in the fridge for a few days.

Oil-in-water emulsions always work better when their ingredients are neither too hot nor too cold. If you're starting with an egg straight from the fridge, bring it up to room temperature before you start. If you're in a hurry, submerge the egg in a bowl of warm tap water for a few minutes to speed things up.

Lightly dampen a kitchen towel and lay it into a small saucepan, then set the mayonnaise-making bowl in it. The wet towel will create enough friction to keep the bowl steady and prevent spillage. Place the yolk(s) in the bowl and start whisking, adding in the oil one drop at a time using a ladle or a spoon. Once you've added half the total volume of oil and created a relatively stable base, start to add the rest of the oil in more swiftly. If the mayonnaise grows so thick it's hard to whisk, add a few drops of water or lemon juice to thin it out and prevent it from breaking. Once you've added all the oil, turn your attention to seasoning the mayonnaise to taste.

Follow these rules, and you'll see that mayonnaise is difficult (but not impossible) to ruin. During one of his cooking lessons with me, Michael Pollan asked me to explain the science at work in an emulsion. I didn't really know, so I responded, "Magic keeps it together." Even now that I understand the science, I still believe there's some magic at work.

Retaining Creaminess: Butter

One of my favourite poets, Seamus Heaney, once described butter as "coagulated sunlight," which might be the most elegant and economical way to describe its special alchemy. To begin with, it's the only animal fat made without killing an animal. Cows, goats, and sheep eat grass, a product of sunlight and photosynthesis, and deliver us milk. We skim the richest cream off the top, and churn it until it transforms into butter. The process is so straightforward that kids can make butter by shaking a glass jar filled with chilled cream.

Remember that butter, unlike oil, isn't pure fat. It's fat, water, and milk solids all held together in a state of emulsion. While most emulsions are stable in a narrow range of temperatures (just a few degrees), butter retains its solid form from freezing temperatures (0°C) until it melts (32°C). Compare this to what happens when you heat or freeze mayonnaise—it'll break quickly!—and the magic of butter will become clear.

This explains why butter sweats when left on the kitchen worktop on a hot day—the water separates from the fat as it melts. At even warmer temperatures—in a pan over a hot burner, or in the microwave—butter's fat and water will immediately separate. Melted butter, then, is a broken emulsion, hardening as it cools, never to return to its former miraculous state.

Take care of its emulsion and butter will lend creaminess to everything from *jambon-beurre*, the classic Parisian ham and butter baguette, to chocolate truffles. The precise temperatures prescribed for butter in recipes are not arbitrary: butter at room temperature is more pliable, allowing air to be worked into it to lighten cakes, or to combine more readily with flour, sugar, and eggs for tender cakes and cookies, or spread evenly onto a baguette, to be topped with ham. As I'll explain later, it's also important to keep butter cold in order to preserve its emulsion and prevent it from interacting with the proteins in flour when making doughs for flaky pastries, including **All-Butter Pie Dough**.

Julia Child once remarked, "With enough butter, anything is good." Put her advice into practice by using butter to make another emulsion: butter sauce. Temperature is crucial with butter-water emulsions. The key is to start with a warm pan and cold butter. For a simple pan sauce, after removing a steak, fish fillet, or pork chop from the pan, tip out any excess fat. Place the pan back over the heat and add just enough liquid—water, stock, or wine—to coat the bottom. Using a wooden spoon, scrape any delicious crusty bits into the sauce and bring it to a boil. Then, for each serving, add 2 tablespoons of very cold butter into the pan and swirl over medium-high heat, letting the butter melt into the liquid. Don't let the pan get so hot that the butter sizzles; as long as there is enough water in the sauce, you'll be fine. Once you see the sauce begin to thicken, turn off the flame and let the butter finish melting over residual heat, but don't stop swirling. Taste for salt and, if needed, add a squeeze of lemon or splash of wine. Spoon over the food and serve immediately.

The same method works for making butter-water sauces to coat noodles or vegetables. Do it directly in the pasta pan, as long as it's hot enough and the butter is cold. Make sure there's enough water in the pan, and swirl, toss, swirl to make the sauce and coat the pasta all at once. Add pecorino cheese and black pepper and you've got ***Pasta Cacio e Pepe***, the classic Roman dish that's even more delicious than macaroni and cheese.

Breaking and Fixing Emulsions

Some emulsions will naturally break with time, and others will break if fat and water are combined too quickly, but the most common way to ruin one is to allow its temperature to swing. Some emulsions must remain cold, and others warm. Yet others must be at room temperature. Heat a vinaigrette, and it will break. Chill a *beurre blanc*, and it will break. Each persnickety emulsion has its comfort zone.

Sometimes, you *seek* to break an emulsion, as when you melt butter to clarify it. Other times, it's a disaster. Heat a chocolate sauce too quickly and it will break into a greasy, undesirable mess that even I wouldn't pour over ice cream after the longest day. But, as important as it is to be careful with emulsions, ruining one isn't the end of the world, and you almost always have some recourse.

If the magic holding together your mayonnaise expires and your emulsion breaks, don't worry! The best way to learn how to fix a broken mayonnaise is to break it once deliberately so you can figure out how to salvage it.

Here's the mind-bogglingly simple solution: get out a new bowl, but keep the same whisk. If you have only one bowl, scrape out the broken mayonnaise into a measuring cup with a spout or, failing that, a coffee cup, and clean the bowl.

Bring the clean bowl to the sink and spoon in half a teaspoon or so of the hottest water you can coax from your tap.

Using your oily, eggy whisk, start whisking the hot water maniacally, until it starts to foam. Then, treating the broken mayonnaise as if it were oil, add it drop by drop, continuing to whisk with the urgency of a swimmer escaping a shark. By the time you've added half of it back, it should start to resemble a proper mayonnaise again, perfect for slathering on a lobster roll. If this fails you, then begin the entire process over with the insurance a new egg yolk provides, and add the broken mayonnaise back in, a drop at a time.

In the future, if, while whisking together any emulsion, you notice things start to head south, keep these tips in mind. First, as soon as you suspect that you are on shaky ground, stop adding fat. If the emulsion isn't thickening and the tines of the whisk aren't leaving visible tracks, then for heaven's sake stop adding oil! Sometimes, all that's called for at this point is a good strong whisking to bring things back together.

You can also add a few chips of ice along with the first whiffs of doubt. If you don't have ice on hand, a tiny splash of cold water from the tap will suffice to regulate temperature and keep the peace.

to MAKE A MAYONNAISE

A Lesson in Fats & Emulsion

1 FIRST THINGS FIRST! MEASURE OUT THE RIGHT AMOUNT of OIL and EGGS →

The Golden Mayo Ratio:

=

and MAKE SURE THAT THE EGG and THE OIL ARE THE SAME TEMPERATURE. SO you'll WANT to LEAVE THE EGG OUT of THE FRIDGE for A BIT or, you CAN RUN IT UNDER SOME WARM WATER.

2 PUT THE YOLKS in A BOWL and **START WHISKING**, ADDING **ONE DROP of OIL** at A TIME.

LIGHTLY DAMPEN A KITCHEN TOWEL. LAY IT in A RING and PUT YOUR BOWL in THE MIDDLE. ≡NO SPILLING≡

ONCE you'VE ADDED ½ THE OIL and IT'S FEELING PRETTY SOLID, ADD THE REST A LITTLE FASTER. IF IT GETS SO THICK IT'S HARD to WHISK, ADD A FEW DROPS of WATER OR LEMON JUICE. AFTER ALL THE OIL IS ADDED, **TASTE**. NEED SALT? ADD SOME. **TASTE AGAIN.**

and to FIX A BROKEN MAYONNAISE

1 STOP. TAKE A DEEP BREATH. IT HAPPENS to EVERYONE.

2 GO GET A NEW BOWL.
ADD ½ teaspoon of THE HOTTEST WATER YOUR TAP CAN MUSTER.

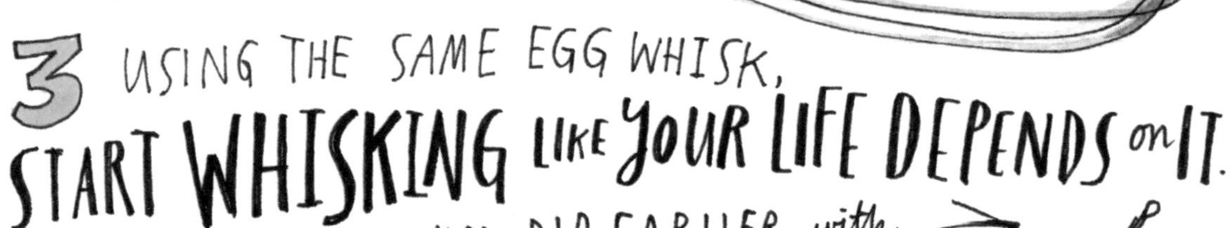

3 USING THE SAME EGG WHISK,
START WHISKING like YOUR LIFE DEPENDS on IT.

THEN, JUST LIKE YOU DID EARLIER with THE OIL, ADD THAT SAD, BROKEN MAYONNAISE, **DROP by DROP** and for HEAVEN'S SAKE,

KEEP WHISKING.

SPEED of LIGHT

THEN, WHEN YOU'VE WHISKED ABOUT ½ of THE MIXTURE, ASK YOURSELF "IS THIS WORKING?"

YES

NO

ALL GOOD.
DEEP BREATH.
RETURN to
STEP 1.

for The FUTURE:

AS SOON AS YOU NOTICE YOUR MAYO ISN'T COMING TOGETHER AS YOU'D LIKE, STOP ADDING FAT, and GIVE IT A GOOD WHISK.

*

YOU COULD ALSO ADD A FEW CHIPS of ICE, OR A TINY SPLASH of COLD TAP WATER.

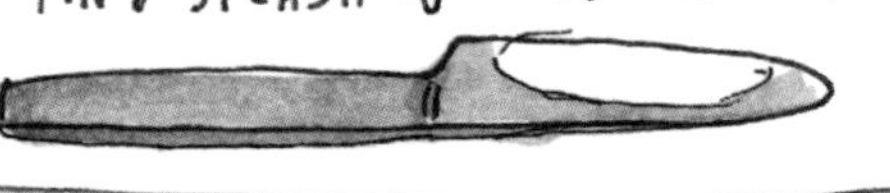

Flaky and Tender

Two proteins in wheat—glutenin and gliadin—comprise **gluten**. When you combine wheat flour and liquid to make dough or batter, these proteins link up with one another into long chains. As dough is kneaded or batter is mixed, the chains develop into strong, extensive webs or the gluten network. The expansion of these webs is called **gluten development**, and it's what makes a dough chewy and elastic.

As gluten develops, dough becomes chewier. This is why bread bakers use flours with relatively high protein content, and work hard to knead doughs for long periods of time to create crusty, chewy country loaves. Salt also preserves the strength of the gluten network. (That's why the mixer strained with effort when I belatedly added the salt to my pizza dough as a young cook at Chez Panisse.) But pastry chefs generally seek tender, flaky, and moist textures, so they do everything they can to *limit or control* gluten development, including using low protein flours and avoiding overkneading. Sugar and acids such as buttermilk or yoghurt also discourage gluten from developing, so adding them early on will tenderise pastries.

Too much fat can also inhibit gluten networks from forming. By coating individual gluten strands, fat prevents them from sticking to one another and lengthening. This is where the term **shortening** comes from, because the gluten strands remain short instead of lengthening.

Four main variables will determine the texture of any baked good (and some nonbaked ones, such as pasta): fat, water, yeast, and how much the dough or batter is kneaded or worked (see illustration on opposite page). The particular way and degree to which fat and flour are blended together, along with the type of flour and type and temperature of the fat, will also affect a pastry's texture:

Short doughs are the epitome of tenderness, crumbling and melting in your mouth. Here, flour and fat are blended together intimately, resulting in a smooth, homogeneous dough. Many of the shortest recipes, such as shortbread cookies, call for very soft or even melted butter, in order to encourage this now fluid fat to quickly coat individual flour particles, preventing gluten webs from forming. These doughs are often soft enough to press into the pan.

Rather than crumbling, **flaky** doughs break apart into flakes when you take a bite. Think of classic American pies and French *galettes*, with crusts sturdy enough to hold up to a mile-high pile of apples or juicy summer fruits, but delicate enough to produce thin, uneven flakes when sliced. To create that strength, some of the fat is worked into

Doughs & Batters

THE VARIABLES THAT DETERMINE TEXTURE

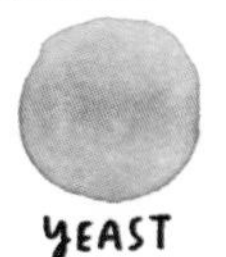
YEAST

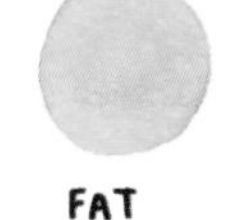
FAT

WATER

KNEADING*

CHEWY & RICH

BRIOCHE, DOUGHNUTS, and DANISHES

CHEWY

SOURDOUGH BREAD, BAVARIAN PRETZELS, BAGELS, PIZZA DOUGH, and FRENCH BAGUETTE

CRUMBLY

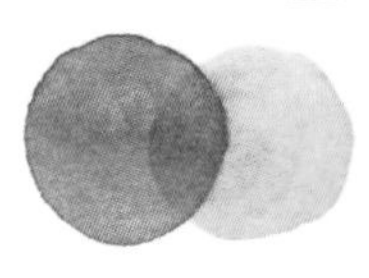

SHORTBREAD, MEXICAN WEDDING COOKIES, and RUSSIAN TEA CAKES

STRUCTURED

PÂTE À CHOUX: ÉCLAIRS, CREAM PUFF, STRUDEL, and PHYLLO

TENDER

MIDNIGHT CAKE, PIE CRUST, GALETTE DOUGH, BISCUITS, CHOCOLATE CHIP COOKIES, and BROWNIES

CHEWY, pt. 2

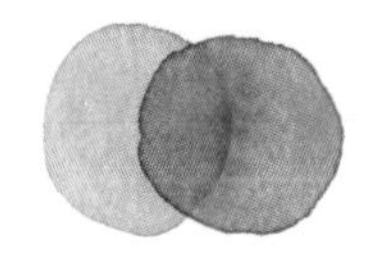

PASTA

FLAKY

PUFF PASTRY (MINIMAL WATER), CHEESE STRAWS, and PALMIERS

*ALSO INCLUDES FOLDING, MIXING, and STIRRING

the flour, and a minimal amount of gluten is developed. To achieve the signature flakes of a perfect pie or *galette* crust, the fat must be very cold so that some of it can remain in distinct pieces. Roll out a properly made pie dough and you'll *see* the chunks of butter. When you slide the pie into a hot oven, the cold pieces of butter, entrapped air, and steam from the water released by the butter, all push apart the layers of dough to create flakes.

The flakiest pastries are made with **laminated** doughs. Picture the flakes on your plate (or shirt) after you've eaten a classic puff pastry, such as a cheese straw, *palmier*, or a strudel. It's a mess! A pile of gorgeous, glassy shards! To achieve this texture, a flaky dough is wrapped around a large slab of butter. This dough-and-butter sandwich is rolled out and then folded back upon itself in a process called a **turn**. Classic puff pastry, when turned six times, will have precisely 730 layers of dough separated by 729 layers of butter! Upon entering a hot oven, each one of those distinct layers of butter will turn to steam, creating 730 layers of flakes. It's crucial, when making laminated doughs, that the fat and workspace remain cold so the butter does not melt, though the butter must be soft enough to roll into a slab.

Yeasted doughs, kneaded to develop gluten, and then treated in this way, can yield laminated breads that exist at that precarious intersection of chewiness and flakiness, including croissants, Danishes, and the Breton speciality called *kouign amann*.

Achieving Tenderness: Shortbread Cookies and Cream Biscuits

Shortbread cookies should be tender, with a fine, sandy crumb. This texture is the result of incorporating fat into flour early in the dough-making process. My favourite shortbread recipe calls for butter so soft it's "spreadable like mayonnaise" so that the fat can readily coat flour particles and keep gluten strands from developing.

Use any soft or liquid fat including cream, crème fraîche, softened cream cheese, or oil to coat flour and achieve tender textures. In classic recipes for cream biscuits, cold whipping cream functions as both the fat and the liquid binder, quickly coating the flour and obviating the need for additional water to develop the gluten network.

Achieving Flakiness: Pie Dough

Guided by lore almost as much as science, the rules of making flaky pastry appeal to my old-wives'-tale-loving heart. Stories of pastry chefs landing jobs due to their cold hands are commonplace since it's so important to keep the fat for flaky pastry dough chilled.

POWERS OF PIE

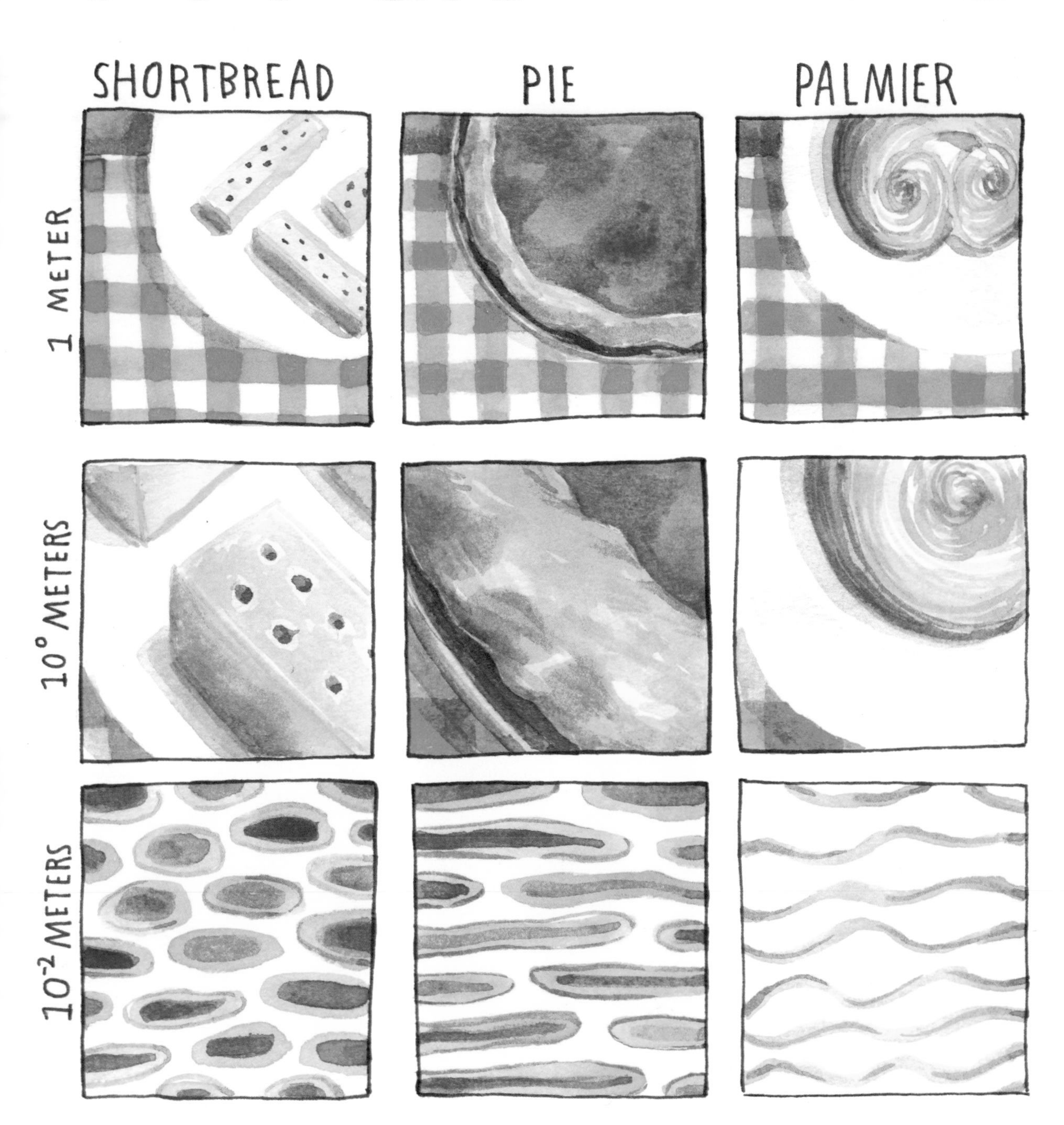

While there's little evidence to prove that rumour, there's plenty to support pastry chefs' compulsion to keep everything cold: they work on cool marble worktops and freeze their mixer bowls and metal tools. One pastry chef with whom I worked for years even insisted on making her doughs in a freezing-cold kitchen. With a sweater and puffy vest layered over her chef's coat, she'd get to work two hours before anyone else, then rush to mix her doughs before the rest of us arrived and lit the ovens, stove, and grill. She made every decision with temperature in mind, and it paid off—her pastries were ethereally flaky.

Cold-handed or not, consider temperature when you seek flakiness to create layers of developed gluten interspersed by pockets of fat. The warmer, and hence softer, your butter, the more readily it will combine with the flour. Because fat inhibits gluten development, the more intimately the two ingredients combine, the more tender—not flaky—a dough will be.

To prevent gluten from developing, keep butter cold. This will protect the delicate bonds of its emulsion while you mix and roll dough. Butter contains about 15 to 20 percent water by weight. If butter softens and melts as it's worked into the dough, its emulsion will break, releasing that water. Water droplets will bind with the flour, developing into long gluten strands that will cause the dough's delicate layers to stick together. If they're stuck together, they can't steam apart and flake as they bake. The pastry will emerge from the oven chewy and elastic.

Vegetable shortening (Trex, for example) is more forgiving of rising temperatures than butter and will remain in solid form even in a warm kitchen, but it *just doesn't taste as good*. By the time it reaches body temperature, butter melts away, leaving behind its rich, satisfying flavour as the tongue's lone souvenir. In contrast, the same chemical qualities that make shortening more stable at warm temperatures keep it from melting away at body temperature, leaving an unpleasant, plasticky residue on the tongue.

I prefer not to sacrifice flavour for the forgiveness that shortening offers. There is a trade-off: certain measures must be taken to achieve a buttery pie crust flaky enough to shatter at the lightest touch of a fork. At home, chill the diced butter, flour, and tools in the freezer before you start, in order to encourage the butter to remain in distinct chunks even as you work it into the dough. Work quickly to reduce the threat of its softening. Don't overmix. And finally, ensure that the dough spends plenty of time chilling in the fridge between the steps of mixing, rolling, assembling, and baking. I find it easiest to make pastry dough in advance and keep it tightly wrapped in the freezer, where it can stay for up to 2 months. That cuts out the most time-intensive step, freeing me to make and bake my pie when the fancy strikes.

It's important to slide the chilled, assembled pie directly into a preheated oven. In a hot oven, the water contained in the butter will quickly evaporate. The steam will push apart layers of dough as it expands with heat, yielding the flakes we so prize. If the oven's not sufficiently hot, the water won't evaporate and the crust won't set before the filling seeps in, and the pie will emerge from the oven disappointingly soggy.

Achieving Flakiness *and* Tenderness: Tart Dough

Prone to bouts of overindulgence at the farmers' market, I tend to find myself with more produce at any given moment than I know I can use up. (You try saying no to ripe Santa Rosa plums, perfectly sweet-tart nectarines, and juicy boysenberries, which always come into season on exactly the same day!) With an understanding of the science of fat, my friend Aaron Hyman sought to develop a tart dough that's structured yet delicate. His ideal dough would stand up to mounds of juicy summer stone fruit but still yield flaky shards when bitten. He wanted a crust that would be both flaky *and* tender. And I wanted a crust that I could bake any time I had extra fruit on hand.

First, he thought about how to achieve flakiness. He decided to keep everything cold, use large chunks of butter, and mix the dough just enough to form a small amount of gluten for the flaky layers. Then, to achieve tenderness, he selected liquid fats to bind the dough—cream and crème fraîche—and to coat the remaining loose flour with fat to prevent further gluten development.

Aaron's method is foolproof. I've always struggled with pastry dough, but his recipe leads me to success every time. With **Aaron's Tart Dough** in the freezer, a regal dinner is always within reach. Stockpile several discs of dough for the moment when you want to invite friends over and have little more in the pantry than a basket of ageing onions, a Parmesan rind, and a can of anchovies. Or when you realise you've committed to bringing dessert to a party but doubt you have the time to make anything special. Or when you go a little overboard at the farmers' market. Tart dough is the key to making something out of nothing.

Tender Cakes

For years I was disappointed by almost every single cake I tasted, whether I'd baked it myself or ordered it in a restaurant or bakery. I dreamed of a cake that was moist yet flavourful. So many cakes were one or the other: store-bought cake mixes yielded the texture I was after but were relatively flavourless, and cakes from fancy patisseries were rich in flavour but often dry or dense. I figured it was an either-or situation. And I resigned myself to it.

Then I tasted a chocolate birthday cake so moist and rich that I nearly fainted from delight. For days, that slice of cake haunted me, so I begged my friend for the recipe. She called it **Chocolate Midnight Cake**, for how darkly rich it was, and when she shared the recipe, I noticed it was made with oil and water rather than butter. When I tasted the **Fresh Ginger and Molasses Cake** at Chez Panisse for the first time a few months later, I was stunned by *its* perfectly moist texture and deep, spicy flavour. I begged for its recipe, too, and noticed that it was eerily similar to my friend's.

There was something to these oil cakes. I flipped through my mental recipe box and realised that many of my favourite cakes, including classic carrot cake and olive oil cake, are made with oil instead of butter. Even cake mixes, which produce the ideal texture I'd been trying to emulate, direct you to add oil. What is it about oil that yields such moist cakes?

Science holds the answer. Oil efficiently coats flour proteins and prevents strong gluten networks from forming, much like soft butter does in shortbread. Gluten development requires water, so this oil barrier significantly inhibits gluten formation, leading to a tender, rather than chewy, texture. As an added bonus, less gluten means more water in the batter, and, ultimately, a moister cake.

Once I discovered the secrets of oil cake, I could anticipate the qualities of a particular cake *without even trying the recipe*. If oil was listed among the ingredients, I knew the recipe would yield the signature moist texture I loved so much. But there were times I craved a buttery cake, too. Rich flavour, rather than a moist texture, took priority in cakes I wanted to enjoy in the afternoon with a cup of tea, or serve to friends at brunch. Emboldened by my discoveries about texture, I began to wonder if I could make a better butter cake. The answer lay not in treating butter like oil and melting it, but rather in capitalising on butter's incredible capacity for lightness.

LIGHT

Lightness might not be the first quality you associate with fat, but its remarkable capacity to entrap air when whipped allows it to act as a **leavening**, or raising, agent in cakes and transform liquid cream into billowy clouds.

Some classic cakes have no chemical leavening—that is, bicarbonate of soda or baking powder—and rely entirely on whipped fat for their cloudlike structure. In pound cake, whipped butter and eggs do all the work of leavening. In *génoise*, a type of sponge cake, whipped eggs, whose fatty yolks entrap the air and protein-rich whites surround air pockets, allow the cake to rise. This is the *only* leavener. There is no baking powder, no bicarbonate of soda, no yeast, and not even any creamed butter to help this cake rise! It is miraculous.

Achieving Lightness: Butter Cakes and Whipped Cream

When seeking rich flavour and a fine, velvety crumb, make a butter cake (or chocolate chip cookies) but take care to aerate this fat by **creaming**, or whipping, butter with sugar to trap air bubbles for leavening. Typically, cool room-temperature butter is beaten together with sugar for 4 to 7 minutes until the mixture is light and fluffy. When done correctly, the butter will act as a net, entrapping millions of tiny air bubbles throughout the mixture.

The key is to work air in slowly, so that many consistently tiny bubbles form and you don't create too much heat through friction. It might be tempting to crank up the mixer so you can get the cake into the oven sooner, but trust me—that'll take you nowhere good, fast. I speak from experience. The road to this chapter is lined with dense, fallen cakes.

As you mix, monitor the butter's temperature; remember, butter is an emulsion and if it gets too warm, it will melt and the emulsion will break or it simply won't be rigid enough to continue trapping air. You'll lose all the air you worked so hard to entrap. If butter is too cold, air won't be able to get in—not evenly at least—and the cake won't rise straight up.

And if fat isn't properly aerated, chemical leavening won't make up for it. Bicarbonate of soda and baking powder don't introduce any new air bubbles into a batter. They simply help expand, via the release of carbon dioxide gas, air bubbles already in place.

Incorporating ingredients delicately is important for the same reason—if you go to great lengths to whip air into your fat, then carelessly combine the cake's dry and wet ingredients, all at once, you'll lose all of the air you whipped up. This is where **folding**, the technique of gently combining aerated ingredients into nonaerated ingredients, becomes important. Try to fold using light movements with a rubber spatula in one hand, while spinning the bowl with the other hand.

Though the chemistry behind whipped cream is slightly different than that of whipped butter—it must be very cold, to begin with—the concept at work here is the same: fat surrounds air bubbles. As cream is whipped, solid fat droplets in the liquid break open and join together (remember that cream is a natural emulsion). Overwhip cream and the fat droplets will warm up and continue to stick to one another, making the cream unappetisingly chunky. Whip it further, and cream's emulsion will break, yielding a watery liquid—buttermilk—and solid fat—butter.

USING FAT

Only on the most special occasions do Persian meals end with dessert, so we never did much baking at our house. Plus, Maman, a health fiend, denied us excess sugar at every turn (though that did little more than encourage my brothers and me to develop fervent sweet tooths). If we wanted cookies or cake, then, we had to make them ourselves, and Maman did her best to ensure it'd be an uphill battle the whole way. She didn't equip the kitchen with either a stand mixer or a microwave for softening butter, and she stored all the extra butter in the freezer.

When it hit, the craving for cookies or cake was always urgent. I was never patient enough to wait for frozen butter to come up to room temperature, as *every single recipe* commanded. And even if I did somehow summon the discipline required to wait for butter to soften, without an electric mixer to help cream it, my cookie dough was always a mess—somehow completely overworked and undermixed at the same time, with huge pieces of unincorporated butter. As a typical teenage know-it-all, I knew I was way more clever than any recipe writer. So I figured I could just *melt* the butter for my baking on the stove and forgo the softening and creaming processes completely. Melted butter was a heck of a lot easier to stir into cookie dough with a wooden spoon, after all, and it sure made cake batter nice and pourable.

What I didn't know then was that by melting the butter, I was destroying any chance I had at working air into it. My cookies and cakes always emerged from the oven disappointingly flat and dense. At an age when my primary goal in baking was to eat something—*anything!*—sweet, this was a minor problem: my brothers and I hungrily gobbled up whatever came out of the oven. As an adult with a slightly more discerning palate, I'm going for more than just a hit of sugar. I want my desserts—and, frankly, everything I cook—to be uniformly delicious, with the ideal texture and flavour. You probably do, too. All it takes is a little forethought.

Layering Fats

Since fats have such a powerful impact on flavour, most dishes will benefit from the use of more than one kind. This is what I call **layering fats**. In addition to considering the cultural appropriateness of a particular fat, think about whether it will harmonise with the other ingredients in a dish. For example, if you're planning to finish a fish dish with butter sauce, use clarified butter to cook the fish so that the two fats will complement each other. Pair blood oranges with creamy avocado in a salad, then drizzle everything with *agrumato* olive oil to amplify the citrus flavour. For perfectly crisp waffles, melt butter to add to the batter, but brush the hot iron with fat that's rendered out of the breakfast bacon.

Sometimes you'll need to use multiple fats to achieve different textures within a single dish. Deep-fry crisp pieces of fish in grapeseed oil, and then use olive oil to make a creamy **Aïoli** to serve alongside it. Use oil to make a supremely moist **Chocolate Midnight Cake**, then slather it in buttercream frosting or softly whipped cream.

Balancing Fat

As with salt, the best way to correct overly fatty food is to rebalance the dish, so the solutions are similar to when you oversalt: add more food to increase total volume, add more acid, water it down, or add starchy or dense ingredients. If possible, chill the dish, let the fat come to the surface and solidify, then skim it off. Alternatively, lift food out of a very greasy pan and dab it on a clean towel, leaving the fat behind.

Foods that are too dry, or need just a bump of richness, can always be corrected with a little olive oil (or other appropriate oil), or another creamy ingredient such as sour cream, crème fraîche, egg yolk, or goat's cheese to improve the texture and get the flavour right. Use vinaigrette, mayonnaise, a soft, spreadable cheese, or creamy avocado to balance out dryness in a sandwich piled high with lean ingredients or built atop thick, crusty bread.

Improvising with Salt and Fat

Follow the tenets I outline in **How Fat Works** to achieve whichever texture you're after, then refer to **The World of Fat** (page 72) to guide you in evoking the flavours of wildly different places. Choose to pan-fry **Finger-Lickin' Pan-Fried Chicken**, for instance, in clarified butter for a classic French flavour. If you're craving an Indian-inspired meal and want to dig into that jar of mango chutney in the refrigerator door, change the cooking fat to ghee. If it's a Japanese chicken cutlet you're craving, use a neutral oil studded with a few drops of toasted sesame oil. In all of these cases, the fat must be sufficiently hot to swiftly lead to browning and deliver a crisp exterior.

Before you bake a birthday cake for your sweetie pie, do a little reconnaissance. Is it the moist, tender crumb of an oil cake she prefers, or the dense, velvety one of a butter cake? Since even I won't recommend improvising when you bake, let this information guide you to a recipe using the right fat to make your honey happy.

With what you know about fat and what you know about salt, you'll find that you're closer to riffing than you might think. Fat has a remarkable capacity to affect texture, while salt and fat can both enhance flavour. Practise using salt and fat to improve flavour and texture every single time you cook. If you intend to finish a salad with a shower of creamy *ricotta salata*, hold back on some of the salt until after you taste a bite of it with its salty garnish. Similarly, when you're dicing *pancetta* to add richness to ***Pasta all'Amatriciana***, wait to season the sauce until after it's absorbed all the salt from the pork. And if a recipe for pizza dough instructs you to add salt *after* kneading in olive oil, think twice about following it word for word. Start to use what you *know* to be true to guide you through the vast forests of myth and misinformation that poorly written recipes comprise.

Improvising begins with notes, and now you have two with which to compose a Salt-Fat melody. Master a third note, and you'll experience the transcendent harmony of Salt, Fat, and Acid.

ACID

In contrast to the revelations I experienced with Salt and Fat, I've learned the value of Acid gradually. It started at home, with the food my mom, grandmothers, and aunts cooked each night.

Maman, who'd grown up eating lemons and limes as an afternoon snack, never thought a dish tasted right unless it made her pucker. She always added a sour element to the plate, to balance the sweet, the salty, the starchy, the rich. Sometimes it was a sprinkle of dried sumac berries over kebabs and rice. With ***Kuku Sabzi***, a frittata packed with herbs and greens, it was a few spoonfuls of my grandmother Parivash's *torshi*, or mixed pickles. For *No-Ruz*, the Persian New Year, my dad would drive down to Mexico to find sour oranges for us to squeeze ceremoniously over fried fish and herbed rice. Into other classic dishes, Maman layered *ghooreh*, sour green grapes, and *zereshk*, the tiny tart fruits known as barberries. But mostly we used yoghurt to achieve that desired tang, spooning it over everything from eggs to soups to stews and rice and, though I wince to think of it now, spaghetti with meat sauce.

I wasn't like the other kids at school. Looking at my classmates' peanut butter sandwiches next to the *kuku sabzi*, cucumbers, and feta Maman packed in my lunch box, it was clear that my home life was dramatically different from theirs. I grew up in a house filled with the language, customs, and food of another place and time. Each year, I eagerly anticipated my grandmother Parvin's visits from Iran. I loved nothing more than watching her unpack while the room flooded with exotic aromas: saffron, cardamom, and rosewater mingled with the humid, slightly mouldy Caspian air that had tucked itself into the fabric lining of her bags over the years. One by one, she'd pull out treats: pistachios roasted with saffron and lime juice, sour cherry preserves, sheets of homemade *lavashak*, plum leather so sour it made my cheeks hurt. Growing up, I learned from my family to delight in sour foods and let my palate become the most Persian part of me. But it wasn't until I left home that I realised that there's so much more to acid than just the pucker.

As part of my parents' ongoing efforts to delay our assimilation for as long as possible, we never celebrated Thanksgiving. I first celebrated the holiday in college, with a friend and her family. I loved the hubbub involved in preparing and gathering for the meal, but the actual *eating* part of Thanksgiving was kind of a letdown. We sat down to a table piled high with food: a humongous whole turkey, roasted and ceremoniously carved;

brown gravy made with the drippings; mashed potatoes thick with butter and cream; creamed spinach spiced with nutmeg; Brussels sprouts boiled so long that my friend's nearly toothless grandmother could easily chew them; and stuffing packed with sausage, bacon, and chestnuts. I *really* love to eat, but these soft, rich, bland foods bored my palate after just a few bites. Spooning more cranberry sauce onto my plate each time the bowl passed my way, I kept eating in hope of tasting something satisfying. But it never happened, and every year on the fourth Thursday of November I ate until I felt mildly ill, like everyone else.

Once I started cooking at Chez Panisse, I began to spend the holiday with friends from the restaurant. At my first Thanksgiving with other cooks, my palate never became bored. I never felt like eating was a chore. I never felt sick afterwards. This certainly wasn't because the foods we'd cooked were somehow healthier or more virtuous. So what was it?

It hit me that the Thanksgiving dinners I'd spent with other cooks mirrored the traditional Persian meals I'd grown up eating. Acid had been tucked into every dish, and it had brought the meal to life. Sour cream lent a tang to mashed potatoes. A splash of white wine added just before serving lightened the gravy. Hidden in the big, beautiful mass of stuffing among torn sourdough croutons, greens, and bites of sausage were prunes soaked in white wine—secret caches of acid, most welcome. Roasted winter squash and Brussels sprouts were tossed in an Italian *Agrodolce,* a sauce made with sugar, chillies, and vinegar. The salsa verde featured fried sage, a welcome partner to the cranberry-quince sauce that I'd made with a nod to the Persian quince preserves Maman jarred every autumn. Even dessert, with a drizzle of dark caramel for the pies and a touch of crème fraîche folded into the whipped cream, had a tang. It dawned on me that the reason why everyone spoons so much cranberry sauce over everything at Thanksgiving is that on most tables, it's just about the only form of acid available.

I began to see that the true value of acid is not its pucker, but rather, *balance.*

Acid grants the palate relief, and makes food more appealing by offering contrast.

Soon after, I learned another of acid's secrets. Late one morning at Chez Panisse, I was rushing to finish a batch of carrot soup in time for lunch. Like most of the soups we served in the café, it was pretty simple. I sweated onions in olive oil and butter. I peeled and sliced the carrots and added them to the pot once the onions were soft. I submerged the vegetables in stock, seasoned with salt, and simmered the soup until everything was tender. Then I blended the contents of the pot into a velvety purée and adjusted the salt.

It tasted perfect. I brought a spoonful to Russ, the eternally boyish chef, as he rushed upstairs for the menu meeting with the servers. He tasted it, and without pausing to turn around, said, "Add a capful of vinegar to the pot before you bring it up!"

Vinegar? Who'd ever heard of putting vinegar in soup? Was Russ crazy? Did I hear him right? I didn't want to ruin the entire pot, so I took a spoonful of my beautiful soup and added a single drop of red wine vinegar. Tasting it, I was floored. I'd expected the vinegar to turn the soup into a sweet-and-sour abomination. Instead, the vinegar acted like a prism, revealing the soup's nuanced flavours—I could taste the butter and oil, the onions and stock, even the sugar and minerals within the carrots. If blindfolded and quizzed, never in a million years would I have been able to identify vinegar as one of the ingredients. But now, if something I cooked and seasoned ever tasted so dull again, I'd know exactly what was missing.

Just as I'd learned to constantly evaluate a dish for salt, now I knew I needed to always taste for acid, too. It was finally clear to me—acid is salt's alter ego. While salt *enhances* flavours, acid *balances* them. By acting as a foil to salt, fat, sugar, and starch, acid makes itself indispensable to everything we cook.

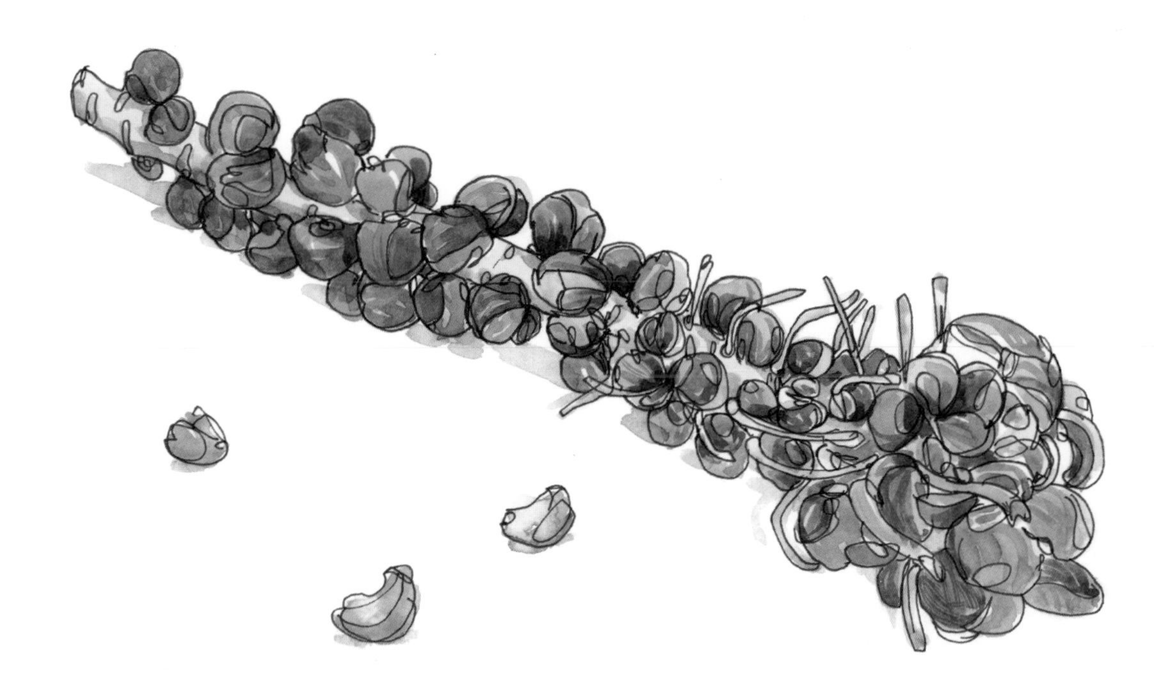

SOURCES OF ACID

ACIDS:

1. VINEGAR and VERJUS (UNRIPE GRAPE JUICE) 2. LEMON and LIME JUICE 3. WINE and FORTIFIED WINE

ACIDIC INGREDIENTS:

4. CONDIMENTS: MUSTARD, KETCHUP, SALSA, MAYONNAISE, CHUTNEYS, HOT SAUCE, etc. 5. FRUIT and DRIED FRUIT 6. CHOCOLATE and COCOA POWDER 7. CURED MEATS 8. CULTURED DAIRY PRODUCTS: CHEESE, YOGURT, BUTTERMILK, CRÈME FRAÎCHE, SOUR CREAM, MASCARPONE 9. PICKLED and FERMENTED VEGETABLES and THEIR BRINES 10. COFFEE and TEA 11. TOMATOES, CANNED OR FRESH 12. BEER 13. SOURDOUGH CULTURES and SOURDOUGH BREAD 14. HONEY, MOLASSES, DARK CARAMEL

WHAT IS ACID?

Technically, any substance that registers below 7 on the pH scale is an acid. I don't have a working pH metre in my kitchen—I broke mine while testing everything in my kitchen for the chart on page 109—and I'm guessing you don't, either. No matter. We've all got a much handier acid sensor—a tongue. Anything that tastes sour is a source of acid. In cooking, acid usually comes in the form of lemon juice, vinegar, or wine. But, like fat, acid has myriad sources. Anything fermented, from cheese and sourdough bread to coffee and chocolate, will lend a pleasant tang to your food, as will most fruits, including that vegetable-posing chameleon, the tomato.

ACID AND FLAVOUR

Acid's Effect on Flavour

The term *mouthwatering* has long been a synonym for *delicious*. Foods that are the most enjoyable to eat cause our mouths to water—that is, to produce saliva. Of the five basic tastes, acid makes our mouths water the most. When we eat anything sour, our mouths flood with saliva to balance out the acidity, as it's dangerous for our teeth. The more acidic the food, the more saliva rushes in. Acid, then, is an integral part of many of our most pleasurable eating experiences.

Yet on its own, acid isn't particularly gratifying. It's the way acid contrasts with *other* tastes that heightens our pleasure in foods. Like salt, acid heightens other flavours. But it works a bit differently: while the salt threshold is absolute, acid balance is relative.

Think of seasoning a simple pot of broth with salt. When the salt concentration passes a certain point, the broth will become inedible. The only way to salvage the broth is to add more unseasoned liquid to reduce the salt concentration, increasing the total volume considerably.

Acid balance is different. Think of making lemonade. Measure out the lemon juice, water, and sugar, but mix together only the lemon juice and water. Take a sip, and it will taste unpalatably sour. Then add the sugar, and taste again. It'll be delicious. Yet the lemonade is *no less acidic*: the **pH**, or measure of acidity, remains constant after the sugar is added. The acidity is simply *balanced* by sweetness. And sugar isn't acid's only counterpoint: salt, fat, bitterness, and starch also invariably benefit from the welcome contrast of acid.

cooks in the American South. Southerners also have an affinity for cane vinegar, which is also the acid of choice in the Philippines, where sugarcane is a major crop.

Citrus

When it comes to citrus, lemon trees are well suited to the coastal climates in Mediterranean countries, so choose lemon to squeeze into *tabbouleh* and hummus, and over grilled octopus, Niçoise salad, or Sicilian fennel and orange salad. Lime trees, on the other hand, grow more readily in tropical climates, so limes are the preferred citrus everywhere from Mexico and Cuba to India, Vietnam, and Thailand. Use limes in guacamole, *pho ga*, green papaya salad, and *kachumbar*, the Indian answer to pico de gallo. One form of citrus you should *never* use, though, is bottled citrus juice. Made from concentrate and doctored with preservatives and citrus oils, it tastes bitter and doesn't offer any of the clean, bright flavour of fresh-squeezed juice.

Pickles

From Indian *achar* to Iranian *torshi*, from Korean kimchee to Japanese *tsukemono*, from German sauerkraut to chow-chow in the American South, every culture has its pickles. A few slices of steak can easily become a bowl of Korean *bibimbap* if piled high with kimchee, or they can become a taco with a few pickled carrots and jalapeños depending on what's in the fridge.

Dairy

Let cultured dairy products be the secret weapon in your quest for acid balance. Change a salad by topping it with cheese, be it Greek feta, Italian gorgonzola, or Spanish Manchego. Spoon sour cream over latkes, Mexican *crema* over tacos, crème fraîche onto a French berry tart, and yoghurt over the little lamb kebabs most of Eastern Asia calls ***Kufte***.

Look at a lamb shoulder and know you can take it to Morocco by braising it with preserved lemons, to the south of France with some white wine and green olives, or to Greece with red wine and tomatoes. The same cabbage slaw can evoke the American South when made with mustard and cider vinegar, Mexico when made with lime juice and coriander, or the Chinese kitchen when spiked with rice wine vinegar, spring onions, and toasted peanuts. Learn to not only consider, but also take advantage of, the flavour of an acid to guide the direction a dish takes.

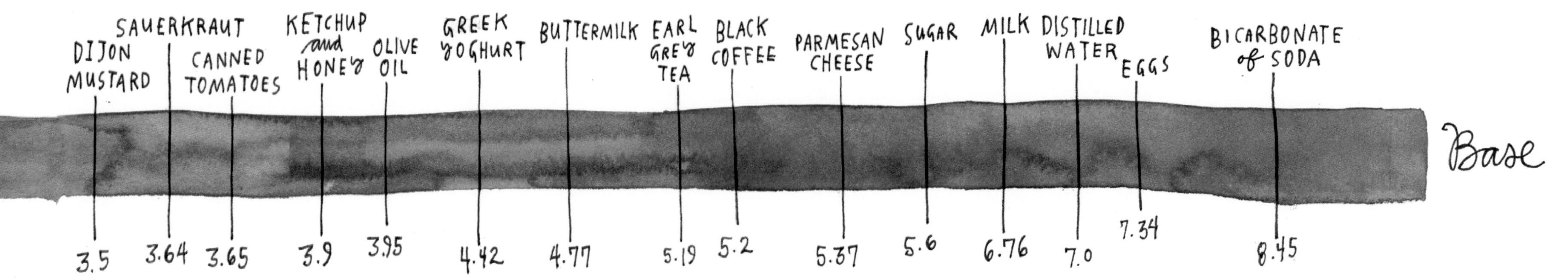

the World of Acid

USE THIS WHEEL to HELP you CHOOSE WHICH COOKING ACIDS (INNER CIRCLE) and GARNISHING ACIDS (OUTER CIRCLE) to USE AS you COOK FOOD from AROUND THE WORLD.

Region	Country	Cooking acids (inner circle)	Garnishing acids (outer circle)
EUROPE	GREECE & CYPRUS	BEER, WINE, VINEGAR, LEMON	TOMATO, OLIVE, YOGURT, FETA CHEESE, HALLOUMI
	SCANDINAVIA	BEER, WINE, VINEGAR	PICKLES, PICKLED HERRING, PICKLED CAPERS, SKYR, HAVARTI, DANISH BLUE CHEESE, BERRIES
	EASTERN EUROPE	WINE, BEER, CIDER, CIDER VINEGAR, WINE VINEGAR	SOUR CREAM, SOUR CABBAGE, YOGURT and QUARK, PICKLES, BRINED CHEESE
	GERMANY	WINE, WINE VINEGAR, CIDER, CIDER VINEGAR, BEER	SOUR CREAM, SAUERKRAUT, MUSTARD, PUMPERNICKEL BREAD, PICKLES
	SPAIN	WINE, SHERRY, WINE & SHERRY VINEGARS, LEMON	OLIVES, ROMANESCO SAUCE, CHORIZO, FRESH GOAT'S CHEESE, MANCHEGO
	ITALY	WINE, WINE VINEGAR, LEMON	BALSAMIC VINEGAR, TOMATO, OLIVES, PARMESAN, PECORINO, BUFALA MOZZARELLA
	FRANCE	WINE, WINE VINEGAR, CIDER, LEMON, VERJUS	DIJON MUSTARD, CRÈME FRAÎCHE, OLIVES, CORNICHONS, SOURDOUGH BREAD, TOMATO, GOAT'S CHEESE, GRUYÈRE, ROQUEFORT
	UNITED KINGDOM	MALT VINEGAR, BEER, CIDER, WINE, FRUIT WINE	CHEDDAR and STILTON, MUSTARD, KETCHUP, TARTAR SAUCE, MINT SAUCE, BUTTERMILK, SALAD CREAM, BROWN SAUCE, HORSERADISH SAUCE
NORTH AMERICA	U.S. & CANADA	CIDER VINEGAR, WHITE VINEGAR, BEER, WINE, WINE VINEGAR	TOMATO, MUSTARD, BUTTERMILK, PICKLES, HOT SAUCE, BACON and HAM, CHEDDAR and CREAM CHEESE
	MEXICO	LIME, SOUR ORANGE, WHITE VINEGAR, BEER	TOMATO, FRESH CHEESES, SALSA, SOUR CREAM, OLIVES, PICKLES, CHORIZO, MOLE, CHOCOLATE, DULCE de LECHE
	CENTRAL AMERICA	LIME, ORANGE, WHITE VINEGAR, BEER	CURTIDO (FERMENTED CABBAGE), AJÍ PEPPER SAUCE, FRESH CHEESE, TAMARIND, TOMATO
	CARIBBEAN	LEMON, LIME, ORANGE, CIDER VINEGAR	TOMATO, MOJO (LEMON-GARLIC MARINADE), OLIVES, PIKLIZ, SOS TI-MALICE (HOT SAUCE)
SOUTH AMERICA	ARGENTINA & URUGUAY	LEMON, WINE, WINE VINEGAR, BEER	CHIMICHURRI, TOMATO, MANCHEGO and PROVOLONE, DRIED FRUIT, PICKLED AUBERGINE
	CHILE, PERU & BOLIVIA	LIME, ORANGE	AJÍ PEPPER SAUCE, TOMATO
	BRAZIL	LEMON, VINEGAR, ORANGE	REQUEIJÃO (CREAMY CHEESE), TOMATO, PINEAPPLE, PASSION FRUIT, PIRIPIRI HOT SAUCE
ASIA	CHINA	RICE WINE, BLACK VINEGAR, MOUTAI LIQUOR	PICKLED VEGETABLES, SOY SAUCE, PLUM SAUCE, FERMENTED BEAN PASTE, OYSTER SAUCE
	JAPAN	RICE WINE VINEGAR, RICE WINE	SOY SAUCE, TAMARI, MISO, PICKLES, PONZU
	KOREA	RICE WINE VINEGAR, RICE WINE, BEER	KIMCHEE, GOCHUJANG (PEPPER PASTE), SOY SAUCE, FERMENTED BEAN PASTE
	THAILAND	LIME JUICE, RICE WINE VINEGAR, RICE WINE, BEER	FISH SAUCE, SRIRACHA, SAMBAL, CURRY PASTE, PICKLES
	VIETNAM	LIME, RICE WINE VINEGAR, RICE WINE, BEER	FISH SAUCE, HOISIN SAUCE, PICKLED SHALLOTS
	INDIA	LIME, BEER	MIXED PICKLES, YOGURT, PANEER, CHUTNEYS, BUTTERMILK, FERMENTED RICE CAKE, TAMARIND
	IRAN	LEMON, LIME, VINEGAR	YOGURT, PICKLES, DRIED FRUIT, BARBERRIES, SUMAC, POMEGRANATES
	MEDITERRANEAN	DATE VINEGAR, LEMON, LIME, WINE, BEER	YOGURT, LABNEH, FETA CHEESE, PEPPER SAUCE, POMEGANATES, PICKLES, SUMAC
AFRICA	HORN of AFRICA	TEJ (HONEY WINE), BEER, WINE	INJERA and CANJEERO, HOT SAUCE, TOMATO, MANGO, GUAVA, GRAPEFRUIT, COTTAGE CHEESE
	NORTH AFRICA	LEMON, LIME, DATE VINEGAR	PRESERVED LEMON, DRIED FRUIT, SUMAC, CHARMOULA, HARISSA, TOMATO, OLIVES, PICKLES
	WEST AFRICA	HONEY, WINE, BEER, PALM WINE	TOMATO, SUMBALA (FERMENTED LOCUST BEAN)

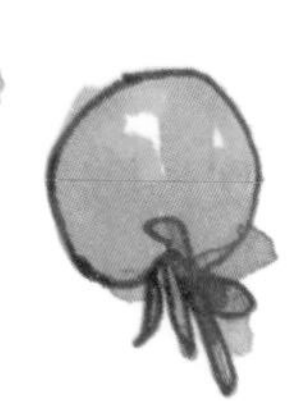

I might have written for the sauce the first week of the summer would have been completely inaccurate by the last week. And these were all the same variety of tomatoes from the same farm! This is another reason why you can't always rely solely on recipes in the kitchen. Instead, taste as you go, develop a sense for acid balance, and trust your instincts.

Acids of the World

Many iconic dishes are defined by their particular acids: a peanut butter sandwich, for example, suffers without the tang jelly provides. No proper Brit would consider eating a plate of fish and chips without malt vinegar. Imagine *carnitas* tacos without a spoonful of salsa. Or *xiao long bao*, the classic soup dumplings of Shanghai, served with anything other than Chinese black vinegar. Just as with cooking fats, acid can change the direction of a dish, so let geography and tradition guide your choice of which one to use.

Vinegars

In general, a region's vinegar reflects its agriculture. Italy, France, Germany, and Spain—countries known for wine production—make good use of wine vinegars in their cooking. Choose sherry vinegar for ***Romesco***, the Catalonian sauce made with peppers and toasted nuts, champagne vinegar for *mignonette* sauce to serve with oysters, and red wine vinegar to dress radicchio and to make *blaukraut*, the classic German braised red cabbage. On the other hand, rice vinegar is a staple in many Asian countries—from Thailand and Vietnam

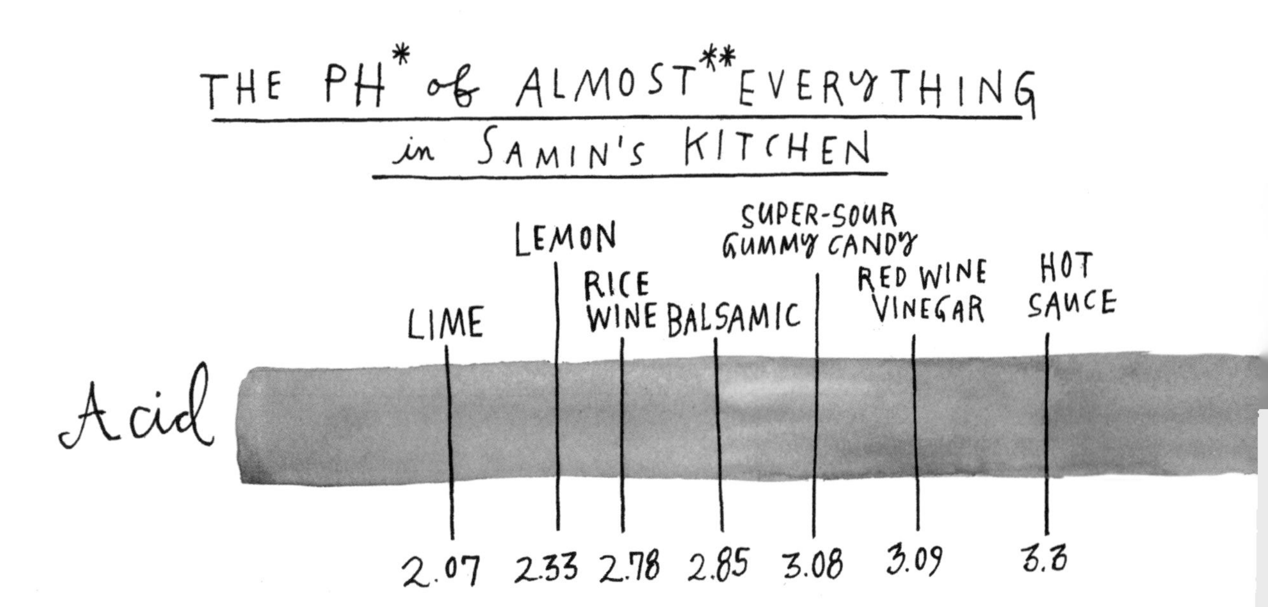

The Flavour of Acid

Pure acid tastes sour—nothing less, nothing more. Sourness isn't necessarily pleasant or unpleasant. Taste a drop of distilled white vinegar—the stuff we all keep around for household tasks like unclogging drains and cleaning the stove. You'll see it's more or less flavourless. It just tastes sour.

Many of the delicious flavours we associate with acidic ingredients—for example, the distinctive, fruity tang of a wine or the funkiness of a cheese—result from *how* these ingredients are produced. Everything from the type of wine used to make a vinegar or the kind of milk or bacteria used to make a cheese will affect the flavours of these acidic ingredients. Even the same cheese, aged for different lengths of time, will taste more acidic and complex in flavour, which is why we call a young cheddar mild and an aged one sharp.

Acids from different sources vary not only in flavour but also in concentration. All vinegars are not equally acidic. Nor is the acidity of citrus juice consistent. In John McPhee's 1966 book *Oranges*, the literary journalist illustrates how natural elements affect flavour. First, he explains how the acidity of oranges diminishes with an orchard's increasing proximity to the equator. One particular Brazilian variety is practically acid-free! He goes on to describe in characteristic detail how not only the location of a tree, but the location of an orange *on* a tree, will affect flavour.

> Ground fruit—the orange that one can reach and pick from the ground—is not as sweet as fruit that grows high on the tree. Outside fruit is sweeter than inside fruit. Oranges grown on the south side of a tree are sweeter than oranges grown on the east or west sides, and oranges grown on the north side are the least sweet of the lot . . . Beyond this, there are differentiations of quality inside a single orange. Individual segments vary from one another in their content of acid and sugar. . . . When [orange pickers] eat an orange . . . they eat the [sweeter] blossom half and throw the rest of the orange away.

These kinds of natural variations mean you can't know whether your orange is as acidic, ripe, or sweet as the one the recipe tester used in some distant kitchen. I once spent an entire summer making and canning sauce with Early Girl tomatoes from a friend's farm. Every single batch I made was different from the last—some tomatoes were watery, others were more flavourful. Some were sweet, others were more acidic. Any recipe

HOW ACID WORKS

Though acid primarily affects flavour, it also can trigger chemical reactions that change the colour and texture of food. Learn to anticipate these effects so you can make better decisions about how, and when, to add acid.

Acid and Colour

Acid dulls vibrant greens, so wait until the last possible moment to dress salads, mix vinegar into herb salsas, and squeeze lemon over cooked green vegetables such as spinach.

On the other hand, acid keeps reds and purples vivid. Cabbage, red chard stems, or beetroots will best retain their colour when cooked with anything slightly acidic, such as apples, lemon, or vinegar.

Raw fruits and vegetables that are susceptible to **oxidation**, the enzymatic browning that results from exposure to oxygen—sliced apples, artichokes, bananas, and avocados—will retain their natural colour if coated with a little acid or kept in water mixed with a few drops of lemon juice or vinegar until they are ready to cook or eat.

	BEFORE ACID	AFTER ACID
GREENS		
REDS and PURPLES		
RAW FRUITS and VEGETABLES		

Acid and Texture

Acid keeps vegetables and legumes tougher, longer. Anything containing cellulose or pectin, including legumes, fruits, and vegetables, will cook much more slowly in the presence of acid. While ten to fifteen minutes of simmering in water is enough to soften carrots into baby food, they'll still be somewhat firm after an hour of stewing in red wine. The acid in tomatoes explains why those pesky onions float to the top of a pot of sauce or soup and stay there, never getting soft, even after hours of cooking. To prevent this crunchy mishap, cook onions until they're tender before adding any tomatoes, wine, or vinegar to the pot.

When cooking beans or any legumes, including the chickpeas for hummus, a pinch of bicarbonate of soda will gently nudge the bean water away from acidity towards **alkalinity**, ensuring tenderness. And, just like those onions, cook legumes until they are completely tender before adding anything acidic. A great Mexican chef once told me that dousing cooked beans with vinegar or vinaigrette sort of "uncooks" them, tightening and toughening the skins a bit. Account for that tightening when preparing beans for a salad, and cook the beans just a touch longer than you might otherwise.

Use this chemistry to your advantage when deciding how to cook vegetables. Boiling dilutes the relatively acidic liquid contained in vegetable cells, so it will generally yield more tender vegetables than roasting will. Roast big, beautiful slices of cauliflower or Romanesco broccoli to ensure they retain their shape. Boil potatoes or parsnips so that they melt into a puddle of tenderness, perfect for puréeing or mashing.

Acid also encourages bonds between **pectin** groups—the gelling agent in fruit—so that they can trap water to help set jam or jelly. Some fruits, such as apples and blueberries, don't contain enough acid to bond the pectin on their own, so we help them along by squeezing some fresh lemon juice into the jam pot and into fruit fillings for pies and cobblers to encourage them to set.

Acid is required when using **chemical leavenings** such as bicarbonate of soda or baking powder. Visualise the bicarbonate of soda and vinegar volcanoes of your elementary school science projects. Just like that, but on a much smaller scale, acid reacts with bicarbonate of soda to release carbon dioxide bubbles to leaven baked goods. Doughs and batters leavened by bicarbonate of soda should also have an acidic ingredient such as natural cocoa powder, brown sugar, honey, or buttermilk. Baking powder, on the other hand, already contains powdered tartaric acid and doesn't need an external source of acid to react.

Acid encourages the proteins in an egg white to assemble, or **coagulate**, more quickly but less densely than they otherwise would. Under normal conditions, strands of egg proteins unravel and tighten when heated. As they do, the strands squeeze out water, causing eggs to toughen and dry out. Acid draws egg proteins together before they can unravel, which inhibits them from joining too closely. A few secret drops of lemon juice will produce creamier, more tender scrambled eggs. For perfect poached eggs, add a capful of vinegar into boiling water to help speed up coagulation of the white and strengthen the outer texture, while preserving the runny yolk.

Acid aids in stabilising whipped egg whites by encouraging more, finer air pockets, helping to increase the volume of the egg white foam. Though cream of tartar—a by-product of wine-making—is the form of acid traditionally added to egg whites as they're whipped for meringues, cakes, and soufflés, a few drops of vinegar or lemon juice per egg white will yield a similar result.

Dairy proteins called **casein** will coagulate, or curdle, with the addition of acid. With the exception of butter and double cream, which are very low in protein, dairy should only be added to acidic dishes at the last minute. While curdled fresh dairy, when unintended, is usually inedible, this same reaction makes cultured dairy—from yoghurt to crème fraîche to cheese—possible, offering us a delicious, entirely new category of acidic ingredients to incorporate into food. Try making your own **crème fraîche**—it couldn't be easier. Just combine 2 tablespoons of crème fraîche or cultured buttermilk with 450ml of double cream. Pour into a clean glass jar, cover loosely or leave uncovered, and leave out at warm room temperature for 2 days, or until it thickens. That's it. Use it in **Blue Cheese Dressing**, **Chicken with Vinegar**, or **Tangy Whipped Cream**. Cover and store it in the fridge for up to two weeks. Use the last few spoonfuls to start the next batch in the same way.

When acid is incorporated into doughs and batters, it will tenderise them, much as fat does. Whether it comes in the form of cultured dairy, natural (nonalkalised) cocoa powder, or vinegar, acid in a dough or a batter will disrupt the gluten network, resulting in a more tender product. If it's chewiness you're after, wait as long as possible into the process of dough-making to add acidic ingredients.

Acid tenderises, then toughens, meat and fish proteins. Imagine protein as coiled strands folded up into bundles. When acid comes into contact with the coils, they unfold and unwind. This process is called **denaturation**. These denatured proteins then begin to bump into each other and **coagulate**, reconnecting into an intimate network. The same thing happens when proteins are heated, which is why acid is sometimes said to cook meat or fish.

PROTEIN BEHAVIOUR

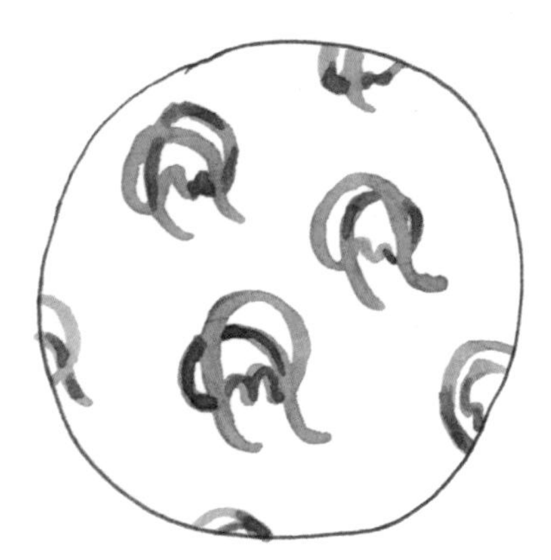

PROTEIN STRANDS *without* ANY ACID OR HEAT

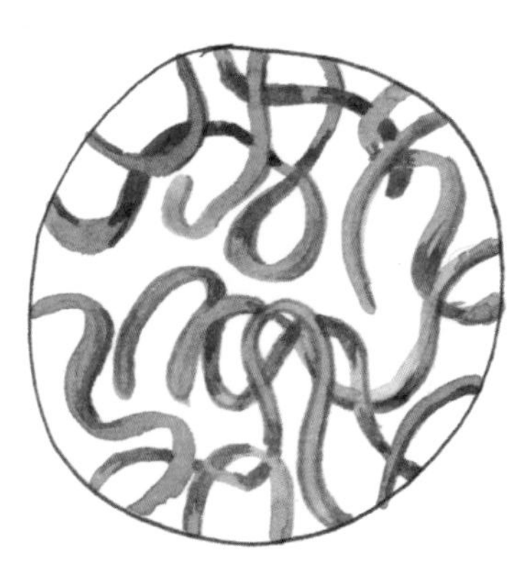

PROTEIN STRANDS *with* SOME ACID, UNWINDING *and* UNFOLDING

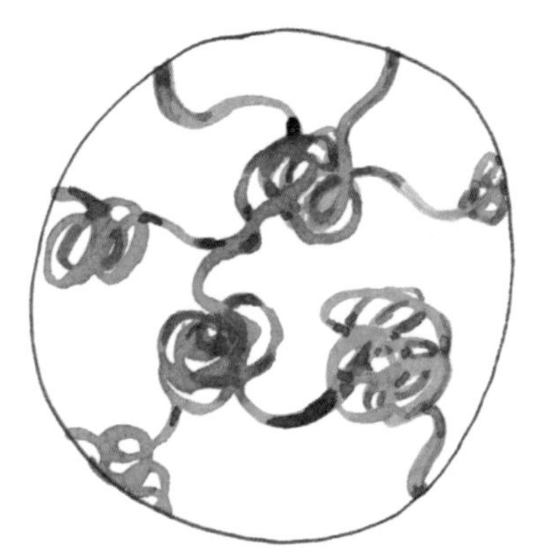

PROTEIN STRANDS RECONNECTED— A.K.A COAGULATED

At first, the intimate network traps water that was previously bound up in muscle fibres, leading to moist, tender food. But if the denaturation conditions persist—that is, if food continues to sit in acid—the protein network will continue to tighten, squeezing water out of the protein altogether, resulting in tough, dry food, much like an overcooked steak.

To understand this progression, consider the way the texture of a piece of sashimi will become tender, bright-tasting fish tartare with the addition of acid, and then turn into a chewy ceviche over time. Fish meant for cooking shouldn't marinate in acid for more than a few minutes, but dip any flaky, white-fleshed fish into buttermilk and flour before frying, or toss sea bass with lemon juice and curry powder just before skewering and grilling, and you'll get the benefit of moist texture along with the pleasant hit of tartness.

Acid also helps break down **collagen**, the main structural protein found in tough cuts of meat. Add wine or tomatoes as you begin to cook braises and stews, since the more quickly the collagen melts, the sooner the meat will grow juicy and succulent.

Producing Acid

While we introduce salt and fat into our food in the form of distinct ingredients, there are two easy ways to *produce* acid in food as we cook. One process is rather fast, the other rather slow.

The fast method? Browning foods. In Salt and Fat, I explained that food begins to brown once its surface temperature climbs considerably beyond the boiling point. This can happen in the toaster to a slice of bread, in the oven to cookies and cake, on the grill to meats, fish and vegetables, or in the pan to caramel. The chemical reaction involved in browning sugars is called **caramelisation**. The chemical reaction involved in browning meats, seafood, vegetables, baked goods, or just about anything else is called the **Maillard reaction**, after Louis-Camille Maillard, the scientist who discovered it. There will be more details about these delicious, mysterious chemical reactions in Heat.

Though they're entirely different processes, caramelisation and the Maillard reaction share some similarities. Both create acidic flavour compounds, in addition to many other tasty molecules, as by-products. As it caramelises, a single sugar molecule will develop into hundreds of new and different compounds, including some acids. In other words, equal amounts of sugar and burnt caramel by weight are not equally sweet, and in fact caramel is *acidic*! Similar acidic compounds are produced in carbohydrates and proteins by the Maillard reaction.

Though producing acidity is rarely a reason to brown food, knowing that the process will develop a host of new flavours, including some sour ones, can be a valuable tool. Imagine tasting two batches of ice cream, both made with the same amount of sugar. In one batch, the sugar was added directly to the dairy. In the other batch, some of the sugar was cooked into dark caramel before being mixed in. The ice cream made with caramelised sugar will not only taste less sweet but will also be far more complex, because it has the vital flavour contrasts that acid provides.

The other, much slower, method for producing acid in the kitchen is **fermentation**, where, in addition to many other flavour-producing processes, carbohydrates transform into carbon dioxide and acids or alcohols using yeasts, bacteria, or a combination thereof. Wine, beer, and cider are of course fermented, but so are naturally leavened breads, all sorts of pickles, cured meats, cultured dairy, and even coffee and chocolate.

Some of the most delicious bread I've tasted is naturally leavened, and has been allowed to rise—which is to say ferment—slowly. According to Chad Robertson, of

Tartine Bakery in San Francisco, who lets his dough rise for more than thirty hours, slow fermentation "improves the flavour, in large part because more sugars are available to caramelise during the baking. The loaves brown faster and the crust gets darker." Subtly sour, Chad's bread is layered with complex flavours; every time I taste it, I enthusiastically declare it the best loaf of bread in the world! Bake a naturally leavened loaf of bread sometime when your schedule allows. The results can be stellar, especially if you bake it Chad's way and let the elements in the crust undergo both caramelisation and the Maillard reaction, yielding layer upon layer of acidity and sweetness.

USING ACID

As with all good cooking, the best way to use acid well is to taste, over and over again. Using acid is much like using salt: if something is noticeably sour, it's probably got too much acid. But if a food tastes bright and clean, then its acid balance is spot-on.

Layering Acid

When considering acid, think about *which* acid or combination of acids to use, and *when* to add them. Just as with salt, and fat, a single dish can often benefit from several forms of acid: think of this as **layering acids** as you cook.

Cooking Acids

Learn to use acid like salt to season food from within. While acid presents many last-second opportunities to adjust dishes—with a final squeeze of lemon, crumble of goat's cheese, or pile of pickles—some acids should be worked into dishes from the start. These are what I call **cooking acids**. Examples include tomatoes in pasta sauce, white wine in **Poultry Ragù**, beer in a pot of chilli, vinegar in **Chicken with Vinegar**, and mirin (rice wine) in **Glazed Five-Spice Chicken**.

Cooking acids tend to be mellow, transforming the foods with which they are cooked slowly, over time. They can be extraordinarily subtle; while their presence may go undetected,

SOURCES of ACID

their absence is sharply felt. I learned this painful lesson when at the request of a distant relative, I tried to make beef bourguignon without the Bourgogne in Iran, where wine isn't readily available. No matter what I did, I couldn't get the dish to taste right without that crucial ingredient.

Give acid the time it needs to do its silent work when macerating shallots and onions. **Macerate**, from Latin, "to soften," refers to the process whereby ingredients soak in some form of acid—usually vinegar or citrus juice—to soften their harshness. Simply coat the shallots or onions in acid—they don't need to be completely submerged. If you plan on using a couple of tablespoons of vinegar for a dressing, just coat the shallots with it first, and wait 15 or 20 minutes before adding oil to build the dressing in the same cup or bowl. It will be enough to prevent dragon breath.

There's no replacement for working acid early into braises and stews; the remarkable alchemy of time and heat will soften any dish's sharp edges. Omit the tomatoes and beer from **Pork Braised with Chillies** and the sweetness of the aromatic base of onions and garlic will dominate. The sweetness resulting from browning needs the foil of acid, too. Deglazing a pan with wine, whether for risotto, pork chops, fish fillets, or a more complex reduction sauce will keep a dish from skewing too sweet.

Garnishing Acids

Garnishing acids, on the other hand, are used to finish a dish. While no amount of salt at the table will make up for underseasoning food from within, a hit of acid at the very last second often improves food, which is why garnishing acids are so important. As the volatile aromatic molecules disperse over time, the flavour of fresh citrus juice will transform, losing some of its brightness—so freshly squeezed juice is best. The application of heat will change the flavours of both citrus juice and vinegar, dulling the former and mellowing the latter, so add them just before serving when you want their full flavour impact.

You can incorporate different garnishing acids into a single dish to increase flavour. Balsamic vinegar isn't always acidic enough to dress a salad on its own, so spike it with red wine vinegar. Or layer vinegar with citrus juice, which is brighter: make **Citrus Vinaigrette** with white wine vinegar *and* blood orange juice to drizzle over an **Avocado Salad**. The strong acidity of the vinegar will balance the richness of the avocado, while the vivid orange juice will round out its flavour.

When you can, use the same kind of acid for cooking and garnishing—spoon tomato salsa, for example, atop pork braised with tomatoes; finish a risotto with a fresh splash of wine from the same bottle used earlier to deglaze the pan. This kind of layering offers multiple tastes of the same ingredient.

And then there are times when a single form of acid isn't enough to accomplish its task. Feta cheese, tomato, olives, and red wine vinegar offer four distinct forms of acid in a Greek salad. To bring out a chorus of bright, happy notes, serve that pork I mentioned above with all kinds of acidic condiments, including *queso fresco*, sour cream, and a **Bright Cabbage Slaw** tossed with vinegar and lime juice.

And think back to that **Caesar** salad, where Parmesan and Worcestershire sauce—sources of acid—both lend the dressing tang as well as salt and umami. Balance the creamy, salty dressing with wine vinegar and lemon juice. Tinker with all four sources of acid as you taste and adjust, little by little, until it's perfect.

PASTA ALLE VONGOLE

3. NOW, MAKE THE WHITE WINE CLAM SAUCE
HEAT UP SOME OIL, ADD DICED ONION, and A PINCH of SALT.
COOK TILL TENDER, THEN ADD A CLOVE or TWO of SLICED GARLIC
and RED PEPPER FLAKES
THEN ADD CHERRYSTONES or MANILAS, CRANK THE HEAT, ADD A SPLASH of CLAM COOKING LIQUID & COVER.
AS SOON AS THEY OPEN, USE A SLOTTED SPOON to ADD LITTLENECK CLAMS
COOK for A MINUTE and THEN
4. ADD NOODLES & TASTE.
ADJUST ACID with SOME WHITE WINE or LEMON JUICE.
TASTE.
ADJUST ACID with SOURDOUGH BREAD CRUMBS and PARMESAN CHEESE. and
TASTE. and EAT.
CHEAP BOTTLE LEFT OVER from A PARTY

Make ***Pasta alle Vongole*** to practise layering acids. I like to make clam pasta with two varieties of clams—littlenecks, which lend an intense brininess to the dish, and cherrystones or Manilas, which are small enough to toss in whole and eat directly out of the shell along with the pasta. First, set a pot of water to boil and season it with salt. Rinse the clams and dice an onion, saving the root ends. Heat a large frying pan over medium heat and splash in some olive oil. Add the root ends of the onion, a few parsley sprigs, and as many littlenecks as will fit in a single layer, then pour in enough wine to cover the bottom of the pan. Turn the heat up and cover the pan. Let the clams steam until they open, which should take two or three minutes. Use tongs to pull the clams from the pan into a bowl as they open. Some of the stragglers might need a little encouragement, so tap them with your tongs if they're taking too long.

Cook the rest of the littlenecks in this way, adding more wine if needed to cover the bottom of the pan. When you've removed all of the clams from the pan, strain the liquid through a fine-mesh strainer or cheesecloth; this clam-cooking liquid is priceless. Plus, it's now the dish's main source of acid. When the clams are cool enough to handle, pluck them from their shells and run a knife through them, then return them to the clam-cooking liquid.

Rinse out the frying pan, then set it over medium heat. Add just enough oil to coat the pan, and when it shimmers, add the diced onion and a pinch of salt. Stirring from time to time, cook the onion until it's tender. It's fine if it picks up a little colour, but don't let it burn; add a splash of water if you need to. Then taste the pasta water, make sure it's as salty as the sea, and cook the linguine until it's not quite al dente, about 6 or 7 minutes.

Add a sliced clove or two of garlic and some red pepper flakes to the onion and allow it to **bloom**, or sizzle gently without taking on any colour, then add the cherrystones or Manilas and crank up the heat to high. Add a healthy splash of the clam-cooking liquid and cover the pan. As soon as the little clams pop open, use a slotted spoon to add the chopped littlenecks into the pan. Cook all of the clams together for about a minute, and then taste and adjust the acid with more white wine or a squeeze of fresh lemon juice.

When the pasta is not yet al dente, drain it, reserving a cup of the pasta water. Add the noodles directly to the pan with the clams. Continue to cook the pasta, swirling the pan, until the noodles are cooked al dente. This way, the pasta will absorb all the briny flavour of the clam liquid as it finishes cooking. Taste again and adjust for salt, acid, and spiciness. If the noodles seem dry, add some of the reserved pasta water.

Now begins the magic of garnishing (and fat). Intensify the creaminess and flavour of the dish by tossing in a knob of butter. Next, add chopped parsley and some freshly grated Parmesan. Some might balk at adding cheese to a seafood pasta, but I learned this trick from the chef at a beloved seafood restaurant in Tuscany, where this pasta was so delicious it helped me overcome my lifelong aversion to clams. The salt, fat, acid, and umami offered by the cheese makes this pasta unforgettable. For a final touch of acid and crunch, sprinkle the dish with toasted sourdough bread crumbs. They'll be crisp when you first dig in, but as they mingle with the pasta, the bread crumbs will absorb the clam juice, becoming little flavour bombs exploding with each bite.

LITTLENECK

Condiments and Umami

Cervantes may have thought that "hunger is the best sauce," but I'd argue that *sauce* is the best sauce—because sauce can complete a dish. Sauce, and in fact most condiments, are sources of both acid and salt; they offer a pretty surefire way to improve flavour. The bonus is that they are often excellent sources of **umami**, which is the word, from Japanese, for the fifth taste we can sense, the other four being sweet, sour, salty, and bitter. The closest translation into English is something like "deliciousness," or "savouriness."

Umami is, in fact, the result of flavour compounds called **glutamates**. The most familiar glutamate is monosodium glutamate, or MSG, the white powder often generously used in the kitchens of Chinese restaurants to enhance flavour. Though MSG is chemically manufactured, there are also many natural sources of glutamates. Two foods most abundant in naturally occurring glutamates are Parmesan and tomato ketchup. Sometimes a grating of Parmesan can make the difference between a good bowl of pasta and a great one (even ***Pasta alle Vongole***). And then, there are those of us who always crave ketchup with our burgers and fries, and not only because of the sweetness, salt, and acid that it provides. A little ketchup—and the umami it offers—makes things taste inexplicably more delicious.

Since the list of foods rich in umami dovetails nicely with many sources of salt and acid, always seek the opportunity to work in a little umami along with salt or acid to heighten flavour without having to do any extra work.

However, as Cal Peternell, the chef who'd shocked me with his palmfuls of salt in that pot of polenta so many years ago, likes to say, there is such a thing as *toomami*, so don't be tempted to pack bacon *and* tomatoes *and* fish sauce *and* cheese *and* mushrooms into a single meal. A little bit of umami can go a long way.

SOURCES OF UMAMI

1. TOMATOES and TOMATO PRODUCTS (THE MORE COOKED DOWN, THE MORE CONCENTRATED THE UMAMI) 2. MUSHROOMS 3. MEAT and MEAT BROTHS, PARTICULARLY CURED MEATS and BACON 4. CHEESE 5. FISH and FISH BROTHS, PARTICULARLY LITTLE FISH SUCH AS ANCHOVIES 6. SEAWEED 7. YEAST ENHANCERS and SPREADS i.e. MARMITE, NUTRITIONAL YEAST FERMENTED THINGS i.e. 8. SOY SAUCE 9. FISH SAUCE, etc.

Balancing Sweetness with Acid

Imagine taking a bite of the perfect peach: it's sweet, juicy, and firm, yet giving.

But is that all? It's also acidic. Without that pucker, it'd be all sugar.

Pastry chefs know that the best thing we can do in our cooking is to mimic this perfection—there's no better model for getting that sweet-sour balance just right than nature itself. The best apples for pie aren't the sweetest, but tart varieties such as Fuji, Honeycrisp, and Sierra Beauty. If a dessert's only quality is sweetness, it stimulates only the taste buds that sense sweetness. Chocolate and coffee are the perfect bases for building desserts because they are bitter, sour, and rich in umami. Once sweetened, they trigger more types of taste buds. Caramel, too. Add salt and suddenly all five of our basic tastes are activated with a single bite. For this reason, **Salted Caramel Sauce** has never gone out of fashion. And it never will.

Always balance sweetness with acid, and not only in desserts. Roasted beetroots, full of sugar, benefit from a splash of red wine vinegar, which offers contrast to the naturally earthy flavour of beetroots that is so off-putting to some. Season them with olive oil and salt, and all of a sudden even the staunchest beet-phobe will be converted. Roasted carrots, cauliflower, and broccoli—or anything that's developed sweetness from browning—will always appreciate a squeeze of lemon or touch of vinegar. A little will go a long way.

Acid Balance in a Meal

From time to time, I travel with Alice Waters to help cook special dinners. During one particularly rich, wintry meal we served in Washington, DC, while the snow piled up outside, I had an epiphany about acid. The last savoury course was a garden lettuce salad, dressed with delicate vinaigrette, which we sent out in big bowls to be eaten family-style. After we served the salad, all the cooks stood in the kitchen, exhausted, absentmindedly shoving lettuce into our mouths with our fingers. After a long day of cooking in a dry, hot, crowded kitchen, none of us had ever tasted anything so delicious. We were all marveling about how refreshing and perfectly dressed the salad was when Alice walked into the kitchen and said it could've used some more acid.

We were confounded! We were downright besotted with this salad, and yet here she was telling us that the balance was off? We all protested, trying to get Alice to admit she was wrong.

But Alice was steadfast. She pointed out that we hadn't been at the table with her, piling salad onto a plate laden with grilled lamb and borlotti beans, garnished with a decadent sauce, following courses of creamy lasagna and rich shellfish soup. On a plate with all of that other stuff it wasn't doing its job—a salad should relieve your palate and leave it clean after rich, muddy foods. It needed more acid to stand up to the other intense flavours.

Alice was right. (That happens a lot.) In order to make the best salad, you have to consider how it fits into the meal. Though each dish, on its own, should always be balanced in Salt, Fat, and Acid, there is also the larger picture to consider—a good meal should also be balanced. Make a caramelised onion tart, with all that butter in the crust and onions, and serve it with garden lettuces dressed with a sharp mustard vinaigrette. Make long-cooked pork shoulder, southern barbecue–style, and pair it with bright, acidic slaw. Make a rich Thai curry, thick with coconut milk, but precede it with a crunchy, light shaved cucumber salad. Begin to incorporate this sort of balance with every meal you plan, then read on to **What to Cook?** for more tips on writing a balanced menu.

Improvising with Salt, Fat, and Acid

Think of any dish you absolutely love to eat. It probably has an ideal balance of Salt, Fat, and Acid, whether it's a bowl of tortilla soup, Caesar salad, a *bánh mì* sandwich, a *margherita* pizza, or a bite of feta cheese tucked with cucumber into a piece of lavash bread. Since the human body can't produce certain essential forms of salt, fat, and acid, our palates have evolved to seek these three elements. This results in a universal appeal to food with Salt, Fat, and Acid all in balance, no matter the cuisine.

On their own, Salt, Fat, and Acid can give shape to the idea for a dish or even a meal. When deciding upon what to make, first answer the questions of which form (or forms) of each element to use, and how, and when. You'll find yourself with a to-do list that resembles—wait for it—a kind of recipe. If you want to turn last night's leftover roast chicken into chicken salad sandwiches, for instance, think first about whether you're craving Indian, Sicilian, or classic American flavours. Once you decide, refer to **The World of Acid** (page 110) to help you choose the forms of Salt, Fat, and Acid that will take you in the right direction. To evoke a taste of India, you might use thick, full-fat yoghurt, coriander, onions macerated in lime juice, salt, and a hint of curry powder. To conjure up a night on the shores of Palermo, you could use lemon juice and zest, onions macerated in red wine vinegar, aïoli, fennel seeds, and sea salt. Or try a chicken salad sandwich inspired by Cobb salad, with huge crumbles of bacon and blue cheese and slices of hard-boiled egg and avocado. Then dress everything with a red wine vinaigrette before loading it onto the bread.

If the thought of improvisational cooking scares you, take it slowly. Try the recipes I've included in this book, grow comfortable with a basic repertoire of dishes, and then start to play with one component at a time. Make **Bright Cabbage Slaw** enough times to memorise its ingredients and method, then adapt it as you like, by varying the Fat, Acid, or both. Use mayonnaise instead of olive oil to make a Classic Southern variation, and rice wine vinegar instead of red wine vinegar to make an Asian one.

Play to each element's strengths: use Salt to enhance, Fat to carry, and Acid to balance flavour. Now, with the knowledge of how they affect various foods, add each to a dish at the right time in order to season it from within. Add salt early to a pot of beans, but acid late. Season meat for a braise in advance, then start it off on the heat with a dose of cooking acid. When it's done and rich in flavour, lighten it with a garnishing acid.

Let Salt, Fat, and Acid work together in concert to improve anything you eat, whether you cooked it or not. Doctor a lacklustre restaurant taco by asking for sour cream, guacamole, pickles, or salsa. Eye the dressings, cheeses, and pickles at the local salad bar with renewed interest. Use yoghurt, tahini, pepper sauce, and pickled onions to amend a dry, bland falafel sandwich.

Harmonise these three notes, and invariably your taste buds will sing with delight.

HEAT

When aspiring chefs ask me for career advice, I offer a few tips: Cook every single day. Taste everything thoughtfully. Go to the farmers' market and familiarise yourself with each season's produce. Read everything Paula Wolfert, James Beard, Marcella Hazan, and Jane Grigson have written about food. Write a letter to your favourite restaurant professing your love and beg for an apprenticeship. Skip culinary school; spend a fraction of the cost of tuition travelling the world instead.

There is so much to learn from travel, especially as a young cook: you collect taste memories, understand the flavours of a place, and gain a sense of context. Eat cassoulet in Toulouse, hummus in Jerusalem, ramen in Kyoto, and ceviche in Lima. Make these classics your beacons so that when you return to your own kitchen and change a recipe, you know precisely how it diverges from the original.

Travel offers another extraordinary value, too: watch and learn from cooks around the world, and discover the universality of good cooking.

For the first four years of my cooking career, Chez Panisse was my only point of reference. Eventually, I couldn't contain my curiosity any longer. I had to go to Europe and cook in the kitchens that inspired the chefs who'd taught me. Arriving in Tuscany, I was surprised by how familiar it felt to cook alongside Benedetta and Dario. Some habits seemed to be common to all good cooks. Benedetta doted on her onions as they browned and brought roasts to room temperature before cooking them, just as the chefs at home had taught me to do. Heating up a pot of oil for deep-frying, she tested its temperature not with a thermometer, but by dropping in a stale crust of bread to see how quickly it turned golden brown, just as I'd learned to do the first time I'd fried glimmering fresh anchovies at Chez Panisse.

Curious, I began to watch others who cooked the foods I loved to eat. Enzo, my favourite *pizzaiolo* in Florence, served only three classic pizzas: Marinara, Margherita, and Napoli. He worked alone, snapped at regulars and tourists alike, and eschewed all luxuries, cooking all night in a kitchen the size of a postage stamp. I never saw Enzo use a thermometer to gauge the temperature of his wood-burning oven. Instead, he paid attention to his pizzas. If they burned before the toppings cooked, the oven was too hot. If they emerged pale, he'd throw another log onto the fire. And his method worked: with its crisp, yet chewy crust and barely melted cheese, I'd never tasted a better pizza.

I left Italy and travelled to visit friends and family around the world. Late one night at a bustling roadside stand, I ate flavourful *chapli kebabs*—Pakistan's mouthwatering answer to the hamburger. The cook flavoured the meat with chillies, ginger, and coriander, flattened each patty, and slid it into hot oil, monitoring the gurgling fat to decide if he should add more coal to the fire beneath the metre-wide iron pan. When the bubbles relented and the meat was as dark as the tea leaves in his cup, he pulled the kebab from the oil. He handed me one, wrapping it with a warm *naan*, and drizzling it with yoghurt sauce. I took a bite: heaven.

I thought back to one of my first nights in the kitchen at Chez Panisse, when I'd watched Amy, a soft-spoken chef, grill steaks for a hundred guests, graceful and skilful as a dancer. She showed me how she watched the surface of each steak. If the meat didn't sizzle as it hit the grill, she'd stoke the fire, pulling more coals beneath the metal grates. If the meat browned too quickly, she'd spread out the coals and wait for the grill to cool before continuing. Amy showed me how to ensure that the heat was just right so that the steaks browned evenly on the surface as the interior cooked, so that by the time they reached medium-rare, the outside was mouthwateringly charred, and the strip of fat lining the edge of each rib eye was perfectly rendered. It was no different than turning up or down the flame on the stove.

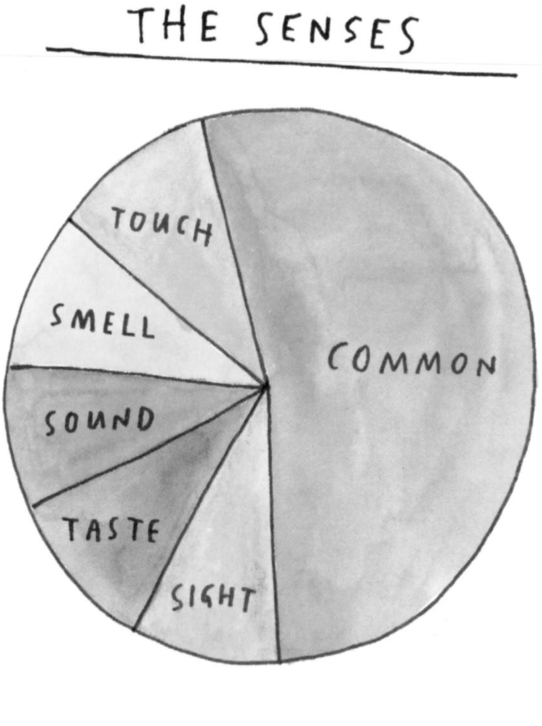

When I left Pakistan, I visited my grandparents' farm on the coast of the Caspian Sea in Iran, where my grandmother spent all day in the kitchen. Though she loved to cook for her family, she nevertheless grumbled about how ours is the most labour-intensive cuisine in the world. She chopped mountains of herbs, peeled and prepared cases of vegetables, and tended to *khoreshs*, complex meat and vegetable stews, as they simmered on the stove for hours. My grandmother watched and stirred the bubbling pots constantly—never still, never boiling—until finally the stews were done. My uncles, on the other hand, would spend all day smoking filterless cigarettes and telling stories before they lit the fire shortly before dinner. They'd thread chicken and lamb onto flat metal skewers and cook the kebabs quickly over grills so hot their arm hairs regularly caught fire. One kind of cooking took all day, the other, minutes. Both kinds were delicious. Our meals wouldn't have been complete without either the tender *khoreshs* or the juicy, charred kebabs.

As I travelled, I noticed that in every country, whether I was watching home cooks or professional chefs, and whether they were cooking over a live fire or on a camp stove, the best cooks *looked at the food, not the heat source.*

I saw how good cooks obeyed sensory cues, rather than timers and thermometers. They listened to the changing sounds of a sizzling sausage, watched the way a simmer becomes a boil, felt how a slow-cooked pork shoulder tightens and then relaxes as hours pass, and tasted a noodle plucked from boiling water to determine whether it's al dente. In order to cook instinctually, I needed to learn to recognise these signals. I needed to learn how food responds to the fourth element of good cooking: Heat.

WHAT IS HEAT?

Heat is the element of transformation. No matter its source, heat triggers the changes that take our food from raw to cooked, runny to set, flabby to firm, flat to risen, and pale to golden brown.

Unlike Salt, Fat, and Acid, Heat is flavourless and intangible. But its effects are quantifiable. Heat's sensory cues, including sizzles, spatters, crackles, steam, bubbles, aromas, and browning, are often more important than a thermometer. All of your senses—including common sense—will help you gauge heat's effects on food.

Exposure to heat changes foods in many different, but predictable, ways. Once familiar with how different foods respond to heat, you'll make better choices about how to shop at the market, plan a menu, and cook every dish. Turn your attention away from the oven dial or the knob of the stove and towards the food you're cooking. Heed the clues: is the food browning, firming, shrinking, crisping, burning, falling apart, swelling, or cooking unevenly?

These cues matter considerably more than whether you're cooking on an electric rather than gas stove, on a makeshift camping grill rather than in a grand marble hearth, or whether your oven is set to 180°C or 190°C.

Just as I learned from watching cooks all around the world, no matter what you're cooking, or what heat source you're using, the aim is always the same: apply heat at the right level, and at the right rate, so that the surface of a food and its interior are done cooking at the same time.

Think about making a grilled cheese sandwich. The goal is to use the right level of heat so that the bread turns golden-brown-toasty-delicious at the same rate that the cheese melts. Heat it too quickly and you'll burn the outside and be left with an under-cooked centre—burnt bread, unmelted cheese. Heat it too slowly, and you'll dry the whole thing out before the surface has a chance to brown.

View everything you cook like that grilled cheese sandwich: Is the skin of the roast chicken golden brown by the time the bird is cooked? Is the asparagus cooked all of the way through by the time it's developed the perfect char from the grill? Is the lamb chop evenly browned, all of its fat rendered by the time the meat is perfectly medium-rare?

Just as with Salt, Fat, and Acid, the first step to getting the results you want from Heat is to *know what you're after*. Know what results you seek, so that you can take the steps to achieve them. Think about your goals in the kitchen in terms of flavours and textures. Do you want your food to be browned? Crisp? Tender? Soft? Chewy? Caramelised? Flaky? Moist?

Next, work backward. Make a clear plan for yourself using sensory landmarks to guide you back to your goal. For example, if you want to end up with a bowl of flavourful, snowy white mashed potatoes, then think about the last step: mashing potatoes with butter and sour cream, and tasting and adjusting for salt. To get there, you'll need to simmer the potatoes in salted water until they're tender. To get there, you'll need to peel and cut the potatoes. There's your recipe. For something more complicated—say, crispy pan-fried potatoes—you'll want to end with a golden-brown crust and a tender interior. So the last step will be frying in hot fat to achieve crispness. To get there, make sure the potatoes are tender inside—simmer them in salted water. To get there, peel and cut them. There's another recipe.

This is good cooking, and it's simpler than you might think.

HOW HEAT WORKS

The Science of Heat

Simply put, heat is energy.

Food is primarily made up of four basic types of molecules: water, fat, carbohydrates, and protein. As food is heated, the molecules within it begin to speed up, colliding with each other as they go.

As molecules gain speed, they also gain the power to break free of the electrical forces uniting their atoms. Some atoms can split off and join up with other atoms to create new molecules. This process is called a **chemical reaction**.

And the chemical reactions initiated by heat affect the flavour and texture of food.

Water, fat, carbohydrate, and protein molecules each react to heat in different, yet predictable, ways. If this seems overwhelming, don't worry—it's not. The science of heat, luckily, adheres to common sense.

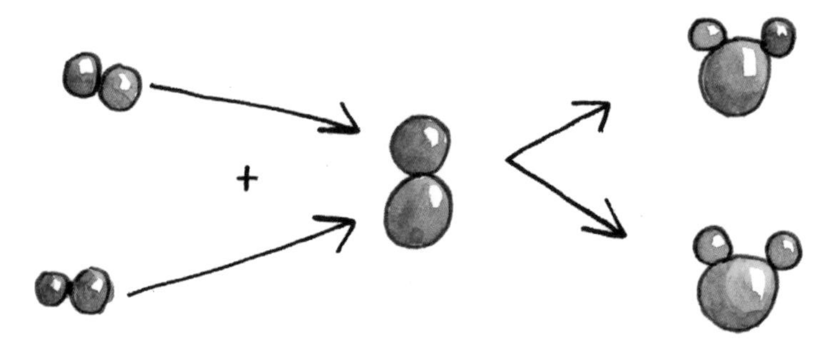

Water and Heat

Water is an essential element of practically all foods. Cook most of its water out, and food will become crisp or dry. Leave its water in—or add water as you cook—to make food moist and tender. Cook water out of scrambled eggs, and they will be dry. Cook the right amount of water into rice, cornmeal, potatoes, or any other starch, and they will be tender. Vegetables that lose water become limp. During years with intense rainy seasons, fruit will taste watery. Overwater your tomato plants and the flavour of the tomatoes will be diluted. When food is weak in flavour, it's "watered down." To intensify flavours in soups, stocks, and sauces, reduce their water content. Use heat to control food's water content to get the texture and flavour you seek.

When frozen, water expands. This is why you must always leave headroom in jars of soup or stock you plan to freeze. Or why a bottle of beer or wine you stick in the freezer to chill will explode if forgotten. On a much, much tinier scale—at the cellular level—a similar phenomenon occurs inside foods: as food freezes, its cell walls, much like your storage containers, will burst when the water they contain expands. Freezer burn and dehydration, then, are the result of water escaping from the inside of a food's cells and then crystallising or vaporising on the surface of the food. Have you ever opened a package of frozen berries or meat and wondered where those Antarctic stalactites came from? Now you know—from inside your food.

This dehydration also sadly explains that leathery steak you forgot about in the freezer for three years, and is helpful to remember when deciding whether or not freezing will damage a particular food. In other words, choose to freeze foods that can withstand a little dehydration, and even be successfully rehydrated—raw braising cuts of meat, stews, soups, sauces, and cooked beans in their liquid.

Water can also be a medium in which we cook other foods. At low temperatures, water is particularly gentle: water baths are ideal for cooking custards; and simmering, braising and poaching provide tough foods with the sustained low heat they need to develop tenderness.

Heat water further, to 100°C at sea level, and it boils, giving us one of the most efficient—and quickest—ways to cook food. Boiling water is one of the most invaluable tools in the kitchen. It's a simple way to gauge temperature without a thermometer. If you see bubbles roiling in a pot of water, you know that it's reached 100°C. At this temperature, water can kill pathogenic bacteria. To be on the safe side, when reheating soupy leftovers or your freezer stash of chicken stock, make sure to bring them to a boil to kill bacteria that may have grown in the meantime.

The Power of Steam

As water is heated beyond 100°C, it transforms into steam, another of the kitchen's most valuable visible cues. Let the sight of steam help you approximate temperature: as long as food is wet and giving off steam, its surface temperature probably isn't hot enough to allow browning to begin. Remember, the reactions that cause food to brown—caramelisation and the Maillard reaction—don't begin until food reaches much higher temperatures. So, if water is present on the surface of a food, it can't brown.

Learn to make decisions in relationship to steam. Encourage steam to escape if you want temperatures to rise and food to brown. Contain and recycle steam with a lid to allow food to cook in a moist environment if you want to prevent or delay browning.

Food piled up in a pan can affect steam levels in a pan by acting like a makeshift lid: both entrap steam. Trapped steam condenses and drips back down, keeping food moist and maintaining the temperature right around 100°C. At first, entrapped steam gently **wilts** food, and then it leads to **sweating**, which is a way to cook food through without allowing it to develop any colour.

Steam replaces some of the air contained in vegetables with water, which is why plants initially transform from opaque to translucent in colour and reduce in volume as they cook. They also begin to intensify in flavour—a mountain of just-washed spinach becomes a molehill of wilted greens and a pan mounded full of sliced onions cooks down into a stewy, flavourful base for **Silky Sweet Corn Soup**.

Pile chard leaves high above the sides of a pan and let steam cook the greens. Cover with a lid if you like, but stir once in a while with tongs to ensure even cooking, because even steam can't navigate the labyrinth of greens as evenly as you might hope. The temperature at the bottom of the pan, closer to the heat source,

will always be higher than the temperature above. Control steam in the oven when roasting or toasting foods using the same variables. How tightly a roasting tray of vegetables is packed is as much of a factor in even browning as the oven temperature. Let courgettes and peppers develop glorious sweetness and flavour by spreading them out so steam can escape and browning can begin sooner. Protect denser vegetables that take longer to cook, such as artichokes or onions, from browning too much before they can cook through by packing them tightly in a pan to entrap steam.

Choose your cooking vessel based on how steam will move within and out of it. Pans with sloped or curved sides are better at allowing steam to escape than pans with straight sides. And the taller the sides of the pan or pot, the longer it will take steam to escape. Deep pots and pans are great for sweating onions and simmering soups, but less ideal for foods you aim to sear and brown quickly, such as scallops and steaks.

Recall the osmosis that salt initiates, and weave that understanding into how you decide to use steam. Let salt do its work, drawing water out of food it touches, to help create steam when you want it in the pan. When the goal is to brown swiftly, wait to salt food until after it begins to crisp or salt far enough in advance to let osmosis occur, pat food dry, and then place into a hot pan. Use the former method for onions you want to sweat and keep translucent for cauliflower soup, and the latter for aubergines and courgettes you plan to grill or roast.

Fat and Heat

In Fat, I explained the main principles that will help you understand how Heat and Fat work together in good cooking. Like water, fat is both a basic component of food and a cooking medium. But fat and water are enemies: they don't mix, and they respond very differently to heat.

Fats are flexible; indeed, the broad range of temperatures fats can withstand allows us to achieve many different textures—crisp, flaky, tender, creamy, and light—that simply cannot be achieved without the proper relationship between Fat and Heat.

When chilled, fats harden—and transform from liquids into solids. Solid fats such as butter and lard are a boon to pastry chefs, who can work them into doughs to achieve flakiness or whip air into them to achieve lightness. But picture the way greens cooked with bacon leave a trail of semisolid grease behind on the platter and you'll see how this quality is less desirable when serving food containing animal fats that congeal at room temperature.

Extended, gentle heat will transform, or **render**, solid animal fats into pure liquid fats such as pork lard or beef tallow. In slow-cooked meats such as **Sage- and Honey-Smoked Chicken**, rendering fats essentially bastes food from within, and this self-basting also explains the exuberantly moist texture of **Slow-Roasted Salmon**. The same gentle heat will cause butter's emulsion to break and then clarify.

At moderate temperatures, fat is an ideal gentle cooking medium, perfect for using in a cooking method called **confit**, which is essentially poaching in fat instead of water. Look ahead to recipes for **Tomato**, **Tuna**, and **Chicken Confit** to put this technique into practice.

While water boils and vaporises at 100°C, fats can climb to staggering temperatures well beyond that point before turning to smoke. As a result, since water and fat don't mix, foods containing water (which is practically all foods) won't dissolve in fat; instead the surfaces of foods exposed to very hot fats can climb to high enough temperatures to develop crisp textures as water evaporates.

Fats are slow to cool and heat—in other words, it takes a lot of energy to heat or cool a unit of fat by even a few degrees. This is a boon to the amateur deep fryer; you can relax when frying **Beer-Battered Fish**, knowing you don't have to act with lightning-quick reflexes when the temperature of the oil starts to rise or fall. If the fat gets too hot, just turn off the heat or carefully add a little more room-temperature oil. If the pot gets too cold, increase the heat and wait before adding more food. The same phenomenon will cause meats with large quantities of fat such as prime rib or pork loin roasts (or those sitting in fat, such as any of the confits mentioned above) to continue cooking slowly even when pulled from the heat.

Carbohydrates and Heat

Found primarily in foods made from plant sources, carbohydrates provide food with both structure and flavour. In Acid, I described three types of carbohydrates—cellulose, sugars, and pectin. Along with a fourth type of carbohydrate—starches—cellulose provides much of the bulk and texture of plant-derived foods, while sugars offer flavour. When heated, carbohydrates generally absorb water and break down.

Understanding a bit of basic **Plant Anatomy** will help you determine how to cook various plant-derived foods (see page 144). If *fibrous* or *stringy* are words that come to mind when you think of a particular fruit or vegetable, it's rich in cellulose, a type of carbohydrate that isn't broken down by heat. Cook cellulose-rich produce, such as collard greens, asparagus, or artichokes, until it absorbs enough water to become tender. Leaves have less cellulose fibres than stems or stalks, which is why kale and chard stems cook at a different rate than their leaves and ought to be stemmed and cooked separately, or simply staggered into the pot.

Starches

Give the starchiest parts of plants, including tubers such as potatoes and seeds such as dried beans, plenty of water and time over gentle heat to coax out their tenderness. Starches absorb liquid and swell or break down, so firm potatoes become delightfully creamy, impossibly hard chickpeas transform into buttery bites, and rice goes from indigestible to fluffy and tender.

Dry seeds, grains, and legumes, including rice, beans, barley, chickpeas, and wheatberries, generally need water and heat to make them edible. To protect the potential for life that they contain, seeds have evolved with tough sheaths that make them nearly impossible for us to digest unless we transform them in some way. Sometimes, this simply means removing the shell, as we do with sunflower and pumpkin seeds. For seeds that need to be cooked in order to become edible, this usually means adding water and heating them until they grow tender. Some starch-rich seeds, including dried beans, chickpeas, and hearty grains like barley benefit from an overnight soak, which gives them a head start at absorbing water. Consider it a sort of inactive cooking.

Some grains are processed to remove some or all of this outer sheath—hence the difference between whole wheat and refined flour or brown and white rice. Without that tough exterior, processed grains cook much more quickly and have a longer shelf-life than their whole-grain counterparts. Ground, or **milled**, grains can be combined with water to make doughs and batters, which firm and set up with exposure to heat.

The key to cooking starches properly is using the correct amount of water and heat. Use too little water or undercook starches and they will be dry and unpleasantly tough in the centre. Cakes and bread baked with too little water are dry and crumbly. Undercooked pasta, beans, and rice are unpleasantly tough in the centre. But use too much water or heat, or simply overcook starches, and they will be mushy (think limp noodles and soggy cakes and rice). Starches are eager to undergo browning and will burn easily if overcooked or exposed to too much heat. I kick myself when this happens—scorched grits at the bottom of an unwatched pot, or bread crumbs blackened after just 90 seconds of neglect in a hot oven.

SOAKING STAGES of DRIED BEANS

Sugars

Odourless and colourless, **sucrose**, or sugar is the pure manifestation of sweetness. When exposed to heat, it melts. Mix granulated sugar with water and heat it to high temperatures to yield myriad confectionery delights with varied textures: marshmallows, meringues, fudge, nougat, butterscotch, brittle, toffee, pralines, and caramel candies.

Working with hot sugar is one of the few temperature-specific endeavours in the kitchen, but it's not a particularly difficult one. At about 143°C, a melted sugar syrup will yield a firm nougat, but just a ten-degree increase will yield toffee. The first time I made caramel candies I was too stingy to buy a twelve-dollar candy thermometer. I figured I could just eyeball the temperature. As a result, my caramels were so sticky that I ended up paying hundreds of dollars for dental work instead. Learn from my stubbornness and invest in a candy thermometer to help monitor temperatures when working with sugar (and use it for deep-frying, too!). Trust me, you'll save money in the long run.

At extremely high temperatures (170°C), sugar molecules begin to darken in colour, in a process that isn't entirely understood, as they decompose and reorganise into hundreds of new compounds, generating abundant new flavours. This is **caramelisation**, and it's one of the most essential ways heat affects flavour. In addition to producing acidic flavour compounds, caramelised sugars introduce a slew of new qualities and flavours, including bitter, fruity, caramel, nutty, sherry, and butterscotch.

In addition to starches that can be broken down into sugars, fruits, vegetables, dairy, and some grains also contain natural simple sugars that can participate in the same reactions as table sugar when cooked. They grow sweeter with heat, and can even caramelise. As heat penetrates a boiling carrot, for example, its starches begin to break down into simple sugars . The cell walls enclosing these sugars begin to disintegrate. This frees the sugars to reach our taste buds more readily, making the cooked carrot taste far sweeter than its raw counterpart.

The small amounts of sugars that most vegetables contain begin to disappear the moment they're picked, which is why just-picked produce is so much more sweet and flavourful than store-bought. I've heard countless stories of Midwestern grandmothers putting the pot of water on to boil before sending the kids out to the garden to pick corn. Just a few minutes, they'd tell the kids, could mean a noticeable loss in sweetness. As it turns out, the grannies were right: just a few hours at room temperature can deprive starchy vegetables like corn and peas of half of their sugars. Potatoes, too, are at their sweetest when first harvested—hence the indescribable pleasure of boiled new potatoes topped with butter. As potatoes sit in storage all year, though, their sugars convert to starches. Fry newly dug potatoes, full of sugar, and they'll burn before they can cook through. Instead, when making potato chips or fries, use starchy, older potatoes and rinse them of excess starches after slicing until the water runs clear. Only then will your fried potatoes emerge from the hot oil of the fry pot crisp but not burnt.

Plants, Above & Below

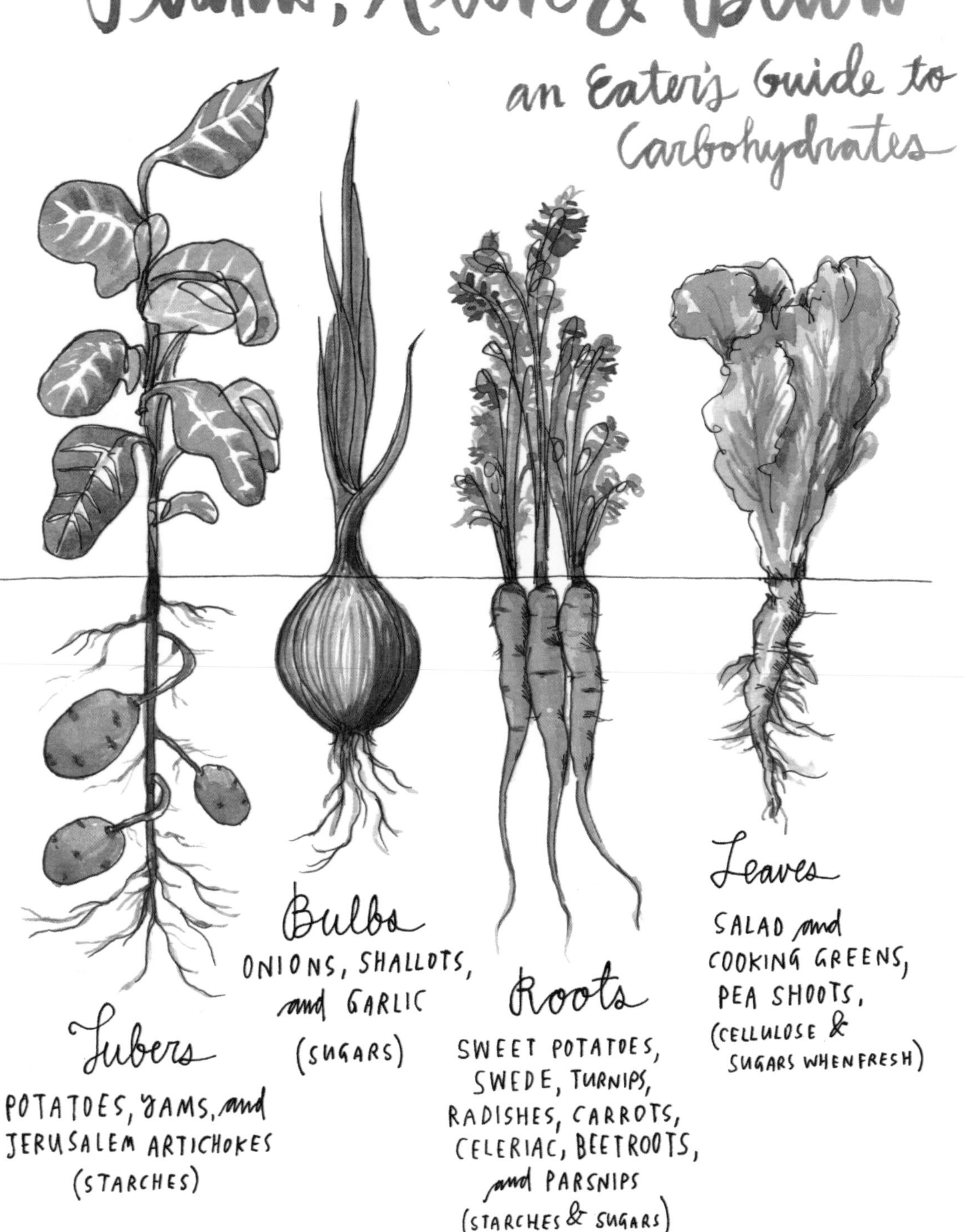

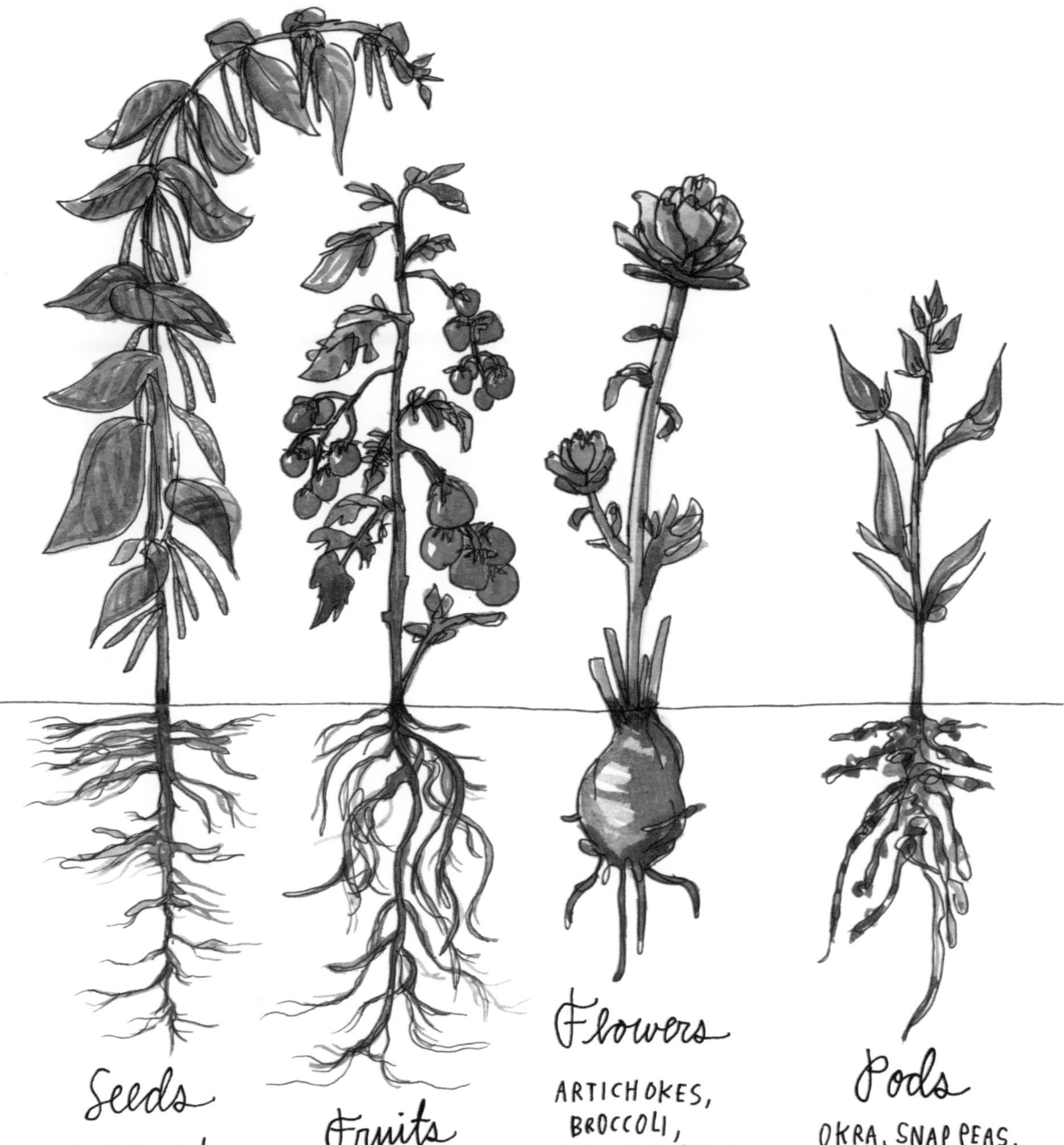
Seeds
FRESH and DRIED BEANS, GRAINS- WHOLE and MILLED, NUTS, PEAS, CORN, and CORNMEAL, GRITS, HOMINY, QUINOA (STARCHES & CELLULOSE)
Fruits
COURGETTES, TOMATOES, AUBERGINES, WINTER SQUASH (SUGARS)
Flowers
ARTICHOKES, BROCCOLI, SQUASH BLOSSOMS, CAULIFLOWER (CELLULOSE & SUGARS WHEN VERY FRESH)
Pods
OKRA, SNAP PEAS, (CELLULOSE & SUGARS WHEN VERY FRESH)

Pectin

Another carbohydrate, **pectin**, is a kind of indigestible fibre, and I like to think of it as fruit- and vegetable-derived gelatin. Found primarily in the seeds and peels of citrus fruits, stone fruits, and apples, pectin functions as a gelling agent when combined with sugar and acid and exposed to heat. Its setting properties make possible fruit preserves and fruit pastes such as *membrillo*, the Spanish quince paste. From June Taylor, a champion of traditional British preserve-making methods, I learned to extract pectin from citrus into my marmalade. She taught me to place a couple of handfuls of membranes and seeds into a cheesecloth pouch and cook it into the marmalade along with the fruit. When the preserves are partially cooked, I remove the bag, let it cool, and then massage it to coax out the pectin. The first time I did this, I was shocked to find that I could actually *see* the pectin—a milky white liquid. When, months later, I opened that jar of marmalade, the pectin's effects were clear: the marmalade was set, not runny, and spread smoothly across my hot, buttered toast.

Proteins and Heat

It helps me to picture proteins as coiled threads floating around in water. This definition proves particularly useful when visualising how temperature affects proteins. As with acid, when exposed to heat, the threads first **denature**, or unwind, and then clump together more tightly, or **coagulate**, entrapping pockets of water, to create structure in foods.

Think of how heat transforms a chicken breast from flabby and watery to firm, tender, and moist when perfectly cooked. But apply too much heat and the protein clumps will continue to tighten, squeezing out the pockets of water. With its water expelled, the chicken becomes dry, stringy, and tough.

This phenomenon is also apparent in scrambled eggs. Cook scrambled eggs too long, or at too high a temperature, and they will dry out. Put them on the plate, and you'll see their poor, oversqueezed proteins continue to wring water out, leaving a puddle behind. Instead, to get the silkiest scrambled eggs, follow Alice B. Toklas's advice and cook them over very low heat. I imagine she learned a thing or two about good cooking from her adopted hometown—Paris—where she was a member of the twentieth-century avant-garde. Crack 4 eggs into a bowl and season them with salt and a few drops of lemon juice, whisking thoroughly to break them up. Gently melt a little butter in a saucepan over the lowest possible heat and pour in the eggs. Continue to stir with a whisk or a fork, while adding 4 or more tablespoons of butter in thumb-size pieces, letting each be absorbed before you add the next. Never stop stirring, and be patient. It'll take several minutes for the eggs to start to come together. When they do, pull them from the stove in anticipation of the cooking that will continue due to residual heat. Serve with—what else?—buttered toast.

JUST RIGHT

SAMIN'S JUST RIGHT

SMOKE ALARM

BASICALLY TOXIC WARFARE

A little salt can help keep proteins from drying out. Recall the many advantages of salting meat in advance. One of its luckiest consequences is that, given enough time, salt will tinker with the structure of meat proteins, reducing their capacity to expel water. Consequently, meat that has been salted early will be indescribably moist when cooked properly, and even forgive being slightly overcooked.

The coiled threads in each type of protein are unique, so the range at which different proteins coagulate is vast. Preserve tender cuts of meat with careful, quick cooking, generally over the intense heat of a grill, preheated frying pan, or hot oven. If cooked to an internal temperature beyond 60°C, the proteins within tender red meats will coagulate entirely, expelling water and yielding tough, chewy, overcooked steaks and lamb chops. Chicken and turkey breasts, on the other hand, don't dry out until temperatures surpass 70°C.

Tougher cuts, rich in sinewy connective tissue, require a slightly more nuanced cooking approach to reveal their tenderness: the investment of gentle heat, time, and water implicit in braising or stewing. Heat metamorphises **collagen**, the main structural protein found in animal connective tissue, into gelatin. The tough and chewy proteins that make undercooked short ribs impossible to chew and unpleasant to eat will transform into gelatin with water, time, and further cooking, yielding the rich, tender textures we associate with barbecued brisket, stewed meats, and properly cooked short ribs. And since acid will further amplify collagen's transformation into gelatin, add an acidic ingredient into the marinade, dry rub, or braise to encourage the process.

The key to this transformation is gentle heat. In contrast to the carefully applied quick heat required to cook tender cuts, time and sustained low heat are essential to transforming dark meat's tough, sinewy connective tissue into luxurious gelatin while its lumps of intermuscular fat render and baste the meat from within.

Browning and Flavour

Continue heating proteins in the presence of carbohydrates, and a remarkable thing happens: the **Maillard reaction**, heat's most significant contribution to flavour. Compare bread to toasted bread, raw to seared tuna, boiled to grilled meat or vegetables. In each case, the browned version is much richer and more delightfully complex in flavour, a result of the Maillard reaction.

This transformation reorganises aromatic compounds into entirely new flavours. In other words, in browned versions of a food we can experience flavours that don't exist in the pale version! In Acid, I described the ways in which the Maillard reaction can produce sour flavours in a food. Any food that undergoes the Maillard reaction—browned meats, vegetables, breads—can also develop savoury aromas such as floral, onion, meaty, vegetal, chocolatey, starchy, and earthy flavours in addition to the flavours of caramelisation. Because surface browning is often accompanied by dehydration and crispness, it can also leads to the contrasts in texture, as well as flavour, that so delight our palates. My very favourite French pastry of all time, the *canelé,* is the pinnacle of this sort of juxtaposition: its tender, custardy centre is enveloped by a dark, chewy crust altered by caramelisation *and* the Maillard reaction.

Browning begins at around 110°C—well past the boiling temperature of water and the coagulation point of proteins. Since the temperatures required to achieve this kind of tasty browning will dry out proteins, beware. Use intense heat to brown the surface of meats and quickly cook tender cuts such as steaks and chops through. After browning a tougher cut such as brisket, on the other hand, use gentle heat to keep its interior from

drying out. Or do the opposite and cook it through with gentle heat. Then, once the meat is tender, increase temperatures to brown the surface.

Browning is an invaluable flavouring technique, but it must be done with care. Heat that's uneven or too powerful can take food straight past golden delicious to charred. But sear a steak too timidly, and you'll overcook it before it has a chance to brown.

Learn to take browning fearlessly to the edge, because that's where the deepest flavours lie. Try another little experiment: make two half-batches of **Salted Caramel Sauce**. Stop cooking one half when you normally would, but cook the other a few shades darker. Drizzle both, side by side, onto vanilla ice cream and taste to understand how much more flavour a few moments on the stove can yield. Or, next time you plan to braise short ribs or chicken legs, brown half of the meat in the dry heat of the oven, and the other half on the stove to see how the different forms of heat in each method yield different results (for a hint, read on to **Roasting**).

As with all good things, including salt, you can take browning too far. The next time you dare to call burnt bacon or nuts "crisp," think of the time one of my cooks at Eccolo did so, only to spot Alice Waters seated at the bar, gingerly picking the too-dark hazelnuts out of her salad. Having just served a culinary legend a dish he'd known was unsatisfactory, he went into the walk-in refrigerator, lay down on the floor, and cried. Though I felt terrible for him when I found out, all I could do was laugh and encourage him to learn from his mistake. Most of the time, you don't need anyone else to tell you things aren't right; be your own Alice Waters.

Temperature's Effects on Flavour

It's tempting to think that cooking begins with the click of the gas burner or the turn of the oven dial. It doesn't. Cooking begins much, much earlier, with the temperature of your ingredients.

To begin with, the temperature—that is, the measure of heat, or of its absence—of an ingredient will affect *how* it cooks. Food at room temperature cooks differently than food straight from the fridge. The same food will cook evenly or unevenly, quickly or slowly, depending on its temperature at the start of cooking. This is particularly true for meat, eggs, and dairy, whose temperamental proteins and fats are deeply affected by temperature swings.

Take, for example, the chicken you're thinking about roasting for dinner. Slide the chicken directly from the fridge into the oven, and by the time enough heat penetrates to cook the legs through, the breast meat will have overcooked, resulting in tough, dry meat. But let the bird come to room temperature on the kitchen worktop before roasting and the bird will spend a shorter time in the oven, limiting the opportunity for overcooking.

Because the chicken is so much more dense than the hot oven air, the fifteen degree difference in the temperature of the bird when you start cooking it—the approximate difference between fridge and room temperature—is substantially more important than a fifteen degree difference in oven temperature. You could cook a room-temperature bird at 200°C or 215°C and not see much of a change in cooking time or result. If you cook a cold bird, the cooking time will increase dramatically and dry, tough breast meat will be apparent from your first bite. Let all meats—except for the thinnest cuts—come to room temperature before you cook them. The larger the roast, the earlier you can pull it out of the fridge. A rib roast should sit out for several hours, while a chicken needs only a couple, but when it comes to tempering meat, any time is better than none at all. Get in the habit of pulling out the meat you plan to cook for dinner right when you get home from work (and salting it, too, if you haven't already), and you'll learn that time can do some of the work of good cooking even better than the oven can.

And just as cooking doesn't begin when the flame is lit, nor does it end when the flame dies out. The chemical reactions generated by heat develop momentum, and they don't stop the second you turn off the flame. Proteins in particular are susceptible to **carryover**—continued cooking that results from residual heat trapped within a food.

Use this knowledge to your advantage, knowing that roasts carry over a couple of degrees Celsius on average after they are removed from heat, and that some vegetables, such as asparagus, do too, as well as fish, shellfish, and custards.

Apart from affecting how food cooks, temperature also affects how it tastes. For example, some tastes, when warm, trigger pleasure responses in our brains.

Many of food's most aromatic molecules are **volatile**, meaning that they can evaporate into the surrounding air. The more of a food's aromatic molecules we can breathe in, the more powerful our experience of its flavour will be. Other flavour molecules are liberated for us to taste as heat degrades the cell walls that confine them. By increasing their volatility, heat sets a greater number of aromatic molecules free, allowing them to permeate the environment more fully. The smell of a tray of warm chocolate chip cookies can fill a room, whereas cookie dough, still clinging to its aromatic compounds, neither smells nor tastes as compelling.

Sweet, bitter, and umami tastes are more intense and send stronger signals to the brain when food is warmer. As any college student can tell you, the same pint of beer, while delicious chilled, will be unpalatably bitter at room temperature. Or try a bite of cheese straight from the fridge. It won't taste like much. Let the cheese come to room temperature. As it warms, its fat molecules relax, releasing entrapped flavour compounds. Taste the cheese again, and you'll perceive new dimensions of flavour that weren't available before. Fruits and vegetables, too, taste different at various temperatures. Volatile compounds in some fruits, such as tomatoes, are so delicate that the cold of the refrigerator can make them less available—making a good case for storing and eating them at room temperature.

There's a case to be made for serving food warm or at room temperature rather than blazing hot. Researchers posit that excessive heat impairs our ability to enjoy the flavour of food. Besides burning our taste buds, hot food is harder to taste. The perception of taste decreases when a food's temperature rises beyond 35°C. While some foods, such as many pasta dishes and fried fish, suffer if they're not served immediately after coming out of the pan, most others are more forgiving.

Over the years, I've grown to prefer serving warm and room-temperature food at gatherings. Try throwing a dinner party where you don't serve anything hot. Prepare marinated roasted or grilled vegetables; sliced roasted meats; grain, noodle, or bean salads; frittatas and hard-boiled eggs. Besides tasting better, hosting a dinner this way is also a lot less stressful than trying to herd guests and rush a soufflé to the table!

The Flavour of Smoke

Smoke, that wispy consequence of heat, conveys a powerful flavour to food. Most of smoke's flavour is in its aroma, and it's one that triggers ancestral memories of the earliest kind of cooking: over fire.

Made up of gases, water vapour, and small particles resulting from combustion, smoke is a by-product of burning wood, which is why I always choose to grill over a live fire rather than gas, even though it takes more time and effort. If all you've got is a gas grill and you want to impart some smokiness to your grilled meats and vegetables, you can use wood chips. Just soak and drain a couple of handfuls—I love the flavours of oak, almond, and fruit woods—in a disposable aluminium baking pan and cover with foil. Poke several holes in the foil to allow the smoke to escape. Turn on some, but not all, of the burners, place the pan over an unlit spot, and close the lid. Begin cooking once you catch the first appetising whiffs of smoke. Close the lid to bathe your meat and vegetables in smoky flavours, which result from a series of chemical reactions, including browning. Heat transforms the flavours of wood into the marvellous flavours of smoke, which include aromatic compounds similar to those found in vanilla and cloves. When food is exposed to smoke, it absorbs the sweet, fruity, caramel, flowery, and bready flavour compounds. You'll see—nothing else compares to the flavour of true wood smoke.

USING HEAT

At the heart of good cooking lies good decision making, and the primary decision regarding Heat is whether to cook food *slowly over gentle heat*, or *quickly over intense heat*. The easiest way to determine which level of heat to apply is to consider tenderness. For some foods, the goal is *creating* tenderness, while for others, it's *preserving* innate tenderness. In general, foods that are already tender—some meats, eggs, delicate vegetables—should be cooked as little as possible to maintain their tenderness. Foods that start out tough or dry and need to be hydrated or transformed to become tender—grains and starches, tough meats, dense vegetables—will benefit from longer, more gentle cooking. Browning, whether for tender or tough foods, will often involve some form of intense heat, meaning that sometimes you have to combine cooking methods to get the different results you're after on the surface and within. For example, brown and then simmer meats in a stew, or simmer and then brown potatoes for hash to ensure browning *and* tenderness in both cases.

A Note on the Oven

Baking, the most precise endeavour in the kitchen, is powered by its most imprecise source of heat: the oven. Humans have never had much control over exact oven temperatures, whether in the first ovens, which were little more than pits in the ground heated by a wood fire, or in today's luxe gas-powered models. The only difference is that when ovens were still powered by a live fire, no one believed that he or she could control temperature with the turn of a dial. Because the truth is, no one can.

Set the average home oven to 175°C, and it'll heat up to about 185°C before the heating element shuts off. Depending on how sensitive the thermostat is, the temperature might drop down to 165°C before the heating element switches on again. Open the oven door to check on the cookies, and cool air will rush in as hot air escapes, dropping the temperature even more. Once the thermostat is triggered, the temperature will head back to 185°C, with the cycle continuing until the cookies are done. The amount of time the oven actually spends at 175°C is negligible. If your oven is miscalibrated—and most are—then 175°C could mean anywhere from 150°C to 200°C, before the heating cycle even begins. It's all mind-bogglingly imprecise.

Don't let the oven's willy-nilly nature scare you. Instead, be bold: don't rely on the oven dial. Paying attention to the sensory cues that indicate *how* food is cooking is far more valuable than minding an arbitrary number. I internalised this lesson the first time I worked the wood-fired spit at Eccolo. I was still a young cook when I arrived back in California, after my travels to Italy and beyond. Constantly doubting myself, I made it easy for the cooks with whom I shared the kitchen to doubt me, too. None of them ever seemed insecure about working the spit, but I was terrified. What did they know that I didn't?

Most nights, we roasted skewers of chickens on the spit, over burning oak and almond wood. I had so many questions: How would I know where to build the fire? How would I know how much wood to add, and when? How would I know if the fire was too hot, or cool, and when the chickens were done cooking? How could they expect me to cook anything properly on this crazy contraption when it had no controls, dials, or thermostat?

Sensing my impending meltdown, the chef, Christopher Lee, took me aside and patiently explained that even though I'd never used a spit, I was prepared. Hadn't I roasted hundreds of chickens over the years? Didn't I know that it takes about 70 minutes for a chicken to roast in the oven? Didn't I know that I could tell when a chicken was cooked when the juice at the thigh ran clear when pricked? I had, and I did. He showed me how heat reflected off the walls of the rotisserie oven just like it did in a gas oven, how it was hotter in the back and cooler in the front just like in an oven, and to treat the birds as if I were roasting them in a big, black box—something I could do with ease. Soon, I realised that spit-roasting looked a lot more complicated than it actually was, and it quickly became my favourite way to cook.

Relinquish the false sense of control an oven offers, just like I did at the spit. Instead pay attention to how your food is cooking. Is it rising? Browning? Setting? Smoking? Bubbling? Burning? Jiggling? When you read recipes, think of temperatures and cooking times as strong suggestions, rather than fixed rules. Set your timer for a few minutes less than a recipe might suggest, then use all of your senses to check for doneness. Always remember the qualities you seek in your food. Adjust course constantly and accordingly to achieve them. This is what good cooking looks like.

Gentle Heat versus Intense Heat

The aim of cooking with **gentle heat** is always the same: tenderness. Use gentle cooking methods to allow delicate foods—such as eggs, dairy, fish, and shellfish—to retain their moisture and delicate texture. Let gentle heat transform the dry and tough into the moist and tender. Choose among **intense heat** cooking methods (apart from boiling, which is intense in its own way) when seeking to brown food. When carefully applied to tender meats, intense cooking methods lead to brown surfaces and moist, juicy interiors. For tough meats and starchy foods, combine these methods with gentler ones, in order to achieve the desired browning on the outside and allow low heat to do its gradual work within.

Gentle Cooking Methods

- Simmering, Coddling, and Poaching
- Steaming
- Stewing and Braising
- Confit
- Sweating
- Bain-marie
- Low-heat Baking and Dehydrating
- Slow-roasting, Grilling, and Smoking

Intense Cooking Methods

- Blanching, Boiling, and Reducing
- Sautéing, Pan-frying, and Shallow- and Deep-frying
- Searing
- Grilling
- High-heat Baking
- Toasting
- Roasting

Cooking Methods and Techniques

Cooking with Water

Simmering

Since the boiling point of water is such an important kitchen landmark, I'd always assumed boiling to be the most straightforward cooking method: just drop food into a pot of bubbling water and pull it out when it's done. Then one day, after about a year in the kitchen, as I turned my hundredth pot of boiling chicken stock down to a simmer, a lightbulb went off: when it comes to cooking food in liquid, *cooking food through at a rolling boil is the exception rather than the rule.*

I realised boiling is called for only when cooking vegetables, grains, and pasta; reducing sauces; and hard-boiling eggs. I could bring everything else—and I mean *everything*—to a boil and then swiftly reduce it to a simmer to cook through, whether I was cooking over a live fire, on the stove, or in an oven. Since simmering water is gentler than boiling water, it won't jostle delicate foods so much that they fall apart or agitate tougher foods so much that they overcook on the surface before cooking through completely.

Beans. Braises. Paella. Jasmine Rice. Chicken Vindaloo. *Pozole*. Quinoa. Stews. Risotto. Chilli. Béchamel sauce. Potato gratin. Tomato sauce. Chicken stock. Polenta. Oatmeal. Thai curry. It didn't matter—this applied to everything cooked in liquid. It was a life-changing revelation!

Depending on whom you ask, the temperature of simmering water can range from 82°C to 96°C. Look at the pot—is it barely bubbling like a just-poured glass of your favourite sparkling water, beer, or champagne? If so, then cheers—it's simmering.

Sauces

Bring tomato sauce, curry, milk gravy, and *mole* sauce alike to a boil, then turn down to a simmer to cook them through. Some sauces, such as *Ragù Bolognese*, take all day. Others, such as pan sauces or Indian butter chicken, cook far more quickly, but the process is the same.

In general, keep sauces containing fresh milk at a simmer, because some of the proteins in milk can coagulate above temperatures of 82°C, resulting in curdled, grainy sauces. Sauces made from cream contain little to no protein and avoid this risk of coagulation. And milk sauces containing flour, such as béchamel or pastry cream, are an exception to this rule, as flour will interfere with coagulation. Still, remember that the natural sugars in milk and cream are eager to scorch, so once these sauces come to a boil, reduce them to a simmer and stir often to prevent burning.

Meats

I used to turn my nose up at boiled meat, which really ought to be called simmered meat, but that was before I discovered Nerbone, a sandwich stand in Florence's Mercato Centrale. The lunch lines at Nerbone were the longest in the market, so I decided to investigate. While I stood in line, I eavesdropped as everyone ahead of me in line ordered, trying to decipher their words. Even though there was a full lunch menu replete with pastas and main courses, everyone disregarded it, instead ordering *panini bolliti*—boiled beef sandwiches—garnished with chilli oil and an herby salsa verde.

When I got to the front of the line, I carefully placed my order in Italian, *"Un panino bollito con tutte due le salse."* A boiled beef sandwich with both sauces. Though I'd been in Italy for less than a week, I'd studied Italian intensively before arriving. I may have overestimated my grasp of the language. When the man at the counter said something to me in Tuscan dialect, I froze. I refused to admit that I had absolutely no clue what he'd just said. I nodded vehemently and paid the cashier. He handed me my sandwich, which I took outside to eat on the steps of the market. I took a bite, expecting to taste the tender, flavourful brisket I'd seen him slicing for the others, but that wasn't what I got. I was totally thrown off at first. I had no idea what was wrong with my sandwich. If this was indeed brisket, it was definitely the weirdest brisket I'd ever had. How could this strange-textured, off-tasting thing be what everyone was lining up for? After a brief panic, I forced myself to continue chewing and swallow. I went back and hovered at the sandwich stand, studying the signs, until I finally figured out that the man at the counter had been trying to tell me he'd sold out of brisket. All he had left was *lampredotto,* a Florentine speciality. With my vehement nodding, I'd signalled that I'd be fine with tripe instead of brisket. I forced myself to eat that sandwich, even though I'd never before—and have never since—enjoyed tripe. It may not have been suited to my tastes, exactly, but I will say—it was the most tender meat I'd ever had. The next time I returned to Nerbone, I got there early to beat the lunch rush. The brisket sandwich was the best I'd ever had. Eventually, when my language skills improved, I asked the counter guy how he got the meat so tender and moist. He looked at me, bewildered. "*È semplice. Arrivo ogni mattina alle sei e lo cuoco a fuoco lento*—It's simple. I get here every morning at six and simmer it."

And then he added, "*L'acqua non dovrebbe bollire mai*—The water must never boil."

He was right—there's no recipe for meat more straightforward than "Simmer in salted water." Such a simple preparation leaves lots of room for exotic or savoury garnishes. That is its beauty. Vietnam's chicken noodle soup ***Pho Gà***, a model of clarity, is most inviting to a long list of garnishes including spring onions, mint, coriander, chillies, and lime.

NERBONE PANINO BOLLITO

Cuts of meat with lots of connective tissue, such as chicken thighs, brisket, and pork shoulder, are perfect for simmering, as the water and gentle heat will transform collagen into gelatin overtime without drying out the exterior. To yield the most flavourful meat, place it in boiling, salted water, then turn it down to a simmer. For tasty meat *and* broth, start with simmering water. Add a few aromatics—half an onion, a few cloves of garlic, bay leaves, or a dried chilli—and leave the slate otherwise blank. Over the course of the week, refer to **The World of Flavour** on page 194 and turn the meat into a different dish each night. How to know when the meat is done? It'll be falling off the bone, or if boneless, it'll be mouthwateringly tender.

Starches

Starchy carbohydrates prosper at a simmer, which rattles their tough skins and encourages water to flow inside. Simmer potatoes, beans, rice, and all manner of grains until they've absorbed enough water to be tender.

As with boiled meat, heighten the flavour of any starch by simmering it in a savoury cooking liquid. Cook rice in unskimmed chicken stock, as Thai cooks do for *khao man gai,* and you'll give a modest meal of rice, greens, and an egg a little meaty edge. When my grandparents took me on a trip into the mountains towering above their village in northern Iran, each morning I eagerly looked forward to a breakfast of *haleem*: the hearty, nutritious porridge of wheat, oats, and turkey simmered slowly together in stock or milk warmed me up in spite of the crisp mountain air.

Porridges, including polenta, grits, and oatmeal, are variations on this theme—simmer these starches in water, milk, or whey, the clear liquid that gathers atop yoghurt, until they

grow tender. Because they are so starchy, stir these dishes often to prevent scorching.

Risotto, paella, and *fideus* react similarly. Make risotto with arborio rice, a variety with a remarkable capacity to absorb an immense amount of liquid without falling apart. After toasting the onions and browning the rice in fat, add flavourful liquids, such as wine, stock, or tomatoes. As the pot simmers, the rice takes on liquid and gives off starch. The more flavourful the liquid, the more flavourful the finished dish will be. *Fideus*, a similar dish from Spain, is made with toasted noodles instead of rice. Paella, too, is built on the concept of a thirsty starch drinking up a flavourful stock. Traditionally, paella isn't stirred but left untouched as it cooks, and is prized for the *soccorat*, or crisp crust of rice that forms at the bottom of the pan as a result.

Pasta will also absorb flavourful liquids. As I described in the step-by-step recipe for ***Pasta alle Vongole***, one of my favourite tricks is to pull the noodles from the boiling water a minute or two early and let them finish cooking in a pan of simmering sauce. This allows the noodles and the sauce to unify into a single entity—as the pasta cooks, it gives off starch and takes on liquid. As a result, the sauce absorbs its starch and thickens. And the pasta takes on the sauce's flavour. There's nothing else like it.

Vegetables

Simmer fibrous or tough vegetables—those particularly rich in cellulose—that require extended cooking to be rendered edible. Spare fennel and artichokes (and cardoons, their thistly cousins) from the tumult of boiling to keep them from falling apart. Instead, simmer them until tender with equal parts water and wine spiked with olive oil, vinegar, and aromatics to cook them *à la grecque*.

Coddling and Poaching

If simmering water resembles a glass of champagne, then the water for poaching and coddling should look like a glass of champagne you poured last night but (somehow!) forgot to drink. The extra-gentle heat of water used for **coddling** and **poaching** is perfect for delicate proteins—eggs, fish, shellfish, and tender meats. Fish poached in water, wine, olive oil, or any combination of the three will emerge with an exceptionally tender texture and clean flavour. A poached or coddled egg can turn toast, salad, or soup into a meal. Poach eggs in spicy tomato sauce and you'll have *shakshuka*, the popular North African dish. Use leftover marinara sauce for the endeavour and garnish with abundant Parmesan or pecorino Romano for *uova al purgatorio*, the Italian version with a slightly sinister name. Either will make a fine meal at any time of day.

Bain-marie

A bain-marie, or water bath, will help expand the narrow margin of error for cooking curds, custards, bread puddings, and soufflés, and for other delicate tasks such as melting chocolate. For these temperamental dishes, where just a few moments of neglect can mean the difference between silky and lumpy or smooth and grainy, welcome the assistance a water bath offers.

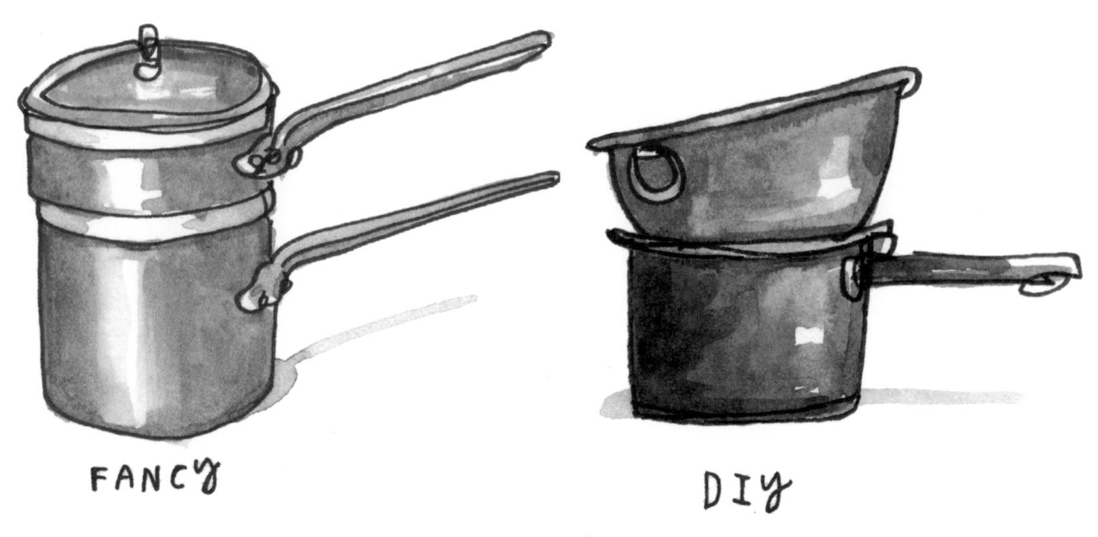

Bains-marie are generally used in the oven to regulate heat; though the oven temperature might be at 175°C, the temperature of the bath won't exceed water's boiling point of 100°C. But overcook a custard, or misjudge how much heat will carry over, and you'll end up with grainy *pot de crème*, stiff *crème caramel*, or cracked cheesecake. Pull custards from the oven and the water bath in anticipation of the residual heat that encourages coagulation to continue even as the egg proteins cool. I once pulled a still-jiggling cheesecake from the oven. Cooling on the worktop, it looked so textbook-perfect that I kept making excuses to walk by and gaze at it. When I passed through the kitchen for the twentieth time—after about four hours—a mighty crack had suddenly appeared, signalling that I'd overcooked it. I'd underestimated the power of carryover; the jiggle hadn't been jiggly enough!

To bake in a bain-marie, put a kettle on to boil while you prepare your custard base. If you have a wire rack, place it into an empty roasting pan—preferably metal—and lay the empty ramekins or cake tin atop it and fill them with custard. If you don't have a wire rack, it's fine—just be a tad more vigilant about checking your custards for doneness. Carefully carry the pan to the oven. Working quickly, open the oven door, place the pan partway on the rack, and pour in enough boiling water to go one-third of the way up the sides of the custards. Slide the pan in, shut the oven door, and set a timer. A baked custard is generally done when a tap to the edge of the dish leaves behind a faint jiggle in its wake, but the centre is no longer liquid. Upon removing them from the oven, carefully pull custards from the water.

For gentle heat on the stove, use a slightly different kind of bain-marie, heated by steam rather than hot water. You don't need the whole setup known as a double boiler; you can simply place a large bowl over a pot of barely simmering water, in order to gently heat eggs and dairy to room temperature for use in baking, to melt chocolate, to make certain sauces that contain egg, such as béarnaise and hollandaise, or sabayon, a classic stovetop custard. Just as the heat of a bain-marie protects custards from overcooking in the oven, it also protects them on the stove.

The gentle heat of a bain-marie is also handy for keeping starchy or temperamental cooked foods such as mashed potatoes, creamy soups, hot chocolate, and gravy warm until serving, without the risk of burning them.

Stewing and Braising

Twentieth-century poet Mark Strand neatly addressed the time-flavour continuum for braised meats in his poem "Pot Roast." Upon inspection of the saucy slices of braised beef on his plate, with mouthwatering anticipation, he declared, "And for once I do not regret / the passage of time."

Reading the poem, I know exactly how he must have felt, impatiently waiting for hours for the tender meat to emerge from the oven. Indeed, the key to any good stew or braise is the passage of time. Though investing time in cooking—or in anything—can turn some of us off from the endeavour, with braises the investment requires little of us but delivers big results.

As my grandmother demonstrated with her flavourful *khoreshs*, it's *time* in braising and stewing, along with water and the implicit gentle heat, which allows for the connective tissue in the tough cuts of meat to transform into gelatin, leaving meat tender, luscious, and moist. The difference between the two methods is minor: braises involve larger pieces of meat—often on the bone—and minimal cooking liquid, while stews are made with smaller pieces of meat cooked with chunky vegetables, typically served together in the plentiful cooking liquid. Greens, dense vegetables, stone fruits, and tofu also lend themselves well to braising.

At Chez Panisse, I watched chefs buy whole animals and devise creative ways to use up all of the tough, sinewy cuts. Some we cured, others we ground into sausage, and the rest we braised and stewed. For months I watched with awe as the cooks set out several cast iron pans to heat up over a medium-high flame, then added a splash of neutral tasting olive oil into the pan and laid in big pieces of beef, lamb, or pork to brown. How did they keep tabs on all of the different pans, all of the different pieces of meat? How could they turn their backs on six pans of cooking meat in order to peel and slice the onions, garlic, carrots, and celery for the aromatic flavour base? How did they know what temperature to set the burner or oven to, and how long to cook the meat? And when could I try?

With the long lens of hindsight at my disposal, I've learned that the best thing about braises is that they're nearly impossible to ruin. If I could go back and tell my nineteen-year-old self to relax, I would. And then I'd walk her through the few important landmarks of setting up and cooking a braise or stew.

Every cuisine around the world has devised ways to turn cartilaginous, bony, and sinewy meats into delicious braises and stews. This is true of Italian *osso buco*, Japanese *nikujaga*, Indian lamb curry, French *boeuf bourguignon*, Mexican pork *adobo*, and Mr. Strand's pot roast. Use the chart of aromatic flavour bases from around the world to determine what vegetables and herbs you'd like to use, and refer to **The World of Flavour** to choose your flavourings.

Think of these long-cooked dishes as opportunities to layer in flavour. Every step of the way, consider how to infuse the most flavour into the dish and extract the deepest flavour out of every individual ingredient. Apply the principles of braising and stewing to any tough cut of meat. To preserve flavour, leave the meat in large pieces and on the bone when possible. And remember to season the meat in advance to let salt do its important work of flavouring from within.

When it's time to cook, preheat a frying pan over a medium-high flame, pour in a thin layer of neutral-tasting oil, and carefully place in the pieces of meat. Make sure none of the pieces touch, to encourage steam to escape and to allow for even browning. Then do what I once found so difficult, and step away. The keys to beautiful, even browning are steady heat and patience. If you move the meat around too often, or just keep picking it up to check on it, it will take an absurdly long time to brown. Resist that urge, and instead work on the aromatic flavour base.

In a separate pan, or perhaps the same casserole you plan to cook the braise, build flavour by cooking down and slightly browning your vegetables, which can be as minimal as an onion and a couple of garlic cloves if you're not feeling up for a hunt for ginger or coriander. As the vegetables cook, check on the meat, turning the pieces and rotating the pan to get even browning. If so much fat renders from the meat that instead of searing the meat begins to fry, remove the meat from the pan and carefully pour some of the hot fat into a metal bowl and set aside. Return the meat to the pan and continue to brown on all sides. It can take upwards of fifteen minutes to properly brown a piece of beef or pork on all its sides. Do not rush this step—you want the meat to reap all of the savoury benefits of the Maillard reaction.

When you've finished browning the meat, dump out any remaining fat and deglaze the pan with your liquid of choice, be it stock or water. Remember, this is an ideal moment to work in a cooking acid, so consider adding some wine or beer. Use a wooden spoon and some elbow grease to get all of the tasty brown bits unstuck so you can add them into the braising pan. Build the braise with the vegetables and herbs on the bottom, then place in the meat—here it's all right if pieces touch as long as they all fit in a single layer, since browning isn't a concern any longer—and then add the deglazing liquid. Top off with more water or stock to come up about a third or halfway up the meat—any more and you'll be poaching rather than braising. Seal the pan with a lid, or parchment paper and foil, and bring everything to a boil, then reduce to a gentle simmer. On the stove, this is simple enough, but in the oven, that means cranking the temperature up to high (220°C and above), and then turning it down to medium-low (140°C to 180°C). The lower the temperature, the longer the braise will take, but the less likely the meat will dry out. If the liquid can't help but boil, flip the lid ajar or tear open the edge of the foil to encourage the temperature inside the pan to drop.

Again, patience is key, but the boon is that this is passive cooking time. As long as you check on the pan from time to time to make sure the liquid remains at a slight simmer and nothing more, you can go about your day as you like. The only hustle involved in braising is setting everything up and getting it into the oven. (Or any source of steady or gentle heat.) Once it's in, you can breathe easy.

How to know when it's done? I wondered the same thing at nineteen, in the kitchen at Chez Panisse. But I soon learned that the meat should fall off the bone at the gentlest touch. In boneless braises, meat should be fork-tender. Pull the pan from the heat and let it cool before straining the cooking liquid. Pass the solids through a food mill for a thicker sauce, and taste it and decide if you'd like to reduce it to intensify flavour before adding any salt.

These techniques are ideal for preparing food in advance. Time performs a potent alchemy on cooked braises and stews, improving flavour with a day or two of rest. Because it liberates the cook from last-minute demands, this kind of cooking is ideal for dinner parties. Braises and stews make for excellent leftovers and freeze well, too. With its basic technique, braising can be the most effortless path towards deeply flavourful food.

BRAISE

1. SALT

AKA SEASON in ADVANCE ← (IDEALLY) YESTERDAY*

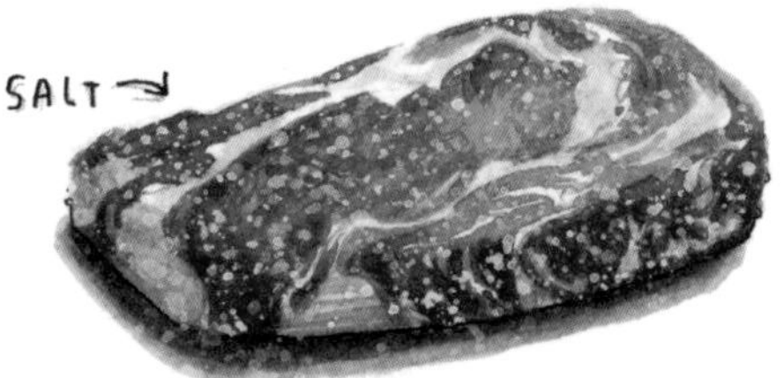

SALT GENEROUSLY on ALL SIDES and LET SIT OVERNIGHT

* OR SALT at LEAST 30 min – 3 HOURS. THE MORE TIME THE BETTER.

2. BROWN

← TODAY

HEAT PAN to MEDIUM-HIGH.

2A. THE MEAT

BROWN MEAT on ALL SIDES – MORE SPACE BETWEEN MEAT GETS IT BROWN(ER)

SET MEAT ASIDE, DRAIN FAT.

DEGLAZE HOT PAN with (ACIDIC) LIQUID (SEE "THE WORLD of ACID") and SET LIQUID ASIDE.

2B. THE AROMATICS

AKA FLAVOUR ENHANCERS

CHECK THE SPICE WHEEL & AROMATIC CHART for TIPS.

(DON'T MATTER IF THESE ARE PRETTY, YOU'RE THE ONLY ONE WHO'S GOING to SEE THEM)

BROWN and COOK DOWN

3. BUILD

LAYER INGREDIENTS into PAN.

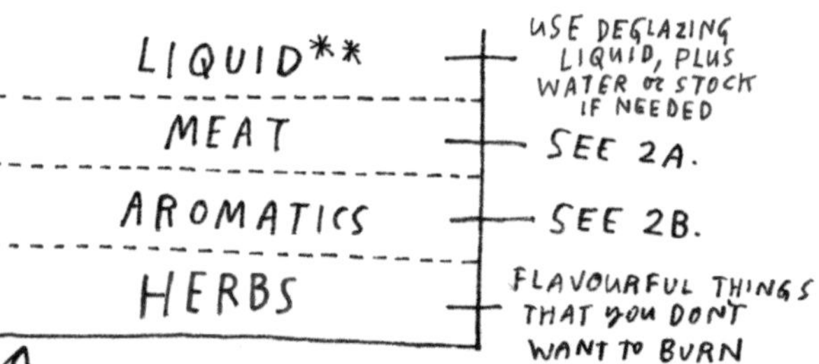

** LIQUID SHOULD GO ⅓ UP MEAT

4. BOIL

PUT in THE OVEN and CRANK UP THE HEAT.

IF PIECES ARE SMALL, LEAVE THEM UNCOVERED.
IF THEY'RE BIG, COVER THEM UP.

5. Then.... SIMMER

TURN DOWN THE HEAT and PREPARE to WAIT. (PATIENCE IS REWARDED.)

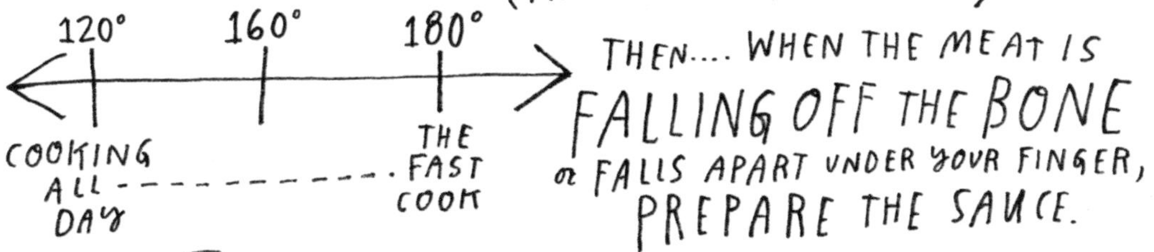

THEN.... WHEN THE MEAT IS FALLING OFF THE BONE or FALLS APART UNDER YOUR FINGER, PREPARE THE SAUCE.

6. SERVE

Blanching and Boiling

Blanching is boiling by another name, and the key to both is to *keep the water at a boil*. In Salt, I described how foods need to frolic when boiled in salty waves to cook evenly.

Add too much food to too little water, and a pot's temperature will drop drastically. A rolling boil will come to a rocking halt. Pasta will clump. Basmati rice for **Persian-ish Rice** will stick. Pencil-thin asparagus spears will pile up on the bottom of the pot and cook unevenly. Do justice to any food you blanch and keep water at a rolling boil by using twice as much as you think you need.

Vegetables

Boiling is an extraordinarily efficient cooking method, perfect for preserving the flavour of fresh vegetables. Boil vegetables long enough to let heat degrade their internal cell walls and release their sugars, and so that their starches can convert to sugars, developing sweetness. But be careful not to cook them so long that their vibrant colours begin to fade or their cell walls break down entirely, resulting in mushy textures. Choose to boil vegetables when you're short on time, or when you're seeking clean flavours. Boil everyday vegetables such as turnips, potatoes, carrots, and broccoli and dress them with good olive oil and flaky salt. You'll be pleasantly surprised by their pristine simplicity.

While some chefs insist on chilling blanched vegetables in ice baths, I generally disagree. The less time a vegetable spends immersed in water, the less chance of its minerals and nutrients leaching out. Instead of bothering with an ice bath, simply cook your vegetables a little less, knowing that they'll continue to cook even after they're pulled from the pot.

Over the years, I've found that vegetables with higher water content, like asparagus and perfect little haricots verts, carry over more than denser, less watery ones, so pull them from the pot just before they're done. Root vegetables, such as carrots and beetroots, won't carry over even if you beg them to so always boil them until they are tender throughout. You can control carryover by slipping trays of vegetables plucked from boiling water straight into the fridge, or onto an icy porch, to chill quickly.

The only way to know when a vegetable should be pulled from its blanching water is to taste it, and quickly. Before you add anything to a pot of boiling water, find your sieve or spider and prepare a landing pad. Instead of piling hot veggies in a bowl, spread them out on a baking sheet lined with parchment paper to prevent overcooking.

To save time in the kitchen, combine blanching with other cooking methods. Blanch tough greens like kale or collards until they are tender, then squeeze them dry, chop them up, and sauté. In Italy, balls of blanched greens are available at every deli, ready for any *mamma* to take home and sauté with garlic and hot pepper. Partially blanch denser vegetables such as cauliflower, carrots, and fennel on Sunday and keep them on hand for the coming week, ready to reheat and brown in the pan or oven at a moment's notice.

Blanching can also be a useful way to facilitate peeling produce with a clinging skin, such as fava beans, tomatoes, peppers, and peaches. Simply blanch them for about thirty seconds—or just long enough for the skin to loosen—and then plunge them into an ice bath to stop them from cooking any further. The skins will slip right off.

Noodles and Grains

Noodles made with wheat flour must be cooked in water at a vigorous boil in order to cook evenly, regardless of whether you call them pasta, ramen, *bakmi*, udon, or elbow macaroni.

The pandemonium keeps the noodles moving, preventing them from sticking to one another as they release starch. Take the guesswork and measuring out of cooking whole grains such as barley, rice, farro, and quinoa by boiling them as you would pasta, until they are completely tender. Drain and serve as a side dish, or spread them out to let them cool, then drizzle with olive oil and add them to soups, grain salads, or store them in the freezer for up to two months for future use.

Once you've grown familiar with the cooking times of various foods, you can stagger multiple ingredients into a single pot of water to save yourself time and a pan. When pasta still has a few minutes of boiling left, add bite-size florets of broccoli or cauliflower, chopped kale, or turnip greens to the water. Delicate spring peas or tiny slices of asparagus or green beans need only about ninety seconds to cook through, so add them just before draining the pot, and taste to determine their doneness.

Reducing

Intensify the flavour and thicken the texture of sauces, stocks, and soups by leaving them at a continuous boil. Recall that while water may evaporate, salt and other seasonings won't, so take care to avoid oversalting reductions. Season cautiously as you go to give yourself a greater margin of error—you can always adjust the salt once you're satisfied with the texture of the sauce.

Extended vigorous boiling can also encourage clear sauces and soups to emulsify if they aren't properly skimmed, so take care to remove fat from sauces or stocks before you set them on the stove. Or simply pull the pan askew on the burner for a moment—as one side of the pan calms and cools, the boiling action will force all of the fat and scum to collect on the side of the pan away from the bubbles. Skim the fat with a spoon or ladle, return the pan to the centre of the burner, and keep boiling.

Finally, remember that reducing food will continue to cook it, deepening and changing its flavour. Increased surface area—that is, using a wider, shallower pan—will speed up reduction. If the amount of liquid you're reducing is beyond 8cm deep, divide it into multiple shallow pans to allow steam to escape more quickly and prevent flavours from changing considerably. Using a second pan is also a great time-saving trick, and one I recently taught to a friend's mom as she struggled to get Christmas Eve dinner on the table on time. Reducing the beef stock for the sauce was taking such a long time that all of the rest of the food was growing cold. When she realised that she'd have to add 450ml of cream to the sauce and reduce it all by half a second time, she started tearing up. Just then, I poked my head into the kitchen to see if I could help, and when I realised what the problem was, I told her not to worry. I just pulled out two more shallow pans, poured half of the reducing beef sauce into one and the cream into the other, and let everything boil at full blast. Ten minutes later, our sauce was done and we were sitting down to eat.

Steaming

Steam trapped in a pan, pot, or packet will efficiently cook food while preserving clarity of flavour. Though oven steaming requires a temperature of at least 230°C, the temperature within the vessel will remain below 100°C due to recycling water vapour. Note that since it's higher in energy than boiling water, steam will cook the surface of a food more quickly. But I've grouped it with the gentle cooking techniques because steaming physically protects delicate foods from the jostling of boiling.

Steam little potatoes in the oven by placing them in a single layer in a roasting dish, seasoning with salt, and adding any aromatics—a sprig of rosemary and a few garlic cloves will do. Add just enough water to cover the bottom of the pan, and tightly seal it up with aluminium foil. Cook until the potatoes present no resistance when pierced with a knife, and then serve with flaky salt and butter or garlicky aïoli alongside hard-boiled eggs or grilled fish.

My favourite steaming technique calls for a parchment-paper package of fish, vegetables, mushrooms or fruit. Upon opening the package (*cartoccio* in Italian or *papillote* in French) at the table, each guest experiences a burst of aromatic steam.

I once collaborated with a group of talented chefs on a special dinner. I was assigned to the dessert course. I suspect the only reason they asked was because I was the only woman in the group. It certainly wasn't because I'm a natural at pastry, where it's essential to follow recipes meticulously (and by now, you know how I feel about that). While the other chefs focused on one-upping each other with complicated techniques, I took one look at the massive oven in our kitchen and decided to take another route. The Blenheim apricots from my favourite farm had just come into season. With blushing orange skin and velvety flesh, these apricots evoke both the quiet awakening of spring and the vibrancy of summer, perfectly balanced in sweetness and acidity, absolutely delicious. If you ever see them at the farmers' market, buy as many as you can carry.

That night, I halved the apricots, removed the pits, and stuffed each half with a filling made of marzipan, almonds, and the little Italian cookies called *amaretti*. Then I placed the apricots on a piece of parchment paper, drizzled them with a few drops of dessert wine, sprinkled them with sugar, and wrapped up the *cartocci*. I baked the parchment packages in the blazing-hot oven for about 10 minutes, until they puffed up with steam, and then rushed them to the table with bowls of whipped crème fraîche. After a refined multicourse dinner, the simple pleasure of tearing open the packets, smelling the apricots' heady perfume, and tasting their balanced sweet-tart flavour delighted our guests no end. Even now, years later, when I bump into folks who were guests at that meal, they dreamily reminisce about the apricot *cartoccio*. I never cease to be amazed at how good a simple preparation can be.

To steam on the stove instead of the oven, set a perforated steamer insert or sieve filled with a single layer of food—anything from vegetables and eggs to rice, tamales, and fish—over a pot of simmering water. Cover with a lid to entrap steam and cook until tender. Traditional Moroccan couscous is cooked in this way—over a water bath spiked with aromatic vegetables, herbs, and spices to lend a whisper of flavour.

Stovetop steaming is also an ideal method for cooking shellfish, such as clams or mussels, in the way I described in the step-by-step recipe for ***Pasta alle Vongole***.

Combine steaming with the browning that comes from intense heat in a method I like to call **steamy sauté**. It's perfect for cooking dense vegetables such as fennel or carrots: add a centimetre of water, salt, a generous splash of olive oil or knob of butter, and aromatics into a pan filled with a single layer of vegetables, and place a lid on ajar. Simmer until the vegetables are tender, remove the lid, pour off any excess water, then turn up the heat and let the Maillard reaction commence.

Cooking with Fat

Confit

Confit is the French word for foods cooked slowly in fat at temperatures low enough to avoid browning. It's one of the few times you'll use fat as a cooking medium *without* the goal of browning.

The best-known, and perhaps the most delicious, confit is made with duck. This dish from Gascony, in the hills of southwest France, evolved as a way to preserve duck legs for later consumption. The process is simple and the results couldn't be tastier. Season the legs, immerse them in rendered duck fat, and cook them gently until they are tender at the bone. You'll know the temperature is right when the duck fat emits a bubble or two every few seconds. When covered with fat and stored in the fridge, the duck will last for months, ready to be turned into the shredded duck *pâté* called *rillettes,* or *cassoulet,* the traditional French dish of duck, beans, and sausage, or simply heated and crisped at a moment's notice and served with boiled potatoes, zesty greens, and a glass of wine.

If you don't have duck on hand, the technique works beautifully with other meats, including pork, goose, and chicken. For a holiday indulgence, remove and prepare a confit from the legs of your Thanksgiving turkey or Christmas goose. Roast the breast and offer your guests a bird prepared two ways. In the summer, try confit of fresh tuna in olive oil spiked with a garlic clove or two and make Niçoise salad. Vegetables, too, are ripe for confits: toss **Artichoke Confit** with pasta and some torn basil for a quick supper, or pair **Cherry Tomato Confit** with fresh beans or poached eggs. Strain and refrigerate the olive oil, which will be as flavourful and valuable as what was cooked in it, to use in vinaigrette or cook with again in the coming days.

Sweating

Sweating is a gentle way of cooking vegetables in minimal fat until they are tender and translucent, without resulting in browning. As they cook, they release some liquid, hence the name. *Mirepoix,* the aromatic combination of onions, carrots, and celery at the root of all French cooking, is typically sweated, rather than sautéed or browned, in an effort to prevent colouring. Sweat onions to add to *risotto bianco,* cauliflower purée, or any other ivory-coloured dish where flecks of browned onions would offer unwelcome punctuation.

A foundation of sweated onions is the secret to delicate-tasting single-vegetable soups such as English pea, carrot, or **Silky Sweet Corn Soup**, whose recipes are identical: sweat onions, add the chosen vegetable, cover with water, season with salt, bring to a boil, reduce to a simmer, and remove from the heat the *moment* the vegetables are cooked, or even just before that moment in anticipation of the carryover that will occur. Place the whole pot in an ice bath to chill immediately, and purée. Stir, taste, adjust, and serve with a tasty garnish, replete with acid and fat, such as an herb salsa or crème fraîche.

To keep temperatures in the sweat zone, watch the pan closely. Add salt to draw water out of the vegetables. Use a pan or pot with tall sides to discourage steam from escaping. Parchment paper or a lid will help entrap and recycle steam, if needed. And don't hesitate to add a splash of water from time to time if you sense a brown spot starting to form.

A note on stirring: it tends to dissipate heat. So, stir regularly when you want to keep food from browning, and stir less often to let browning take its course. Stir with a wooden spoon, which is both strong and soft, to prevent sugars or starches from building up at the bottom of pots of caramelising onions, béchamel sauce, or polenta. You don't have to get too crazy about stirring—just add it to the toolbox of tricks you can use to encourage or discourage browning.

The Frying Continuum

In Fat, I explained that the various names for frying methods generally refer to the amount of fat used in each preparation. Whether you're deep-, shallow-, pan-, or stir-frying or sautéing, the concept is the same: preheat the pan and the fat long enough so that food immediately begins to brown once it's added, but regulate the temperature so that the food cooks through at the same rate its surface browns. Always resist overcrowding the pan and moving food around too much, too soon. Proteins in particular will stick to the pan as they begin to cook. Leave fish, chicken, and meat be for a few minutes, and once they begin to brown, they will release from the pan.

The term ***sauté*** is derived from the French word for "jump," and it refers to the little jag of the wrist used to flip all of the food in a pan. Use minimal fat when sautéing to avoid burning yourself with a splash of hot oil—just enough to barely coat the bottom of the pan (about 2mm) will do. Sauté small foods that will cook through at the same rate their surfaces will brown, such as prawns, cooked grains, small pieces of vegetables or meat, and greens.

Sautéing saves both time and a utensil, and also ensures even browning on all sides, so it's a good skill to cultivate. Don't worry if you don't have the flipping action down—it took me years to master. Just lay an old sheet on the living room floor and practise: place a handful of rice or dried beans in a frying pan with curved sides, tilt the pan down and your elbow up, and flip fearlessly until you get the action right. In the meantime, use metal tongs or a wooden spoon to move your sautéing food around the pan.

To **pan-fry**, use enough fat to generously cover the bottom of the pan (about 5mm). Pan-fry larger foods—such as fish fillets, steaks, pork chops, or **Finger-Lickin' Pan-Fried Chicken**—that need more time to cook through. Let the pan and the fat preheat long enough so that any food you add will immediately start to sizzle, but don't crank the heat: the food should brown at the same rate it cooks through. Since chicken breasts and fish fillets take longer to cook through than bite-size pieces of meat or prawns, the temperature here should be slightly lower than when sautéing.

Shallow- and **deep-frying** are fraternal twins, both ideal for cooking starchy vegetables, or battered and breaded foods. Appearances aside, the two methods are nearly identical. Submerge foods in fat a little more than halfway to shallow-fry. Submerge foods completely to deep-fry.

Whichever form of frying you're undertaking, the temperature of the oil should be right around 185°C. (Just think, *I wish I were eating fried food 365 days a year!* to remember the right temperature for frying. Or simply mark 185°C on your frying thermometer with a permanent marker.) Much lower, and a crust won't form quickly enough, resulting in soggy food. Much higher, and the batter will burn before the food it encases has a chance to cook. The only exception to this rule: dense, tough foods that take a while to cook through, such as chicken thighs, which can fry for upward of 15 minutes. Add chicken thighs to oil at about 185°C to get that desired crust, but let the temperature drop to 160°C, where they can cook through without burning.

Like that roadside cook I watched making *chapli kebabs* in Pakistan, pay attention to the signals frying foods emit as they cook, and eventually you won't need to get your thermometer out every time you fry. Steam, bubbles, food rising to the top of the pot, and browning are all clues to heed. When the temperature is hot enough, food sizzles and browns—but not too violently or quickly—upon entering the pot. When the bubbling ceases and steam slows down, batter is done cooking. When food is crisp and golden, it's ready to pull from the oil.

The amount of food you add into a pot of oil will affect its temperature. The more, bigger, colder, and denser the food you add, the farther its temperature will drop. If the oil takes too long to climb back to 185°C, the food will overcook before it has a chance to brown properly. Preemptively heat oil just past the ideal zone or add less food at once in anticipation of a big drop in temperature, and always let oil temperature return to the ideal point in between batches.

Since the ideal frying temperature is so far beyond 100°C, any water in the batter or on the surface of a frying food will immediately vaporise—the source of all of the bubbling. The key to getting a crisp, golden-brown crust is to encourage that

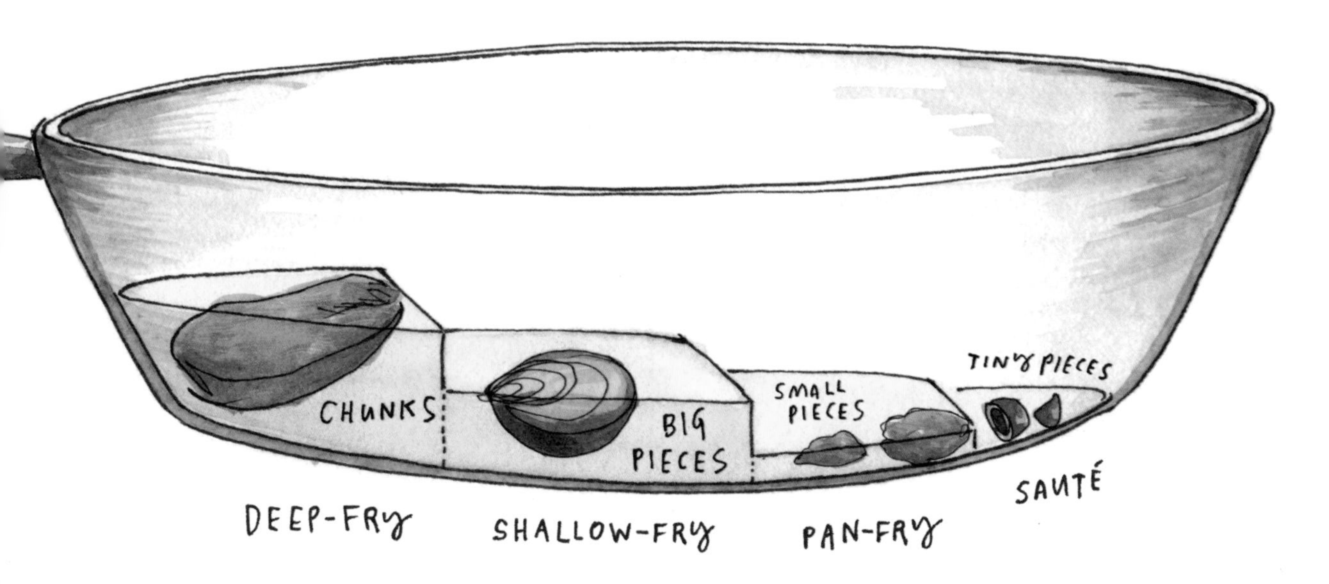

vapour—steam—to escape as quickly as possible. In other words, don't overpack the pot. Battered foods must never touch or be more than a single layer deep in the oil—otherwise they'll cook into a big, soggy mass. While foods fried sans batter—such as potato, kale, or beetroot chips—can and will touch, stir them often to prevent them from sticking together, and to encourage them to brown evenly on all sides.

Choose to shallow-fry delicate foods that could be broken apart by the bubbling tumult of deep-frying, such as crab or fish cakes, little chard fritters, or breaded green tomatoes. Deep-frying is a better choice for chips of all kinds, battered foods, and more substantial foods that need total immersion to cook evenly, such as soft-shell crabs.

Searing

It doesn't matter whether you use a grill, a cast iron pan, or a baking sheet preheated in the oven—the main requirement for **searing** is a blazing-hot cooking surface. Preheat the surface over high heat, then add the fat and let it approach its smoke point before adding meat to sear. Once Eccolo closed, I began to cook more and more in my home kitchen. It was hard to give up the restaurant's turbo-charged stove and get used to my apartment's no-frills one with its weak burners. At first, no matter how long I preheated my cast iron pan on the stove, it never got hot enough to properly sear a steak without overcooking it. After a few tough steaks, I started preheating the pan in a blasting hot oven for at least 20 minutes before bringing it up to the stovetop to begin searing over high heat. It works like a charm.

When browning, frying, or searing, the first side of a food to be browned will always be the most beautiful, so lay food in a pan or on the grill with its presentation side down. For poultry, that means skin side down, for fish that means skin side up. For meat, use your judgment and put the prettiest side down.

The purpose of searing isn't so much to cook as it is to brown meat or seafood in order to get the flavour benefits of the Maillard reaction. The penetrative heat of searing can be sufficient to cook the most tender cuts of meat and fish that are best served rare or barely cooked, such as tuna, scallops, or beef tenderloin. But for everything else, searing is for *browning* rather than *cooking*. Sear larger cuts of meat to achieve the flavour hits of Maillard before transferring the meat to braise over a gentle heat. Sear racks of lamb, pork loin roasts, or thick pork chops over direct heat before rendering and cooking them through with gentler heat, whether on the stove or grill, or in the oven.

Cooking with Air

Grilling

The number one rule of **grilling**: never cook directly over the flame. Flames leave soot, unpleasant flavours, and carcinogens on food. Instead, let the flames subside and cook over smouldering coals and embers. Picture toasting the perfect marshmallow for s'mores—you've got to patiently perch the coat hanger over the coals, turning the marshmallow for even browning. Get that puppy too close to the flames and it'll taste gassy and burnt on the outside, while remaining untoasted within. The same thing will happen to any food you grill directly over flames.

Different fuels—whether fruit woods, hard woods, charcoal, or gas—reach different temperatures on the grill. Hard woods such as oak and almond catch fire quickly and burn slowly, so they're ideal when you need sustained heat. Fruit woods—including grapevines and fig, apple, and cherry woods—tend to burn hot and fast and are great for quickly reaching browning temperatures. Never grill over soft woods such as pine, spruce, or fir, which can lend pungent, and not altogether pleasant, flavours to food.

The benefit of charcoal is that it burns more slowly yet hotter than wood. Lump charcoal in particular lends a delicious smoky flavour to food. Though the flavour of food cooked over a live fire will always be superior, the convenience of a gas grill can't be beaten. Use gas grills with an understanding of their limitations—because they do not burn wood, they will not lend smokiness to food. (You can, however, use smoking chips to make up for this, as described on page 153.) And because gas doesn't burn as hot as wood or charcoal, gas grills can't achieve the blazing-hot temperatures of live fires, so they aren't able to brown food as quickly or efficiently.

Leave grilling meat unsupervised and as fat renders and drips into the coals, flare-ups will occur, engulfing food in flames and leaving behind unwelcome flavours. Prevent flare-ups by moving food around a grill and keeping very fatty cuts away from the hottest coals. Before I learned to cook, I always assumed that perfect crosshatched grill marks were the sign of a talented cook. Watching Alice grill piles of quail and sausages in her yard one afternoon, a few years after I started at Chez Panisse, I suddenly realised why the cooks I worked with never bothered with grill marks. As diminutive as a hummingbird, and just as restless, Alice hovered over the grill, moving the birds and sausages as soon as they began to take on colour, or just as they began rendering fat and threatening to cause a flare-up. As she flipped the meat, it was obvious that their even golden-brown sheen was the direct consequence of her feverish tending. This way, every single bite would be bestowed with the flavourful molecules resulting from the Maillard reaction, instead of just the spots lucky enough to be marked by crosshatching.

Whether you're working with gas or a live fire, create different temperature zones on your grill, like various burners on a stove. Use **direct heat** over the hottest coal beds for the littlest, most tender foods: thin steaks, little birds such as quail, sliced vegetables and thin toasts, chicken breasts, and burgers you might want to leave rare. Use the suggestion of heat from nearby coals to create cooler spots for cooking meats on the bone, larger cuts, and chickens that need time to cook through. Cooler zones are also ideal for sausages and fatty meats that will cause flare-ups and for keeping foods warm.

Indirect heat is at work in the kind of slow, gentle grilling known in the south as barbecue, and in smoking meats, such as **Sage- and Honey-Smoked Chicken**. In both of these methods, the grill is essentially turned into an oven and kept at temperatures between 95°C and 150°C. The key to gentle grilling and smoking is slow, constant heat, which can be a challenge when working with live fire. A digital meat thermometer can be helpful here, letting you know when the temperature of the grill drops or rises too far.

A digital meat thermometer came in handy one summer after Eccolo closed, when my journalism teacher and cooking student Michael Pollan accidentally ordered three times as much pork shoulder as he'd thought. Panicked, he called me over. He taught me how to make pork shoulder barbecue and we had an emergency slow-cooking session in his yard—a contradiction in terms, perhaps, but a delicious one involving a lot of thumb-twiddling. He rubbed the meat with salt and sugar in advance, and then cooked it on a gas grill fortified with wood chips for six hours over indirect heat. I suspect that he may have been a southern pitmaster in a past life, for this yielded the smokiest, most fork-tender meat I'd ever tasted. Since there wasn't much active meat-cooking to do, we also made **Simmered Beans**, **Bright Cabbage Slaw**, and **Bittersweet Chocolate Pudding** in our downtime and threw a pretty sweet Pork 911 Dinner Party that night.

Don't own a grill? Live in an apartment? Think of **oven-grilling** as upside-down, indoor grilling. While most grilling is done outdoors, with the heat source below the food, oven-grilling happens inside the oven, with the heat radiating from above. Oven grills can get really, really hot—much hotter than a typical grill, since the food is usually much closer to the heat source. Use an oven grill to cook very thin steaks or chops, or to brown foods under careful supervision, since just twenty seconds can mean the difference between delicious and carbonised. Use an oven grill to melt cheese on cheesy toast, to brown bread crumbs atop mac and cheese, and crisp the skin of leftover **Glazed Five-Spice Chicken**.

Whether grilled, oven-grilled, or roasted, allow all tender meats to rest after cooking and before carving. In addition to allowing time for carryover to occur, resting gives the proteins in meat a chance to relax. Rested meat retains water better after carving, yielding a juicier piece of meat. For large cuts, this can take up to an hour, while steaks need only 5 or 10 minutes. For the most tender slices, cut meat **against the grain**, or the direction in which the muscle fibres run. Let your knife do the hard work of shortening the fibres by cutting right through them. The meat will be much more tender, and chewing it will be a lot more enjoyable.

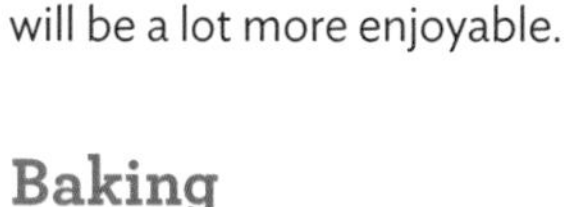

Baking

Oven temperatures fall into four general categories: **low** (80°C to 135°C), **medium-low** (135°C to 180°C), **medium-high** (180°C to 220°C), and **high** (220°C and above). Within any one of these categories, food will cook in more or less the same way. If you don't know where to start, start at 180°C, the "middle C" note of baking. Start here if you misplaced your recipe. 180°C is hot enough to encourage browning but gentle enough to allow most food to cook through.

Low temperatures (80°C to 135°C) offer enough heat to leaven and dry out **Marshmallowy Meringues** but are also gentle enough to prevent browning. One superstitious pastry chef I know will only ever bake meringues in her antique gas oven overnight. Before going to sleep, she preheats the oven to 95°C and then shuts it off as she slips in the cookies. The minimal heat generated by the pilot light slows the cooling of the oven, and by morning, her meringues are always snow-white and crisp, without being overly dry. In other words, they're perfect.

Most baked goods prosper with the delicate heat **medium-low** temperatures

(135° C to 180°C) offer. Proteins set, doughs and batters dry out—but not too much—and gentle browning ensues. Cakes, cookies, and brownies alike do well at these temperatures, as well as many pies and tender doughs including shortbreads and biscuits. Think of 160°C as a more forgiving version of 180°C; it's more likely to yield chewy rather than crisp cookies and golden rather than golden-brown cakes.

In contrast, higher temperatures swiftly lead to browning. Cook savoury dishes through at **medium-low** temperatures, then crank them up to **medium-high** (180°C to 220°C) to develop the golden-brown tops we love to see on gratins, lasagna, pot pies, and casseroles.

High (220°C and above) oven temperatures lead to rapid, though sometimes uneven, browning. Using high temperatures when achieving structure quickly is important, as it is for cream puffs and flaky crusts. As water vaporises into steam in a hot oven, it leads to **oven spring**, which is the initial increase in the volume of a baking dough. This burst of rising steam pushes apart layers of a baking dough, yielding a flaky crust, like **Aaron's Tart Dough**. Some baked goods, such as soufflés and popovers, rely entirely on oven spring to rise, while others, such as **Lori's Chocolate Midnight Cake,** also depend on chemical leaveners. Either way, this initial rise is generally the most substantial in the baking cycle. To achieve the most powerful oven spring, leave the oven door shut for the first 15 to 20 minutes of high-heat baking. After the proteins in the dough have set and the basic structure has formed, you can turn down the heat to prevent burning and ensure that the food cooks through.

Dehydrating (less than 95°C)

Think of **dehydrating** as baking at the lowest possible temperatures. As its name suggests, its aim is to remove water from food, often to preserve it, without reaching browning temperatures. Meat and fish jerky, dried peppers, fruit leather, and tomato paste, dried fruit and tomatoes are all dehydrated foods. While you can buy special dehydrators to heat food gently, the lowest setting on the oven, or even just leaving food in there overnight with the pilot light on, is generally just right. At Eccolo, during the hottest, dryest days of summer, I'd dry fresh peppers and fresh haricot beans on the roof, spreading them out in a single layer on a wire rack. I quickly learned to move the trays indoors at night to discourage nighttime critters and the morning dew from interfering with my work. Each round took several days and some careful tending, but I was always grateful for my summer diligence, come winter. To make juicy, oven-dried tomatoes, cut small, flavourful tomatoes such as Early Girls in half. Pack them snugly onto a parchment-lined baking sheet, cut side up. Season them with salt and a light sprinkling of sugar, then slide them into an oven set to 95°C (or lower, if possible) for about 12 hours, checking on them once or twice along the way. You'll know the tomatoes are done when none of them is soupy or wet. Pack into a glass jar and cover with olive oil and refrigerate, or freeze in a resealable plastic bag, for up to 6 months.

Toasting (180°C to 230°C)

My ideal piece of toast is crisp on the surface, golden brown in colour, and rich with all of the flavours produced by the Maillard reaction. Aim for these three qualities whether you're **toasting** a bagel, bread crumbs, or shredded coconut. Nuts, too, will only improve with toasting. To avoid doing the sort of euphemistic overtoasting carried out by my young cook at Eccolo, set a timer to remind you to check on toasting foods from time to time. Always toast in a single layer, stir often, and pull bits and pieces as they are done.

Toast thin slices of bread, to be smeared with chicken liver paste or broad bean purée at medium-low heat (about 180°C) so they don't burn or dry out, which will result in mouth-damaging shards. Thicker slices of bread, to be topped with poached eggs and greens or tomatoes and ricotta, can be toasted at high heat (up to 230°C), or on a hot grill, so they brown quickly on the surface and remain chewy in the centre.

At 230°C and above, coconut flakes, pine nuts, and bread crumbs will go from perfect to burnt in the time it takes to sneeze. Knock 10 to 25°C off the temperature, and you'll buy yourself the luxury of time. If a sneezing fit hits, your toasted foods will be safe. And when you deem the toastiness of these delicate foods sufficient, remove them from their hot trays (not doing so may lead to carryover and your perfectly toasted food will blacken while your back is turned).

Slow-Roasting, Grilling, and Smoking (95°C to 150°C)

Meats and fish that are rich in fat can be cooked slowly in the oven or on the grill at very low temperatures so that their own fats render and moisten them from within. I love to **slow-roast** salmon, a method that works equally well for a single serving or a whole side. Simply season the fish with salt on both sides and tuck it, skin side down, into a bed of herbs. Drizzle a tiny bit of good olive oil on top and rub it in evenly with your hands, then place the fish in an oven preheated to 110°C. Depending on the size of your portion, it can take anywhere from 10 to 50 minutes to cook, but you'll know it's done when the fish begins to flake in the thickest part of the fillet when poked with a knife or your finger. Because this method is so gentle on its proteins, the fish will appear translucent even when it's cooked. **Slow-Roasted Salmon** is luscious and succulent—perfect for serving warm, at room temperature, or chilled in a salad. (For a more detailed recipe and serving suggestions, turn to page 310.)

Roasting (180°C to 230°C)

The difference between **roasting** and toasting is simple: toasting implies browning the surface of a food, while roasting also cooks food through. Originally, roasting referred to cooking meat on a spit above or beside a fire. What we think of as roasting today—cooking meat in a dry, hot oven—was known as baking until about two hundred years ago.

While the chickens—and everything else I so came to love roasting on that spit at Eccolo—invariably emerged with evenly cooked meat as a result of their constant rotation, the birds I roast at home brown differently due to the different forms of heat at work in the oven. The **radiant** heat emitted from the heating element dries out exposed foods as it cooks them, leading to crisp, dry skin on a chicken, or wrinkly, leathery skin on little potatoes. In a **convection** oven, one or two fans consistently circulate hot air, so food browns, dries out, and cooks more quickly than in a conventional oven. When using convection, reduce the temperature by approximately 15°C or monitor foods with extra vigilance.

On the other hand, the surface of any food touching hot metal will brown via **conduction**, the principle at work in stovetop frying: the burner heats the pan, which heats the fat in the pan, which heats the food. It's the same in the oven: the oven heats the pan, which heats the fat, which heats the food. Lay oiled slices of sweet potatoes on a pan and slide it into a hot oven. Though both sides of each slice will brown, they'll cook differently due to the various modes of heat transfer at work. The tops will be slightly dry and leathery, while the bottoms will be golden and moist, as if they'd been pan-fried. Any roasting food will suffer from this sort of uneven browning—unless it's cooking on a wire rack and air can circulate beneath it. Flip, rotate, and move roasting foods around in the oven as they cook. Oven browning gains momentum, so start food that must brown quickly at high temperatures and then turn the oven down as browning begins, to prevent overcooking.

Thin foods, or foods that can't risk being overcooked before they brown, can benefit from a head start: preheat the baking sheet in the oven before adding oiled and salted courgette slices, or heat up a cast iron pan on the stove before tossing in prawns dressed in **Harissa** and sliding it into a hot oven. Use slightly milder temperatures for foods you expect to leave in the oven for long periods of time. Taste food as it cooks. Touch it. Smell it. Listen to it.

If you sense browning is happening too quickly, turn down the temperature, loosely cover the dish with a piece of parchment paper or foil, and move the rack away from the heating element. If you sense browning is happening too slowly, crank up the temperature, push food back into your oven's hot spots, which are typically the back corners, and move it closer to the heating element.

To further encourage steam to escape and browning to commence, use a shallow pan for roasting. Most of the time, a baking sheet with a lip or a cast iron pan is the way to go. If the meat you're roasting has lots of fat to render (goose, duck, rib roast, or pork loin, for example), consider using a wire rack so that your roast doesn't end up frying on the bottom as a pool of fat collects in the pan.

Vegetables

Timely salting, combined with the Maillard reaction, leads to perfect roast vegetables that are brown and sweet on the outside, tender and delicious on the inside (refer to the **Salting Calendar** on page 40 for a refresher on when to salt). Make 200°C your default temperature for roasting vegetables, but know that it will change based on the size of the vegetables, their density and molecular makeup, as well as the depth and material of your roasting pan and the amount of food on the tray or in the oven.

I once horribly miscalculated how many courgettes I had to roast at Chez Panisse. There was only enough room in the oven for two trays, and I was running short on time. I figured I'd just squeeze all of the courgettes onto two trays to get the task done. Like puzzle pieces, I packed the first tray so tightly that each piece seemed to hold all the others in place. I slipped the tray into the oven and set about doing the same with the rest of the summer squash. It never occurred to me to wonder why I'd never seen any other cooks pack so many vegetables onto a single tray—I was just doing what I needed to do to get the work done!

When I piled the remaining courgettes onto the second tray, though, it was clear I'd made a mistake. There was barely enough squash to fill a second tray, leaving ample room between the pieces. With the first tray already heating up in the oven and a long list of other tasks to get done, I couldn't bring myself to take the extra step and even out the two trays of courgettes, so I just slid the second tray into the hot oven.

I lived to regret this shortcut. When I went to rotate the trays, the packed courgettes were floating in a lake of their own juices, while the spread-out courgettes were browning nicely. Between the weeping brought on by osmosis and the lack of room for steam to escape, the first tray of squash emerged from the oven a sopping, soggy mess. I'd unwittingly made steamed courgette soup. The only positive result from that experiment was that I've never again overstuffed a tray of roasting vegetables.

For even browning, don't pack too many vegetables on a tray. Leave space between the pieces for steam to escape and allow temperatures to rise high enough for browning to begin. Tend to your vegetables as they roast—stir them, turn them, rotate trays, and change the oven racks.

Resist the urge to combine vegetables with vastly different sugar, starch, or water contents on a single tray when roasting. They will not cook evenly—some will steam, some will burn, and none will be satisfying to eat. Refer to **Plants, Above and Below** on page 144 for a refresher on which vegetables will cook similarly. If you only have one baking sheet to your name, get thee to a thrift store! And in the meantime, roast your potatoes on one side of the pan, the broccoli on the other, and remove each as it's finished cooking.

Meats

Well-marbled, tender cuts of meat such as prime rib and pork loin are ideal for roasting, because they're juicy enough to stand up to the dry heat of the oven. As I explained earlier, as meat cooks, rendering fat bastes it from within. With the built-in safeguard of copious fat, then, tougher cuts of meat such as pork shoulder or chuck are also apt for roasting.

Take preemptive measures if you plan to roast very lean meats such as turkey breasts by **brining** or **barding**, or wrapping them with a layer of fat to ensure moistness.

For even cooking, remember to season roasts in advance to give salt the time it needs to penetrate the meat and impede proteins from relinquishing all their entrapped water as they cook. Bring meats for roasting to room temperature (this can take several hours for very large cuts). Start roasts in a hot oven (about 200 to 220°C) and then gradually decrease the temperature in 15°C increments after browning commences, until done.

And any time you think of cooking bacon or browning meat in an oven hotter than 200°C in order to save a few minutes, remember this cautionary tale. A few years ago, I was running behind on the prep for a dinner party I was catering out of my tiny apartment kitchen. I cranked the oven up and threw in a pan of short ribs to brown. Though I hadn't thought much of it at the time, I'd noticed earlier that the ribs were extraordinarily fatty. A few minutes later, smoke started billowing out of the stove at an alarming rate. It was so dramatic, it looked staged! I realised all that fat was rendering from the short ribs and immediately turning to smoke. Before I had a chance to do anything, some of the rendering fat splattered onto the oven grill and caught fire. I whipped open my cupboards and grabbed the first thing I saw that could extinguish the flames: a five-pound bag of flour. Let's just say I didn't serve the short ribs that night. (Another kitchen shortcut that backfired. Sometimes the long way is the best—and only—way.)

Learn from my mistake. Once fat begins to render, cook meat at temperatures below 190°C—the smoke point of most animal fats—to prevent repeatedly setting off the smoke alarm, or worse.

Invest in an instant-read meat thermometer for roasting meats (and use it for smoking meats, too). Check large roasts in multiple spots, because one part can appear done while another is undercooked. An internal temperature variance of just a few degrees can mean the difference between juicy and dry. My rule of thumb for cooking a large roast is once its internal temperature hits 37°C, it'll start climbing at a rate of about two-thirds of a degree a minute, if not faster. So if you're aiming for medium-rare, around 48°C to 49°C, then know that you've got about 15 minutes before it's time to pull. Large roasts carry over about 8°C, while steaks and chops will carry over about 3°C, so account for this any time you pull meat off the heat.

If you prefer the kind of crust **searing** produces, start your roast on the stove. This can also be a handy way to speed up a weeknight roast—I do it all the time with my **Crispiest Spatchcocked Chicken**: I brown it breast side down in a cast iron pan, then flip and slide it into the oven to halve the time it takes to roast a chicken. This technique also works beautifully for pork, lamb, and beef loins and sirloins and, if you're feeling decadent, fillet mignon.

Layering Heat

Just as with Salt, Fat, or Acid, sometimes you'll need to use more than one type of heat to get the results you need. This is what I call **layering heat**.

Toasted bread is a great example. As with any starch, wheat needs water and heat to cook through. In bread, that's done in the form of combining milled wheat with water to make a dough, and then baking that dough in the oven until it's cooked through. When we toast bread, we cook it a second time.

Learn to break down the cooking process into chunks so that you can finish cooking delicate things at the time of serving, preventing the inevitable overcooking associated with reheating. This is exactly the kind of thinking restaurant cooks employ to cut down on the time it takes to prepare a dish to order without compromising quality. Foods that require long exposure to gentle heat—tough meats, dense vegetables, and hearty grains—are entirely or partially cooked in advance and reheated to order. Delicate foods that will cook quickly or suffer from reheating—fried foods, tender meats, fish and shellfish, and baby vegetables—are cooked to order.

Braise pork shoulder overnight, but grill it up for tacos for a party the next day. To achieve depth of flavour, gently roast or blanch any number of tough vegetables—broccoli, cauliflower, turnips, or winter squash—before sautéing them. Simmer chicken thighs until they're falling off the bone, then shred the meat to use in a pot pie.

Learn to combine two different cooking methods to get the flavour and texture contrasts that so please our palates—such as crisp, brown crusts and soft, tender insides.

Measuring Heat: Sensory Cues

As American poet Mary Oliver wrote, "To pay attention, this is our endless and proper work." She must be a great cook. Indeed, the best cooks I've ever met—whether in home or professional kitchens—are careful observers.

With Salt, Fat, and Acid, your tongue can guide you as you cook. Other senses take on greater importance when considering Heat, since generally you can't taste its effects until its work is done. Use these sensory cues to help you determine when various foods are cooked, or nearly there.

See

- Cakes and quick breads develop a golden-brown colour and pull away from the sides of a pan. A toothpick inserted into the centre will come out with just a couple of crumbs, or totally clean when inserted, depending on the type of cake.

- Fish will change from translucent to opaque. Fish on the bone starts to peel away from the bone. The flesh of flaky fish, such as salmon and trout, begins to break apart into flakes.

- Shellfish, such as clams and mussels, open up as they are cooked. Lobster and crab meat won't cling to the shells. Scallops should remain translucent inside. Prawns change colour and begin to curl.

QUINOA

BEFORE AFTER

WHEAT BERRIES

BEFORE AFTER

- When quinoa is cooked through, its germ, which looks like a little tail, will stick out. Fully cooked whole grains, including barley and wheat berries, will just begin to split. Fresh pasta droops when it's cooked, and lightens in colour. Dried pasta also lightens in colour, though when broken open or bitten into it should still be white in the centre, indicating it's al dente.

- Gauge deep-fried foods not only by their surface colour but also by the rate of bubbles they're giving off. As deep-fried foods cook further, they emit fewer bubbles because there is less moisture left to escape from the food.

- When properly cooked, chicken meat turns from pink to opaque but is still juicy. You can always nick and peek at poultry, meat, or fish. Cut into the thickest part of the piece and see if it's cooked. Roast chicken is done when pricked at the thigh and the juice runs clear.

- Custards jiggle at the centre, but not around the edges, when cooked. Egg whites no longer appear slimy.

Smell

- The aromas of cooking are among the most rewarding sensory treats, second only, perhaps, to its flavours. Familiarise yourself with the smells of cooking onions at different degrees of browning. Do the same for caramelising sugars. This will help when you're in the other room, with roasting vegetables in the oven—often the nose is the first to know.

- Spices toasting in a hot pan will often emit an aroma long before they change in colour, which is a good sign to take them off and let residual heat continue to do its work.

- Always heed the smell of burning and find its source.

Hear

- Food should almost always sizzle when it's added to a pan, signalling that the pan and the fat are both preheated.
- But there are different qualities of sizzle . . . once sizzling slows and becomes more pronounced and aggressive, it's a sputter. Sputtering is a sign that there's a lot of hot fat present, and can often mean that it's time to tip some fat out of the pan, flip the chicken breast to the other side, or pull the browning short ribs out of the oven.
- Listen for a boil. Especially when you need to be prepared to turn it down to a simmer. You'll find that you can hear whether foil-wrapped pans have come to a boil in the oven if you listen carefully enough. It'll save you from having to peel back the foil to check.

Feel

- Tender meats firm up as they cook.
- Tough meats also firm up as they cook, but they won't be done until they relax again, and fall apart at the touch or are tender at the bone.
- Cakes spring back at the touch.
- Starches sticking together at the bottom of the pot, difficult to stir, or creating an impenetrable crust at the bottom of the pot are teetering on the edge of burning. Either scratch them off, or switch pots to avoid scorching.
- Beans, grains, and starches of all kinds are tender throughout when cooked.
- Pasta is chewy, with the tiniest bit of resistance in the centre.
- Vegetables are done when they are tender at their thickest points.

Improvising with Salt, Fat, Acid, and Heat

Now for the fun part: using Salt, Fat, Acid, and Heat to compose great dishes and menus. Answer the basic questions for each element to give yourself the clearest idea of how to proceed. How much Salt, Fat, and Acid, and when, and in what forms? Will the ingredients benefit most from gentle or intense Heat? Line up the answers to these questions and a theme will emerge, upon which you can begin to improvise.

For example, next Thanksgiving, use what you've learned about Salt, Fat, and Heat, to cook the juiciest, tastiest roast turkey you've ever had. Salt or brine it well in advance for tender, flavourful meat. Sneak slices of herbed butter underneath the skin to baste the lean breast as it cooks. Pat its skin dry before you stick it in the oven, so it can brown, instead of steam. Bring it to room temperature before cooking and remove its backbone (this is called **spatchcocking**, see page 317) so that it can lie flat, absorbing the intense heat of the oven evenly and quickly. And, of course, let the bird rest for at least 25 minutes before you carve it to allow its proteins to relax. Then, savour every single bite with some sweet, bright cranberry sauce.

Or, when your family asks you to make short ribs for dinner tonight, disappoint them at first by saying no. Instead, feed them **Slow-Roasted Salmon**, or **Finger-Lickin' Pan-Fried Chicken** tonight, knowing you can season and cook either properly on short notice. Promise to reward them for their patience. When you're ready to make them, season the short ribs generously with salt and let them sit overnight. The next day, get the braise together, softening the aromatic vegetables while the meat browns. Take care to work wine and tomatoes into the base. Slip the pan into the oven and let it simmer, growing ever richer, more tender, and more flavourful. Ponder which herb salsa you'll make to play the foil, and when you bring it all to the table, watch as their eyes grow large with disbelief. They will swoon with each bite. They'll ask how you managed such a feat. And you'll say, "It's simple—Salt, Fat, Acid, and Heat."

WHAT TO COOK

Now that you know *how* to cook, all that remains is to decide *what* to cook. Menu writing is one of my favourite parts of the cooking process, and I think of it as a simple puzzle: first, figure out one part, and then fit everything else in around that.

Anchoring

Choose one element of a dish and make it the foundation upon which you build a meal. This is what I call **anchoring**, and it's the best way to create a menu unified in flavour and concept.

Sometimes the anchor will be a particular ingredient, such as the chicken you salted two days ago. It may be a cooking method; perhaps it's the first day of summer and you're eager to light the grill. Maybe there's a specific recipe you're eager to try. Sometimes the mere thought of leaving the house to buy groceries is overwhelming and the anchor becomes the scraps you've got in the fridge, freezer, and pantry.

At times, the anchor will be a limitation—of time, space, resources, or stove or oven capacity. At Thanksgiving, when oven space is at a premium, make the oven your anchor. Decide which of your menu items must be cooked in the oven, and choose to make other dishes that can be cooked on the stove or grill, or served at room temperature. On a weeknight, your anchor may be the lack of time you have to spend on dinner, so let that guide you in the choice of meat to build a dish around. On a leisurely Sunday, the opposite may be true, and you can build not only your menu but your entire day around slow cooking.

When you're craving Mexican, Indian, Korean, or Thai food, let the flavours of those places be your anchor. Think about the ingredients that define the cuisine that inspires you, and start to build a meal around that. Consult cookbooks, memories of your own childhood or travel, or call your grandmother or auntie for counsel. Decide whether you want to go the traditional route and follow your grandmother's advice, or whether you'd prefer to refer to **The World of Flavour** (page 194) and simply infuse the spirit of the place into a dish you already know how to cook.

If you're overenthusiastic at the farmers' market, as I often am, and come home with more food than you could possibly use, let the produce be your anchor. Sit down with a cup of coffee at the kitchen table and pull your favourite cookbooks down from the shelf—or flip to the recipe section in this book—in search of inspiration.

One of the first jobs I had at Chez Panisse was called *garde-manger*—French for "eating guard." I started every morning at six o'clock, and my first task was to walk through each of the four walk-in refrigerators and inventory every single item of food. I quickly learned to wear a sweatshirt beneath my chef's coat, because the walk-ins are quite literally bone-chilling. I also learned how this task affected the chefs' menu writing each morning. Only when they had a complete picture of what was on hand, and what was being delivered that day by the farmers, ranchers, and fishermen who supplied us, could they set about creating the best possible menu. If I didn't do my job well, they couldn't do theirs.

I came to love that quiet time in the walk-ins each morning, before the kitchen sprang to life with the busyness of the other cooks and the din of the dishwasher filled the restaurant with noise. Soon I realised that taking note of everything on hand was just the first step in deciding *what* to cook, whether at the restaurant or at home. I also learned that implicit in this style of cooking is an emphasis on the quality of the ingredients. If something doesn't taste good to begin with, no amount of Salt, Fat, Acid, Heat trickery will change that. Try to buy the best tasting ingredients available, when you can.

As a rule, the fresher the produce, meat, dairy, or fish, the better it will taste. In general, foods grown locally and in season are the freshest, and so they taste the best. By shopping before deciding on a specific menu, you'll ensure that your meal starts with the most flavourful ingredients instead of crossing your fingers and hoping to find a way to work in the perfectly ripe figs or tender baby lettuces you unexpectedly find at the farmers' market.

And when you can't get to a farmers' market, scour the produce aisles of the grocery store in search of the freshest-looking stuff. In the store, as in the kitchen, let all your senses guide you. If the greens look wilted, or the tomatoes don't smell like much, head to the freezer section and choose from the produce hidden over there. Frozen fruits and vegetables are easy to forget about, but they tend to be harvested and flash-frozen at the peak of freshness. In the depths of winter—or at other times when nothing much else looks very good—frozen peas and corn can offer a welcome dose of spring and summer flavour.

WHAT SHOULD I COOK?

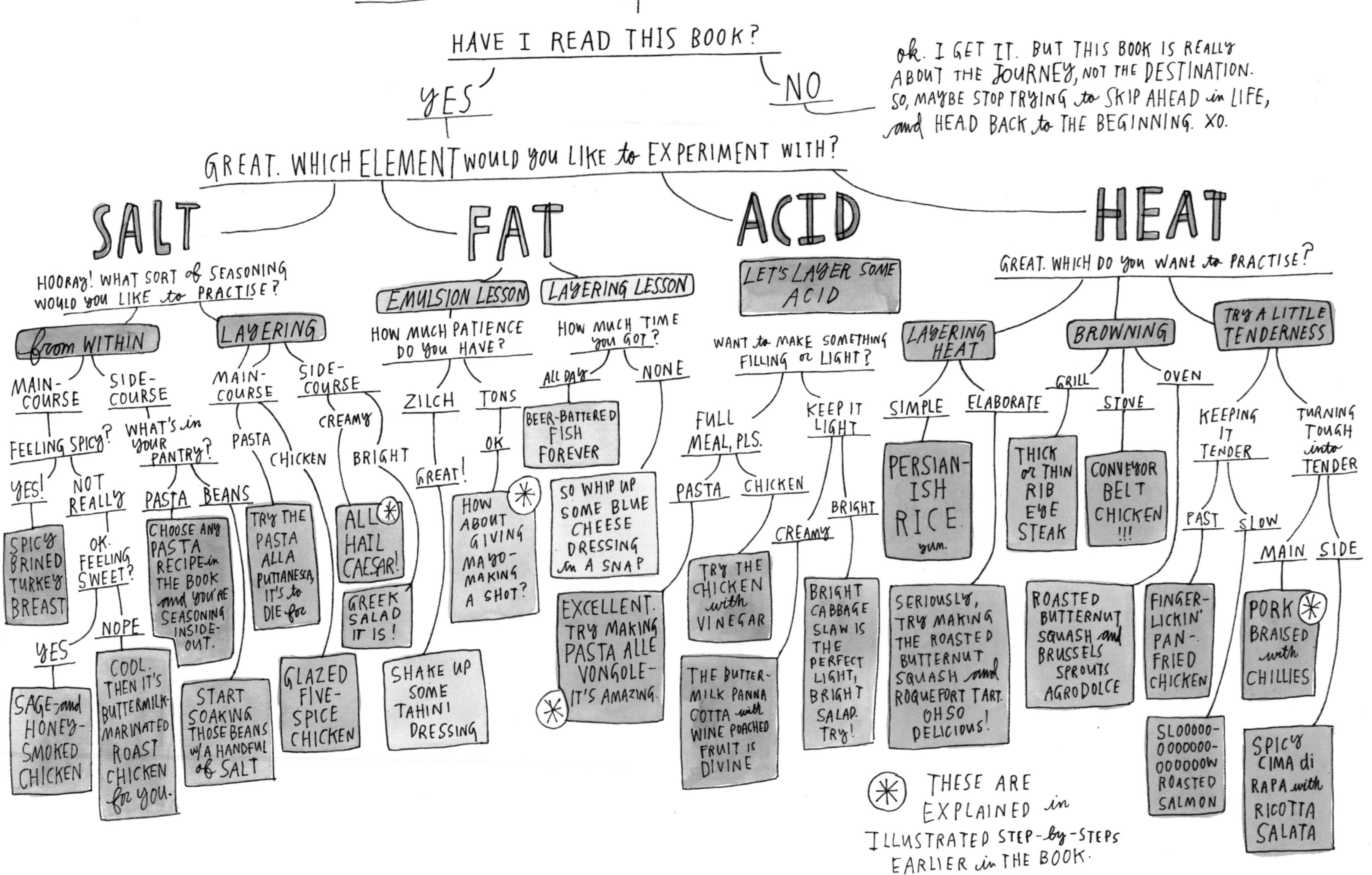

The World of Flavour

USE THIS WHEEL to HELP CHOOSE WHICH FLAVOURINGS to USE AS you COOK FOODS from AROUND THE WORLD. LAYER HERBS and SPICES into AROMATIC BASES and GARNISHES to ADD MULTIPLE DIMENSIONS of THE SAME FLAVOUR THROUGHOUT THE DISH.

EUROPE

- **GREECE & CYPRUS**: MINT, DILL, PARSLEY, OREGANO, BASIL
- **SCANDINAVIA**: CARDAMOM, CINNAMON, DILL, GINGER, JUNIPER BERRIES, NUTMEG, BAY LEAF, ALLSPICE, MUSTARD, and SAFFRON
- **EASTERN EUROPE**: ALLSPICE, CARAWAY SEEDS, CINNAMON, CLOVES, DILL, GINGER, JUNIPER, PAPRIKA, BLACK PEPPER, SAVORY
- **GERMANY**: ALLSPICE, ANISE, BAY LEAF, CARAWAY, CHIVES, CINNAMON, DILL SEED & WEED, GINGER, JUNIPER, HORSERADISH, PAPRIKA, PARSLEY, WHITE & BLACK PEPPER, CELERY SEED
- **SPAIN**: SAFFRON, THYME, PARSLEY, SWEET & SMOKY PAPRIKA, BAY LEAF, CHILLIES, CORIANDER, LAVENDER, TARRAGON, BASIL
- **ITALY**: BASIL, FENNEL SEEDS & FRONDS, BLACK PEPPER, ROSEMARY, SAGE, CHILLIES, OREGANO, and SAFFRON
- **FRANCE**: PARSLEY, TARRAGON, THYME, BASIL, FENNEL SEEDS, LAVENDER, ROSEMARY, SAGE, BAY, CHERVIL, HERBES de PROVENCE, QUATR'EPICES
- **UNITED KINGDOM**: PARSLEY, CELERY, MINT, DILL, CURRY POWDER, CARDAMOM, GINGER, CINNAMON, NUTMEG

NORTH AMERICA

- **USA & CANADA**: MUSTARD, PAPRIKA, BLACK PEPPER, CAYENNE, CHILLIES, PARSLEY, CELERY, DILL, MINT, CINNAMON, NUTMEG
- **MEXICO**: FRESH & DRIED CHILLIES, FRESH & DRIED CORIANDER, CUMIN, CINNAMON, EPAZOTE, OREGANO, CLOVE, ALLSPICE, and THYME
- **CENTRAL AMERICA**: CHILLIES, EPAZOTE, CORIANDER, MUSTARD, TURMERIC
- **CARIBBEAN**: ALLSPICE, HOT PEPPERS, CALLALOO, GINGER, HIBISCUS, OREGANO, CUMIN, BASIL, BAY LEAVES, PAPRIKA, SAFFRON, CURRY POWDER, JERK SPICES

SOUTH AMERICA

- **ARGENTINA & URUGUAY**: PARSLEY, OREGANO, CHILLIES, PAPRIKA
- **CHILE, PERU & BOLIVIA**: PERUVIAN BLACK MINT, MINT-MARIGOLD, AJI PEPPER, BASIL, PARSLEY, CORIANDER, CHILLIES
- **BRAZIL**: CARDAMOM, CHILLIES, CORIANDER, CLOVES, GINGER, NUTMEG, PARSLEY, BLACK PEPPER, SAFFRON, THYME

ASIA

- **MEDITERRANEAN**: SUMAC, OREGANO, THYME, CUMIN, MARJORAM, DRIED MINT, BLACK PEPPER, FENNEL, ZA'ATAR, BAHARAT, PARSLEY
- **IRAN**: SAFFRON!, CUMIN, CARDAMOM, ROSE, DILL, MINT, BASIL, PARSLEY, CORIANDER, TARRAGON, DRIED LIME, ORANGE FLOWER WATER, and ADVIEH
- **INDIA**: CHILLIES, CORIANDER, TURMERIC, CUMIN, GINGER, CURRY, GARAM MASALA, PANCH PHORAN, ANISE, CARDAMOM, CINNAMON, CLOVES, CURRIES, MINT, BLACK PEPPER, SAFFRON, MUSTARD
- **VIETNAM**: THAI BASIL, CHILLIES, CORIANDER, GINGER, LEMONGRASS, MINT, SPRING ONIONS, STAR ANISE, PERILLA, RAU RĂM
- **THAILAND**: THAI BASIL, CHILLIES, CORIANDER, CUMIN, CURRY PASTE, GINGER, LEMONGRASS, MINT, TURMERIC, KAFFIR LIME, GALANGAL
- **KOREA**: CHILLIES, GARLIC, SESAME SEEDS, GINGER, and PERILLA
- **JAPAN**: CHILLIES, GINGER, WASABI, SHISO, SHITAKE MUSHROOMS, YUZU, KOMBU, MUSTARD POWDER, NORI, SHICHIMI TOGARASHI
- **CHINA**: CHILLIES, GARLIC, GINGER, SZECHUAN PEPPERCORN, STAR ANISE, BLACK PEPPER, SESAME SEEDS, and FIVE SPICE

AFRICA

- **HORN of AFRICA**: BERBERE SPICES, MITMITA
- **NORTH AFRICA**: SAFFRON, HARISSA, CINNAMON, MINT, CUMIN, SUMAC, PARSLEY, CORIANDER, LA KAMA, DUKKAH, RAS EL HANOUT
- **WEST AFRICA**: NUTMEG, GINGER, CURRY, ADOBO, PEANUTS

BALANCE, LAYERING, AND RESTRAINT

Once you've chosen your anchor, begin to balance the meal. Precede long-cooked, rich dishes with light, fresh-tasting ones. If you plan to serve a bready appetiser—perhaps **Winter Panzanella**, or **Tomato and Ricotta Toasts**—then avoid heavy starches throughout the rest of the meal—no pasta, no cake, no bread pudding. If a custardy **Chocolate Pudding Pie** will conclude the meal, don't serve rich **Pasta Alfredo**, or steak doused in creamy béarnaise sauce before it.

Incorporate contrasting textures and flavours, as well as ingredients, and avoid repetition—unless you're purposely celebrating the height of a season, with tomato soup, salad, and *granita*, for example. Garnish soft comfort foods with crunchy crumbs, toasted nuts, or crisp bits of bacon to make things interesting. Serve rich meats with bright, acidic sauces and clean-tasting blanched or raw vegetables. Serve mouth-drying starches with mouthwatering sauces, and recognise that a well-dressed, juicy salad can serve as both a side dish and a sauce. On the other hand, pair simply cooked meats, such as grilled steak or poached chicken, with roasted, sautéed, or fried vegetables glazed with Maillard's dark lacquer.

Let the seasons inspire you; foods that are in season together naturally complement one another on the plate. For example, corn, beans, and squash grow as companions in the field, then the three sisters find their way together into succotash. Tomatoes, aubergines, courgettes, and basil become *ratatouille, tian*, or *caponata* depending on where you are on the Mediterranean coast. Sage, a hardy winter herb, is a natural complement to winter squash because its leaves—and its flavour—stand up to the cold of winter.

Pair delicate ingredients that could easily be overwhelmed with clean, bright flavours—light broths, tender herbs, a squeeze of citrus at the end, no browning. Think of spring peas and asparagus, delicate salmon or halibut, or a salad of summer fruits. Other times, the weather, the season, or the occasion demands depth of flavour: aggressive browning of both the aromatics and the meat in a braise, rich stocks, cheeses, mushrooms, anchovies, and savoury other ingredients rich in umami. Generally, aim to strike a balance of cleanliness *and* depth.

Heavily spice one part of a dish or meal, then keep the rest more or less neutral, echoing a few of the same spices here and there if you like, to prevent overloading your taste buds. Garnish a simple puréed carrot soup with a yoghurt *raita* replete with spices sizzled in ghee. Add just a few cumin seeds to beans and rice, but use them in abundance with chillies and garlic to rub all over skirt steak for tacos.

If food doesn't taste right—first turn to the lessons of Salt, Fat, and Acid. Make sure that those three elements are in balance. Most often, that'll be enough. If a dish still needs something, turn next to umami. Is it falling a little flat? Perhaps a little soy sauce, pounded anchovy, or Parmesan will make the difference. Finally, texture. Is the reason for the dullness its one-note texture? Perhaps it needs the crunch of bread crumbs, toasted nuts, or a pickle to add contrast.

Scientists have found that we all prefer to eat foods that engage our senses with these kinds of contrasts—including light and dark, sweet and salty, crunchy and silky, hot and cold, and, of course, sweet and sour.

And then there are herbs and spices, which can wake up the plainest foods. Herb salsas, pepper sauces, a sprinkle of chopped parsley, Lebanese *za'atar*, or Japanese *shichimi togarashi* can enliven any dish.

Invest in the flavours of a dish by layering each upon one another to create a tightly woven matrix of tastes and aromas. Use a single ingredient in multiple ways to add dimension to a dish: a lemon's zest *and* its juice; coriander seeds *and* leaves; fennel seeds, fronds, *and* bulbs; fresh peppers *and* dried chillies; toasted hazelnuts *and* their oil.

And if menu writing grows overwhelming, just remember: you already have a lifetime of balanced menu creation under your belt. Whenever you've ordered multiple courses at a restaurant, you have practised this kind of thinking. Every time you choose to order a salad, then split a pasta, main course, and dessert with

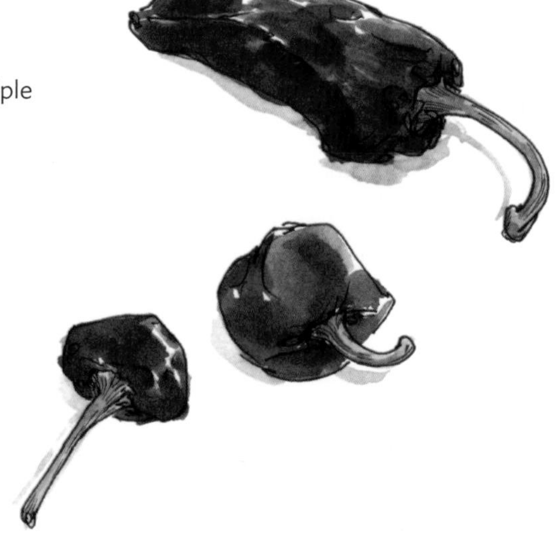

your dining companion, you're intuitively creating a balanced meal. Though it can be tempting to order Caesar salad *and* meatballs *and* pasta *and* fried chicken *and* ice cream, you rarely do, instinctively aware of the price you'll pay for that kind of excess.

Every choice you make in the kitchen should have a clear reason. Rare is the kitchen-sink dish or meal that doesn't taste like a kitchen-sink dish or meal. This is not to say you should never take action to clear out the pantry or the fridge with a meal—quite the contrary!—but that you should decide carefully which ingredients belong together, and which will bring out the best in the others.

USING RECIPES

Chef Judy Rodgers once said, "Recipes do not make food taste good; people do." I couldn't agree more. Most of the time, the path to good food is simple: get the Salt, Fat, and Acid right, and apply the right type of Heat, for the right amount of time. At other times, you'll need to consult a recipe. Whether for general inspiration or precise step-by-step instruction, a good recipe can be invaluable.

But recipes lead us to believe that cooking is a linear process, while most good food results from a circular one; like a spiderweb, touch one part and the entire thing will quiver. Earlier in this book, I described the alchemy of the perfect Caesar dressing. Here, for example, the amount of anchovies you add will affect the amount of salt, which will affect the amount of cheese you add, which will affect how much vinegar you need, which may need to be lightened by lemon juice. Every choice is part of a greater whole, with the ultimate goal of achieving the deepest flavour possible.

Think of a recipe as a snapshot of a dish. The better the recipe, the more detailed, in focus, and striking the photo. But even the most beautiful photos can't replace the experience of being in a place, smelling its smells, tasting its tastes, hearing its sounds. Just as photos can't satisfy all of our senses, nor should recipes subvert them.

A great recipe, like a great photo, tells a story, and it tells it well. Lesser recipes may not connect all the dots. There are plenty of reasons for this, and while some of them may have to do with the skill of the cook or the accuracy of the recipe tester, or frankly, whether the recipe has been tested at all, they're not important. Simply put, *no recipe is infallible*. You are the one cooking, you are the one who is present, you are the one who must use all your senses—most of all, common sense—to guide you to the result you hope for. Over the years I've constantly been amazed by the way good cooks give up thinking critically and independently when they begin following recipes.

Instead, once you've chosen a recipe, don't let your own intimate knowledge of your own ingredients and kitchen and, most important, your own taste be overridden by what you're reading. Be present. Stir, taste, adjust.

Certain kinds of recipes—particularly those involving desserts—must be followed to the letter. But I believe that most savoury recipes are little more than guides, and some guides are better than others. Learn to decipher the secret codes within recipes to see where they are leading you.

Once you understand that braising, stewing, and making *ragù* or beef chilli all follow the same general trajectory, I hope you'll feel liberated. Use your judgment to help decide which pan to use, how high to heat it, what fat to use for browning, and how to judge doneness, no matter what the recipe directs.

Sometimes, you can't go wrong when you begin with the recipe on the package. The best pumpkin pie I've ever tasted was a version of the recipe on the Libby's canned pumpkin label, with double cream substituted for the prescribed canned evaporated milk (indeed, this is the inspiration for the recipe I've included in Part Two). The go-to recipe for corn bread at Chez Panisse is a slight variation on the recipe from the back of the Alber's cornmeal box, made instead with freshly milled Antebellum cornmeal from Anson Mills in South Carolina. And my very favourite chocolate chip cookie of all time involves a tiny riff on the original Toll House recipe: a 50g increase in the amount of brown sugar and a corresponding decrease in the amount of white sugar.

When making a dish for the first time, read several different recipes for the same dish and compare notes. Notice which ingredients, techniques, and flavourings are common to the recipes, and which are different. This will give you an idea of which aspects of the dish you must not compromise on, and where a little improvisation is welcome. Over time, as you get to know which chefs and writers are traditionalists, and which take more liberties, you'll grow better equipped to decide between recipes and cooking styles.

When making foods from far-off lands, perhaps no ingredient is as important as curiosity. Cooking, and eating, foods from places we've never seen is as good a way as any (and better than most!) to expand your horizons, to remember that the world is a big, beautiful place of endless magic and surprise. Let curiosity lead you to new books and magazines, websites, and restaurants, cooking classes, and of course, cities, countries, and continents.

The nature of cooking is ever-changing. Even the same pile of peas will taste different when cooked on two different days, as their innate sugars transform into starches. They'll have to be treated differently in order to extract the best flavour from them, and that means you need to pay attention and ask yourself what will work best today, here, with these ingredients.

With all of this—and everything I've taught you in Part One—in mind, I've compiled my most essential and versatile recipes and recommendations in Part Two. Organised somewhat differently from the recipes in a traditional cookbook, they reflect the patterns and lessons I've uncovered in Salt, Fat, Acid, and Heat. Refer to the charts and infographics to set your course. These resources are kind of like training wheels: use them until you feel comfortable cooking without them. Then abandon them, using only the four elements of good cooking as a guide. They are all you will need.

• • •

The other night, as I was watching *The Sound of Music* for the umpteenth time, unabashedly singing along, I heard a line from "Do-Re-Mi" in a whole new way. It goes: "Once you know the notes to sing, you can sing most anything." Feel free to imagine my off-key belting as you let this idea sink in. Once you know the basics of Salt, Fat, Acid, and Heat, you can cook most anything, and do it well.

These are the four notes of the culinary scale; learn your way around them. Verse yourself in the classics, and then begin to improvise like a jazz musician, putting your own spin on the standards.

Think about Salt, Fat, Acid, and Heat every single time you set out to cook. Choose the right type of Heat for the particular foods you're cooking. Taste and adjust Salt, Fat, and Acid as you go. Be thoughtful, and use your senses. Consider these four elements when making dishes you've made hundreds of times, and use them to find your bearings when cooking exotic foods for the first time. They'll never let you down.

and NOW THAT
you KNOW
HOW to COOK...

PART TWO

RECIPES and RECOMMENDATIONS

KITCHEN BASICS

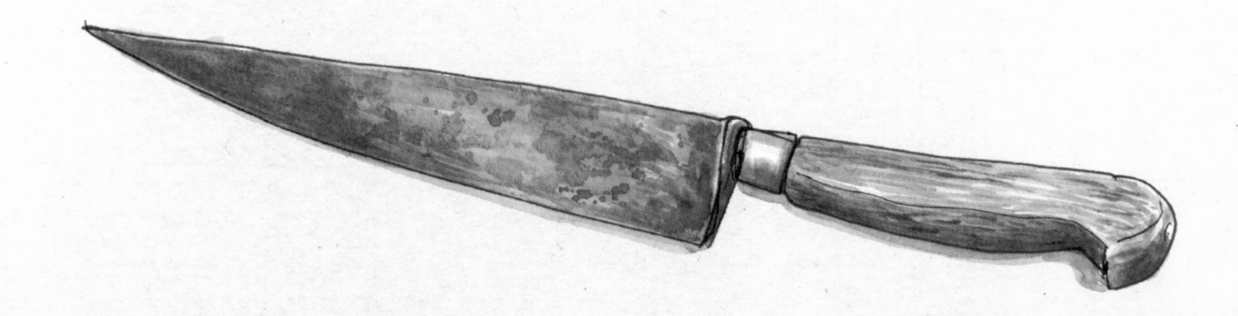

CHOOSING TOOLS

Use this list to help you choose the right tool for every task.

Serrated Knife vs. Chef's Knife vs. Paring Knife

There are only a few proper uses for a serrated knife: slicing bread, tomatoes, and layer cakes. For everything else, use a chef's knife—the sharper the better. Use a paring knife whenever a task requires precision.

Wooden Spoon vs. Metal Spoon vs. Rubber Spatula

Stir cooking foods with a wooden spoon, which is soft enough to avoid damaging the pan but strong enough to scrape off all the browned bits that might stick to the bottom. A metal spoon is ideal for browning ground meat for chilli or *ragù*—you can use the edge to break up the pieces. Use a rubber spatula any time you need to scrape every last drop out of the bowl or pan.

Frying Pan vs. Cast Iron Casserole

Use a frying pan for searing, sautéing, or any cooking method where the goal is to brown foods quickly. Use a cast iron casserole, with its taller sides, to entrap steam and encourage tough foods to become tender. As it's deep enough to keep oil from bubbling over, the casserole is also great for deep-frying.

Baking Sheet vs. Bowl

A baking sheet lined with parchment paper is the ideal landing pad for blanched vegetables, browned meats, cooked grains, or anything else that needs to cool off quickly without overcooking. When roasting vegetables, croutons, or anything else, toss them together with oil and salt in a bowl to ensure even coverage, and then lay them out on a baking sheet.

CHOOSING INGREDIENTS

A Note on Salt

I've got a lot to say about salt. So much, in fact, that I wrote an entire chapter on it. While I recommend reading the Salt chapter before heading into the kitchen with these recipes, I certainly understand if you can't help yourself.

If you get to a recipe that doesn't specify the type or amount of salt to use, use what you've got on hand (unless it's iodised table salt, in which case you should throw it out and head straight to the store to buy kosher or sea salt). Start with a pinch or two of salt, then taste early and often in the cooking process to get where you want to go, adjusting the seasoning along the way.

Refer to the **Salting Guidelines** on page 43 to see just how much the weight (and saltiness!) of a single tablespoon of salt will vary depending on the type. Hint: it's a lot. For this reason, I encourage you to start with my guidelines as your benchmarks until you get a feel of how much salt it takes to properly season various foods. I've tested these recipes with both Diamond Crystal brand kosher salt (the red box) and fine sea salt from the grocery store. We can get Diamond Crystal online and Morton's on Amazon. Morton brand kosher salt (the blue box) is almost twice as salty by volume, so if you're cooking with that, use *half as much* kosher salt as the recipes indicate.

Where Not to Skimp

Most of the recipes that follow call for ingredients that can be found in any grocery store. But I splurge on a few items, and I suggest you do too. Good cooking starts with good ingredients. You'll thank me when you're sitting down to the most delicious dinner you've ever cooked.

Buy the best you can afford

- Extra-virgin Olive Oil, pressed in the last calendar year
- Whole chunks of Parmigiano-Reggiano from Italy
- Chocolate and Cocoa Powder

Buy whole and prepare yourself

- Pick and chop **fresh herbs** (and always use Italian or flat-leaf parsley).
- Juice **lemons** and **limes**
- Peel, chop, and pound **garlic**
- Grind **spices**
- Soak, rinse, fillet, and chop **salt-packed anchovies**
- Make **chicken stock** when you can (see page 271 for a recipe). Or buy fresh or frozen stock from your butcher, rather than the boxed or canned stuff (it never tastes as good). Failing that, use water.

For more details about selecting ingredients, flip a few pages back to **What to Cook**?

A FEW BASIC HOW-TOS

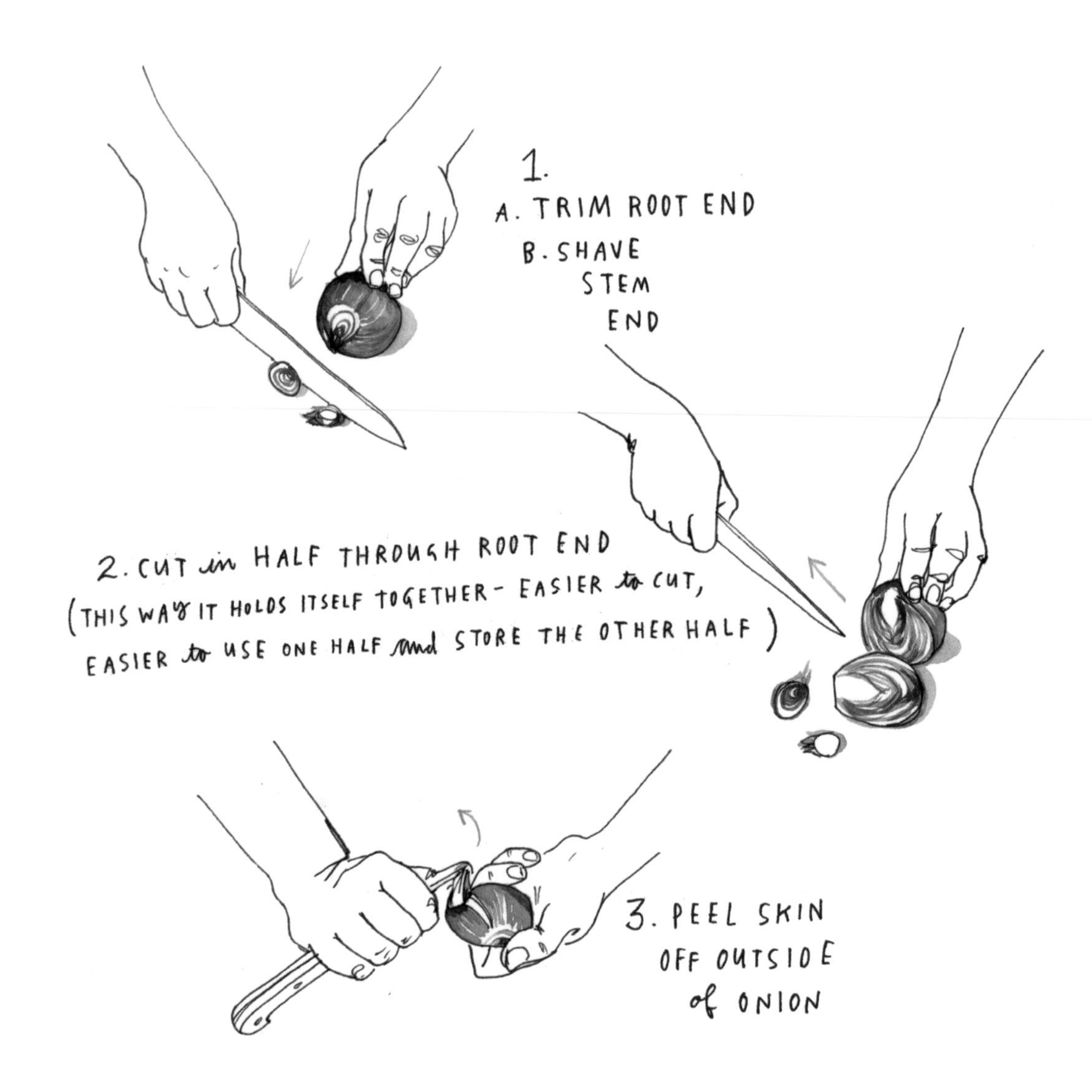

How to Slice an Onion

FOLLOW PREP STEPS 1-3, and THEN:

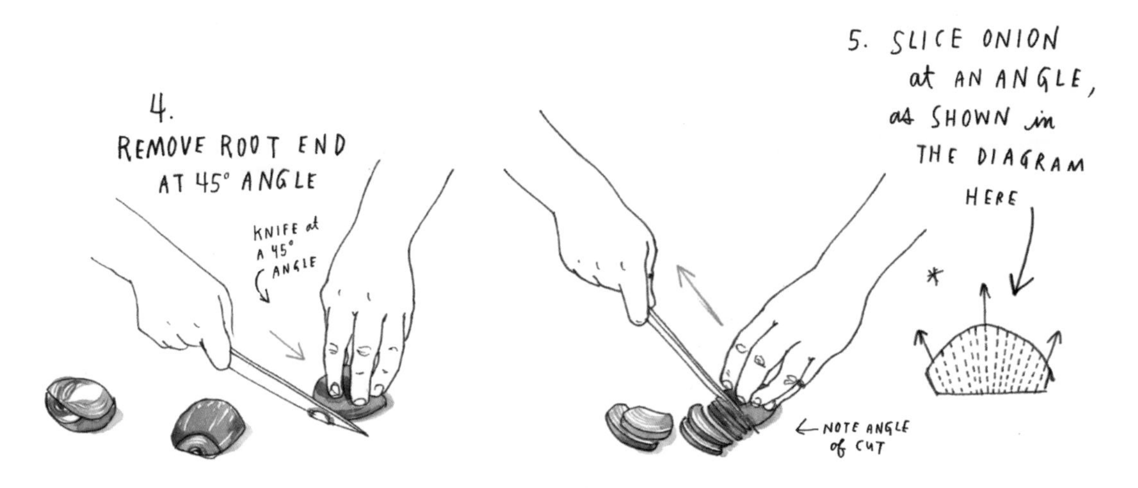

How to Dice an Onion

FOLLOW ONION PREP STEPS 1-3, and THEN:

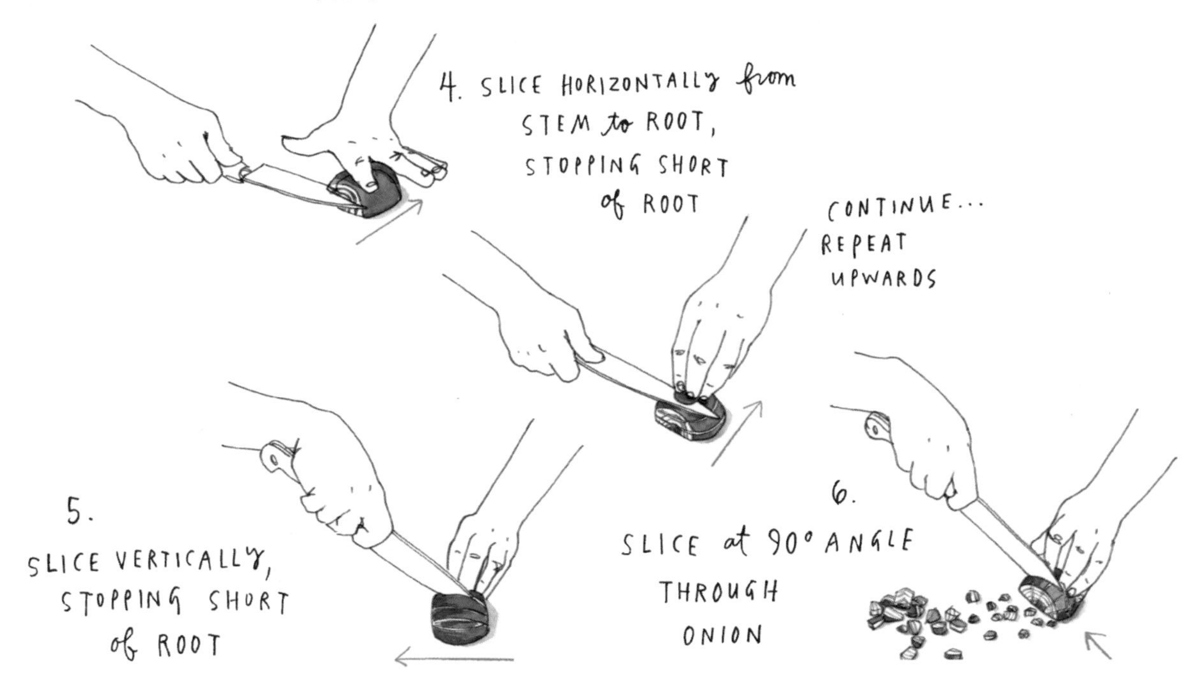

How to Turn Garlic into a Smooth Paste

1. PEEL A CLOVE OR TWO and REMOVE THE GREEN STEM

2. SLICE THINLY

3. CHOP FINELY

4. ADD A PINCH of SALT to CREATE FRICTION

5. USE THE BLADE of YOUR KNIFE to SMEAR THE GARLIC AGAINST THE CUTTING BOARD UNTIL IT BREAKS DOWN into A SMOOTH PASTE

6. IF NOT USING IT IMMEDIATELY, PUT THE GARLIC PASTE into A SMALL BOWL and COVER with OLIVE OIL to KEEP from OXIDIZING

How to Chop Parsley

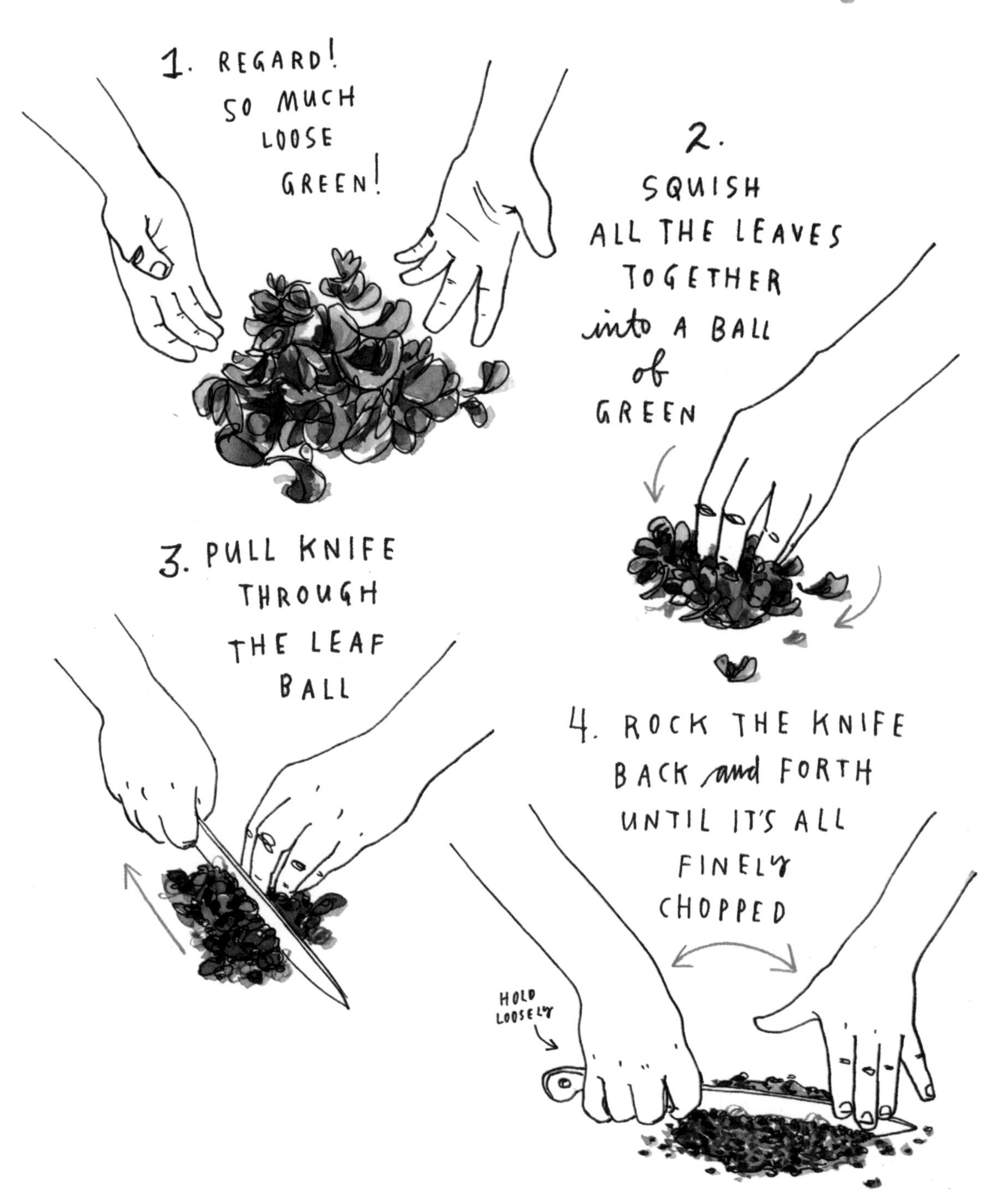

KNIFE CUTS to SCALE

DRAWN to REAL, ACTUAL SIZE

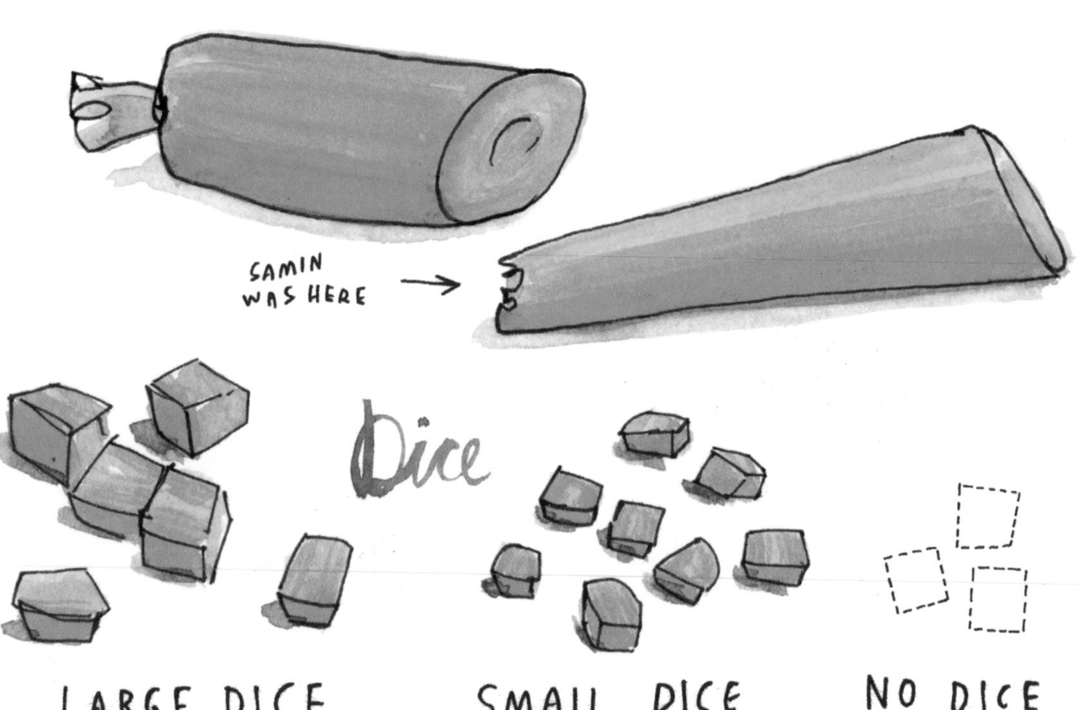

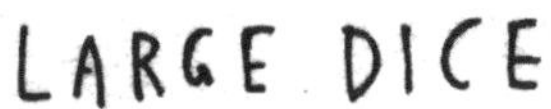

Leaf and or Sprig
PARSLEY
Chop
COARSE CHOP
FINE CHOP
FETA CHEESE
CELERY (CUT)
Crumble
Slice
THICK SLICE
THIN SLICE

RECIPES

SALADS

My *maman* is a fantastic cook. Her kitchen boasts a broad variety of foods and flavours, from tender lamb shanks to puddings scented with rosewater. But she only ever serves one of two salads at our dinner table: Persian cucumber, tomato, and onion, or ***Shirazi* Salad** (page 230), and a romaine-pecorino-sun-dried tomato number. As a child, I quickly grew bored with salad. By the time I left for college, I'd disavowed it altogether.

Then I ended up at Chez Panisse, which may as well be called Alice's House of Salads because if there were ever a restaurant built on the supremacy of salad, it's Chez Panisse. I once heard Jacques Pépin say he could judge a cook's skill by how well he cooks an egg. For Alice—and by extension all of us who've worked for her—salad reveals everything she needs to know about a cook.

At Chez Panisse, I learned to build a salad—a great one—out of anything: any vegetable, fruit, or herb, beans, grains, fish, meat, eggs, or nuts. As with all good cooking, get the Salt, Fat, and Acid in a salad right, and it will be delicious. For bonus points, add crunchy ingredients for textural variety and umami-rich ingredients for a flavour boost. For inspiration, look to salads such as Wedge, Caesar, and Cobb, which remain classics precisely because they achieve this ideal balance of tastes and textures.

Familiarise yourself with the following basic salad recipes, then begin to improvise with the ideal salad checklist in mind. Choose a flavour direction, and use the fat, acid, and herb combinations that reflect the tastes you seek.

From vibrant, raw seasonal produce to fresh-tasting herbs and vinaigrettes, every ingredient in a salad can be beautiful *and* delicious. Learn to dress salads properly, by tossing ingredients in a bowl with your hands, which will do an immeasurably better job than tongs or a wooden spoon. Let your fingers feel when all of the leaves are coated, then taste and adjust the seasoning as needed.

For salads with multiple components, such as **avocado with heirloom tomato and cucumber** (page 217), dress the less delicate cucumber slices in a bowl with salt and vinaigrette. Alternate various colours of tomato slices on the platter, then top with spoonfuls of avocado and season with salt and vinaigrette, then spoon the cucumbers around. Finish the salad—and indeed any salad—with the most delicate ingredients of all, a billowing nest of herbs or tiny rocket leaves tossed with a whisper of dressing and a little more salt.

Ideal Salad

LET'S BREAK IT DOWN.	The WEDGE	The CAESAR	The COBB	The GREEK
SALT	BACON and BLUE CHEESE	ANCHOVY, PARMESAN, and WORCESTERSHIRE	BACON and BLUE CHEESE	FETA CHEESE and OLIVES
FAT	BACON, BLUE CHEESE, and OLIVE OIL	EGG, OLIVE OIL, and PARMESAN	AVOCADO, EGG, BLUE CHEESE, and OLIVE OIL	OLIVE OIL and FETA CHEESE
ACID	BLUE CHEESE and VINEGAR	LEMON, VINEGAR, WORCESTERSHIRE, and PARMESAN	VINEGAR, MUSTARD, and BLUE CHEESE	VINEGAR or LEMON, MACERATED ONION, FETA, and TOMATO
CRUNCH	ICEBERG LETTUCE and BACON	ROMAINE LETTUCE and CROUTONS	ROMAINE, WATERCRESS, and BACON	CUCUMBERS
UMAMI	BACON and BLUE CHEESE	PARMESAN, ANCHOVY, and WORCESTERSHIRE	BLUE CHEESE, BACON, TOMATO, and CHICKEN	TOMATO, FETA CHEESE, and OLIVES

Avocado Salad Matrix

Rich and creamy, avocados are one of my favourite affordable luxuries. You can easily build an elegant salad out of a ripe one. And since avocados pair well with all sorts of crunchy and acidic fruits and vegetables, instead of giving you a single recipe for avocado salad, I've organised a bunch of possibilities into this matrix.

An avocado salad will make any meal more special, a point I once proved by bringing avocados, blood oranges, salt, and good olive oil to a yoga workshop. During our lunch break, we had a surprise birthday potluck for one of our classmates. I made a simple salad by slicing the citrus and laying it out on a platter, spooning the avocado on top, and then seasoning both with olive oil and salt. Served in the back of the gym, the salad was so refreshing and unexpected that everyone who tasted it still tells me it was the best salad of their life, even a decade later!

To make enough salad for about 4 people, begin with one ripe avocado (you can always add more to your liking!), and refer to the chart to see which other ingredients and dressings to add into your salad. Let the rest of your meal dictate the direction of the salad, from Morocco to Mexico to Thailand. No matter how you proceed, every single version will be improved by the counterpoint of a big pile of herbs, some shaved fennel bulb, or a handful of rocket.

Avocado

Hass avocados are the most widely available variety. They're also one of my favourites, with their silky texture and rich, nutty flavour. You can use any variety you like, as long as it's perfectly ripe: the avocado is ready when it's tender to the touch.

A friend who's been a hand surgeon for nearly forty years told me that avocados and bagels are the two most common causes of hand injuries. So please, please, please put the avocado down on the board when you whack at the pit with your knife to remove it.

Use one avocado for this salad, and wait until the last minute to cut into it, because it will oxidise quickly, changing in both flavour and colour.

Once you've halved the avocado and removed the pit, use a spoon to scoop out rustic spoonfuls and place them directly onto the platter. Season each bite of avocado with flaky salt and drizzle with vinaigrette. If you have any mild pepper flakes, such as Aleppo, on hand, sprinkle them on top for a little hint of spice and a welcome colour contrast.

Beetroots

Use 2 to 3 small beetroots, tops and ends trimmed and rinsed. I've found that red beetroots are the most consistently delicious, but gold beetroots and the candy cane–striped variety called Chioggia lend stunning beauty to the plate. Even someone like me, who is obsessed with flavour, can make an exception for these varieties from time to time.

Preheat the oven to 220°C. Place the beetroots in a baking dish in a single layer and fill the pan with 5mm water—just enough to create steam in the pan without simmering the beetroots. Lay a piece of parchment paper over the beetroots and cover the dish tightly with foil. Roast for an hour, or until completely tender when pierced with a paring knife—there are few things less appetising than undercooked beetroots. Pay attention to the aromas emitted from the oven—if you smell sugars caramelising, it means all the water has evaporated, and you'll need to add more to prevent the beetroots from burning.

Let the beetroots cool just enough so you can handle them, and then peel by rubbing with a paper towel. The skins will slip right off. Cut into bite-size wedges and toss in a bowl along with 1½ teaspoons wine vinegar, 1 tablespoon extra-virgin olive oil, and salt. Let sit for 10 minutes, then taste and adjust seasoning as needed—remember that the right amount of Acid and Salt will amplify the beetroots' natural sweetness.

To serve, arrange the wedges on the platter—the rule when plating beetroots is: put them down confidently, and do not move them or they will stain, leaving a messy trail in their wake.

Citrus

Use 2 to 3 citrus fruits of any variety, including grapefruits, pomelos, oranges, blood oranges, even mandarins. Combine a couple of different varieties of citrus to enhance the flavour and aesthetics of the dish.

Cut off the tops and bottoms of the fruits. Place on a cutting board, then remove the peel and the pith in strips with a sharp knife. Carefully slice oranges and mandarins crosswise, about 5mm thick, removing seeds as you encounter them. To *supreme*—or segment—grapefruits and pomelos, hold the peeled fruit over a bowl in one hand. Carefully use a knife with a sharp, thin blade to cut along the membrane down to the centre of the orange. Continue cutting along both sides of each membrane to release every segment. When you're done, squeeze all of the remaining juice from the fruit into a separate bowl and use it to make **Citrus Vinaigrette** (page 244), ***Granita*** (page 404), or just drink it! Season the slices or segments lightly with salt as you place them on the platter.

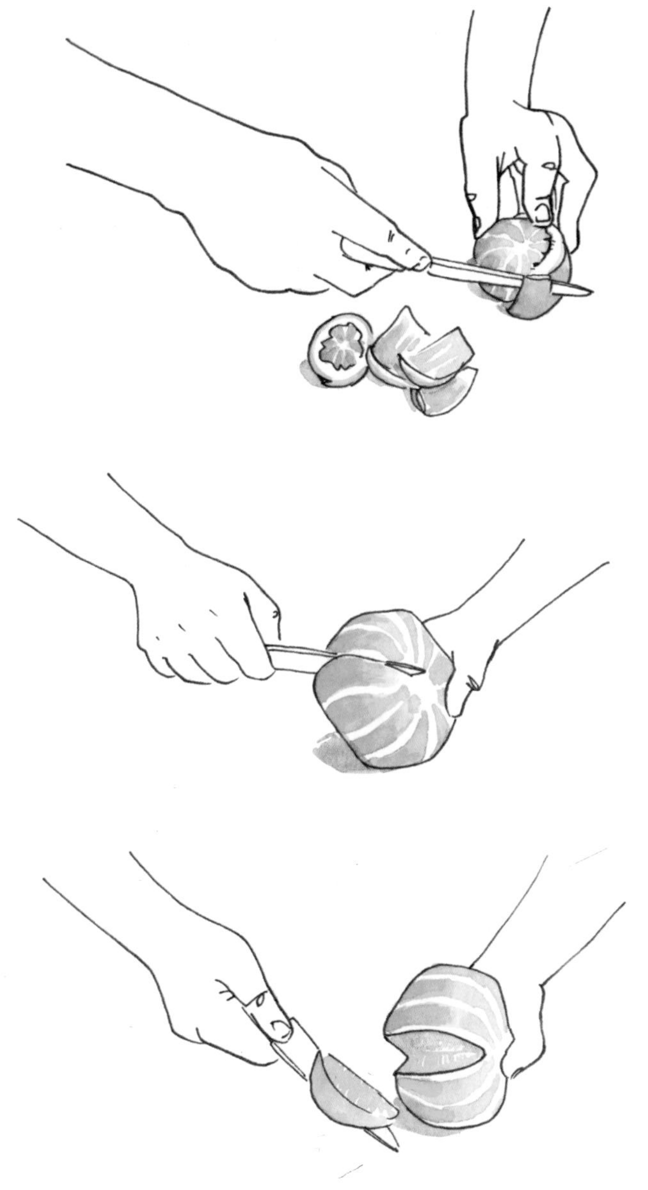

Tomatoes

Use 2 to 3 tomatoes when they're ripe and in season during the summer months. A few contrasting slices of heirloom tomatoes—try Green Zebra, Great White, a yellow variety such as Marvel Stripe or Hawaiian Pineapple, a pink one such as Brandywine, or a dark one such as Cherokee Purple—will likewise enhance how the salad looks and tastes.

Core the tomatoes with a paring knife, then carefully slice them horizontally, about 5mm thick. Season the slices with salt as you place them on the platter. As with the beetroots or citrus, arrange with an eye towards beauty, alternating colours of tomatoes with the other elements of the salad.

Cucumbers

While almost all of the other ingredients in this matrix are soft in texture and rich in flavour, cucumbers are crisp and light. Use about 225g of any flavourful, thin-skinned variety. This works out to about two Persian, Japanese, or lemon cucumbers, or one small Armenian cucumber. Remove the peel in alternating strips. This is what I call a **stripey peel**, and I use it for all sorts of produce when I want to remove some but not all of the skin (leaving some peel behind is both a handy aesthetic trick and a technical one, since it provides structure and prevents delicate vegetables such as aubergines and asparagus from completely disintegrating as they cook). Halve the cucumbers lengthwise, and if the seeds are bigger than a peppercorn, use a teaspoon to scrape them out. Slice the cucumbers on the bias for a longer, more elegant, half-moon shape. Toss with salt and vinaigrette before spreading out onto the salad.

Macerated Onion

Place half a red onion down on the cutting board and cut it in half, parallel to the root end. Holding the two quarters together, slice the onion thinly to yield quarter slices. Place the slices in a bowl and dress with 2 tablespoons wine vinegar or citrus juice. Toss to coat. Let the onions sit in the acid, or macerate (see page 118), for at least 15 minutes before using. This process tones down their acrid bite. Keep in mind that as onions macerate, they'll absorb the acid, so as you incorporate them into the salad they'll add both tartness and a pleasant oniony crunch. If you like, drain the macerating acid and use it to build the vinaigrette.

Optional Additions

- Gently tear **Slow-Roasted Salmon** (page 310) or **Tuna Confit** (page 314) into two-bite-size pieces, then arrange atop the salad. Drizzle with vinaigrette and sprinkle with flaky salt.
- Halve 2 **Eight-Minute Eggs** (page 304) and sprinkle them with flaky salt and freshly ground black pepper. Drizzle with extra-virgin olive oil, and if you like, lay an anchovy fillet over each half. Arrange atop the salad.

the Avocado Matrix

	AVO, BEETROOT & CITRUS	AVO & BEETROOT	AVO & CITRUS	AVO & TOMATO	AVO, TOMATO & CUKE	AVO, BEETROOT & CUKE
AVOCADO (OBVIOUSLY)	✓	✓	✓	✓	✓	✓
SALAD BASE						
BEETROOTS	✓	✓				✓
CITRUS	✓		✓			
TOMATO				✓	✓	
CUCUMBER					✓	✓
LAYER MACERATED ONIONS			✓	✓	✓	
OPTIONAL ADDITION						
SALMON or TUNA	✓	✓	✓	✓	✓	✓
EGG & ANCHOVY		✓		✓	✓	✓
VINAIGRETTE						
ANY CITRUS	✓	✓	✓			✓
LEMON	✓	✓	✓	✓	✓	✓
LIME	✓	✓	✓	✓	✓	✓
TOMATO				✓	✓	
RICE WINE		✓		✓	✓	✓
GREEN GODDESS		✓				✓

AVOCADO, BEETROOT, and CITRUS SALAD

1. ARRANGE CITRUS

2. LAYER BEETROOTS

3. LAYER ONIONS

4. LAYER AVOCADO

5. LAYER GREENS

6. EAT.

Bright Cabbage Slaw

Serves 4 generously

I know that some people hate coleslaw. But I've converted even the most fervent among them with this version, which bears no resemblance to the cloying stuff many of us grew up eating. Light and clean, it'll lend crunch and brightness to any plate. Serve the Mexican variation with **Beer-Battered Fish** (page 312) and tortillas for delicious fish tacos. Make **Classic Southern Slaw** to serve alongside **Spicy Fried Chicken** (page 320). And remember, the richer the food you plan to serve with it, the more acidic the slaw should be.

½ medium head of red or green cabbage
½ small red onion, thinly sliced
55ml lemon juice
Salt
15g coarsely chopped parsley leaves
3 tablespoons red wine vinegar
6 tablespoons extra-virgin olive oil

Quarter the cabbage through the core. Use a sharp knife to cut the core out at an angle. Thinly slice the cabbage crosswise and place in a colander set inside a large salad bowl. Season with two generous pinches of salt to help draw out water, toss the slices, and set aside.

In a small bowl, toss the sliced onion with the lemon juice and let it sit for 20 minutes to macerate (see page 118). Set aside.

After 20 minutes, drain any water the cabbage may have given off (it's fine if there's nothing to drain—sometimes cabbage isn't very watery). Place the cabbage in the bowl and add the parsley and the macerated onions (but not their lemony juices, yet). Dress the slaw with the vinegar and olive oil. Toss very well to combine.

Taste and adjust, adding the remaining macerating lemon juice and salt as needed. When your palate zings with pleasure, it's ready. Serve chilled or at room temperature.

Store leftover slaw covered, in the fridge, for up to two days.

Variations

- If you don't have cabbage on hand, or simply want to try something new, make an **Alterna-slaw**, using 1 large bunch raw kale, 675g raw Brussels sprouts, or 675g raw kohlrabi instead.

- For **Mexi-Slaw**, substitute a neutral-tasting oil for the olive oil, lime juice for the lemon juice, and coriander for the parsley. Add 1 sliced jalapeño pepper to the cabbage along with the macerated onions. Taste and adjust seasoning with the macerating lime juice and salt.

- To make **Asian Slaw**, toss the cabbage with just one generous pinch of salt and add 2 teaspoons soy sauce. Substitute lime juice for the lemon juice. Skip the parsley and add 1 small garlic clove, finely grated or pounded; 2 thinly sliced spring onions; 1 teaspoon finely grated ginger; and 25g chopped, toasted peanuts to the cabbage along with the macerated onions. Skip the red wine vinegar and olive oil and dress with **Rice Wine Vinaigrette** (page 246). Taste and adjust seasoning with the macerating lime juice and salt.

- To make **Classic Southern Slaw**, substitute 115g stiff **Classic Sandwich Mayo** (page 375) for the olive oil and vinegar. Add 1 teaspoon sugar, 135g julienned or grated carrots, and 1 julienned or grated tart apple, such as Honeycrisp or Fuji, to the cabbage along with the macerated onions.

Three Classic Shaved Salads

I inherited my fondness for shaved salads from my friend Cal Peternell, the chef who taught me exactly how much salt it takes to season a pot of polenta (hint: a lot) during my early days at Chez Panisse. One out of three salads I eat at Cal's house is shaved. While I can't speculate on why he seems to have such a soft spot for them, my own reasons are clear: they're easy to make and lend crunch and brightness to any meal.

Vietnamese Cucumber Salad

Serves 4 to 6

900g (about 8) Persian or Japanese cucumbers, **stripey peeled** (see page 220)
1 large jalapeño, seeds and veins removed if desired, thinly sliced
3 spring onions, finely sliced
1 garlic clove, finely grated or pounded with a pinch of salt
15g coarsely chopped coriander leaves
16 large mint leaves, coarsely chopped
50g toasted peanuts, coarsely chopped
55ml neutral-tasting oil
4 to 5 tablespoons lime juice
4 teaspoons seasoned rice wine vinegar
1 tablespoon fish sauce
1 teaspoon sugar
Pinch of salt

Using either a Japanese mandoline or a sharp knife, thinly slice the cucumbers into coins, discarding the ends. In a large bowl, combine the cucumbers, jalapeño, spring onions, garlic, coriander, mint, and peanuts. In a small bowl, whisk together the oil, 4 tablespoons lime juice, the vinegar, fish sauce, sugar, and a small pinch of salt. Dress the salad with the vinaigrette and toss to combine. Taste and adjust seasoning with salt and more lime juice as needed. Serve immediately.

Shaved Carrot Salad with Ginger and Lime

Serves 6

210g golden or black raisins

1 tablespoon cumin seeds

900g carrots

4 teaspoons finely grated ginger

1 garlic clove, finely grated or pounded with a pinch of salt

1 to 2 large jalapeños, seeds and veins removed if desired, minced

60g coarsely chopped coriander leaves and tender stems, plus a few sprigs for garnish

Salt

Lime Vinaigrette (page 243)

In a small bowl, submerge the raisins in boiling water. Let them sit for 15 minutes to rehydrate and plump up. Drain and set aside.

Place the cumin seeds in a small, dry frying pan and set over medium heat. Swirl the pan constantly to ensure even toasting. Toast until the first few seeds begin to pop and emit a savoury aroma, about 3 minutes. Remove from the heat. Immediately dump the seeds into the bowl of a mortar or a spice grinder. Grind finely with a pinch of salt. Set aside.

Trim and peel the carrots. Using either a Japanese mandoline or a sharp knife, thinly slice the carrots lengthwise. Use a sharp knife to cut the slices into matchsticks. If that seems too troublesome, you can use a vegetable peeler to make thin ribbons or just slice the carrots into thin coins.

Combine carrots, ginger, garlic, jalapeño, coriander, cumin, and raisins in a large bowl. Season with three generous pinches of salt and dress with lime vinaigrette. Taste and adjust seasoning with salt and more lime juice as needed. Refrigerate the salad for 30 minutes to allow flavours to come together. To serve, toss to distribute seasonings, heap onto a large platter, and garnish with a few sprigs of coriander.

Shaved Fennel and Radishes

Serves 4 to 6

3 medium fennel bulbs (about 675g)

1 bunch radishes, trimmed and washed (about 8 radishes)

30g parsley leaves

Optional: 30g chunk of Parmesan

Salt

Freshly ground black pepper

About 75ml **Lemon Vinaigrette** (page 242)

Trim the fennel by removing any stalks and the very tip of the bottom end, leaving the bulb intact. Halve the bulbs through the root and remove any fibrous outer layers. Using either a Japanese mandoline or a sharp knife, cut the fennel bulbs crosswise into paper-thin slices, discarding the cores. Reserve the discarded fennel for another use, or sneak it into **Tuscan Kale and Bean Soup** (page 274). Slice the radishes just a hair thicker, about 3mm, discarding the ends.

In a large bowl, combine the fennel, radishes, and parsley leaves. If using Parmesan, use a vegetable peeler to shave shards directly into the bowl. Just before serving, season with two generous pinches of salt and a small pinch of pepper. Dress with vinaigrette. Taste and adjust, adding more salt and vinaigrette as needed, then arrange on a serving platter. Serve immediately.

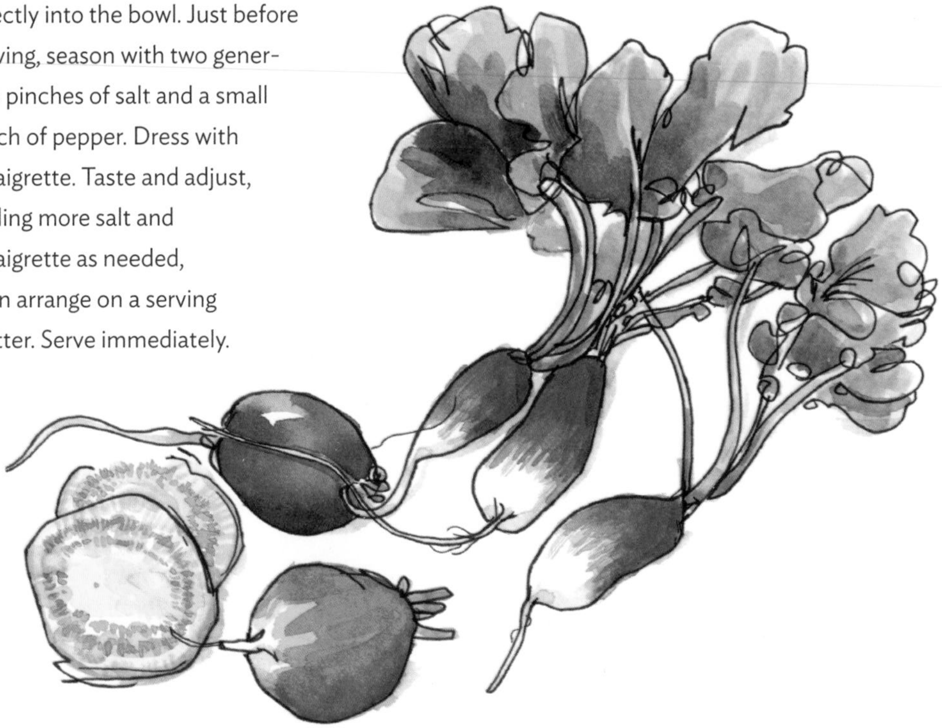

Summary Tomato and Herb Salad

Serves 4 to 6

Is there anything more refreshing to eat than a perfect tomato salad showered with herbs? If there is, I can't think of it. Add this salad to your summer repertoire, changing the tomatoes and the herbs with each passing week. If you grow tired of green basil, look for less common herbs such as anise hyssop, also known as liquorice mint, or opal or Greek basil at the farmers' market. Indian, Mexican, and Asian grocery stores are also great places to find special herbs including all sorts of mint, shiso, Thai basil, and Vietnamese coriander, any one of which will work nicely in this salad.

2 to 3 mixed heirloom tomatoes, such as Marvel Stripe, Cherokee Purple, or Brandywine, cored and sliced into 5mm slices
Flaky salt
Freshly ground black pepper
225ml **Tomato Vinaigrette** (page 245). *Hint*: use the cores and end slices of the salad tomatoes
400g cherry tomatoes, rinsed, stemmed, and halved
60g any combination of freshly picked leaves of basil, parsley, anise hyssop, chervil, tarragon, or 2.5cm pieces of chives

Just before serving, lay out the heirloom tomato slices on a serving platter in a single layer and season with salt and pepper. Drizzle lightly with vinaigrette. In a separate bowl, combine the cherry tomatoes and season liberally with salt and pepper. Dress with vinaigrette, taste and adjust salt as needed, and carefully mound the cherry tomatoes over the tomato slices.

Place the fresh herbs in the salad bowl and dress lightly with vinaigrette, salt, and pepper to taste. Pile herb salad over the tomatoes and serve immediately.

Variations

- To make **Caprese Salad**, alternate heirloom tomato slices with 1cm slices of fresh mozzarella or burrata cheese before seasoning and dressing. Skip the herb salad. Instead, when seasoning the cherry tomatoes in a separate bowl, add 12 torn basil leaves. Mound the cherry tomatoes over the tomato slices. Serve with warm, crusty bread.

- To make **Ricotta and Tomato Salad Toasts**, whip together 325g fresh ricotta cheese with extra-virgin olive oil, flaky salt, and freshly ground black pepper. Brush 4 2.5cm slices of crusty bread with extra-virgin olive oil and toast until golden brown in a 200°C oven for about 10 minutes. Rub each toast lightly with a raw garlic clove on one side. Spread 5 tablespoons ricotta onto the garlic side of each toast. Lay slices of heirloom tomatoes over the ricotta and then pile sliced heirloom tomatoes on top. Divide 30g herb salad atop the toasts and serve immediately.

- To make **Persian *Shirazi* Salad**, toss ½ thinly sliced red onion in 3 tablespoons red wine vinegar in a small bowl and let sit for 15 minutes. Stripey peel 4 Persian cucumbers, cut into 1cm slices, and place in a large bowl. Add cherry tomatoes and 1 pounded or finely grated garlic clove to the cucumbers. Mix in the onions (but not their vinegar, yet). Season with salt and pepper and dress with **Lime Vinaigrette** (page 243). Taste the mixture and add some of the reserved vinegar if needed, then continue as above, mounding the mixture atop the sliced tomatoes. Top with an herb salad of dill, coriander, parsley, and mint, also dressed with Lime Vinaigrette.

- To make **Greek Salad**, toss ½ thinly sliced red onion in 3 tablespoons red wine vinegar in a small bowl and let sit for 15 minutes. Stripey peel 4 Persian cucumbers, cut into 1cm slices, and place in a large bowl. Add cherry tomatoes, 1 pounded or finely grated garlic clove, 125g rinsed, pitted black olives, and 115g rinsed and crumbled feta cheese to the cucumbers. Mix in the onions (but not their vinegar, yet). Season with salt and pepper and dress with **Red Wine Vinaigrette** (page 240). Taste the mixture and add some of the reserved vinegar if needed, then continue as above, mounding the mixture atop the sliced tomatoes. Skip the herb salad.

A *Panzanella* for Every Season

Panzanella is the ultimate proof that Tuscan cooks excel at making something out of nothing. Traditionally made with little more than stale bread, tomatoes, onions, and basil, *panzanella* is as much about texture as it is about flavour. If the croutons aren't soaked in vinaigrette long enough, they'll scrape the roof of your mouth. Let the bread get too soggy, though, and the salad will bore you. Aim for a broad spectrum of crunchiness by staggering the addition of croutons. Your mouth will thank you.

A memorable summer *panzanella* requires good bread and great tomatoes, so vary the ingredient combinations as the seasons shift to delight in bread salad year round.

Summer: Tomato, Basil, and Cucumber

Serves 4 generously

½ medium red onion, sliced thinly

1 tablespoon red wine vinegar

225g **Torn Croutons** (page 236)

Double batch of **Tomato Vinaigrette** (page 245)

450g cherry tomatoes, stemmed and halved

675g Early Girl or other flavourful small tomatoes (about 8 tomatoes), cored and wedged into bite-size pieces

4 Persian cucumbers, **stripey peeled** (page 220) and cut into 1cm slices

16 basil leaves

Flaky sea salt

In a small bowl, toss the sliced onion with the vinegar and let it sit for 20 minutes to macerate (see page 118). Set aside.

Place half the croutons in a large salad bowl and toss with 125ml of vinaigrette. Place the cherry and wedged tomatoes on top of the croutons and season with salt to encourage them to release some of their juices. Let sit for about 10 minutes.

Continue assembling the salad: add the remaining croutons, cucumbers, and macerated onions (but not their vinegar, yet). Tear in the basil leaves in large pieces. Dress with another 125ml of vinaigrette and taste. Adjust seasoning as needed, adding salt, vinaigrette, and/or the macerating vinegar to taste. Toss, taste again, and serve.

Refrigerate leftovers, covered, for up to one night.

Variations

- To make ***Fattoush***, the Middle Eastern tomato and bread salad, substitute 5 torn and toasted pitta breads for the croutons, 10g parsley leaves for the basil, and **Red Wine Vinaigrette** (page 240) for the Tomato Vinaigrette.
- To make a **Grain or Bean Salad**, substitute about 400g cooked, drained farro, wheatberries, barley, or beans for the croutons in any of the seasonal variations.

Autumn: Roasted Squash, Sage, and Hazelnut

Serves 4 generously

1 bunch kale, preferably Cavolo Nero, or Tuscan variety
1 large butternut squash (900g), peeled
Extra-virgin olive oil
½ medium red onion, sliced thinly
1 tablespoon red wine vinegar
Double batch of **Brown Butter Vinaigrette** (page 241)
225g **Torn Croutons** (page 236)
About 450ml neutral-tasting oil
16 sage leaves
100g hazelnuts, toasted and coarsely chopped

Preheat the oven to 220°C. Line a baking sheet with paper towels.

Strip the kale. Gripping at the base of each stem with one hand, pinch the stem with the other hand and pull upward to strip the leaf. Discard the stems or save for another use, such as **Tuscan Bean and Kale Soup** (page 275). Cut the leaves into 1cm slices. Set aside.

Halve, seed, slice, and roast the butternut squash as directed on page 263. Set aside.

Toss the sliced onion in a small bowl with the vinegar and let it sit for 20 minutes to macerate. Set aside.

Place half the croutons and the kale in a large salad bowl and toss with 75ml of vinaigrette. Let sit for 10 minutes.

In the meantime, fry the sage. Pour 2.5cm of neutral oil into a small, heavy-bottomed pot and heat it over a medium-high flame to 180°C. If you don't have a thermometer, just test the oil after a few minutes by dropping in a sage leaf. When it sizzles immediately, it's ready.

Add the sage leaves in batches. Be aware that the oil will bubble up a lot at first, so let it die down, then stir in the sage. After about 30 seconds, as soon as the bubbles die down, pull them out of the oil with a slotted spoon, and spread the sage onto the prepared baking sheet. Let the sage dry on the prepared baking sheet in a single-ish layer, and sprinkle with salt. It'll get crisp as it cools.

Add the remaining croutons, squash, hazelnuts, and macerated onions (but not their vinegar, yet) into the salad bowl. Crumble in the fried sage. Dress with the remaining vinaigrette, toss to combine, and taste. Adjust seasoning with salt, the sage-frying oil, and the macerating vinegar as needed. Toss, taste again, and serve.

Refrigerate leftovers, covered, for up to one night.

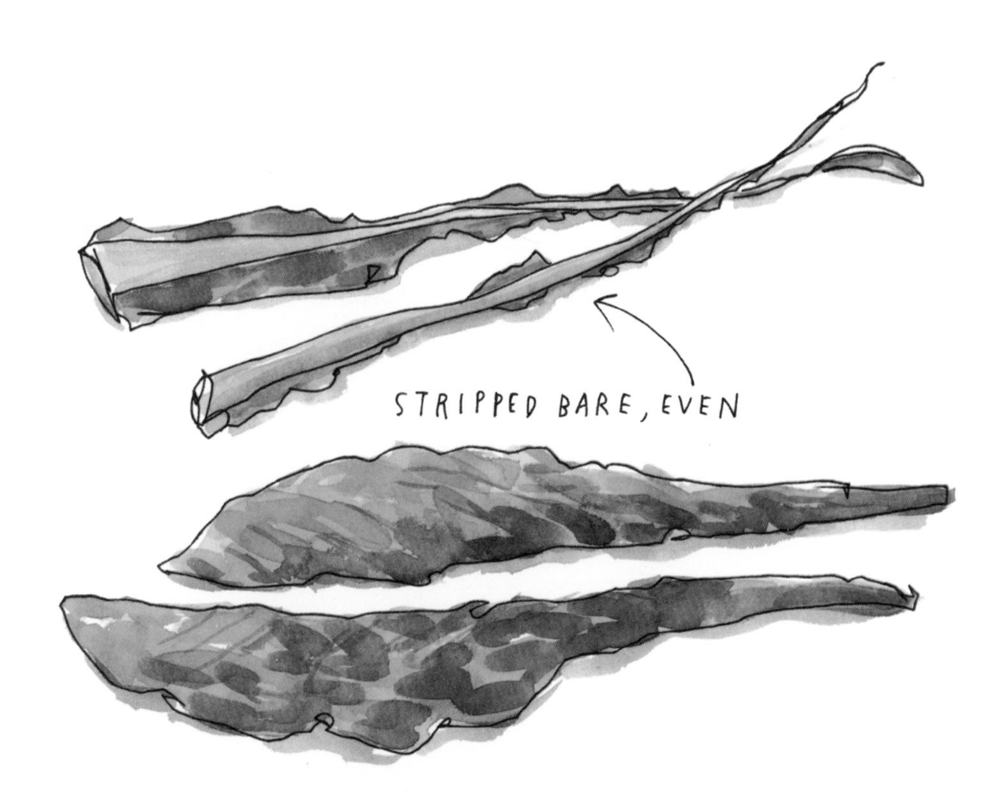

Winter: Roasted Radicchio and Roquefort

Serves 4 generously

2 heads radicchio

Extra-virgin olive oil

Salt

2 medium onions, peeled

225g **Torn Croutons** (page 236)

Double batch of **Brown Butter Vinaigrette** (page 241)

10g parsley leaves

140g toasted walnuts

Coarsely ground black pepper

115g Roquefort cheese

Red wine vinegar, as needed to adjust acid

Preheat the oven to 220°C.

Halve each head of radicchio through the root end. Cut each half into quarters. Drizzle generously with olive oil to coat. Handling the radicchio pieces carefully, spread them out in a single layer on a baking sheet, leaving space between each piece. Drizzle with more olive oil and season with salt.

Halve the onions through the root end. Wedge each half into quarters for a total of 8 pieces. Drizzle generously with olive oil to coat. Handling the onion pieces carefully, spread them out in a single layer on a baking sheet, leaving space between each piece. Drizzle with more olive oil and season with salt.

Place the prepared vegetables into the preheated oven and cook until tender and caramelised, about 22 minutes for the radicchio, and 28 minutes for the onions. Check on the vegetables after about 12 minutes. Rotate the pans and switch their positions to make sure the vegetables are browning evenly.

Place half of the croutons in a large salad bowl and toss with 75ml of vinaigrette. Let sit for 10 minutes.

Add the remaining croutons, radicchio, onions, parsley, walnuts, and black pepper. Crumble in the cheese in big pieces. Dress with remaining vinaigrette and taste. Adjust seasoning with salt and, if needed, a small amount of red wine vinegar. Toss, taste again, and serve at room temperature.

Refrigerate leftovers, covered, for up to one night.

Spring: Asparagus and Feta with Mint

Serves 4 generously

Salt

½ medium red onion, sliced thinly

1 tablespoon red wine vinegar

675g asparagus (about 2 bunches), woody ends removed

225g **Torn Croutons** (page 236)

24 large mint leaves

85g feta cheese

Double batch of **Red Wine Vinaigrette** (page 240)

Set a large pot of water on to boil over high heat. Season it with salt until it tastes like the summer sea. Line two baking sheets with parchment paper. Set aside.

Toss the sliced onion in a small bowl with the vinegar and let it sit for 20 minutes to macerate (see page 118). Set aside.

If the asparagus is thicker than a pencil, stripey peel it, pressing lightly with a vegetable peeler to remove only the outermost skin from about 2.5cm below the blossom to the base. Slice the asparagus into 4cm-long pieces on a bias. Blanch the asparagus in boiling water until it's just tender, about 3½ minutes (less for thinner stalks). Taste a piece to determine doneness—it should still have the faintest crunch in the centre. Drain and allow to cool in a single layer on the prepared baking sheets.

Place half of the croutons in a large salad bowl and toss with 75ml of vinaigrette. Let sit for 10 minutes.

Add the remaining croutons, asparagus, and macerated onions (but not their vinegar, yet). Tear in the mint leaves in small pieces. Crumble in the feta in large pieces. Dress with another 75ml vinaigrette and season with salt, then taste. Adjust seasoning with salt, vinaigrette, and the macerating vinegar as needed. Toss, taste again, and serve at room temperature.

Refrigerate leftovers, covered, for up to 1 night.

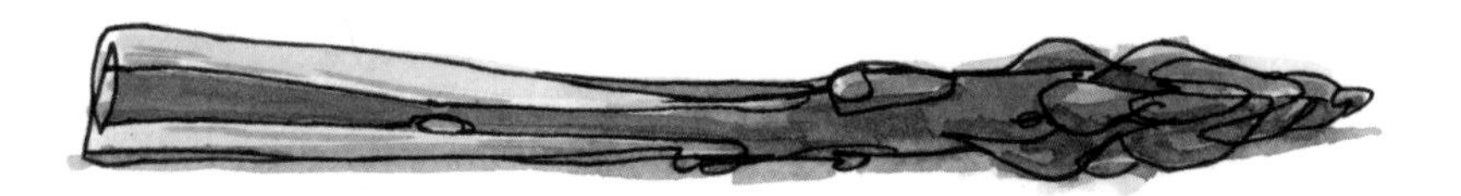

Torn Croutons

Makes 450g

Store-bought croutons simply can't compete with homemade ones. To begin with, your raw ingredients are almost certainly of a higher quality, and hence more delicious, than the stuff anyone else will use. What's more, the rustic, uneven shape of torn croutons lends a variety of textures to your salads. Dressing clings to them better, and they're also just more lovely to look at. That, and they are less likely to scratch the roof of your mouth. If these reasons don't convince you, come over to my house for some Caesar salad. I'll get you that way.

450g loaf day-old country or sourdough bread

75ml extra-virgin olive oil

Preheat the oven to 200°C. For more tooth-friendly croutons, remove the crusts from the bread, then cut the loaf into 2.5cm-thick slices. Cut each slice into 2.5cm-wide strips. Working over a large bowl, tear each strip into 2.5cm-size pieces. Alternatively, you can just tear croutons directly off the loaf, as long as you get somewhat evenly sized pieces—I find that preslicing speeds up the whole process and yields even, yet rustic-looking croutons, so it's my preferred method.

Toss the croutons with the olive oil to coat them evenly, then spread them out in a single layer on a baking sheet. Use a second sheet as needed to prevent crowding, which will entrap steam and keep the croutons from browning.

Toast the croutons for about 18 to 22 minutes, checking them after 8 minutes. Rotate the pans, switch their oven positions, and use a metal spatula to turn and rotate the croutons so that they brown evenly. Once they begin to brown, check them every few minutes, continuing to turn and rotate. Some croutons might be done when others still need a few more minutes of baking, so remove them from the tray and let the rest finish cooking. Bake the croutons until they're golden brown and crunchy on the outside, with just a tiny bit of chew on the inside.

Taste a crouton and adjust the seasoning with a light sprinkling of salt if needed.

When done, let the croutons cool in a single layer on the baking sheet. Use immediately or keep in an airtight container for up to 2 days. To refresh stale croutons, bake for 3 to 4 minutes at 200°C.

Freeze leftover croutons for up to 2 months and use in ***Ribollita*** (page 275).

Variations

- To make **Classic Torn Croutons**, stir 2 cloves finely grated or pounded garlic into the olive oil before dressing the croutons. Toss with 1 tablespoon dried oregano and ½ teaspoon red pepper flakes before toasting.
- To make **Cheesy Torn Croutons**, toss the torn bread with the olive oil, then add 85g very finely grated Parmesan and lots of coarsely ground black pepper to the bowl, and toss until combined. Toast as directed above.
- To make about 450g of **Sprinkling Crumbs**, don't bother tearing the bread. Instead, grind 5cm pieces of bread into pea-size crumbs in a food processor. Increase the olive oil to 125ml and toast in a single layer until golden, 16 to 18 minutes.

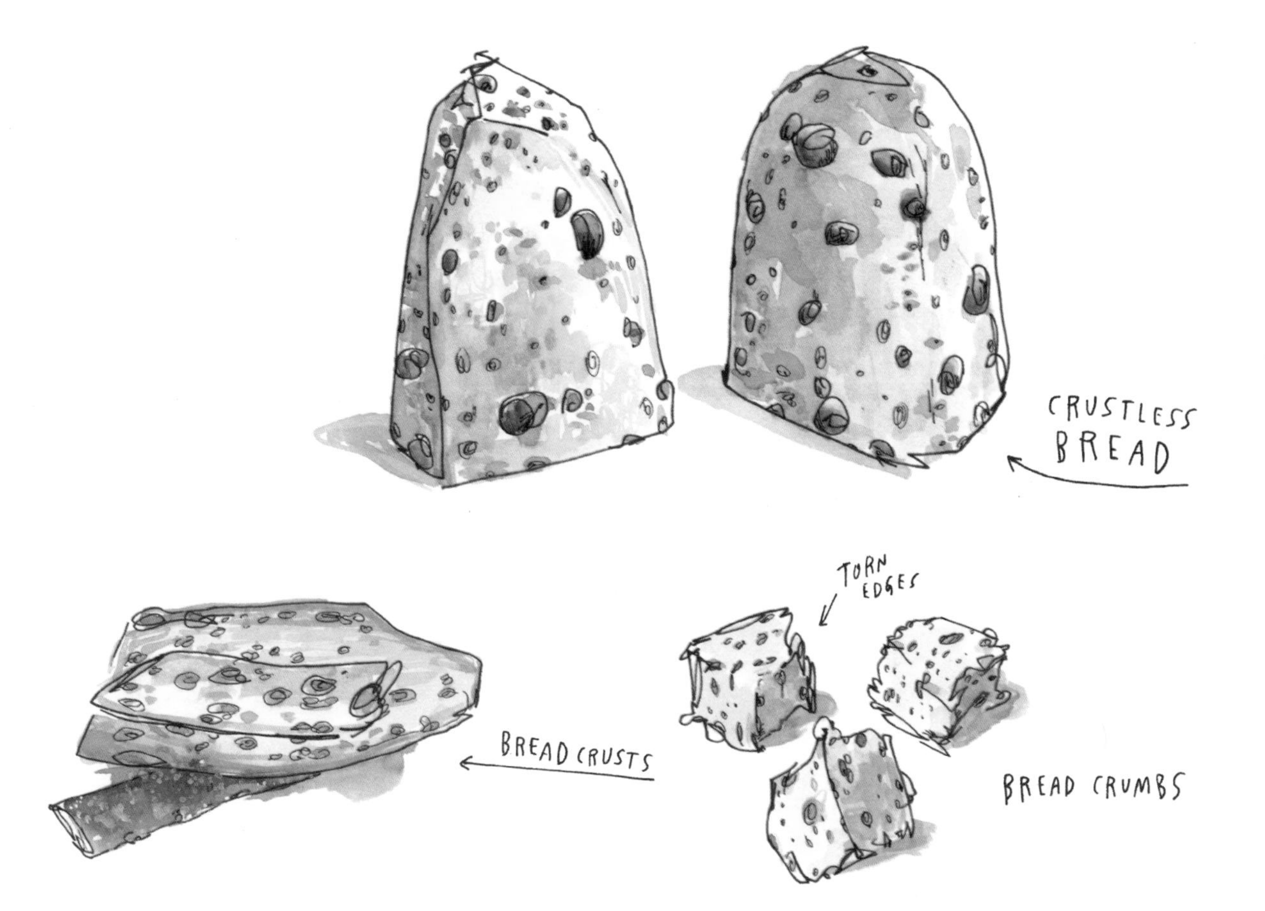

DRESSINGS

The most important thing about any dressing is to strike a proper balance of Salt, Fat, and Acid. Get that right, and any salad will taste good.

To rid shallots (and onions) of their harsh bite, give them ample time to **macerate** in acid. That's just a fancy way of saying, toss shallots with vinegar or citrus juice and let them steep for a bit before adding the oil and other ingredients.

Pairing salads with the right dressings is as important as pairing a meal with the right wine. Some foods require richness, while others ask for brightness. Use this chart to inspire and guide you.

For tossed salads, place the greens in a large bowl and season lightly with salt. Add a conservative amount of dressing and toss with your hands to coat the leaves. Taste a leaf, then add salt and more dressing as needed.

For composed salads, always make sure that every element is seasoned and dressed. Marinate beetroots before setting them down on the plate and drizzling them with **Green Goddess**. Season every slice of tomato and fresh mozzarella before spooning **Balsamic Vinaigrette** over them. Dress both **Slow-Roasted Salmon** (page 310) and the shaved fennel salad you serve alongside it with **Any-Other-Citrus Vinaigrette** made with blood oranges. Make every bite of every salad delicious. You'll start to look forward to salad with a fervour you never expected.

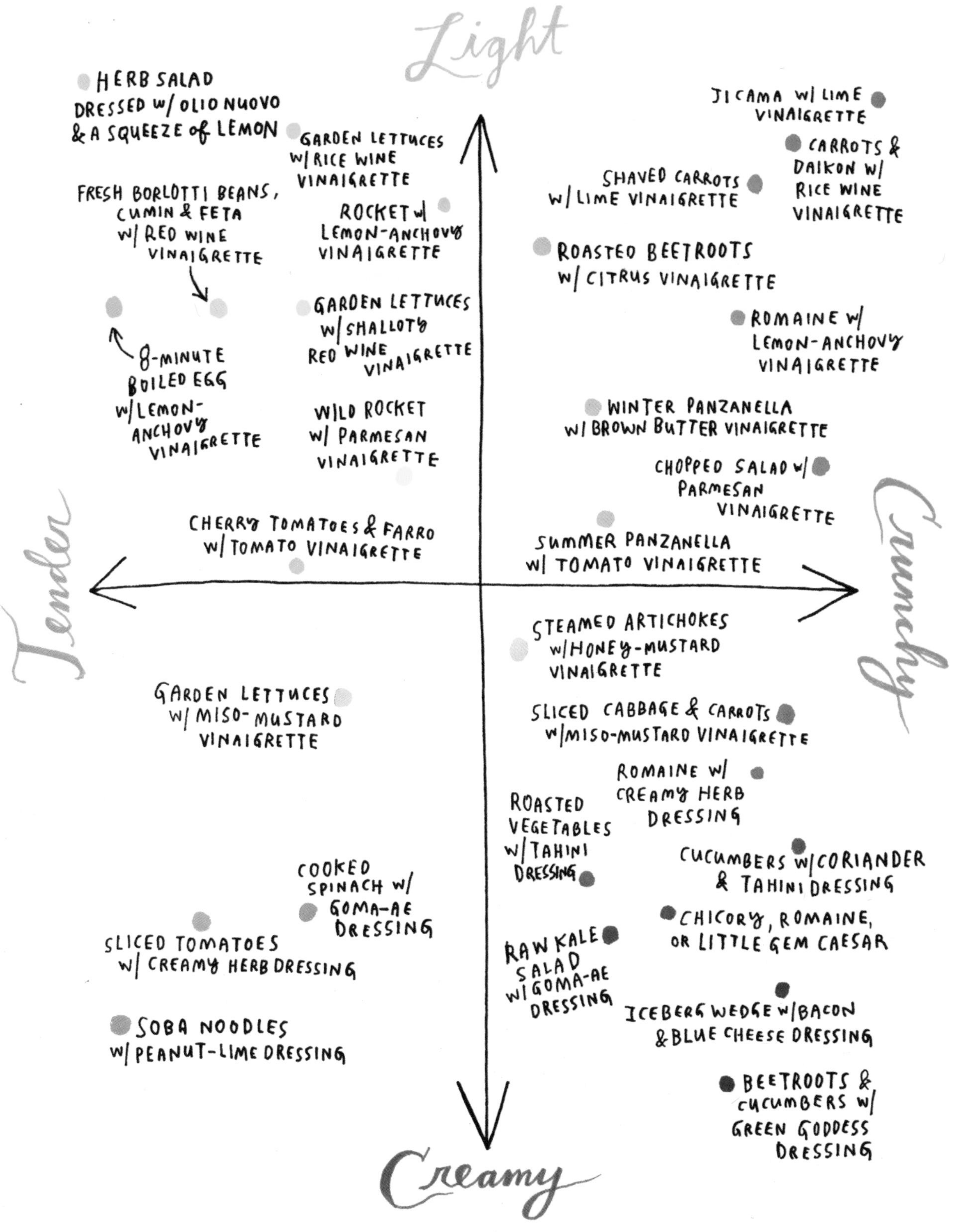

Light

HERB SALAD DRESSED W/ OLIO NUOVO & A SQUEEZE of LEMON

JICAMA W/ LIME VINAIGRETTE

GARDEN LETTUCES W/ RICE WINE VINAIGRETTE

CARROTS & DAIKON W/ RICE WINE VINAIGRETTE

SHAVED CARROTS W/ LIME VINAIGRETTE

FRESH BORLOTTI BEANS, CUMIN & FETA W/ RED WINE VINAIGRETTE

ROCKET W/ LEMON-ANCHOVY VINAIGRETTE

ROASTED BEETROOTS W/ CITRUS VINAIGRETTE

GARDEN LETTUCES W/ SHALLOTY RED WINE VINAIGRETTE

ROMAINE W/ LEMON-ANCHOVY VINAIGRETTE

8-MINUTE BOILED EGG W/ LEMON-ANCHOVY VINAIGRETTE

WILD ROCKET W/ PARMESAN VINAIGRETTE

WINTER PANZANELLA W/ BROWN BUTTER VINAIGRETTE

CHOPPED SALAD W/ PARMESAN VINAIGRETTE

CHERRY TOMATOES & FARRO W/ TOMATO VINAIGRETTE

SUMMER PANZANELLA W/ TOMATO VINAIGRETTE

Tender

Crunchy

STEAMED ARTICHOKES W/ HONEY-MUSTARD VINAIGRETTE

GARDEN LETTUCES W/ MISO-MUSTARD VINAIGRETTE

SLICED CABBAGE & CARROTS W/ MISO-MUSTARD VINAIGRETTE

ROMAINE W/ CREAMY HERB DRESSING

ROASTED VEGETABLES W/ TAHINI DRESSING

CUCUMBERS W/ CORIANDER & TAHINI DRESSING

COOKED SPINACH W/ GOMA-AE DRESSING

CHICORY, ROMAINE, OR LITTLE GEM CAESAR

SLICED TOMATOES W/ CREAMY HERB DRESSING

RAW KALE SALAD W/ GOMA-AE DRESSING

ICEBERG WEDGE W/ BACON & BLUE CHEESE DRESSING

SOBA NOODLES W/ PEANUT-LIME DRESSING

BEETROOTS & CUCUMBERS W/ GREEN GODDESS DRESSING

Creamy

Red Wine Vinaigrette

Makes about 125ml

1 tablespoon finely diced shallot

2 tablespoons red wine vinegar

6 tablespoons extra-virgin olive oil

Salt

Freshly ground black pepper

In a small bowl or jar, let the shallot sit in the vinegar for 15 minutes to macerate (see page 118), then add the olive oil, a generous pinch of salt, and a small pinch of pepper. Stir or shake to combine, then taste with a leaf of lettuce and adjust salt and acid as needed. Cover and refrigerate leftovers for up to 3 days.

Ideal for garden lettuces, rocket, chicories, Belgian endive, Little Gem and romaine lettuce, beetroots, tomatoes, blanched, grilled, or roasted vegetables of any kind, and for **Bright Cabbage Slaw**, **Fattoush**, **Grain or Bean Salad**, **Greek Salad**, **Spring Panzanella**.

Variation

- To make **Honey-Mustard Vinaigrette**, add 1 tablespoon Dijon mustard and 1½ teaspoons honey and continue as above.

Balsamic Vinaigrette

Makes about 75ml

1 tablespoon finely diced shallot

1 tablespoon aged balsamic vinegar

1 tablespoon red wine vinegar

4 tablespoons extra-virgin olive oil

Salt

Freshly ground black pepper

In a small bowl or jar, let the shallot sit in the vinegar for 15 minutes to macerate (see page 118), then add the olive oil, a generous pinch of salt, and a pinch of pepper. Stir or shake to combine, then taste with a leaf of lettuce and adjust salt and acid as needed. Cover and refrigerate leftovers for up to 3 days.

Ideal for rocket, garden lettuces, Belgian endive, chicories, romaine and Little Gem lettuce, blanched, grilled, or roasted vegetables of any kind, and for **Grain** or **Bean Salad**, **Winter Panzanella**.

Variations

- To make **Parmesan Vinaigrette**, which is perfect for hearty chicories and grain salads, add 40g finely grated Parmesan and continue as above.
- To make **Brown Butter Vinaigrette** for dressing bread salads or roasted vegetables, substitute 4 tablespoons brown butter for the olive oil and continue as above. Bring refrigerated leftovers back to room temperature before using.

Lemon Vinaigrette

Makes about 125ml

½ teaspoon finely grated lemon zest (about ½ lemon's worth)

2 tablespoons freshly squeezed lemon juice

1½ teaspoons white wine vinegar

5 tablespoons extra-virgin olive oil

1 garlic clove

Salt

Freshly ground black pepper

Pour the lemon zest, juice, vinegar, and olive oil into a small bowl or jar. Smash the garlic clove against the worktop with the palm of your hand and add to the vinaigrette. Season with a generous pinch of salt and a pinch of pepper. Stir or shake to combine, then taste with a leaf of lettuce and adjust salt and acid as needed. Let sit for at least 10 minutes, and remove the garlic clove before using.

Cover and refrigerate leftovers for up to 2 days.

Ideal for herb salad, rocket, garden lettuces, romaine and Little Gem lettuce, cucumbers, boiled vegetables, and for **Avocado Salad**, **Shaved Fennel and Radish Salad**, **Slow-Roasted Salmon**.

Variation

- To make **Lemon-Anchovy Vinaigrette**, coarsely chop 2 soaked, filleted salt-packed anchovies (or 4 fillets), then pound them into a fine paste in a mortar and pestle. The more you break them down, the better the dressing will be. Stir the anchovies and an additional ½ clove of finely grated or pounded garlic into the dressing and continue as above. Serve with rocket, Belgian endive, boiled vegetables of any kind, chicories, or shaved winter vegetables such as carrots, turnips, and celeriac.

Lime Vinaigrette

Makes about 125ml

2 tablespoons freshly squeezed lime juice (from about 2 small limes)

5 tablespoons extra-virgin olive oil

1 garlic clove

Salt

Pour the lime juice and olive oil into a small bowl or jar. Smash the garlic clove and add to the vinaigrette, along with a generous pinch of salt. Stir or shake to combine, then taste with a leaf of lettuce and adjust salt and acid as needed. Let sit for at least 10 minutes, and remove the garlic before using.

Cover and refrigerate leftovers for up to 3 days.

Ideal for garden lettuces, Little Gem and romaine lettuce, sliced cucumbers, and for **Avocado Salad**, **Shaved Carrot Salad**, ***Shirazi* Salad**, **Slow-Roasted Salmon**.

Variation

- To add a little heat, add 1 teaspoon minced jalapeño.

Any-Other-Citrus Vinaigrette

Makes about 150ml

1 tablespoon finely diced shallot

4 teaspoons white wine vinegar

55ml citrus juice

55ml extra-virgin olive oil

½ teaspoon finely grated zest

Salt

In a small bowl or jar, let the shallot sit in the vinegar for 15 minutes to macerate (see page 118), then add the citrus juice, olive oil, zest, and a generous pinch of salt. Stir or shake to combine, then taste with a leaf of lettuce and adjust salt and acid as needed.

Cover and refrigerate leftovers for up to 3 days.

Ideal for garden lettuces, romaine and Little Gem lettuce, blanched asparagus, and for **Avocado Salad**, **Slow-Roasted Salmon**, **Grilled Artichokes**.

Variation

- To make a sweet-tart **Kumquat Vinaigrette**, add 3 tablespoons finely diced kumquats to the shallots and continue as above.

Tomato Vinaigrette

Makes about 225ml

Make this dressing with the ripest tomatoes, or better yet, with the cores and ends from the tomatoes you plan to use in your salad. You'll know a tomato is ripe when it smells woody and sweet at the stem, and feels firm when pressed, with just a little bit of give.

2 tablespoons diced shallots
2 tablespoons red wine vinegar
1 tablespoon aged balsamic vinegar
1 large or two small very ripe tomatoes (about 225g)
4 basil leaves, torn into large pieces
55ml extra-virgin olive oil
1 garlic clove
Salt

In a small bowl or jar, let the shallot sit in the vinegars for 15 minutes to macerate (see page 118).

Halve the tomato crosswise. Grate on the largest hole of a box grater and discard the skin. You should be left with 100g grated tomato. Add it to the shallot. Add the basil leaves, olive oil, and a generous pinch of salt. Smash the garlic against the worktop with the palm of your hand and add to the dressing. Shake or stir to combine. Taste with a crouton or slice of tomato and adjust salt and acid as needed. Let sit for at least 10 minutes, and remove the garlic before using.

Cover and refrigerate leftovers for up to 2 days.

Ideal for sliced tomatoes, and for **Avocado Salad**, **Caprese Salad**, **Summer *Panzanella***, **Ricotta and Tomato Salad Toasts**, **Summer Tomato and Herb Salad**.

Rice Wine Vinaigrette

Makes about 75ml

2 tablespoons seasoned rice wine vinegar

4 tablespoons neutral-tasting oil

1 garlic clove

Salt

Pour the vinegar and olive oil into a small bowl or jar. Smash the garlic clove against the worktop with the palm of your hand and add to the dressing. Stir or shake to combine, then taste with a leaf of lettuce and adjust salt and acid as needed. Let sit for at least 10 minutes, then remove garlic before using dressing.

Cover and refrigerate leftovers for up to 3 days.

Ideal for garden lettuces, romaine and Little Gem lettuce, shaved daikon radish, carrots, or cucumbers, and for any **Avocado Salad**.

Variations

- To add a little heat, add 1 teaspoon minced jalapeño.
- To evoke the flavours of Korea or Japan, add a few drops of toasted sesame oil.

Caesar Dressing

Makes about 350ml

4 salt-packed anchovies (or 8 fillets), soaked and filleted

175ml stiff **Basic Mayonnaise** (page 375)

1 garlic clove, finely grated or pounded with a pinch of salt

3 to 4 tablespoons lemon juice

1 teaspoon white wine vinegar

3-ounce chunk of Parmesan, finely grated, plus more for serving

3/4 teaspoon Worcestershire sauce

Freshly ground black pepper

Salt

Coarsely chop the anchovies and then pound them into a fine paste in a mortar and pestle. The more you break them down, the better the dressing will be.

In a medium bowl, stir together the anchovies, mayonnaise, garlic, lemon juice, vinegar, Parmesan, Worcestershire sauce, and pepper. Taste with a leaf of lettuce, then add salt and adjust acid as needed. Or, practising what you learned about **Layering Salt**, add a little bit of each salty ingredient to the mayonnaise, bit by bit. Adjust the acid, then taste and adjust the salty ingredients until you reach the ideal balance of Salt, Fat, and Acid. Has putting a lesson you read in a book into practice ever been this delicious? I doubt it.

To make the salad, use your hands to toss the greens and **Torn Croutons** with an abundant amount of dressing in a large bowl to coat evenly. Garnish with Parmesan and freshly ground black pepper and serve immediately.

Refrigerate leftover dressing, covered, for up to 3 days.

Ideal for romaine and Little Gem lettuce, chicories, raw or blanched Kale, shaved Brussels sprouts, Belgian endive.

Creamy Herb Dressing

Makes about 275ml

1 tablespoon finely diced shallot

2 tablespoons red wine vinegar

100ml **crème fraîche** (page 113), double cream, sour cream, or plain yoghurt

3 tablespoons extra-virgin olive oil

1 small garlic clove, finely grated or pounded with a pinch of salt

1 spring onion, white and green part finely chopped

10g finely chopped soft herbs, in whatever proportions you like. Use any combination of parsley, coriander, dill, chives, chervil, basil, and tarragon

½ teaspoon sugar

Salt

Freshly ground black pepper

In a small bowl, let the shallot sit in the vinegar for 15 minutes to macerate (see page 118). In a large bowl, whisk together the shallot and macerating vinegar with the crème fraîche, olive oil, garlic, spring onion, herbs, sugar, a generous pinch of salt, and a pinch of black pepper. Taste with a leaf of lettuce, then adjust salt and acid as needed.

Refrigerate leftovers, covered, for up to 3 days.

Ideal for romaine, Iceberg wedges, Little Gem lettuce, beetroots, cucumbers, Belgian endive, and for serving with grilled fish or roast chicken, dipping crudités, serving alongside fried foods.

Blue Cheese Dressing

Makes 275ml

140g creamy blue cheese, such as Roquefort, Bleu d'Auvergne, or Maytag Blue, crumbled

100ml **crème fraîche** (page 113), sour cream, or double cream

55ml extra-virgin olive oil

1 tablespoon red wine vinegar

1 small garlic clove, finely grated or pounded with a pinch of salt

Salt

In a medium bowl, use a whisk to thoroughly combine the cheese, crème fraîche, olive oil, vinegar, and garlic. Alternatively, place everything into a jar, seal the lid, and shake vigorously to combine. Taste with a leaf of lettuce, then add salt and adjust acid as needed.

Refrigerate leftovers, covered, for up to 3 days.

Ideal for Belgian endive, chicories, Iceberg wedges, Little Gem and romaine lettuce. This dressing also works beautifully as sauce for steak or dip for carrots and cucumbers.

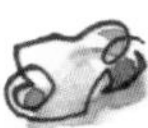

Green Goddess Dressing

Makes about 450ml

3 salt-packed anchovies (or 6 fillets), soaked and filleted
1 ripe medium avocado, halved and pitted
1 garlic clove, sliced
4 teaspoons red wine vinegar
2 tablespoons plus 2 teaspoons lemon juice
2 tablespoons finely chopped parsley
2 tablespoons finely chopped coriander
1 tablespoon finely chopped chives
1 tablespoon finely chopped chervil
1 teaspoon finely chopped tarragon
125ml stiff **Basic Mayonnaise** (page 375)
Salt

Coarsely chop the anchovies and then pound them into a fine paste in a mortar and pestle. The more you break them down, the better the dressing will be.

Place the anchovies, avocado, garlic, vinegar, lemon juice, herbs, and mayonnaise in a blender or food processor with a generous pinch of salt and blend until creamy, thick, and smooth. Taste and adjust salt and acid as needed. Leave the Green Goddess thick to use as a dip, or thin with water to desired consistency for a salad dressing.

Refrigerate leftovers, covered, for up to 3 days.

Ideal for romaine, Iceberg wedges, Little Gem lettuce, beetroots, cucumbers, Belgian endive, for serving with grilled fish or roast chicken, dipping crudités, and for **Avocado Salad**.

Tahini Dressing

Makes about 225ml

½ teaspoon cumin seeds, or ½ teaspoon ground cumin

Salt

225g tahini

55g freshly squeezed lemon juice

2 tablespoons extra-virgin olive oil

1 garlic clove, finely grated or pounded with a pinch of salt

¼ teaspoon ground cayenne pepper

2 to 4 tablespoons ice water

Place the cumin seeds in a small, dry frying pan and set over medium heat. Swirl the pan constantly to ensure even toasting. Toast until the first few seeds begin to pop and emit a savoury aroma, about 3 minutes. Remove from the heat. Immediately dump the seeds into the bowl of a mortar or a spice grinder. Grind finely with a pinch of salt.

Place the cumin, tahini, lemon juice, oil, garlic, cayenne, 2 tablespoons ice water, and a generous pinch of salt in a medium bowl and whisk to combine. Alternatively, blend everything together in a food processor. The mixture might look broken at first, but trust that it'll come together into a smooth, creamy emulsion with stirring. Add water as needed to thin it out to desired consistency—leave it thick to use as a dip, and thin it out to dress salads, vegetables, or meat. Taste with a leaf of lettuce, then adjust salt and acid as needed.

Refrigerate leftovers, covered, for up to 3 days.

Variation

- To make ***Goma-Ae*** (Japanese sesame seed dressing) substitute 55ml seasoned rice wine vinegar for the lemon juice. Omit the cumin, salt, olive oil, and cayenne and add 2 teaspoons of soy sauce, a few drops of toasted sesame oil, and 1 teaspoon mirin (rice wine). Whisk together with garlic as directed above. Taste and adjust salt and acid as needed.

Ideal for drizzling over roasted vegetables, grilled fish, or chicken; tossing with blanched broccoli, kale, green beans, or spinach; or serving as a dipping sauce with cucumbers and carrots.

Miso-Mustard Dressing

Makes 175ml

4 tablespoons white or yellow miso paste

2 tablespoons honey

2 tablespoons Dijon mustard

4 tablespoons rice wine vinegar

1 teaspoon finely grated ginger

In a medium bowl, use a whisk to thoroughly combine everything until smooth. Alternatively, place all the ingredients in a jar, seal the lid, and shake vigorously to combine. Taste with a leaf of lettuce, then adjust acid as needed.

Ideal for tossing with sliced, raw cabbage or kale, garden lettuces, romaine and Little Gem lettuce, Belgian endive, and drizzling over grilled fish, leftover roast chicken, or roasted vegetables.

Peanut-Lime Dressing

Makes about 400ml

55ml freshly squeezed lime juice

1 tablespoon fish sauce

1 tablespoon rice wine vinegar

1 teaspoon soy sauce

1 tablespoon finely grated ginger

55g peanut butter

½ jalapeño pepper, stemmed and sliced

3 tablespoons neutral-tasting oil

1 garlic clove, sliced

Optional: 10g coarsely chopped coriander leaves

Place all the ingredients in a blender or food processor and blend until smooth. Thin with water to desired consistency—leave it thick to use as a dip, and thin it out to dress salads, vegetables, or meat. Taste with a leaf of lettuce, then adjust salt and acid as needed.

Refrigerate leftovers, covered, for up to 3 days.

Ideal for cucumbers, rice or soba noodles, romaine, and serving alongside grilled or roasted chicken, steak, or pork.

VEGETABLES

Cooking Onions

The longer you cook onions, the deeper their flavour will be. But you don't need to caramelise every onion you cook. In general, cook *all* onions, no matter how you intend to use them, at least until they've lost their crunch. Only when they've reached this point will they truly deliver sweetness to a dish.

Blond onions are cooked until they're soft, remaining translucent. Cook them over medium-low heat to keep them from taking on colour. If you notice them starting to stick, discourage browning by splashing a little water into the pan. Use blond onions for **Silky Sweet Corn Soup** (page 276) or any recipe where retaining the light colour of a dish is a priority.

Browned onions are cooked until they take on some colour, and begin to deepen in flavour as a result. They're ideal for pasta sauces, **Chicken with Lentil Rice** (page 334), and as the base for countless braises and soups.

Caramelised onions are taken to the edge of browning and hence boast the deepest flavour. Use them to make a **Caramelised Onion Tart** (page 127), toss them with blanched broccoli or green beans, pile them atop burgers and steak sandwiches, or chop them finely and stir into crème fraîche for an unbelievable onion dip.

Though their name may be a misnomer (Maillarded onions just doesn't sound right!), there's nothing wrong about caramelised onions. Since they take so long to make, and since they are so good, make more caramelised onions than you'll need for a single meal. Use them over the course of four or five days as the base of any of the many dishes that benefit from deeply flavoured onions.

Start with at least 8 thinly sliced onions. Set your largest frying pan, or a large cast iron casserole, over medium-high heat. Add enough butter, olive oil, or some of each, to generously coat the bottom of the pan. Let the fat heat up until it shimmers, then add the onions and season lightly with salt. Though this will draw water out and delay browning initially, it will also soften the onions and lead to more even browning in the long run.

COOKING ONIONS

BLOND (ABOUT 15 MIN.)

BROWNED (ABOUT 25 MIN.)

CARAMELISED (ABOUT 45 MIN.)

Reduce the heat to medium, and keep an eye on the onions, stirring as necessary to keep from burning, or from browning too quickly in any one spot of the pan. It'll take a while for them to cook all the way through—at least 45 minutes, and up to an hour.

When the onions are done cooking, taste and adjust seasoning with salt and a rumour of red wine vinegar to balance out their sweetness.

Cherry Tomato Confit

Makes about 1kg

At the height of summer, make cherry tomato confit once a week and use it as a quick pasta sauce, spoon it over grilled fish or chicken, or serve it alongside fresh ricotta and grilled croutons rubbed with garlic. Use the sweetest, most flavourful tomatoes you can find—they'll explode on your tongue.

Strain, save, and reuse the confit oil for a second batch, or use it to make **Tomato Vinaigrette** (page 245).

675g cherry tomatoes, stemmed

Small handful basil leaves or stems (the stems are packed with flavour!)

4 garlic cloves, peeled

Salt

450ml extra-virgin olive oil

Preheat the oven to 150°C.

Lay the cherry tomatoes in a single layer into a shallow roasting dish over a bed of basil leaves and/or stems and garlic cloves. Cover with about 450ml of olive oil. While the tomatoes don't have to be totally submerged, they should all be in contact with the oil. Season them liberally with salt, give them a stir, and then stick them in the oven for about 35 to 40 minutes. At no time should the dish ever boil—a simmer, at most, is fine.

You'll know they're done when they are tender all the way through when pierced with a skewer and the first skins start to split. Pull them from the oven and let them cool a bit. Discard the basil before using.

Serve warm, or at room temperature. Keep tomatoes refrigerated, in their oil, for up to 5 days.

Variations

- To **confit large tomatoes**, peel them first. Use the tip of a small, sharp knife to core 12 Early Girls or tomatoes of similar size, then turn them over and make a small X at the base. Blanch in boiling water for 30 seconds, or just until the skin starts to loosen. Drop them into an ice bath to prevent them from cooking further, then remove the skins. Cook as directed above, in a single layer, with enough oil to go two-thirds of the way up the sides. Adjust cooking time to about 45 minutes, or until the tomatoes are soft all the way through.

- For **artichoke confit**, remove the tough outer leaves of 6 large or 12 baby artichokes. Use a vegetable peeler or sharp paring knife to peel away the dark green, fibrous skin at the base and along the stem of each artichoke. Halve the artichokes and use a spoon to scoop out the hairy chokes (refer to page 267 for an illustrated guide to preparing artichokes). Cook as directed above, in a single layer, with enough oil to go two-thirds of the way up the sides, until they are completely tender when pricked with a fork or paring knife, about 40 minutes. Toss with pasta, lemon zest, and pecorino cheese; chop up with a few mint leaves, a clove of pounded garlic, and a squeeze of lemon juice to spread atop crostini; or serve room temperature as an antipasto alongside cured meats and cheeses.

Six Ways to Cook Vegetables *

Every time I sat down to narrow the recipes for this section, the cracks in my heart deepened a bit. Vegetables are my favourite things to eat and cook. For example, I love broccoli, *cima di rapa* (also known as broccoli raab or *rapini*), *and* Romanesco broccoli (that fractal wonder) in equal measure. But with room for only a handful of recipes in each section, there was no way I could
include one for each variety. And choosing between them felt like choosing a single album to listen to *for the rest of my life:* impossible.

The problem persisted: how could I ever convey my fervent love for vegetables and demonstrate their endless variety in just a few pages? As I compiled list after list of my favourite vegetable recipes, I realised that nearly all of them involved one of six cooking methods. These are the simplest, most useful methods for every cook to master. Once you do, go fearlessly to the market, knowing you can—and will—turn any vegetable you find into something delicious.

Use **Vegetables: How and When** (page 268) to help you choose which vegetables to cook each season, and how to best prepare them. Refer to **The Worlds of Fat, Acid, and Flavour** (pages 72, 110, and 194) to vary the way you flavour and garnish your vegetables. But cook your vegetables properly to make them universally delicious, no matter what cuisine inspires you.

Blanch: Greens

When you're unsure about what to do with your greens, begin by setting a big pot of water over high heat. While the water comes to a boil, decide if you'd rather use the greens for ***Kuku Sabzi*** (page 306), ***Pasta alle Vongole*** (page 300), ***Ribollita*** (page 275), or something entirely different. Line a baking sheet or two with parchment paper and set aside. (If the greens have tough stems, strip the leaves as directed on page 232. Save kale, collard, and chard stems and blanch them in a separate batch after you cook the leaves.)

Once the water's at a rolling boil, season it until it tastes like the summer sea, then add your greens, whatever kind they may be. Do what the Italians do: first cook the greens just until they're tender. Chard will take about 3 minutes, while collards can take upwards of 15 minutes. Pluck a leaf from the pot and taste it. If it's tender to the bite, it's ready. Use a spider or sieve to pull the greens from the water, then spread them onto the baking sheet in a single layer. Let them cool, grab handfuls of greens and squeeze out the excess

* and MUSHROOMS

water, then chop them coarsely.

Sauté blanched chard leaves and stems with **browned onions**, saffron, pine nuts, and currants, for a side dish inspired by the Sicilian seaside. Toss blanched spinach, chard, kale (or green beans, or asparagus) with ***Goma-Ae* Dressing** (page 251) to make your own version of that sushi joint staple to serve with **Glazed Five-Spice Chicken** (page 338). Sauté blanched bok choy with red pepper flakes and minced garlic—a preparation so simple you might assume it'll underwhelm you. Don't. Cook blanched collards with bacon and **browned onions** to serve with **Spicy Fried Chicken** (page 320). Treat blanched beetroot and turnip tops like you would **Indian Garlicky Green Beans** (page 261), and make yourself something delicious to serve alongside **Indian-Spiced Salmon** (page 311).

And if you have any greens left, ball them up, then wrap and refrigerate for 2 or 3 days, until you decide what you'd like to do with them. You can also freeze balls of greens in a single layer overnight, then transfer into resealable zipper bags. Keep frozen for up to 2 months, until the hankering for *kuku sabzi*—or any other verdant dish—returns. Just defrost and continue cooking as above.

CHARD BALL

Sauté: Snap Peas with Chillies and Mint

Serves 4 generously

You might remember my mentioning that the word *sauté* refers to the flip of the wrist that makes all the food cooking in a pan jump. If you haven't got the movement down, practise (look back to page 173 for tips on learning how to sauté). And in the meantime, just use tongs! Sauté vegetables that will cook quickly, in just a few minutes, and whose texture, colour, or flavour will suffer from overcooking.

About 2 tablespoons extra-virgin olive oil
675g sugar snap peas, trimmed
Salt
12 mint leaves, julienned
Finely grated zest of 1 small lemon (about 1 teaspoon)
½ teaspoon red chilli flakes

Set a large frying pan over high heat. When it's nice and hot, add just enough olive oil to barely coat the bottom of the pan. When the oil shimmers, add the snap peas and season with salt. Cook over high heat, sautéing the peas as they start to brown, until they are sweet but still crisp, about 5 to 6 minutes. Remove the pan from the heat and stir in the mint, lemon zest, and chilli flakes. Taste and adjust salt as needed. Serve immediately.

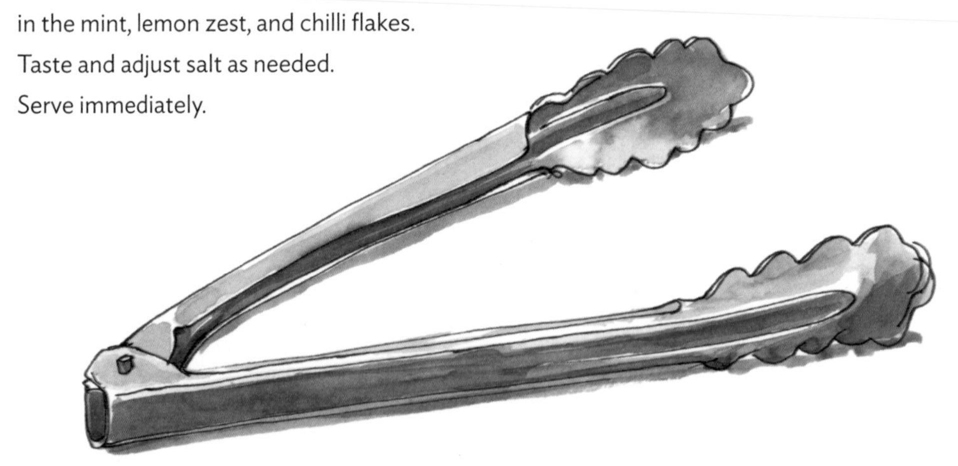

Steamy Sauté: Garlicky Green Beans

Serves 6 generously

Steamy sautéing is a method for vegetables that are a little bit too dense to sauté directly. By cooking them with water for a few minutes before turning up the heat and letting them brown, you'll ensure they're cooked all the way through.

900g fresh green beans, yellow wax beans, Romano beans, or haricots verts, trimmed

Salt

2 tablespoons extra-virgin olive oil

3 garlic cloves, minced

Set your largest frying pan over medium-high heat and bring 125ml of water to a simmer. Add the green beans, season with a couple of generous pinches of salt, and cover, removing the lid every minute or so to stir the beans. When they are almost completely tender, about 4 minutes for haricots verts and 7 to 10 minutes for more mature beans, tip any remaining water out of the pan, using the lid to keep in the beans. Return the pan to the stove, increase the flame to high, and dig a little hole in the centre of the pan. Pour the olive oil into the hole and add the garlic. Let the garlic sizzle gently for about 30 seconds, until it releases an aroma, and immediately toss it with the beans before it has a chance to take on any colour. Remove from the heat. Taste, adjust seasoning, and serve immediately.

Variations

- For **classic French flavours**, replace the olive oil with unsalted butter, omit the garlic, and toss with 1 teaspoon finely chopped tarragon before serving.
- For **Indian flavours**, replace the olive oil with ghee or unsalted butter and add 1 tablespoon minced fresh ginger to the garlic.

Roast: Butternut Squash and Brussels Sprouts in *Agrodolce*

Serves 4 to 6

Roasted vegetables develop unparalleled sweetness both on the inside and on the surface due to caramelisation, the Maillard reaction, and the release of their internal sugars. In other words, roasting is the best way to coax out sweetness.

With this in mind, I always aim to balance that sweetness with an acidic condiment, whether it's an **Herb Salsa** (page 359), a **Yoghurt Sauce** (page 370), or a vinegar-based *agrodolce*. This dish always finds its way onto my table at Thanksgiving, a meal so rich and starchy that extra acid is always welcome.

1 large butternut squash (900g), peeled, halved lengthwise, seeds discarded
Extra-virgin olive oil
Salt
450g Brussels sprouts, trimmed, outer leaves removed
½ red onion, thinly sliced
6 tablespoons red wine vinegar
1 tablespoon sugar
¾ teaspoon red chilli flakes
1 garlic clove, finely grated or pounded with a pinch of salt
16 fresh mint leaves

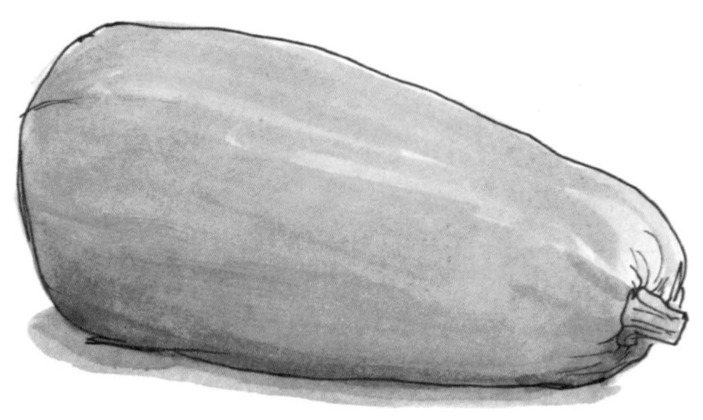

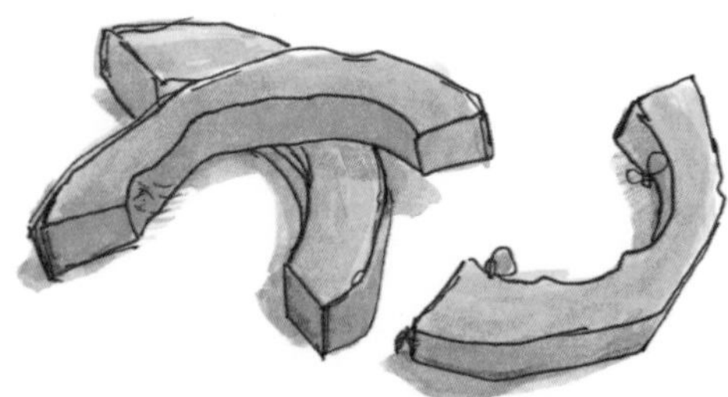

Preheat the oven to 220°C.

Slice each half of the squash crosswise into 1cm thick crescents and place in a large bowl. Toss with enough olive oil to coat, about 3 tablespoons. Season with salt and place in a single layer on a baking sheet.

Halve the Brussels sprouts through the stems, then toss in the same large bowl, adding more olive oil as needed to coat. Season with salt and place in a single layer on a second baking sheet.

Place the squash and sprouts into the preheated oven and cook until tender and caramelised, about 26 to 30 minutes. Check on the vegetables after about 12 minutes. Rotate the pans and switch their positions to ensure even browning.

Meanwhile, in a small bowl, toss the sliced onion and vinegar and allow to sit for 20 minutes to macerate (see page 118). In another small bowl, stir together another 6 tablespoons extra-virgin olive oil, sugar, chilli flakes, and garlic, and a pinch of salt.

When the roasted vegetables are brown on the outside and completely tender when pierced with a knife, remove them from the oven. The sprouts might cook a little more quickly than the squash. Combine the vegetables in a big bowl. Stir the macerated onions and their vinegar into the olive oil mixture, then pour half of the marinade over the vegetables. Toss to combine, taste, and add more salt and marinade as needed. Garnish with torn mint leaves and serve warm or at room temperature.

RED ONIONS MACERATED in RED WINE VINEGAR

Long-Cook: Spicy *Cima di Rapa* with Ricotta Salata

Serves 6

There's overcooking and then there's long-cooking. Overcooked vegetables are the ones that are forgotten in the blanching water or sauté pan for a few minutes, emerging wilted, brown, and sad. Long-cooked vegetables, on the other hand, are carefully tended until they grow tender and sweet—and they're one of my favourite ways to use up the overlooked vegetables in the produce drawer.

2 bunches (about 900g) *cima di rapa*, rinsed
Extra-virgin olive oil
1 medium onion, thinly sliced
Salt
Big pinch red pepper flakes
3 garlic cloves, sliced
1 lemon
55g ricotta salata cheese, coarsely grated

Cut off and discard the woody ends of the *cima di rapa*. Slice the stems into 1cm pieces, and the leaves into 2.5cm pieces.

Set a large cast-iron casserole or similar pot over medium heat. When it's hot, add 2 tablespoons olive oil to coat the bottom of the pot. When the oil shimmers, add the onion and a pinch of salt. Cook, stirring occasionally, until the onion is soft and beginning to brown, about 15 minutes.

Increase the heat to medium-high, add another tablespoon or so of oil, and the *cima di rapa* to the pot, and stir to combine. Season with salt and red pepper flakes. You might need to mound the *cima di rapa* to make it fit, or wait for some of it to cook down before you add the rest. Cover the pan and cook, stirring occasionally, until the *cima di rapa* is falling-apart tender, about 20 minutes.

Remove the lid and increase the heat to high. Let the *cima di rapa* begin to brown, then use a wooden spoon to move it around the pan. Continue cooking until all the *cima di rapa* has evenly browned, about 10 minutes, then move it all to the outer edges of the pan. Add a tablespoon of olive oil into the centre, then add the garlic into the oil and let it sizzle gently for about 20 seconds, until it starts to release an aroma. Before the garlic begins to brown, stir to combine it with the *cima di rapa*. Taste and adjust the salt and red pepper flakes as needed. Remove from the heat and squeeze the juice of half a lemon over the *cima di rapa*.

Stir, taste, and add more lemon juice if needed. Heap onto a serving platter and shower with coarsely grated ricotta salata. Serve immediately.

Variations

- If you don't have ricotta salata on hand, substitute Parmesan, pecorino Romano, Manchego, Asiago, or dollops of fresh ricotta.
- To round out the flavour with a little meatiness, reduce the total amount of olive oil to 1 tablespoon and add 115g bacon or pancetta, sliced into matchsticks, in with the onion.
- To bump up the umami, add 4 minced anchovy fillets in with the onion. Everyone will notice that the greens are unusually flavourful, though most people won't be able to pinpoint precisely why.

Grill: Artichokes

Serves 6

Recall the miraculous way Heat transforms the flavours of wood into the extraordinary flavours of smoke and you'll intuit why any vegetable will be improved by time spent on the grill. But only a handful of them can be properly grilled from a raw state. Think of grilling as a finishing touch for most starchy or dense vegetables, such as these artichokes, fennel wedges, or baby potatoes. Treat them right, by parcooking them on the stove or in the oven until they are tender, then skewer and grill them for a dose of smoky aroma.

6 artichokes (or 18 baby artichokes)
Extra-virgin olive oil
1 tablespoon red wine vinegar
Salt

Set a large pot of water on to boil over high heat. Build a charcoal fire, or preheat a gas grill. Line a baking sheet with parchment paper.

Remove the tough, dark outer leaves from the artichokes until the remaining leaves are half yellow, half light green. Cut away the woodiest part of the stem end and the top 4cm of every artichoke. If there are any purple inner leaves, cut them out, too. You may need to remove more in order to cut away everything fibrous. It might seem like you're trimming a lot, but remove more than you think you should, because the last thing you want is to bite into a fibrous or bitter bite at the table. Use a sharp paring knife or a vegetable peeler to remove the tough outer peel on the stem and at the base of the heart, until you reach the pale yellow inner layers. As you clean them, place the artichokes in a bowl of water with the vinegar, which will help keep them from oxidising, which makes them turn brown.

Cut the artichokes in half. Use a teaspoon to carefully scoop out the choke, or fuzzy centre, then return the artichokes to the acidulated water.

Once the water has come to a boil, season it generously until it's as salty as the sea. Place the artichokes in the water and reduce the heat so the water stays at a rapid simmer. Cook the artichokes until they are just tender when pierced with a sharp knife, about 5 minutes for baby artichokes and 14 minutes for large artichokes. Use a spider or strainer to carefully remove them from the water, and place them on the prepared baking sheet in a single layer.

Drizzle the artichokes lightly with olive oil and season with salt. Place the artichokes cut-side down on the grill over medium-high heat. Don't move them until they begin to brown, then rotate the skewers until the cut side is evenly brown, about 3 to 4 minutes per side. Flip, browning the other side in the same way.

Remove from the grill and drizzle with **Mint Salsa Verde** (page 361), if desired, or serve with **Aïoli** (page 376) or **Honey-Mustard Vinaigrette** (page 240). Serve hot, or at room temperature.

How to Get to the Heart of an Artichoke

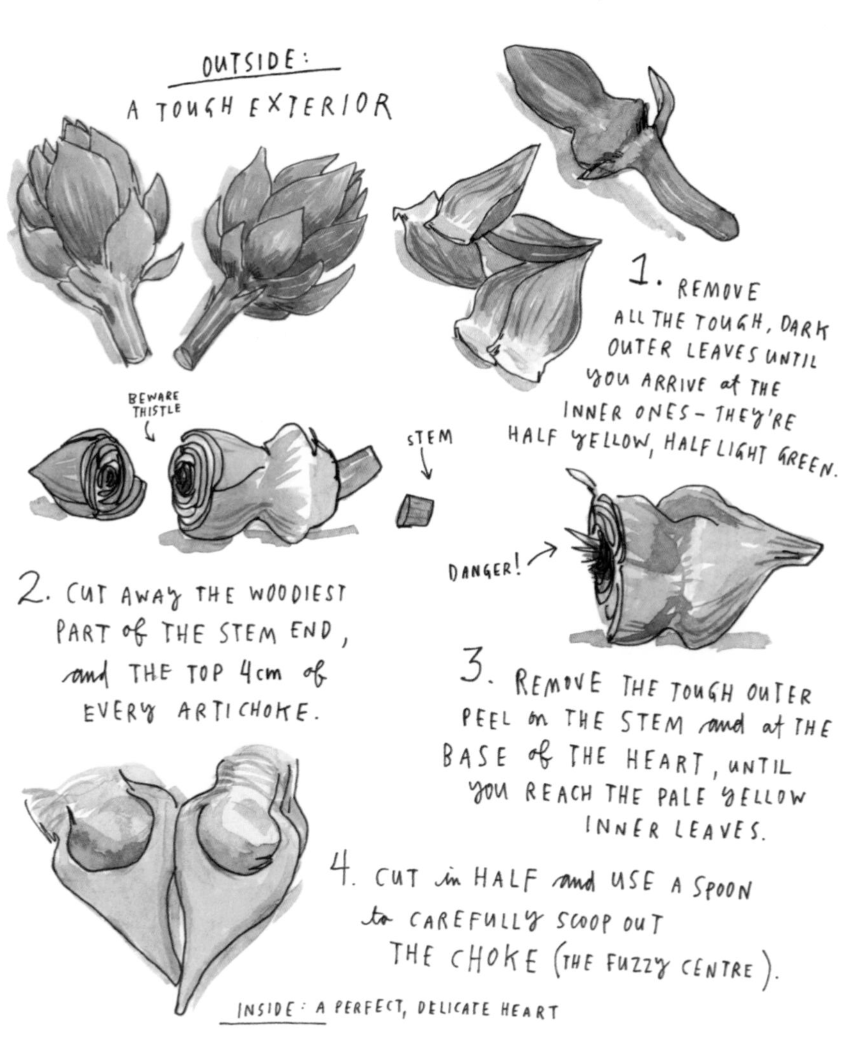

VEGETABLES : HOW and WHEN

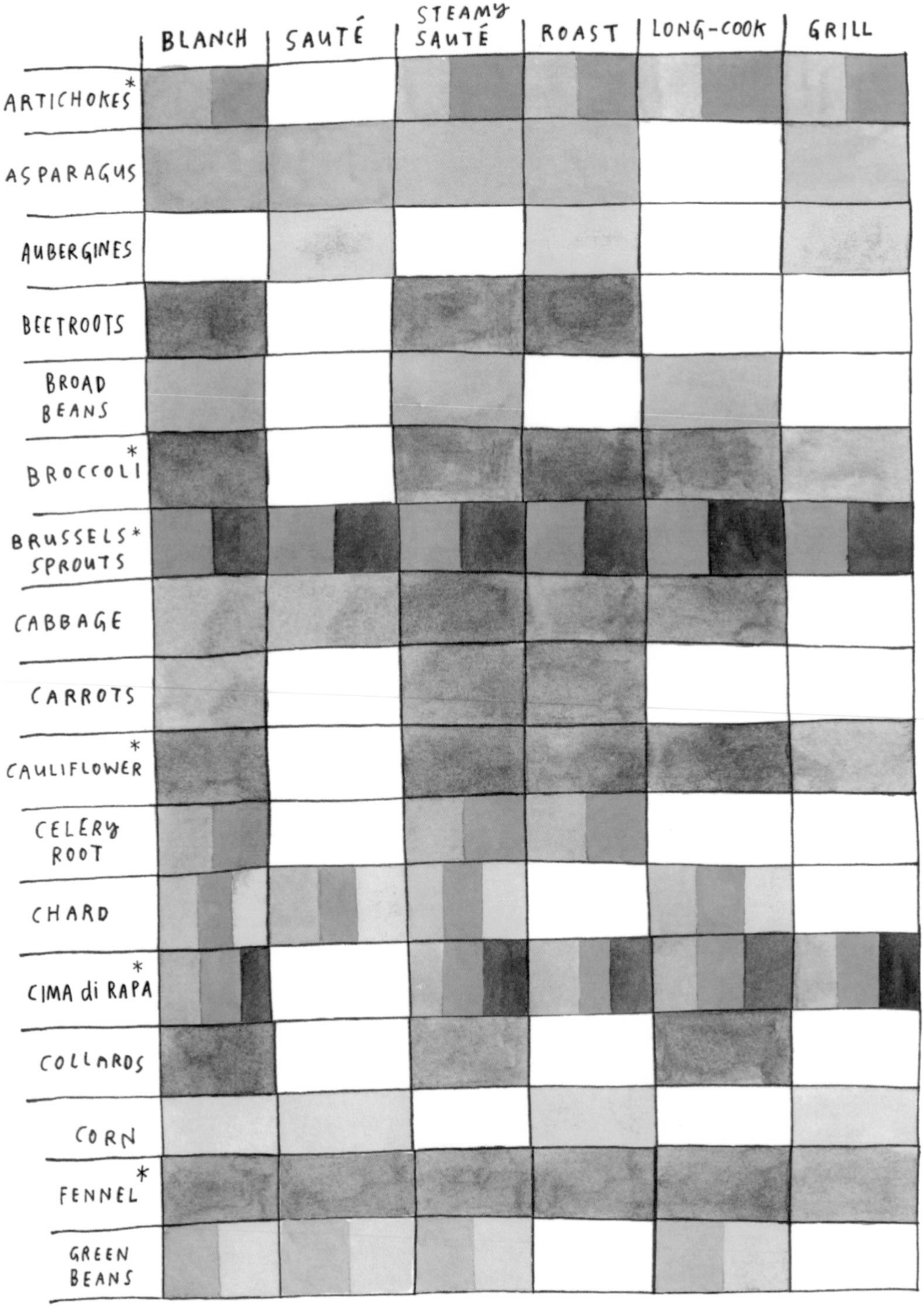

	BLANCH	SAUTÉ	STEAMY SAUTÉ	ROAST	LONG-COOK	GRILL
ARTICHOKES*						
ASPARAGUS						
AUBERGINES						
BEETROOTS						
BROAD BEANS						
BROCCOLI*						
BRUSSELS* SPROUTS						
CABBAGE						
CARROTS						
CAULIFLOWER*						
CELERY ROOT						
CHARD						
CIMA di RAPA*						
COLLARDS						
CORN						
FENNEL*						
GREEN BEANS						

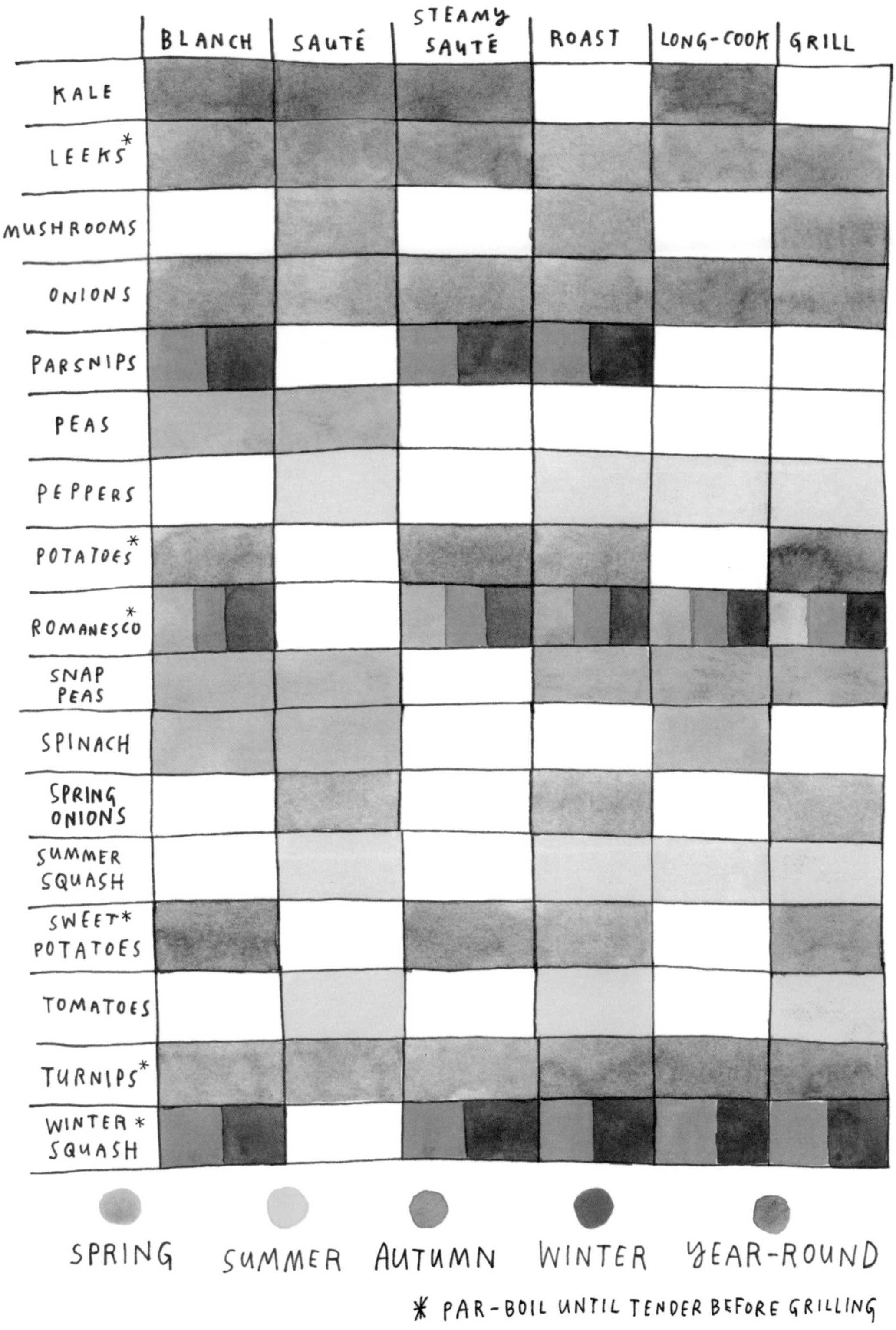

	BLANCH	SAUTÉ	STEAMY SAUTÉ	ROAST	LONG-COOK	GRILL
KALE						
LEEKS*						
MUSHROOMS						
ONIONS						
PARSNIPS						
PEAS						
PEPPERS						
POTATOES*						
ROMANESCO*						
SNAP PEAS						
SPINACH						
SPRING ONIONS						
SUMMER SQUASH						
SWEET* POTATOES						
TOMATOES						
TURNIPS*						
WINTER* SQUASH						

SPRING SUMMER AUTUMN WINTER YEAR-ROUND

* PAR-BOIL UNTIL TENDER BEFORE GRILLING

STOCK AND SOUPS

Stock

With stock on hand, dinner is always within reach. A tasty, simple, quick dinner that can take one of countless forms—soup, yes of course, but also stuffing and *panade*, a gratin made with bread and abundant stock. Or grains cooked in stock, which deliver flavour and protein without relying on meat. Or a poached egg and just-wilted spinach drowned in stock. And then, of course, there are the endless braises, soups, and stews that stock will enrich.

Every time you roast a chicken, cut off the neck or head, feet, and wingtips (and even the backbone, when **spatchcocking**) before salting, and throw them all into the freezer in a plastic bag. Then, after dinner, add the carcass into the plastic bag. One chicken carcass isn't really enough to warrant a pot of stock, so save up three or four and make stock every month or two. You can also save onion ends, the last stalk of celery that's about to go rubbery, parsley stems, and carrot ends and store these in a bag in the freezer. When your freezer can no longer contain the mess, empty it all out into a big pot and prepare to make stock.

If all you have on hand is roasted bones, it's worth making a trek out to the butcher shop to buy a couple of kilos of chicken heads and feet, or some wingtips. The gelatin the raw bones contain will add a ton of body and richness to the stock.

Chicken Stock

Makes about 9 litres

3.2kg chicken bones (at least half should be raw)

8.5 litres water

2 onions, unpeeled, quartered

2 carrots, peeled and halved crosswise

2 celery stalks, halved crosswise

1 teaspoon black peppercorns

2 bay leaves

4 thyme sprigs

5 parsley sprigs or 10 stems

1 teaspoon white wine vinegar

Put everything but the vinegar in a large stockpot. Bring the stock to a boil over high heat, then turn down to a simmer. Skim any foam that rises to the surface. Now add the vinegar, which will help draw out nutrients and minerals from the bones into the stock.

Simmer uncovered for 6 to 8 hours. Keep an eye on it to make sure it stays at a simmer. If stock boils, its bubbles will recirculate fat that rises to the top of the stock. With the sustained heat and agitation, the stock will emulsify. This is one of the times you're not looking for an emulsion, because beyond looking cloudy, emulsified stock also tastes cloudy and clings to the tongue in an unpleasant way. One of the best things about good stock is that though its flavour is rich, it's also clean.

Strain through a fine-meshed sieve and cool. Scrape the fat that rises to the top and save it in the fridge or freezer for **Chicken Confit** (page 326).

Refrigerate for up to 5 days, or freeze for up to 3 months. I like to freeze stock in old yoghurt containers, which have the added benefit of premeasurement.

Variations

- To make **Beef Stock**, follow the same process, but replace the chicken with 2.7kg meaty beef bones (such as knuckle bones) and 450g beef marrow bones. Brown the bones on a rimmed baking sheet in a single layer in a 200°C oven for about 45 minutes. Brown the aromatics in the recipe above in the stockpot with a few tablespoons of olive oil before adding the bones, 3 tablespoons tomato paste, and water. Set the baking sheet over a burner set to low heat, and pour in 225ml dry red wine. Use a wooden spoon or spatula to loosen all of the caramelised bits from the pan, and add them, along with the wine, into the stockpot. Bring to a boil, then reduce to a simmer and cook for at least 5 hours before straining. To make a **Super-Rich Beef Stock**, begin with chicken stock instead of water.

Soup

Beethoven once said, "Only the pure in heart can make a good soup."

Oh, that guy—what a romantic! But clearly, not much of a cook. While I agree that a pure heart is an ideal attribute for any cook, it certainly isn't necessary when making soup (though a clear mind certainly helps).

Soup is exceptionally easy to make. It's also economical. But all too often, it becomes an easy way to clear out the fridge. You must have a reason for every ingredient you choose to add into a soup in order for it to taste good. Get into the habit of making soup with the fewest—and most flavourful—possible ingredients, and you'll find it's so delicious it might even purify your heart.

Soups fall into three categories—**brothy**, **chunky**, and **smooth**—and each will satisfy a different kind of hunger. Though each type calls for different elements, all soups start with a flavourful liquid, whether it's stock, coconut milk, or bean-cooking broth. Master one soup from each category, then let taste and whimsy guide your clear mind *and* your pure heart in making delicious soup.

Brothy soups are clear and delicate, perfect for serving as a light meal or appetiser, or to an ailing friend with a meagre appetite. With only three or four ingredients, there isn't much in a brothy soup to distract the palate from an inferior broth, so wait to make this kind of soup until you have homemade stock on hand.

Chunky soups, by contrast, are robust and rich. Make a pot of chilli or Tuscan bean soup and let it fill and warm you up all week long. With longer ingredient lists and cooking times, there are more ways to build flavour in a chunky soup, so here you can start with water if you don't have homemade stock on hand.

Smooth soups will lie somewhere between **brothy** and **chunky** on the spectrum from light to hearty, depending on the main ingredient. No matter what vegetable or root you use, though, the result will be smooth and elegant. Smooth, puréed soups make for delightful dinner party first courses, or light lunches on warm summer afternoons.

The formula for any puréed soup is simple. Start with fresh, flavourful ingredients. Then cook a few onions through, add the chosen ingredients, and stew everything together for a few minutes. Add enough liquid to cover, bring it up to a boil, then reduce to a simmer and cook until everything is just tender. (Anticipate the way the greenest vegetables will fade and brown if even slightly overcooked; pull English pea, asparagus, or spinach soup off the heat a minute before it's done, knowing the residual heat will continue to cook it. Add a few ice cubes to speed up the chilling.) Remove from the heat, purée, and adjust the salt and acid. Then choose your garnish. As paragons of simplicity, puréed soups eagerly welcome crunchy, creamy, acidic, and rich garnishes alike. Use the list of variations on page 278 for inspiration.

Brothy: *Stracciatella*
Roman Egg Drop Soup

Makes 2.25 litres (serves 4 to 6)

2 litres **Chicken Stock** (page 271)

Salt

6 large eggs

Freshly ground black pepper

20g chunk of Parmesan, finely grated, plus more for serving

1 tablespoon finely chopped parsley

Bring the stock to a simmer in a medium pot and season with salt. In a measuring cup with a spout (you can also use a medium bowl), whisk together the eggs, a generous pinch of salt, pepper, Parmesan, and parsley.

Pour the egg mixture into the simmering stock in a thin stream while gently stirring the soup with a fork. Avoid overmixing, which will cause the eggs to break up into tiny, unappetising bits, instead of the *stracci*, or rags, for which the soup is named. Let the egg mixture cook for about 30 seconds, then ladle the soup into bowls. Garnish with more Parmesan, and serve immediately.

Cover and refrigerate leftovers for up to 3 days. To reheat, gently return soup to a simmer.

Variation

- To make a **Classic Egg Drop Soup**, simmer 2 litres of stock with 2 tablespoons of soy sauce, 3 sliced cloves of garlic, a thumb-size piece of ginger, a few sprigs of coriander, and 1 teaspoon peppercorns for 20 minutes, then strain into another pot. Taste and adjust salt as needed. Return the broth to a simmer. Place 1 tablespoon cornflour in a medium bowl and add in 2 tablespoons of the stock. Whisk to combine, then whisk in 6 eggs and a pinch of salt. Drizzle into simmering broth as directed above. Garnish with sliced spring onions and serve immediately.

Chunky: Tuscan Bean and Kale Soup *Makes about 2.25 litres (serves 6 to 8)*

Extra-virgin olive oil

Optional: 55g pancetta or bacon, diced

1 medium onion, diced

2 celery stalks, diced

3 medium carrots, peeled and diced

2 bay leaves

Salt

Freshly ground black pepper

2 garlic cloves, thinly sliced

400g crushed canned or fresh tomatoes in their juice

400g cooked beans, such as cannellini, corona, or cranberry, cooking liquid reserved (from about 175g raw; feel free to use canned beans in a pinch!)

25g freshly grated Parmesan, rind reserved

675-900ml **Chicken Stock** (page 271) or water

2 bunches kale, thinly sliced

½ small head green or Savoy cabbage, core removed and thinly sliced

Set a large cast-iron casserole or stockpot over medium-high heat and add 1 tablespoon olive oil. When the oil shimmers, add the pancetta, if using, and cook, stirring, for 1 minute, until it just begins to brown.

Add the onion, celery, carrots, and bay leaves. Season generously with salt and pepper. Reduce the heat to medium and cook, stirring occasionally, until the vegetables are tender and just starting to brown, about 15 minutes. Dig a little hole in the centre of the pot, then add another tablespoon of olive oil. Add the garlic and let it sizzle gently until it gives off an aroma, about 30 seconds. Before the garlic has a chance to brown, add the tomatoes. Stir, taste, and add salt as needed.

Let the tomatoes simmer until they cook down to a jammy consistency, about 8 minutes, then add the beans and their cooking liquid, half the grated Parmesan and its rind, and enough stock or water to cover. Add two immoderate splashes of olive oil, about 55ml. Stirring occasionally, bring the soup back to a simmer. Add the kale and cabbage and bring to a simmer again, adding more stock or water as needed to cover.

Cook until the flavours have come together and the greens are tender, about 20 minutes more. Taste and adjust for salt. I like this soup to be very thick, but add more liquid if you like a lighter soup. Remove the Parmesan rind and bay leaves.

Serve with a drizzle of the best olive oil you have on hand, and grated Parmesan.

Store covered in the refrigerator for up to 5 days. This soup also freezes exceptionally well for up to 2 months. Return the soup to a boil before using.

Variations

- To make ***Pasta e Fagioli*** (Tuscan Pasta and Bean Soup), add about 75g uncooked *ditalini*, *tubetti*, or other small pasta shape along with the beans. Stir frequently, as the starch released by the pasta is apt to form a crust on the bottom of the pot and burn. Cook until the pasta is tender, about 20 minutes. Thin out with more stock or water as needed to desired consistency. Serve as directed above.

- To make ***Ribollita*** (Tuscan Bread, Bean, and Kale Soup), add 225g **Torn Croutons** (page 236) when the soup returns to a simmer, just after you add the kale and cabbage. Stir frequently, as the starch released by the bread is apt to form a crust on the bottom of the pot and burn. Cook until the bread has completely absorbed the stock and fallen apart, about 25 minutes. There should be no distinct pieces of bread at the end—instead, it's all just one delightfully tender mess. *Ribollita* should be very, very thick—at Da Delfina, my favourite restaurant in the Tuscan hills, it's served on a plate!

Smooth: Silky Sweet Corn Soup

Makes 2.5 litres (serves 6 to 8)

I'm a firm believer that the best cooking is not so much about fancy techniques and expensive ingredients. Sometimes the tiniest—and most inexpensive—thing will make all the difference. Nothing demonstrates that idea as well as this soup, whose secret ingredient is a quick stock made using nothing more than cobs and water. Use the freshest, sweetest summer corn you can find and you'll see how five simple ingredients can add up to a singularly flavourful soup.

8 to 10 ears corn, husks, stalks, and silk removed
115g butter
2 medium onions, sliced
Salt

Fold a kitchen towel into quarters and set it inside a large, wide metal bowl. Use one hand to hold an ear of corn in place upright atop the kitchen towel—it helps to pinch the ear at the top. With your other hand, use a serrated knife or sharp chef's knife to cut off two or three rows of kernels at a time by sliding the knife down the cob. Get as close to the cob as you can, and resist the temptation to cut off more rows at once—that'll leave behind lots of precious corn. Save the cobs.

In a soup pot, quickly make a corn cob stock: cover the cobs with 2 litres water and bring to a boil. Reduce heat and simmer for 10 minutes, then remove the cobs. Set stock aside.

Return the pot to the stove and heat over medium heat. Add the butter. Once it has melted, add the onions and reduce heat to medium-low. Cook, stirring occasionally, until the onions are completely soft and translucent, or **blond**, about 20 minutes. If you notice the onions starting to brown, add a splash of water and keep an eye on things, stirring frequently, to prevent further browning.

As soon as the onions are tender, add the corn. Increase the heat to high and sauté just until the corn turns a brighter shade of yellow, 3 to 4 minutes. Add just enough stock to cover everything, and crank up the heat to high. Save the rest of the stock in case you need to thin out the soup later. Season with salt, taste, and adjust. Bring to a boil, then simmer for 15 minutes.

If you have an immersion blender, use it to carefully blend the soup until it is puréed.

If you don't have one, work carefully and quickly to purée it in batches in a blender or food processor. For a very silky texture, strain the soup one last time through a fine-mesh sieve.

Taste the soup for salt, sweetness, and acid balance. If the soup is very flatly sweet, a tiny bit of white wine vinegar or lime juice can help balance it out.

To serve, either ladle chilled soup into bowls and spoon salsa over it to garnish, or quickly bring the soup to a boil and serve hot with an acidic garnish, such as **Mexican-ish Herb Salsa** (page 363) or **Indian Coconut-Coriander Chutney** (page 368).

Variations

Follow this method and the basic formula I described above—about 1.2kg of vegetables or cooked legumes, 2 onions, and enough stock or water to cover—to turn practically any other vegetable into a velvety soup. The cob stock is unique to corn soup; don't try to replicate it when making any of the variations. Carrot peel stock won't do much for a soup!

And there's no cooking whatsoever required to make **Chilled Cucumber and Yoghurt** soup! Just purée seeded, peeled cucumbers and yoghurt, then thin with water to your desired consistency.

Turn the page for some some soup-and-garnish combinations to inspire your soup-making.

SMOOTH SOUP SUGGESTIONS

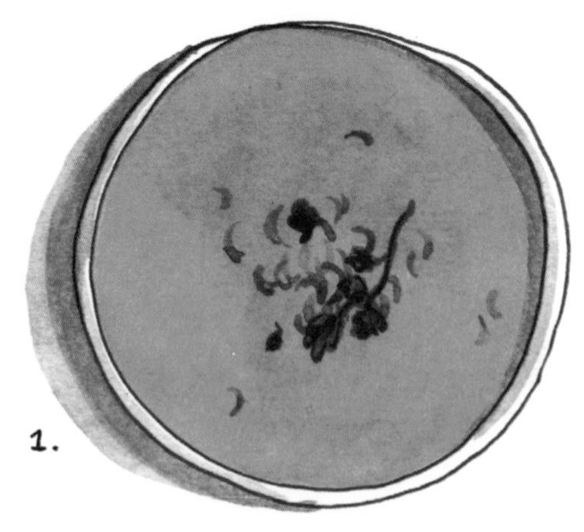

1.

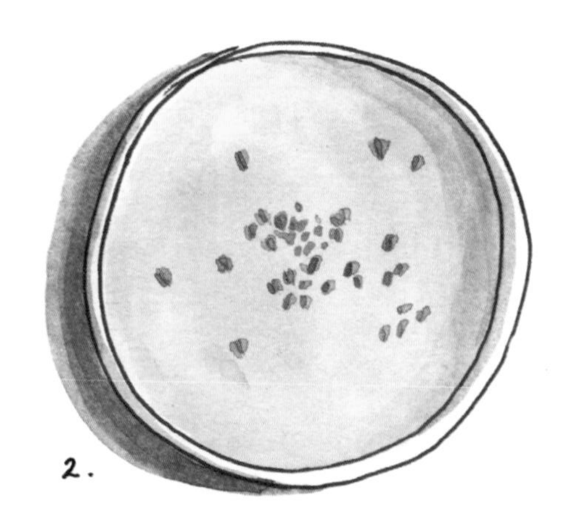

2.

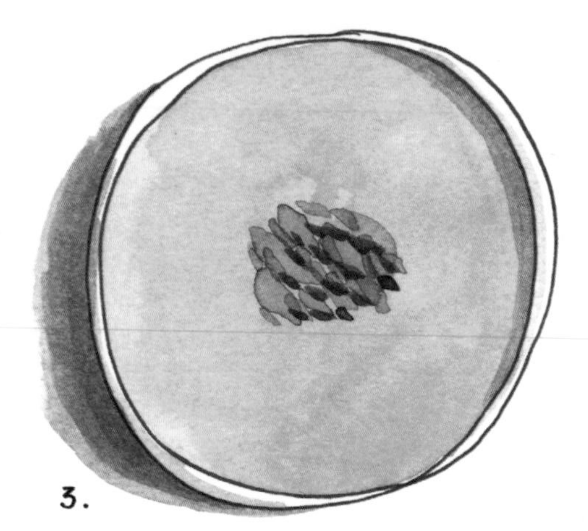

3.

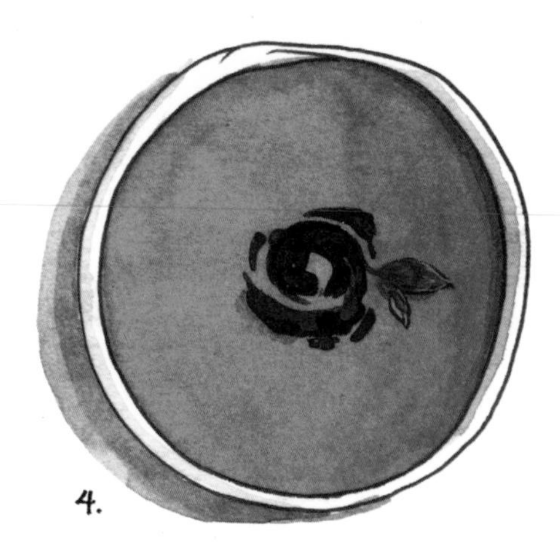

4.

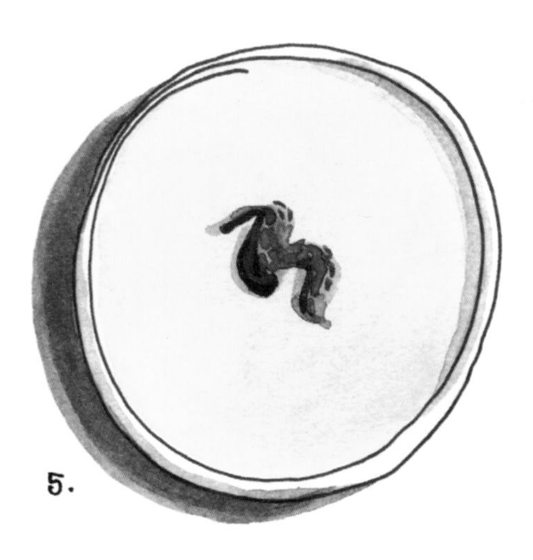

5.

1. BUTTERNUT SQUASH and GREEN CURRY SOUP w/ FRIED SHALLOTS and CORIANDER
2. CHILLED CUCUMBER and YOGURT SOUP w/ TOASTED SESAME SEEDS
3. ENGLISH PEA SOUP w/ MINT SALSA VERDE
4. TOMATO SOUP w/ BASIL PESTO
5. TURNIP SOUP w/ TURNIP TOP PESTO

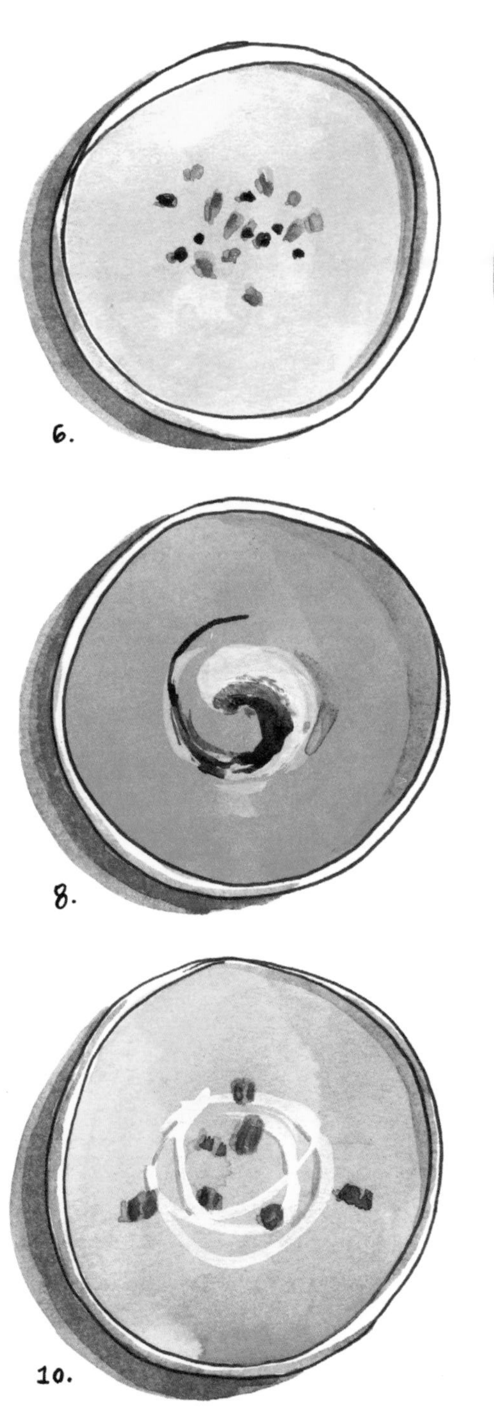

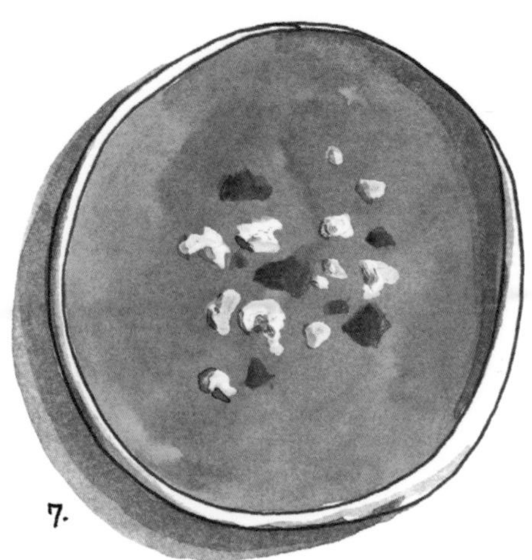

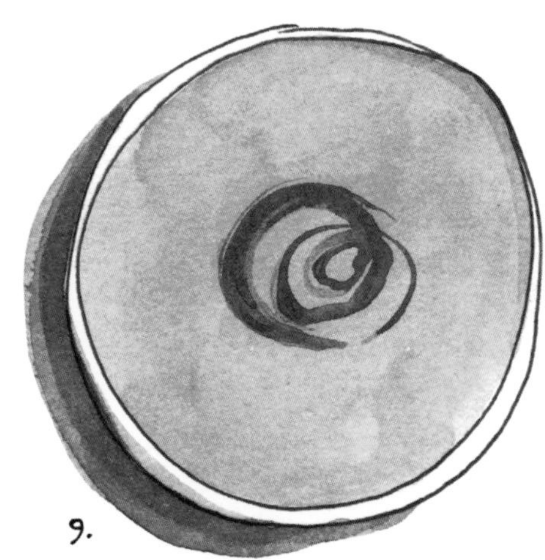

6. CAULIFLOWER SOUP w/ TOASTED PINE NUTS and CURRANTS
7. SPINACH and DILL SOUP w/ CRUMBLED FETA and TOASTED PITA CRUMBS
8. CARROT SOUP w/ YOGURT and CHARMOULA
9. ROASTED AUBERGINES SOUP w/ HARISSA
10. POTATO-LEEK SOUP w/ CRÈME FRAÎCHE and CRUMBLED BACON

BEANS, GRAINS, AND PASTA

Cooking beans, whether dried or freshly shelled, is as simple as can be. In fact, the basic recipe for **Simmered Beans** can be summed up in one short sentence: Cover with water and simmer until tender.

While fresh borlotti beans can cook in about 30 minutes, it can take several hours for dried beans to transform into their most tender selves. To reduce the cooking time, soak them overnight.

I'm a tireless champion of soaking beans in advance. And since one measure of any properly cooked starch is whether or not it's absorbed enough water to become tender, think of soaking as a head start. It's the easiest kind of cooking you'll ever have to do.

When soaking beans, keep in mind that 175g of dried beans will triple in size when cooked, yielding about 6 servings. Add a palmful of salt, and a generous pinch of bicarbonate of soda, which will tip the pH of the pot towards alkalinity and help coax even more tenderness from the beans. Soak beans in the same vessel in which you plan to cook them, to save yourself a dish, and either refrigerate or keep in a cool spot on the worktop overnight (or over 2 nights, for chickpeas or big, creamy beans such as *gigantes*).

Once cooked, consider beans a blank slate, ready to be transformed into whatever you like. Properly cooked and seasoned dried beans, garnished with nothing more than a dousing of extra-virgin olive oil, are a revelation for most people, including those who consider themselves to be bean-haters. And, as with most foods, a showering of chopped fresh herbs or a spoonful of **Herb Salsa** (page 359) never hurts.

Beans and eggs are a classic pairing. Crack eggs into a shallow pan of beans in their liquid

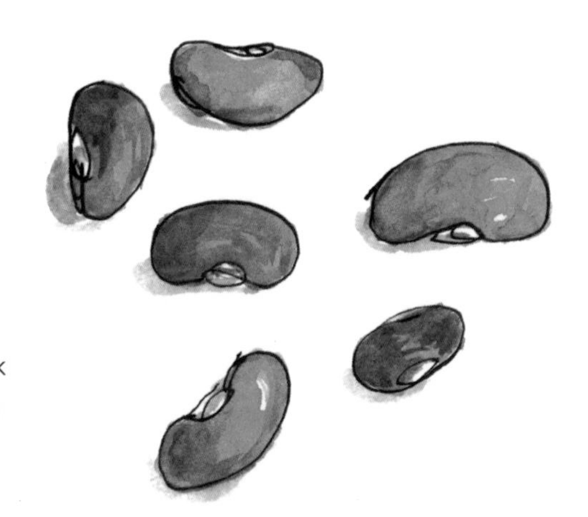

and slide it into a hot oven. Bake until the whites are just set. Garnish with feta cheese and ***Harissa*** (page 380) and serve with warm, crusty bread for any meal.

Beans, more so than most other starches, will happily share the plate with a second starch. Rice and beans, matched together in almost every culture's cuisine, are especially delicious in El Salvadoran cooking, where they are cooked together into a crispy cake known as *casamiento*; in Cuban cooking, where they are called *Moros y Cristianos*; in Persian cooking, where they come together in ***Adas Polo*** (page 334); and of course inside a classic rice and bean burrito. In Italy, beans join bread in the soup known as ***Ribollita*** (page 275) and pasta in another called ***Pasta e Fagioli*** (page 275). And in any kitchen, anywhere in the world, creamy beans have perhaps no better foil than crunchy, golden, **Sprinkling Crumbs** (page 237).

I once brought a simple salad of dried borlotti beans tossed with macerated onions, toasted cumin seeds, feta cheese, and coriander sprigs to a lunch honouring the ground-breaking vegetarian chef Deborah Madison. Even though the table was laden with impressive dishes made by all of the other accomplished cooks at the meal, I continued to receive requests for the recipe for that "amazing bean salad" for nearly a year.

Any beans, not just chickpeas, can be turned into a delicious hummus-ish spread by puréeing them with abundant amounts of olive oil, garlic, herbs, chilli flakes, lemon juice, and also tahini, if you like. Adjust the salt and acid, and serve with crackers, bread, or just sneak spoonfuls, like I do.

Mash cooked beans together with softened onions, herbs, an egg, grated Parmesan, and enough cooked rice or quinoa to bind the mixture, and fry little patties to serve with a **Yoghurt Sauce** (page 370), ***Harissa*** (page 380), ***Charmoula*** (page 367), or any **Herb Salsa** (page 359). Top with a fried egg for a perfect breakfast.

Freeze extra cooked beans, in ample water, to later defrost and slip into soups.

And finally, while canned beans cannot compare in flavour to beans you cook yourself, the convenience they offer is unparalleled. I always keep a few cans of chickpeas and black beans on hand, just in case a feverish hunger strikes.

Three Ways to Cook Grains (and Quinoa*)

* IT'S A PSEUDOGRAIN.**

Steam

Every time I see all the fancy rice makers lined up on the shelf at an Asian grocery, I convince myself that I need one. After all, I do eat a lot of rice, and the machines are all so cute! Then I snap out of it. For one thing, I don't have the space for another kitchen machine. And, more important, I already know how to cook rice!

My theory is that marketing geniuses have planted false seeds of rice-making despair in the minds of home cooks around the world. Think about it: rice is one of the oldest cultivated foods on the planet. If cooks hadn't figured out how to make it properly, I'm fairly certain the human race wouldn't have made it.

It's really not so hard. Steaming is my preferred way to cook rice for weeknight dinners, because it's quick and simple, yet the grains have the chance to absorb the flavours of the cooking liquid.

Find a variety of rice you love to eat, and grow comfortable cooking it, over and over again. My standbys are basmati, jasmine, and a Japanese variety called *haiga*, which is milled to preserve its nutritious germ yet cook quickly. As with everything, the more often you cook rice, the more proficient you'll grow to be. The most important variable when cooking rice is to get the right ratio of liquid to grain.

Basmati and jasmine rices are traditionally both rinsed multiple times until the water runs clear, but for a typical weeknight dinner, I don't usually bother. Save the rinsing step for dinner parties.

Refer to the following chart for liquid-to-grain ratios and remember the rule of thumb, **200g of uncooked rice will serve 2 to 3 people.** Simply bring your chosen liquid—water, stock, and coconut milk all work well—to a boil, season it generously with salt, and add the rice (or quinoa, which I like to cook the same way).

Reduce to a very gentle simmer, cover, and cook until the liquid has all been absorbed and the grains are tender. Let it rest covered for 10 minutes after you turn off the heat. And, apart from risotto—which is an entirely different story—never, ever stir rice while it's cooking. Just fluff it with a fork before serving.

** NO REALLY. IT IS!

grain : water

THE PERFECT RATIOS

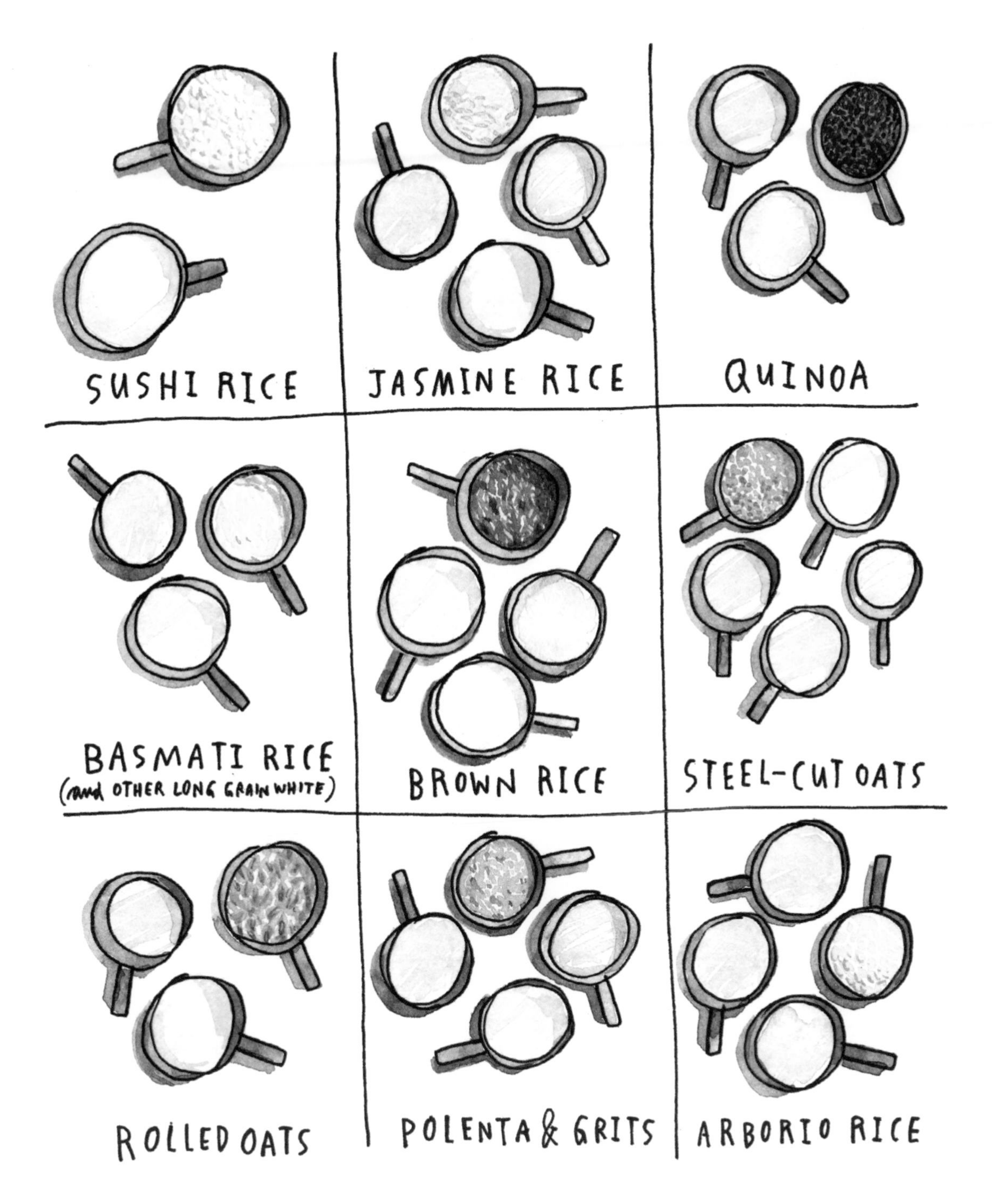

Simmer and Stir until Tender

Steel-cut and rolled oats: Bring very lightly seasoned liquid to a boil, add oats, turn down to a simmer, and stir continuously until tender.

Polenta and grits: Add polenta or grits in a thin stream to boiling, seasoned water while whisking. Stir continuously and cook until tender, about an hour, adding more water as needed. Adjust seasoning and stir in butter and grated cheese before serving.

Arborio rice for risotto: First, mince and cook ½ onion per cup of rice in butter until soft and translucent, then add rice and toast until golden brown, then deglaze with 125ml white wine. Stirring continuously, add stock gradually in 125ml increments, waiting until it's been absorbed to add more. Cook until rice is tender but still al dente. The consistency should be that of thin oatmeal, so thin with stock or a splash of fresh wine if needed. Adjust seasoning and finish with finely grated Parmesan. Serve immediately.

Boil

Cook **pasta**, **farro**, **spelt**, **wheat** or **rye berries**, **barley**, **amaranth**, or **wild rice** in ample salted water until tender. This method also works well for **quinoa**, **brown**, or **basmati rice**.

Persian-ish Rice

Serves 4 to 6

Every Persian has a special relationship with rice, and particularly with *tahdig*, the crispy crust by which every Iranian *maman*'s culinary prowess is measured. Judged on its even browning, perfect crispness, and whether it emerges from the pot in a beautiful cake, as well as its taste, a good *tahdig* is something to be proud of. Since traditional Persian rice can take years to perfect and hours to make, I'm including this Persian-ish variation, which I accidentally devised one night when I found myself with some extra just-boiled basmati rice on my hands.

400g basmati rice
Salt
3 tablespoons plain yoghurt
3 tablespoons butter
3 tablespoons neutral-tasting oil

Fill a large stockpot with 4.8 litres of water and bring it to a boil over high heat.

In the meantime, place the rice in a bowl and rinse with cold water, swirling vigorously with your fingers and changing the water at least five times, until the starch has run off and the water runs clear. Drain the rice.

Once the water comes to a boil, salt it heavily. The precise amount will vary depending on what kind of salt you're using, but it's about 6 tablespoons fine sea salt or a generous 75g kosher salt. The water should taste saltier than the saltiest seawater you've ever tasted. This is your big chance to get the rice seasoned from within, and it's only going to spend a few minutes in the salted water, so don't panic about oversalting your food. Add the rice, and stir.

Set a fine-mesh sieve or colander in the sink. Cook rice, stirring from time to time, until it's al dente, about 6 to 8 minutes. Drain into the sieve and immediately begin rinsing with cold water to stop the rice from cooking further. Drain.

Remove 125g of the rice and combine it with the yoghurt.

Set a large, very well seasoned 25cm cast iron or nonstick frying pan over medium heat, then add the oil and butter. When the butter melts, add the yoghurt-rice mixture into the pan and level it out. Pile the remaining rice into the pan, mounding it gently towards the centre. Using the handle of a wooden spoon, gently dig five or six holes into the rice down to the bottom of the pot, which will be gently sizzling. The holes will allow steam to escape from the bottommost layer of rice so that a crisp crust can form. There should be enough oil in the pan so that you can see it bubbling up the sides. Add a little more oil if needed to see these bubbles.

Continue cooking the rice over medium heat, turning the pan a quarter turn every 3 or 4 minutes to ensure even browning, until you start to see a golden crust begin to form at the sides of the pan, about 15 to 20 minutes. Once you see the crust turn from pale amber to gold, reduce the heat to low and continue cooking for another 15 to 20 minutes. The edges of the crust should be golden, and the rice should be cooked completely through. There isn't a way to tell what *tahdig* will look like until you flip it, so I prefer to err on the side of overbrowning, but if that makes you uncomfortable, pull the rice after about 35 total minutes in the pan.

To unmould the rice, carefully run a spatula along the edges of the pan to ensure that no part of the crust is sticking. Tip out any excess fat at the bottom of the pan into a bowl, gather your courage, and then carefully flip it onto a platter or cutting board. It should look like a beautiful cake of fluffy rice with a golden crust.

And if for any reason your rice doesn't slip out in one piece, do what every Persian grandmother since the beginning of time has done: scoop out the rice, chip out the *tahdig* in pieces with a spoon or metal spatula, and pretend you *meant* to do it this way. No one will be the wiser.

Serve immediately with **Slow-Roasted Salmon** (page 310), ***Kufte* Kebabs** (page 356), **Persian Roast Chicken** (page 341), or ***Kuku Sabzi*** (page 306).

Variations

- To make a **Bread *Tahdig***, cut a 25cm circle out of a piece of lavash bread, or use a 25cm flour tortilla. Mix the yoghurt into the entire amount of parcooked rice. Preheat the pan as directed above, add the butter and oil, and then lay the bread circle or tortilla into the pan. Spoon the rice in and continue as above. A Bread *Tahdig* will brown more quickly than one made with only rice, so keep a vigilant eye on the pan and turn the heat down to low after about 12 minutes, rather than 15 to 20.

- To make **Saffron Rice**, make **saffron tea** by grinding a generous pinch of saffron to a powder with a pinch of salt in a mortar and pestle. Add 2 tablespoons of boiling water and allow it to steep for 5 minutes. Drizzle over drained, parcooked rice and continue adding the rice to the frying pan as directed above. Serve with ***Kufte* Kebabs** (page 356).

- To make **Herbed Rice**, stir 6 tablespoons of finely chopped parsley, coriander, and dill in any combination into cooked, drained rice. Cook as directed above. Serve with **Slow-Roasted Salmon** (page 310) and **Herbed Yoghurt** (page 370).

- To make **Broad Bean and Dill Rice**, stir 10g finely chopped dill and fresh or thawed frozen, peeled broad beans into drained, cooked rice. Cook as directed above. Serve with **Persian Roast Chicken** (page 341).

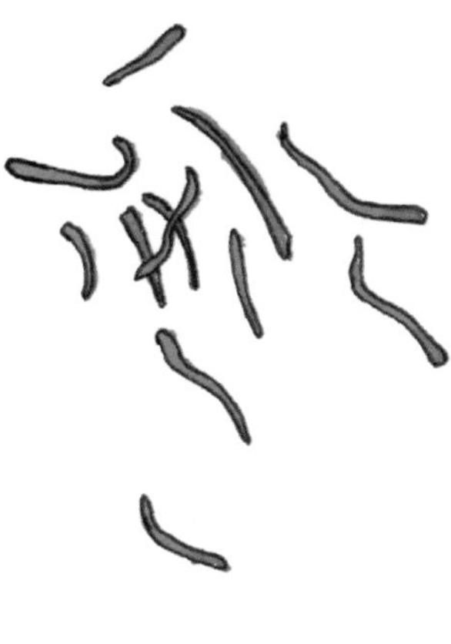

SAFFRON

Five Classic Pastas

My appreciation for pasta is profound. After all, I made and ate it nearly every day for over ten years, two of which were spent in Italy. When the time came for me to decide which handful of pasta recipes to include here, I nearly had a breakdown. How would I ever be able to reduce everything I have to say about pasta into just a few basic recipes?

I realised that before I could narrow anything down, I needed to see all the possibilities, so I made a list of all my favourite pasta and sauce combinations. As the list grew absurdly long, a pattern emerged. Every single sauce on my list fell into one of five families: cheese, tomato, vegetable, meat, and (shell)fish.

Master one sauce from each family, and the path to countless variations will become clear. Eventually, you'll be able to improvise as you wish. Just remember, every ingredient should have a role in the dish—kitchen sink pastas are generally disastrous. As a general rule, if you're improvising with what you've got on hand, stick to a six-ingredient limit, beyond the pasta, olive oil, and salt. And remember to get the Salt, Fat, and Acid just right before serving.

Two last things: with the exception of **Pesto** (page 383)—traditionally made of crushed garlic, pine nuts, Parmesan, and basil, salt, and olive oil—which will take any excuse to turn brown, hot, just cooked pasta should always be tossed with hot sauce. And, pasta is about the pasta just as much as it is about the sauce, so take care to cook the noodles properly and salt the water just right. The water should be as salty as the summer sea, which works out to about 2 scant tablespoons of kosher salt or 4 teaspoons of fine sea salt per quart.

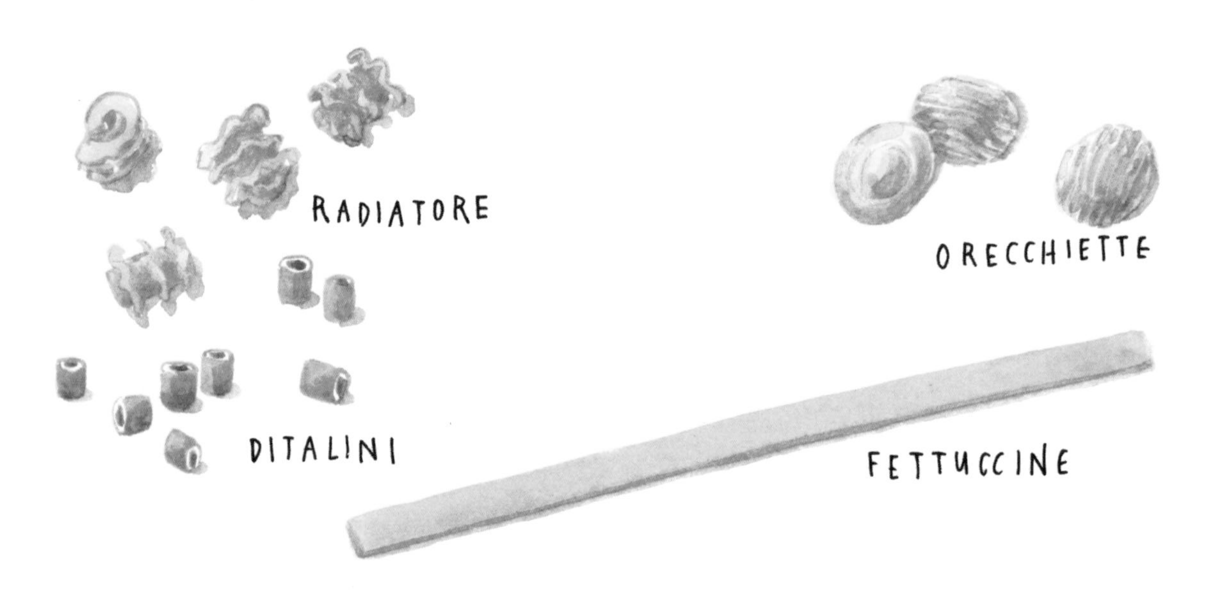

the Pasta Nostra

THE INTERMARRIAGE of FIVE GREAT FAMILIES

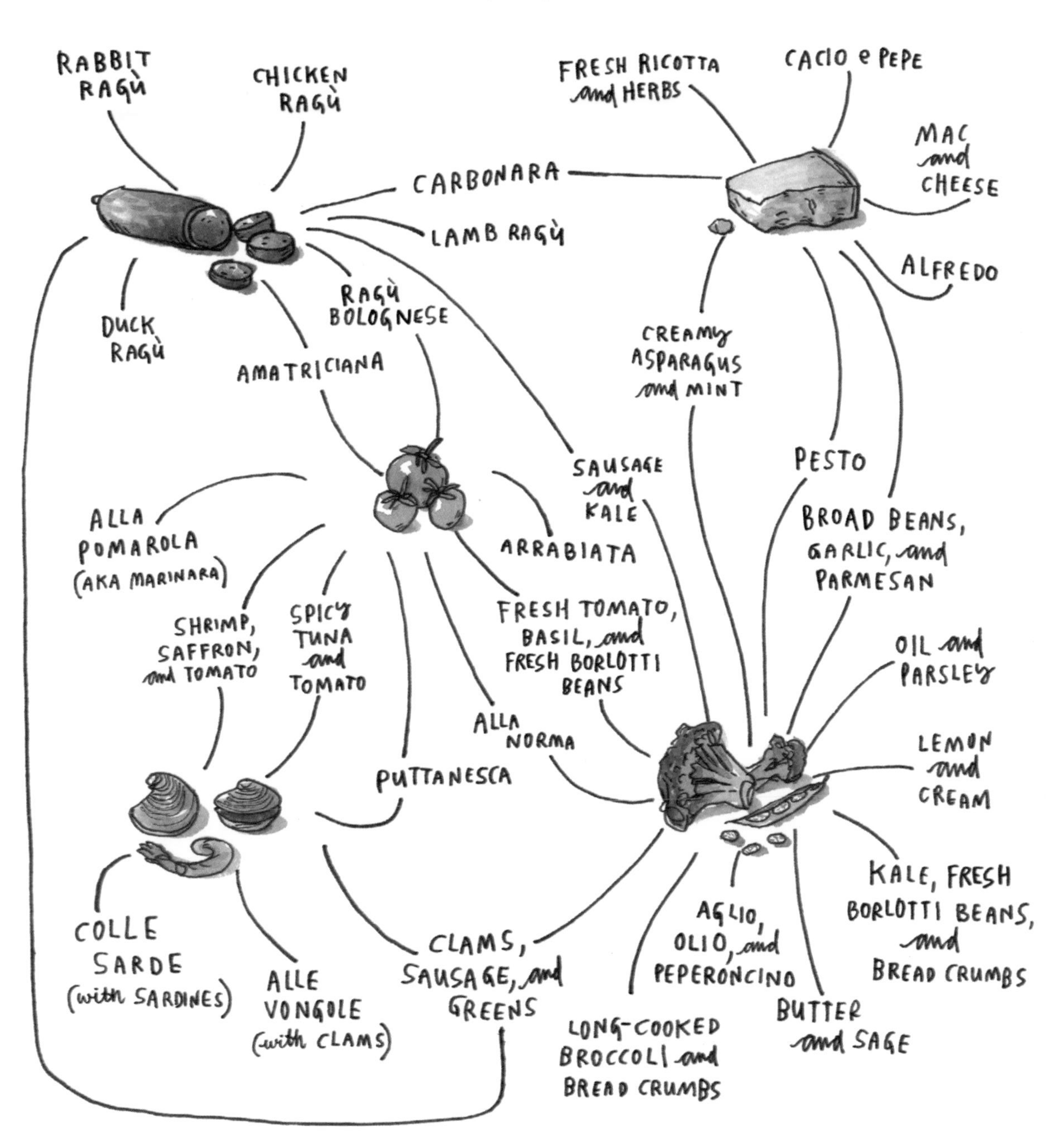

Cheese: *Pasta Cacio e Pepe*

Serves 4 to 6

Cacio e pepe is the Roman (and, dare I say, better) answer to macaroni and cheese. It's traditionally made with pecorino Romano, a salty sheep's milk cheese, and abundant ground black pepper. Take a few measures to prevent the sauce from clumping: first, use the finest grater you have to grate the cheese so it can melt readily. Next, encourage an emulsion in the pan by swirling together the pepper, oil, and starchy pasta water until it comes together. And finally, if your pan isn't roomy enough to toss the pasta, place everything in a big bowl and toss with tongs, adding a little pasta cooking water at a time, until the sauce comes together.

Salt
450g spaghetti, bucatini, or tonnarelli pasta
Extra-virgin olive oil
1 tablespoon very coarsely ground black pepper
115g pecorino Romano, very finely grated

Set a large pot of water over high heat and bring to a boil. Season generously with salt until it tastes like the summer sea. Add the pasta and cook, stirring occasionally, until al dente. Reserve 450ml of the cooking water as you drain the pasta.

In the meantime, heat a large pan over medium heat and add enough olive oil to just coat the bottom. When it shimmers, add the pepper and cook until fragrant, about 20 seconds. Add 175ml of the pasta cooking water into the pan and let it boil—this will encourage an emulsion to form.

Add the drained pasta to the hot pan, toss to coat the noodles, then sprinkle in all but a handful of the cheese. Use tongs to vigorously toss the pasta, adding more pasta water as needed to create a creamy sauce that clings to the pasta without clumping. Taste and adjust salt as needed. Garnish with remaining cheese and more coarsely ground pepper and serve immediately.

Variations

- For **Pasta Alfredo**, simmer 900ml double cream until reduced to 450ml, about 30 minutes. Set a large frying pan over medium heat and add 3 tablespoons of butter. Once the butter has melted, add 3 minced garlic cloves. Cook gently until the garlic starts to give off an aroma, about 20 seconds. Before the garlic begins to take on any colour, add the reduced cream and bring to a simmer. Cook 450g fettuccine until al dente and drain, reserving 225ml pasta water. Add hot noodles into pan and toss with 115g finely grated Parmesan, and abundant freshly ground black pepper. Add more pasta water as needed to achieve creamy consistency. Taste and adjust for salt. Serve immediately.

- To make **Creamy Asparagus and Mint Pasta**, set a large frying pan over medium heat and add enough olive oil to coat the pan. When the oil shimmers, add 1 finely diced onion (or two spring onions) and a generous pinch of salt. Reduce the heat to medium-low and cook, stirring occasionally, until tender, about 12 minutes. Add 3 minced garlic cloves. Cook gently until the garlic starts to give off an aroma, about 20 seconds. Before the garlic begins to take on any colour, add 450ml double cream and simmer until reduced by half, about 25 minutes.

  In the meantime, snap the woody ends off 675g of asparagus and discard. Cut the asparagus into 5mm slices on the bias and set aside. When the cream is almost done reducing, cook 450g of fettuccine or penne pasta until nearly al dente. A minute before the pasta is done cooking, add the sliced asparagus into the pasta water and cook. When pasta is al dente and asparagus is barely cooked, drain, reserving 225ml of the pasta cooking water. Add the noodles and asparagus into pan and toss with cream, 85g finely grated Parmesan, 10g chopped mint leaves, and freshly ground black pepper. Add a little pasta cooking water if needed to loosen the sauce and achieve a creamy consistency. Taste and adjust for salt. Serve immediately.

Tomato: *Pasta alla Pomarola*

Makes about 1.8 litres sauce; pasta recipe serves 4

Ever since that sauce-making competition at Chez Panisse, I've learned dozens and dozens of different methods for making basic tomato sauce, but the truth of the matter is that all of the variations—using onion or not, adding basil or oregano, puréeing or milling—offer little more than personal flourish. You can do it however you like; most important is to use the best-tasting tomatoes and olive oil you can find, and to get the salt right. Do that, and you've got yourself a wonderful blank slate, ready to use in pasta and pizza, of course, but also in dishes as diverse as *shakshuka*, braised Moroccan lamb, Mexican rice, or Provençal fish stew.

Extra-virgin olive oil
2 medium onions, sliced thinly
Salt
4 garlic cloves
1.8kg fresh, ripe tomatoes, stemmed, or four (400g) cans whole San Marzano or Roma tomatoes in their juice
16 fresh basil leaves or 1 tablespoon dried oregano
350g spaghetti, bucatini, penne, or rigatoni
Parmesan, pecorino Romano, or ricotta salata for serving

Set a large, heavy-bottomed, nonreactive pot over medium-high heat. When the pot is hot, add just enough olive oil to coat the bottom. When the oil shimmers, add the onions.

Season with salt and reduce the heat to medium, stirring from time to time to prevent burning. Cook until the onions are soft and translucent, or blond, about 15 minutes. A little browning is fine, but don't let the onions burn. If the onions begin to brown too quickly, turn down the heat and add a splash of water.

While the onions cook, slice the garlic, then quarter the tomatoes, if using fresh. If using canned, pour them into a large, deep bowl and crush with your hands. Swirl about 50ml of water in one can, then pour it into the second can and swirl, then add into the tomatoes. Set aside.

Once the onions are soft, push them to the outer edges of the pot and add a spoonful of oil into the centre. Add the garlic to the oil. Gently sizzle the garlic until it starts to give off an aroma, about 20 seconds, and before it begins to brown, add the tomatoes. If using fresh tomatoes, use a wooden spoon to smash them a bit and encourage the juice to come out. Bring the sauce to a boil, then reduce to a simmer. Season with salt and tear in basil leaves or add oregano, if using.

Cook over low heat, stirring the sauce often with a wooden spoon. Scrape the bottom of the pot to ensure that nothing sticks. If the sauce does start to stick and scorch, then do just the opposite. Don't stir! That'll just mix the burnt taste into the rest of the unaffected sauce. Instead, immediately transfer the sauce to a new pot without scraping the bottom, and leave the scorched pot to soak in the sink. Take extra care to prevent the new pot from burning again.

Put a large pot of water on to boil over high heat. Cover with a lid to prevent too much evaporation.

The sauce will be done when its flavour shifts from raw to cooked, about 25 minutes. Dipping your spoon into the sauce, you'll be reminded less of the garden or the farmer's market and more of a comforting bowl of pasta. If you're using canned tomatoes, the shift is subtler: wait for the moment when the tomatoes lose their tinny taste from the can, which can take closer to 40 minutes. When the tomatoes are cooked, bring the sauce to a rapid simmer and stir in 175ml of olive oil. Let it simmer together for a couple of minutes; the *pomarola* will transform into a rich sauce as it emulsifies. Remove it from the heat.

Purée the sauce with a stick blender, blender, or food mill, then taste and adjust seasoning. Keep covered in the refrigerator for up to a week, or freeze for up to 3 months. For storing *pomarola*, process jars filled with sauce in a water bath for 20 minutes, and use within a year.

To serve 4 people, season the pot of water with salt until it tastes like the summer sea. Add the pasta, give it a stir, and cook until it's just al dente. While the pasta cooks, bring 450ml of *pomarola* sauce to a simmer in a large sauté pan. Drain the pasta, reserving 225ml of pasta water. Add the pasta to the sauce and toss, thinning as needed with pasta water and olive oil. Taste and adjust salt as needed. Serve immediately, with Parmesan, pecorino Romano, or ricotta salata cheese.

Variations

- To add some creaminess to the pasta, add 125ml **crème fraîche** (page 113) to 450ml *pomarola* sauce and bring to a simmer just before adding cooked pasta, or add 115g of fresh ricotta cheese in large dollops into the pasta after tossing with tomato sauce.

- To make ***Pasta alla Puttanesca***, set a large frying pan over medium heat and add enough olive oil to coat the bottom of the pan. When the oil shimmers, add 2 cloves minced garlic and 10 minced anchovy fillets and cook gently until the garlic starts to give off an aroma, about 20 seconds. Before the garlic begins to take on any colour, add 450ml *pomarola* sauce, 55g rinsed and pitted and black olives (preferably oil-cured), and 1 tablespoon rinsed salt-packed capers. Season to taste with red pepper flakes and salt and simmer for 10 minutes, stirring occasionally. In the meantime, cook 350g of spaghetti until al dente and drain, reserving 225ml of the pasta cooking water. Toss the pasta with the simmering sauce and thin as needed with pasta water. Taste and adjust salt as needed. Garnish with chopped parsley and serve immediately.

- To make ***Pasta all'Amatriciana***, set a large frying pan over medium heat and add enough olive oil to coat the bottom of the pan. When the oil shimmers, add 1 finely diced onion and a generous pinch of salt. Stirring occasionally, cook until the onion is soft and brown, about 15 minutes. Slice 175g *guanciale* (cured pork jowl), pancetta, or bacon into matchsticks and add to the onion. Cook over medium heat until the meat is barely crisp, then add 2 cloves minced garlic and cook gently until the garlic starts to give off an aroma, about 20 seconds. Before the garlic begins to take on any colour, add 450ml *pomarola* sauce and season to taste with salt and crushed red pepper flakes. Simmer for about 10 minutes. In the meantime, cook 350g of spaghetti or bucatini until al dente and drain, reserving 225ml of the pasta cooking water. Toss the pasta with the simmering sauce and thin as needed with pasta water. Taste and adjust salt as needed. Garnish with abundant grated pecorino Romano or Parmesan and serve immediately.

Vegetable: Pasta with Broccoli and Bread Crumbs

Serves 4 to 6

This is the dish I cook when I've got no juice left at the end of the day. I pretend to choose to eat a bowl of noodles dressed with broccoli sauce because it's virtuous. In reality, I choose it out of pleasure; the depth of the browned onions, the umami lent by the extravagant dose of Parmesan, and the sweetness of the softened broccoli add up to an unexpected dose of luxury. While Tuscan peasants historically used bread crumbs as an economical alternative to cheese for garnishing pasta, I support the use of both, for crunch *and* flavour. And don't discard the broccoli stems! They're often the sweetest parts of the plant. Just remove their tough skins with a vegetable peeler, slice them, and cook them alongside the florets.

Salt
900g broccoli, florets and peeled stems
Extra-virgin olive oil
1 large onion, finely diced
1 to 2 teaspoons red pepper flakes
3 garlic cloves, minced
450g orecchiette, penne, linguine, bucatini, or spaghetti
40g **Sprinkling Crumbs** (page 237)
Freshly grated Parmesan, for serving

Set a large pot of water over high heat. When it comes to a boil, season it generously with salt until it tastes like the summer sea.

Cut the broccoli florets into 1cm pieces, and stems into 5mm slices.

Set a large cast-iron casserole or similar pot over medium-high heat. Once it's hot, add just enough olive oil to coat the bottom of the pot. When the oil shimmers, add the onions, a generous pinch of salt, and 1 teaspoon pepper flakes. As soon as the onions begin to brown, give them a stir and reduce the flame to medium. Stirring occasionally, cook the onions until they are tender and golden brown, about 15 minutes. Move the onions to the edge of the pot, clearing a spot in the centre. Add a tablespoon or so of olive oil, and then the garlic. Cook gently until the garlic starts to give off an aroma, about 20 seconds. Before the garlic begins to take on any colour, stir it into the onions and reduce the heat to low to keep the garlic from browning.

Drop the broccoli into the boiling water and cook until tender, about 4 to 5 minutes. Remove the pieces from the pot with a spider or slotted spoon and add them directly to the pan of onions. Cover the pot of water to prevent evaporation and leave it boiling on the stove for cooking the pasta. Increase the heat to medium, and continue to cook, stirring occasionally, until the broccoli begins to break down and combines with the onions and olive oil into a sauce, about 20 minutes. If the mixture appears dry, rather than saucy, add a spoonful or two of the cooking water to moisten it.

Add the pasta to the water and give it a stir. As it cooks, continue cooking and stirring the broccoli. The key is to make sure there's enough water in the pan so the broccoli, oil, and water emulsify and become saucy and sweet. Keep cooking, and stirring, and add water as needed.

When the pasta is al dente, drain it, reserving 450ml of the cooking water. Toss the hot noodles into the pan with the broccoli, and stir. Add another, final splash of olive oil and the salty pasta water to ensure the noodles are all well coated, moist, and seasoned. Taste and adjust the salt and pepper flakes as needed.

Serve immediately, topped with bread crumbs and generous amounts of snowy grated Parmesan.

Variations

- To add an umami power punch, add 6 minced anchovy fillets to the onions alongside the garlic.
- To make **Pasta with Beans and Broccoli**, add 150g cooked beans (any kind!) to the broccoli and onions while the pasta is cooking.
- To make **Pasta with Sausage and Broccoli**, crumble 225g mild or spicy Italian sausage in walnut-size pieces into the onions once they are soft, increase the heat to high, and brown.
- To add a little acid and sweetness, stir 225ml ***pomarola*** sauce (page 292) into the cooked onions before adding broccoli.
- To add a little briny kick, add 55g coarsely chopped, pitted black or green olives to the broccoli and onions.
- Substitute kale, cauliflower, *cima di rapa*, or Romanesco for the broccoli and cook as directed above. Or skip the blanching step and substitute long-cooked artichokes, fennel, or summer squash (page 264).

Meat: *Pasta al Ragù*

Makes about 1.5 litres sauce; pasta recipe serves 4

I learned to make meat sauce, or *ragù*, from Benedetta Vitali, the Florentine chef who took me into her kitchen, and her family, when I was twenty-two. We made a pot of *ragù* at her restaurant, Zibibbo, every few days. Like most dishes at the restaurant, it starts with *soffritto*, a foundation of finely chopped, deeply browned aromatic vegetables. From Benedetta I learned to dote on my *soffritto*, first when I finely minced it with the biggest knife I'd ever seen, and then when I browned it using an inordinate amount of olive oil. Nothing is as important to the flavour of a *ragù* as browning, so take your time with the *soffritto* and the meat. After that, it's just a matter of time before you can sit down to a bowl of pasta that tastes as magnificent as afternoon sunlight reflecting off a Tuscan hillside.

And if mincing all of those vegetables by hand is simply out of the question for you, then go ahead and use a food processor. Just pulse each vegetable separately in the machine, stopping to push everything down with a rubber spatula from time to time to make sure you get even pieces. Because the blade of the food processor will burst open more cells than a knife, vegetables chopped in a machine will turn out much more watery. Put the celery and onion in a fine sieve and press firmly to drain as much liquid out as you can, then combine with the carrots and proceed as if you'd done it all by hand. No one will be the wiser.

Extra-virgin olive oil
450g coarsely ground beef chuck
450g coarsely ground pork shoulder
2 medium onions, minced
1 large carrot, minced
2 large celery stalks, minced
350ml dry red wine
450ml **Chicken or Beef Stock** (page 271) or water
450ml whole milk
2 bay leaves
28cm by 8cm strip of lemon zest
28cm by 8cm strip of orange zest
1cm piece cinnamon stick
5 tablespoons tomato paste
Optional: Parmesan rind
Whole nutmeg
Salt
Freshly ground black pepper
450g tagliatelle, penne, or rigatoni
4 tablespoons butter
Freshly grated Parmesan, for serving

Set a large cast-iron casserole or similar pot over high heat and add enough olive oil to coat the bottom. Crumble the beef into the pot in walnut-size pieces. Cook, stirring and breaking up the meat with a slotted spoon until it sizzles and turns golden brown, 6 to 7 minutes. Do not season the meat yet—salt will draw out water and delay browning. Use the slotted spoon to transfer the meat to a large bowl, leaving the rendered fat in the pot. Brown the pork in the same way.

Add the onions, carrots, and celery—the *soffritto*—to the same pot and cook over medium-high heat. The amount of fat should be sufficient to nearly cover the *soffritto,* so add more olive oil as needed, at least another 175ml. Cook, stirring regularly, until the vegetables are tender and the *soffritto* is a deep brown, 25 to 30 minutes. (You can cook the *soffritto* in olive oil a day or two in advance, if you like, to break up the time-intensive steps in the recipe. *Soffritto* also freezes well for up to 2 months!)

Return the meat to the pot, increase the heat to high, and add the wine. Scrape the bottom of the pot with a wooden spoon to release any browned bits into the sauce. Add stock or water, milk, the bay leaves, zests, cinnamon, tomato paste, and Parmesan rind, if using. Add 10 zips of fresh nutmeg by grating it on a nutmeg grinder or other fine grater. Season with salt and freshly ground pepper to taste. Bring to a boil, then reduce to a simmer.

Let the sauce continue to simmer, stirring occasionally. Once the milk breaks down and the sauce starts to look appetising, between 30 to 40 minutes, start tasting the mixture and adjusting salt, acid, sweetness, richness, and body. If it needs some acid, add a secret splash of wine. If it seems bland, add tomato paste to bring it to life and lend sweetness. If it needs to be richer, add a little milk. If the *ragù* seems thin, add a generous splash of stock. It'll reduce as it simmers, leaving behind its gelatin to help thicken the sauce.

Simmer over the lowest possible heat, skimming off the fat from time to time and stirring often, until the meat is tender and the flavours have melded, about 1½ to 2 hours. When you are satisfied that the *ragù* is done, use a spoon or ladle to skim off the fat that has risen to the surface and remove the Parmesan rinds, bay leaves, citrus peels, and cinnamon. Taste and adjust the salt and pepper again.

For 4 servings, toss 450ml of hot *ragù* with 450g of pasta cooked al dente and 4 tablespoons of butter. Serve with ample freshly grated Parmesan.

Cover and store the remaining *ragù* in the refrigerator for up to 1 week, or in the freezer for up to 3 months. Return to a boil before using.

Variations

- For **Poultry *Ragù***, use 1.8kg whole legs. If using whole legs, simply shred the meat and skin once the sauce is cooked, discarding bones and gristle. This works equally well with duck, turkey, or chicken. Brown the meat in batches—avoid crowding the pan—and prepare *soffritto* as directed above. When the *soffritto* is brown, add 4 sliced garlic cloves into the pot and sizzle gently for about 20 seconds until they give off an aroma, but do not let them brown. Substitute white wine for red, add an herb sachet with 1 fresh rosemary sprig and 1 tablespoon juniper berries to the sauce, and add 10g dried porcini mushrooms. Increase stock to 675ml. Omit milk, nutmeg, orange zest, and cinnamon, but keep the bay leaves, lemon zest, tomato paste, salt, pepper, and Parmesan rind. Simmer until tender, about 90 minutes. Skim fat and remove aromatics as directed on the previous page. Taste and adjust the salt and pepper. Serve as directed.

- For **Sausage *Ragù***, replace the beef and pork with 900g of mild or spicy Italian sausage. Brown the meat and prepare *soffritto* as directed above. When the *soffritto* is brown, add 4 sliced garlic cloves into the pot and sizzle gently for about 20 seconds until they give off an aroma, but do not let them brown. Substitute white wine for red, and 400g of diced canned tomatoes and their juice for the tomato paste. Omit the milk, nutmeg, orange zest, and cinnamon, but keep the stock, bay leaves, lemon zest, salt, pepper, and Parmesan rind. Add 1 tablespoon dried oregano and 1 teaspoon red pepper flakes. Simmer until tender, about 1 hour. Skim fat and remove aromatics as directed above. Taste and adjust the salt and pepper. Serve as directed on the previous page.

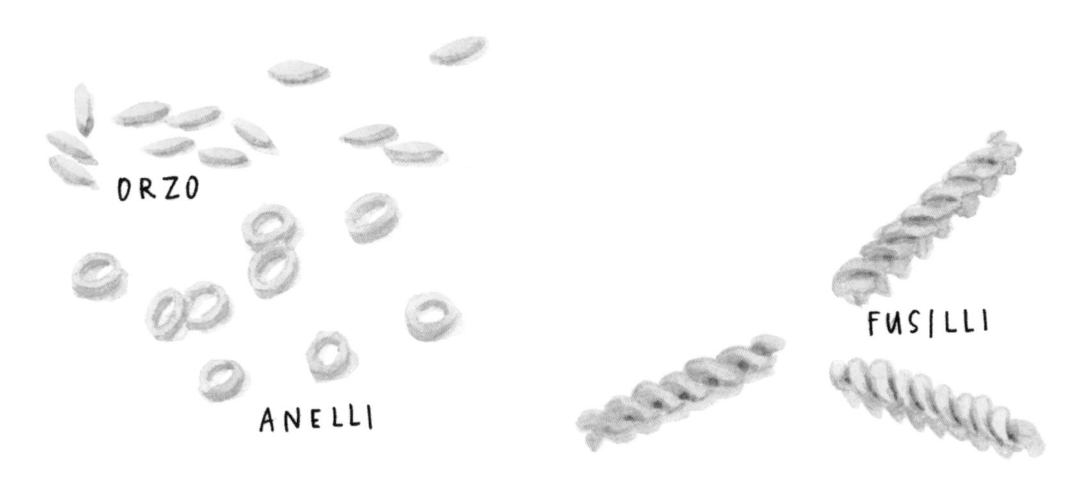

(Shell)fish: *Pasta alle Vongole*
Pasta with Clams

Serves 4 to 6

I didn't taste a clam or mussel until I was twenty. Even now, I'll only rarely choose to eat a bowl of shellfish when given another option. Clam pasta, though? That's another story. *Pasta alle Vongole* is one of those mystical dishes where an alchemy so delicious occurs that a list of ingredients does little to account for its depth of flavour. Pasta with clams tastes like the perfect day of surfing—salty and rich, fresh and bright, entirely satisfying. For an illustrated step-by-step of this recipe, turn back to page 120.

I like to use two kinds of clams in this pasta: larger littlenecks, which have a deeper clammy flavour, and smaller Manilas or cherrystones, which are really fun to pluck out of the shell at the table. If you can't find both kinds, don't sweat it, just use 1.8kg of whichever variety you can find, and treat them all like littlenecks.

Salt
Extra-virgin olive oil
1 medium onion, finely diced, root ends saved
2 or 3 parsley sprigs, plus 10g finely chopped leaves
900g littleneck clams, scrubbed well
225ml dry white wine
2 garlic cloves, minced
About 1 teaspoon red pepper flakes
450g linguine or spaghetti
900g Manila or cherrystone clams, scrubbed well
Juice of 1 lemon
4 tablespoons butter
25g Parmesan, finely grated

Bring a large pot of generously salted water to a boil.

Heat a large frying pan over medium-high heat and add a tablespoon of oil. Add the root ends of the onion, the parsley sprigs, and as many littlenecks as will fit in one layer, then pour in 175ml wine.

Crank the heat up to high, cover the pan, and let clams steam until they open, 3 to 4 minutes. Remove the cover and use tongs to transfer clams to a bowl as they open.

If there are any stubborn clams, tap them gently with your tongs to encourage them to open. Discard any clams that don't open after 6 minutes of cooking. Add the remaining littlenecks to the pan and cook the same way with the remaining wine.

Strain the cooking liquid through a fine-mesh strainer and set aside. Once the clams are cool enough to handle, pluck them from their shells and chop coarsely. Set aside in a small bowl with just enough cooking liquid to cover. Discard the shells.

Rinse the pan, then set over medium heat. Add just enough oil to coat the bottom of the pan, and add the diced onion and a pinch of salt. Cook until tender, stirring occasionally, about 12 minutes. It's fine if the onion picks up colour, but don't let it burn; add a splash of water if you need to.

Meanwhile, cook the pasta until not quite al dente.

Add the garlic and ½ teaspoon pepper flakes to the onion and sizzle gently. Before the garlic has a chance to brown, add the Manila or cherrystone clams and crank up the heat to high. Add a healthy splash of the clam cooking liquid or wine and cover the pan. As soon as the clams open, add the chopped littlenecks. Cook together for a couple of minutes, then taste and adjust acid with lemon juice or more white wine as needed.

Drain the pasta, reserving 225ml of cooking liquid, and immediately add to the pan with the clams. Let the noodles continue cooking until al dente in the clam liquid so that they can absorb all the briny goodness.

Taste and adjust for salt, spiciness, and acid. Pasta should be quite juicy—if it isn't, add more spoonfuls of clam cooking liquid, wine, or pasta water. Add the butter and cheese and allow them to melt, then toss to coat the pasta. Sprinkle with the chopped parsley leaves and spoon into bowls.

Serve immediately with crusty bread for sopping up the sauce.

Variations

- To make **Pasta with Mussels**, substitute 1.8kg scrubbed, bearded mussels for the clams, but steam and shell them all like the littlenecks on the previous page. Add a generous pinch of saffron threads to the diced onion along with the salt. Omit the Parmesan, but otherwise cook and serve as directed above.

- To make **Pasta with Clams and Sausage**, crumble 225g spicy or mild Italian sausage into the cooked onions in walnut-size pieces, increase the heat to high, and brown. Add the Manila clams and continue cooking as directed above. Serve as directed above.

- To make **White Clam Sauce**, add 225ml cream to the pan of onions after gently sizzling the garlic for about 20 seconds. Simmer for 10 minutes before adding the clams. Continue cooking as directed on the previous page.
- To make **Red Clam Sauce**, add 400g chopped fresh or canned tomatoes to the pan of onions after gently sizzling the garlic. Simmer for 10 minutes before adding clams. Continue as in the recipe on the previous page.
- To work some greens into the dish, add 200g of chopped, balled-up **Blanched Greens** (page 258)—kale and *cima di rapa* work especially well—to the cooked onion before adding the garlic.
- For a textural contrast, top any of the above pasta dishes with **Sprinkling Crumbs** (page 237) before serving.

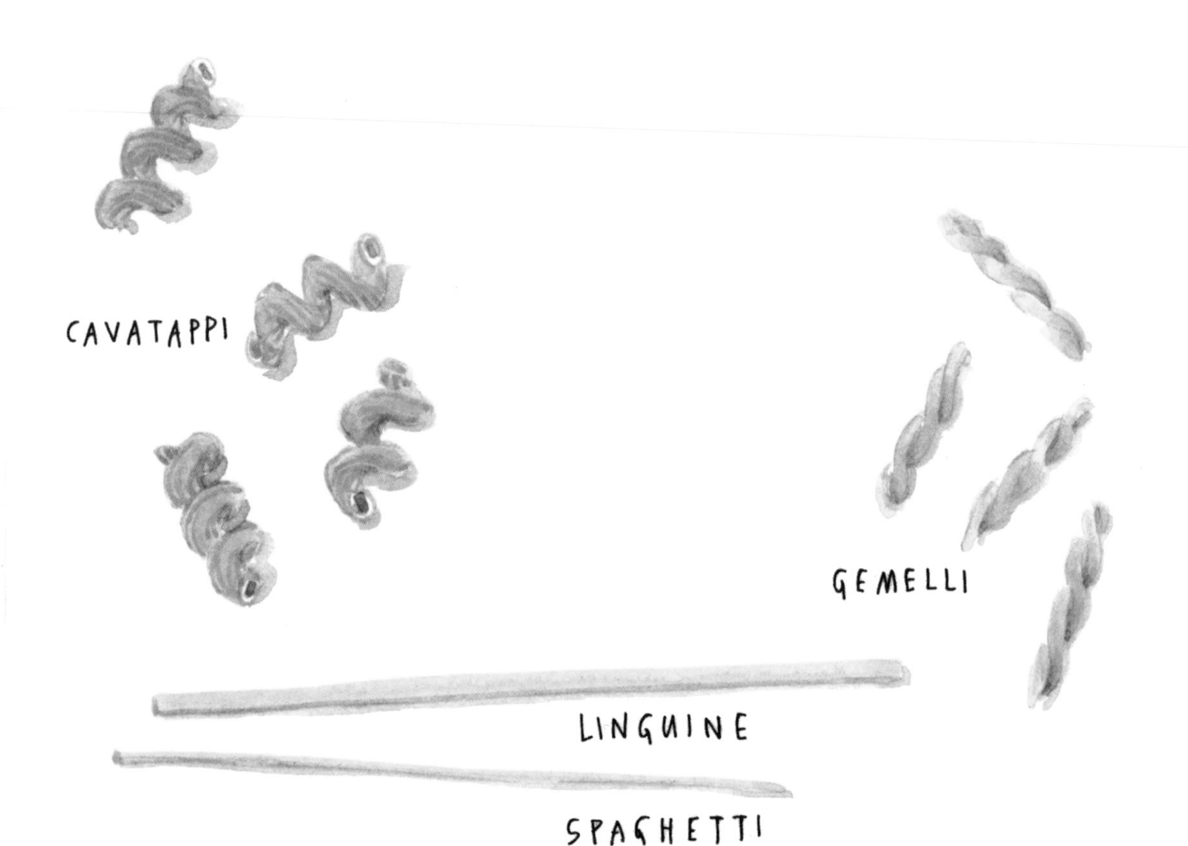

EGGS

Armed with an egg and some courage, you can perform any one of a hundred kitchen miracles. Add oil infused with fearlessness, to an egg yolk, drop by drop, and you'll get **Basic Mayonnaise** (page 375) and all the sauces and dips—from **Aïoli** to **Tartar**—it makes possible. Use the classic ratio of 1 egg to 1 yolk and 225ml of cream as the base for any sweet or savoury ***pots de crème*** you can dream up. Season the cream with freshly ground black pepper, herbs, and Parmesan for a classic savoury custard. Steep lavender in gently warmed cream, then sweeten with honey, and strain before mixing with eggs, for a simple, fragrant dessert. Bake in ramekins set in a water bath (see page 161) at 160°C until they're just barely set.

Whip leftover whites with sugar and top with cream and fruit to make marshmallowy **pavlova** (page 421), or, when you're feeling extra-courageous, try your hand at an angel food cake.

Commit another classic ratio to memory, and you can make **fresh egg pasta** anytime you like. Slowly mix 1 egg and 1 yolk into 135g flour, and knead until it all comes together, before resting, rolling, and cutting into noodles to toss with ***Ragù*** (page 297).

To **fry the perfect egg**, heat a small pan over high heat, further than you normally might, add enough fat to coat the pan, and crack in the egg. Add a small amount of butter and, tipping the pan with one hand, spoon the melting butter onto the egg white with the other hand. This bastes the egg so the top and the bottom of the white cook at the same rate, and the yolk just barely sets.

Slip an uncracked egg into boiling water, and pull it out 9 minutes later. Drop it into a bowl of ice water, and peel

EGG WHITES WHIPPED with SUGAR

it once it's cooled to find **The Perfect Boiled Egg**, replete with a creamy, glossy yolk. The freshest eggs, when boiled, can be difficult to peel, so roll them on the worktop once they're cooked, and leave them in the bowl of ice, where water will make its way under the papery layer between the shell and the white and uncomplicate the task of peeling. To make an egg choppable, and suitable for egg salad, leave it in boiling water for 10 minutes. For a slightly glossier yolk, remove after 8 minutes.

Add a **poached egg** to a bowl of rice, noodles, or broth with greens to transform it into dinner. Fill a large saucepan with at least 5cm of water, and add a light splash of white wine vinegar, which will gently encourage the egg white to coagulate. Over medium heat, bring to a brisk simmer. Gently crack the egg into a coffee cup or ramekin, and then carefully slip the egg into the pan, right where the bubbles are originating. If the temperature of the pan drops and bubbles disappear, turn up the heat, but be careful not to let the water boil because it may break off chunks of white or crack open a yolk. Repeat with 1 egg for each serving, and poach until just set, about 3 minutes. Remove cooked eggs from the water with a slotted spoon, dab on a clean kitchen towel, and slide into bowls.

If poached eggs aren't your miracle of choice, then whisk one together with a little bit of Parmesan and drizzle into simmering stock for a comforting bowl of ***Stracciatella*** (page 273).

For creamy, custardy **scrambled eggs**, look back to page 147 for advice from Alice B. Toklas. Whatever you do, cook the eggs over the gentlest heat and turn off the flame 30 seconds before you think you're done—let your courage carry you, and the eggs, to the finish line.

And of course, a little courage won't hurt when it comes to flipping ***Kuku Sabzi*** (page 306), the Persian answer to frittata.

Boiling an Egg

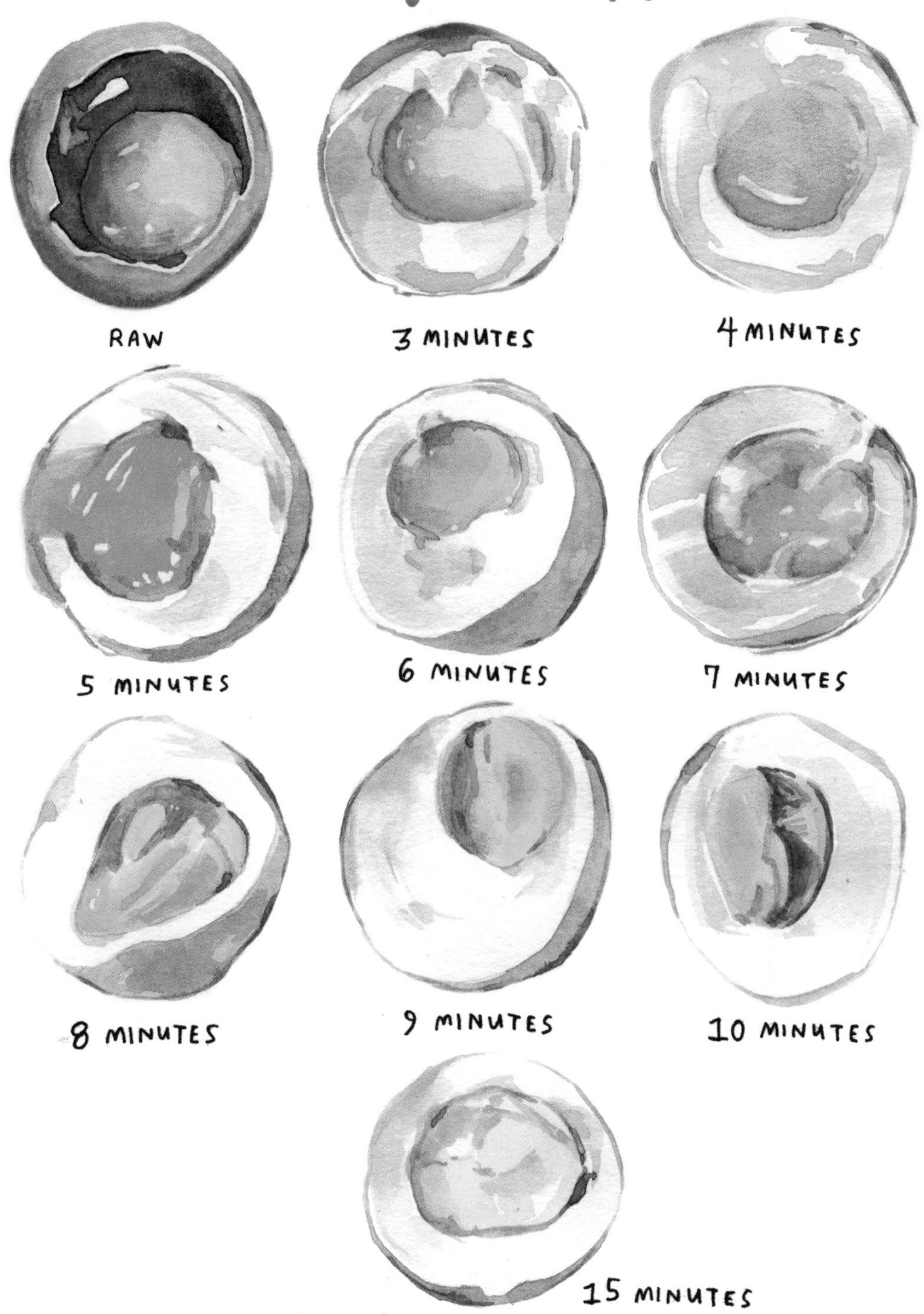

Kuku Sabzi
Persian Herb and Greens Frittata

Serves 6 to 8

The perfect light lunch or appetiser, *kuku sabzi* differs from a typical frittata in two important ways. To begin with, the ratio of greens to eggs is heavily skewed in favour of greens—in fact, I use just enough eggs to bind the greens together. And *kuku* isn't *kuku* without a deeply browned crust to provide a textural and flavour contrast to its bright, custardy centre. Eat *kuku* warm, at room temperature, or cold, with feta cheese, yoghurt, or pickles to offer the balance of acidity.

Washing, chopping, and cooking down all the greens for a *kuku* can be overwhelming if you're not used to staring down a mountain of produce, so feel free to prep the greens a day in advance.

2 bunches green chard, washed
1 large leek
Extra-virgin olive oil
Salt
6 tablespoons unsalted butter
150g finely chopped coriander leaves and tender stems
55g finely chopped dill leaves and tender stems
8 to 9 large eggs

Preheat the oven to 180°C if you do not want to flip your *kuku* partway through cooking. (See pages 307 and 308 for more on flipping.)

Strip the chard leaves. Gripping at the base of each stem with one hand, pinch the stem with the other hand and pull upwards to strip the leaf. Repeat with the remaining chard, reserving the stems.

Remove the root and top 2.5cm of the leek, then quarter it lengthwise. Cut each quarter into 5mm slices, place in a large bowl, and wash vigorously to remove dirt. Drain as much water as possible. Thinly slice the chard stems, discarding any tough bits at the base. Add to the washed leek and set aside.

Gently heat a 25 or 30cm cast iron or nonstick frying pan over medium heat and add enough olive oil to coat the bottom of the pan. Add the chard leaves and season with a generous pinch of salt. Cook, stirring occasionally, until the leaves are wilted, 4 to 5 minutes. Remove the chard from the pan, set aside, and allow to cool.

Return the pan to the stove and heat over a medium flame. Add 3 tablespoons of butter. When the butter begins to foam, add the sliced leeks and chard stems, along with a pinch of salt. Cook until tender and translucent, 15 to 20 minutes. Stir from time to time, and if needed, add a splash of water, reduce the flame, or cover with a lid or a piece of parchment paper to entrap steam and keep colour from developing.

In the meantime, squeeze the cooked chard leaves dry, discard the liquid, then chop them coarsely. Combine in a large bowl with the coriander and dill. When the leeks and chard stems are cooked, add them to the greens. Let the mixture cool a bit, then use your hands to mix everything up evenly. Taste and season generously with salt, knowing you're about to add a bunch of eggs to the mixture.

Add the eggs, one at a time, until the mixture is just barely bound with egg—you might not need to use all 9 eggs, depending on how wet your greens were and how large your eggs are, but it should seem like a ridiculous amount of greens! I usually taste and adjust the mixture for salt at this point, but if you don't want to taste raw egg, you can cook up a little test piece of *kuku* and adjust the salt if needed.

Wipe out and reheat your pan over medium-high heat—this is an important step to prevent the *kuku* from sticking—and add 3 tablespoons butter and 2 tablespoons olive oil, then stir to combine. When the butter begins to foam, carefully pack the *kuku* mixture into the pan.

To help the *kuku* cook evenly, in the first few minutes of cooking, use a rubber spatula to gently pull the edges of the mixture into the centre as they set. After about 2 minutes of this, reduce the heat to medium and let the *kuku* continue to cook without touching it. You'll know the pan is hot enough as long as the oil is gently bubbling up the sides of the *kuku*.

Because this *kuku* is so thick, it'll take a while for the centre to set. The key here is not to let the crust burn before the centre sets. Peek at the crust by lifting the *kuku* with a rubber spatula, and if it's getting too dark too soon, reduce the heat. Rotate the pan a quarter turn every 3 or 4 minutes to ensure even browning.

After about 10 minutes, when the mixture is set to the point of no longer running and the bottom is golden brown, gather all of your courage and prepare to flip the *kuku*. First, tip out as much of the cooking fat as you can into a bowl to prevent burning yourself, then flip the *kuku* onto a pizza pan or the back of a baking sheet, or into another large frying pan. Add 2 tablespoons olive oil into the hot pan and slide the *kuku* back in to cook the second side. Cook for another 10 minutes, rotating the pan every 3 or 4 minutes.

If something goes awry when you try to flip, don't freak out! It's only lunch. Just do your best to flip the *kuku*, add a little more oil into the pan, and get it back into the pan in one piece.

If you prefer not to flip, then slip the whole pan into the oven and bake until the centre is fully set, about 10 to 12 minutes. I like to cook it until it is *just* set. Check for doneness using a toothpick, or just shake the pan back and forth, looking for a slight jiggle at the top of the *kuku*. When it's done, carefully flip it out of the pan onto a plate. Blot away the excess oil. Eat warm, at room temperature, or cold. *Kuku* makes for amazing leftovers!

Variations

- If you want to use up what's in your fridge, substitute 675g of any tender cooking greens for the chard. Wild nettles and spinach are both delicious, though you could also use escarole, lettuce, rocket, beetroot greens, or any other green you can think of.
- For a hint of garlic, add 2 stalks thinly sliced green garlic to the leeks.
- For an authentic Persian touch, add 115g lightly toasted walnuts, coarsely chopped, or 30g barberries to the mixture before cooking.

- To make a *frittata*, as opposed to *kuku*, reverse the ratio of filling to eggs. While *kuku* is about packing in as much green as possible, a frittata is about its delightful eggy texture. Use 12 to 14 eggs and add 125ml milk, cream, sour cream, or **crème fraîche** (page 113) to the egg base for a custardy texture. Stick to a six-ingredient limit: eggs, something sweet, something creamy or rich, something green, salt, and oil. Classic quiche or pizza topping combos are often good starting points, including mushroom and sausage, ham and cheese, spinach and ricotta. Or, as with all of your cooking, find frittata inspiration in produce at the peak of its season:

Spring

Asparagus, spring onion, and mint
Artichoke Confit (page 172) and chives

Summer

Cherry tomato, crumbled feta, and basil
Roasted peppers, *cima di rapa*, and crumbled, cooked sausage

Autumn

Wilted chard, dollops of fresh ricotta
Brussels sprouts and cubes of cooked bacon

Winter

Roasted potato, caramelised onion, and Parmesan
Roasted radicchio, fontina cheese, and parsley

FISH

Slow-Roasted Salmon

Serves 6

This is my favourite way to cook salmon, mostly because the gentle heat makes it almost impossible to overcook the fish. While the method works particularly well with salmon because of its high fat content, you can absolutely try it with other types of fish, including steelhead trout and Alaskan halibut. And in the summer, turn your grill into a slow-cooking oven by placing the baking sheet on the grill grates over **indirect heat** and closing the lid. I have a feeling this'll become your favourite way to cook salmon too.

1 generous handful of fine herbs, such as parsley, coriander, dill, or fennel fronds or 3 fig leaves
900g salmon fillet, skin removed
Salt
Extra-virgin olive oil

Preheat the oven to 110°C. Make a bed of herbs, or if using fig leaves, lay them out in the centre of a baking sheet. Set aside.

Each side of salmon has a line of thin pin bones that reaches about two-thirds of the way down the fillet. Using tweezers or needle-nosed pliers, lay the fillet skin-side down on a cutting board. Run your fingers lightly over the fish from head to tail to locate the bones, and coax their ends out of the flesh. Starting at the head end, pull out the bones one by one, tugging at them with your tweezers at the same angle at which they are lodged in the fish. Once you get the bone out, dip your tweezers in a glass of cold water to release the bone. When you've finished, run your fingers over the fish once more to make sure you've got all the bones. That's it!

Season both sides of the fish with salt and tuck it into the bed of herbs. Drizzle a tablespoon of olive oil onto the fish and rub it in evenly with your hands. Slide the pan into the oven.

Roast for 40 to 50 minutes, until the fish begins to flake in the thickest part of the fillet when you poke it with a knife or your finger. Because this method is so gentle on its proteins, the fish will appear translucent even when it's cooked.

Once the salmon is cooked, break it into large, rustic pieces and spoon **Herb Salsa** of any kind on top in generous amounts. **Kumquat Salsa** (page 363) and **Meyer Lemon Salsa** (page 366) work particularly well here. Serve alongside white beans or potatoes and **Shaved Fennel and Radishes** (page 228).

Variations

- To make **Soy-Glazed Salmon**, reduce 225ml soy sauce, 2 tablespoons toasted sesame seeds, 100g brown sugar, and a pinch of cayenne pepper in a saucepan over high heat until it's the consistency of maple syrup. Add 1 clove pounded or finely grated garlic and 1 tablespoon finely grated fresh ginger. Skip the bed of herbs, line the baking sheet with parchment paper, and brush the glaze onto a 900g fillet of salmon immediately before cooking, basting every 15 minutes or so as it roasts.

- For a bright **Citrus Salmon**, season the fish with salt, then rub the surface with 1 tablespoon finely grated citrus zest mixed with 2 tablespoons olive oil. Skip the bed of herbs. Instead, line a baking sheet with parchment paper and arrange the fish over a bed of thinly sliced blood oranges or Meyer lemons and roast as directed above. Serve in torn chunks atop an **avocado and citrus salad** (page 217).

- For **Indian-Spiced Salmon**, toast 2 teaspoons cumin seeds, 2 teaspoons coriander seeds, 2 teaspoons fennel seeds, and 3 cloves in a dry frying pan over medium-high heat and then grind finely with a mortar and pestle or in a spice grinder. Transfer to a small bowl. Add ½ teaspoon cayenne pepper, 1 tablespoon turmeric, and a generous pinch of salt to the spice mixture, then add 2 tablespoons melted ghee or neutral-tasting oil and combine. Season the fish with salt, then rub the spice paste on both sides of the fish, and refrigerate covered, for 1 to 2 hours. Bring to room temperature, skip the bed of herbs, and bake as directed above.

Beer-Battered Fish

Serves 4 to 6

I clearly remember the first time I battered and fried fish; the way the batter puffed up when it hit the hot oil seemed like a miracle. Considering how frying had always intimidated me, the way the fish turned out—crisp and delicious—was an even bigger miracle. By the time I had frying *down*, about a decade into my frying career, I came across British chef Heston Blumenthal's recipe for fried fish. By replacing some of the water in the batter with vodka, which is only about 60 percent water, he reduced the amount of water available to create gluten. As a result, the crust is unbelievably tender. By adding fizzy beer and baking powder to the batter, and keeping everything ice-cold, he tipped the scales even further in favour of lightness. As a result, the crust is *even more* unbelievably tender. Some might call it, you know, a miracle.

325g plain flour
1 teaspoon baking powder
½ teaspoon ground cayenne pepper
Salt
675g flaky white fish, such as halibut or sole, boned and trimmed
1.3 litres grapeseed or peanut oil for frying
275ml vodka, ice-cold
About 350ml lager beer, ice-cold
Optional: For extra crispness, substitute rice flour for half of the plain flour

In a medium bowl, mix together the flour, baking powder, cayenne pepper, and a generous pinch of salt. Place in the freezer.

Cut the fish into 8 equal pieces on the diagonal, each about 2.5 by 8cm long. Season generously with salt. Keep on ice, or in the refrigerator, until ready to cook.

Place a wide, deep pan over medium heat. Add enough oil to reach a depth of 4cm, and heat to 185°C.

When the oil is hot, make the batter: add the vodka to the bowl of flour while slowly stirring with the fingertips of one hand. Then, gradually add enough beer to thin out the batter to about the same consistency as pancake batter—it should easily drip from your fingertips. Don't overmix—the lumps will turn into a light, crisp crust when fried.

Place half the fish in the bowl of batter. One at a time, completely coat the pieces of fish and then carefully lower them into the hot oil. Do not overpack the pot—at no time should there be more than a single layer of fish in the oil. As the pieces fry, use tongs to gently make sure they don't stick together. After about 2 minutes, when the undersides are golden brown, flip the pieces and cook the second side. When the second side is golden, use tongs or a slotted spoon to remove the fish from the oil. Season with salt and drain on a baking sheet lined with paper towels.

Fry any remaining fish in the same way, letting the oil temperature return to 185°C between batches.

Serve immediately with lemon wedges and **Tartar Sauce** (page 378).

Variations

- To make a ***Fritto Misto***, use this batter to coat and fry a mixture of fish and shellfish, such as prawns halved lengthwise, sliced squid, and soft-shell crab, along with colourful vegetables such as asparagus spears, green beans, bite-size pieces of broccoli or cauliflower, wedges of spring onion, squash blossoms, and raw kale leaves. Serve with lemon wedges and **Aïoli** (page 376).

- For a crisp, **Gluten-Free Batter**, use 200g rice flour, 3 tablespoons potato starch, 3 tablespoons cornflour, 1 teaspoon baking powder, ¼ teaspoon cayenne pepper, a pinch of salt, 225ml vodka, 225ml chilled soda water. Follow the method as directed on the previous page.

Tuna Confit

Serves 4 to 6

This tuna will be a revelation for anyone who has spent her entire life eating tuna from a can, as I had when I first tasted it. Poached gently in olive oil, the tuna remains moist for days. Eat it at room temperature with a salad of white beans, parsley, and lemon, as the Italians do in their classic dish *tonno e fagioli*. Or wait for the peak of summer and make a juicy *pan bagnat*, the superlative Provençal tuna sandwich. Use the crustiest bread you can find and slather one side with **Aïoli** (page 376), then layer torn pieces of tuna confit, a sliced **Ten-Minute Egg** (page 304), ripe tomatoes and cucumbers, basil leaves, capers, and olives. Dip the top piece of bread in the tuna oil, and press the sandwich together. If eating this sandwich sounds like a messy endeavour, imagine making 700 of them for the summer party we threw every year at Eccolo!

- 675g fresh albacore or yellowfin tuna, cut into 4cm thick pieces
- Salt
- 575ml olive oil
- 4 garlic cloves, peeled
- 1 dried red pepper
- 2 bay leaves
- 2.5cm strips of lemon zest
- 1 teaspoon black peppercorns

Season the tuna with salt about 30 minutes before you plan to cook it.

To confit the tuna, place the oil, garlic, red pepper, bay leaves, lemon zest, and peppercorns in a cast iron casserole or deep, heavy sauté pan. Heat to about 82°C—the oil should be warm to the touch, but not hot. Cook for about 15 minutes to infuse the oil with the aromatics and also to pasteurise everything to allow for a long shelf life.

Slip the tuna into the warm oil in a single layer. The tuna must be covered by oil, so add more if needed. You can also cook the fish in batches if necessary. Return the oil to about 65°C, or just until you see the fish emitting a bubble or two every few seconds. The precise temperature of the oil isn't so important, and it will fluctuate as you turn the flame up and down and add and remove the fish. The important thing is to cook the fish slowly, so err on the low side if needed. After about 9 minutes, remove a piece from the oil and check for doneness. The fish should be barely medium-rare—still quite pink in the centre—as heat will continue to carry over. If it's too rare, return the fish to the oil and cook for another minute.

Pull the cooked fish from the oil and allow to cool on a plate in a single layer, then place in a glass container and strain the cooled oil back over the fish. Serve at room temperature or chilled. The fish will keep in the fridge, covered in oil, for about 2 weeks.

THIRTEEN WAYS OF LOOKING AT A CHICKEN

"I DO NOT KNOW WHICH *to* PREFER..."

~WALLACE STEVENS

Crispiest Spatchcocked Chicken

Serves 4

Two tricks make this simple recipe the most extraordinary way I know to cook a whole chicken. First, spatchcocking. **Spatchcocking** is the term for removing a bird's backbone and then splaying it so it lies flat, but I like to think of it as a way to increase surface area for browning while decreasing cooking time. (It's also my favourite way to cook Thanksgiving turkey, cutting down cooking time by nearly half!)

The second trick is one I stumbled on by mistake at Eccolo, when one of my cooks seasoned a few chickens and left them uncovered in the walk-in overnight. When I came in the next day, I was annoyed by his negligence. The constantly circulating air of the walk-in—like that of any refrigerator—had dried out the chicken skin, and the birds looked scarily fossilized. But I had no choice, so I cooked them anyway. The dried-out skin cooked up golden and glassy. It was the crispiest roast chicken skin I'd ever seen, even after the bird had rested.

If you don't have a chance to season the chicken and let its skin dry out overnight, season it as early as possible, then pat it dry with a paper towel before you begin to cook it. It'll help achieve a similar effect.

1.8kg whole chicken

Salt

Extra-virgin olive oil

The day before you plan to cook the chicken, spatchcock it (or ask your butcher to help!). Use heavy-duty kitchen shears to snip down along both sides of the spine (the underside of the bird) and remove it. You can start from the tail or neck end, whichever you prefer. Once you've removed the spine, reserve it for stock. Remove the wingtips and reserve them for stock, too.

Lay the chicken on the cutting board, breast side up. Push down on the breastbone until you hear the cartilage pop and the bird lies flat. Generously season the bird with salt on both sides. Place it breast side up into a shallow roasting dish and refrigerate, uncovered, overnight.

Pull the bird out of the fridge an hour before you plan to cook it. Preheat the oven to 220°C, with a rack positioned in the upper third of the oven.

Heat a 25 or 30cm cast iron pan or other ovenproof frying pan over medium-high heat. Add just enough olive oil to coat the bottom of the pan. As soon as the oil shimmers, place the chicken in the pan, breast side down, and brown for 6 to 8 minutes, until golden. It's fine if the bird doesn't lie completely flat as long as the breast is in contact with the pan. Flip the bird over (again, it's fine if it doesn't lie entirely flat) and slide the entire cast iron pan into the oven on the prepared rack. Push the pan all the way to the very back of the oven, with the handle of the pan facing left.

After about 20 minutes, carefully use an oven mitt to rotate the pan 180 degrees so the handle faces right and return it to the very back of the top rack.

Cook until the chicken is brown all over and the juices run clear when you cut between the leg and the thigh, about 45 minutes.

Let rest 10 minutes before carving. Serve warm or at room temperature.

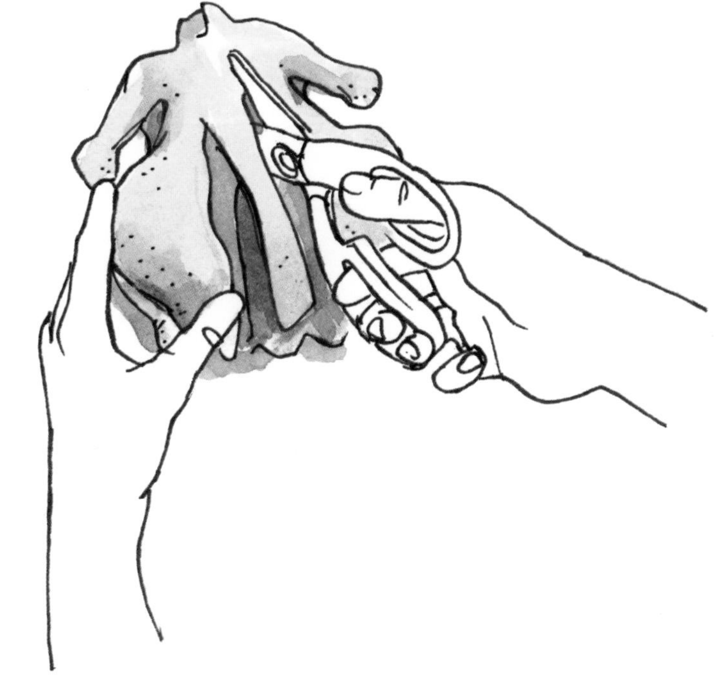

HOW to BREAK DOWN A WHOLE DARN CHICKEN

in A FEW SIMPLE STEPS

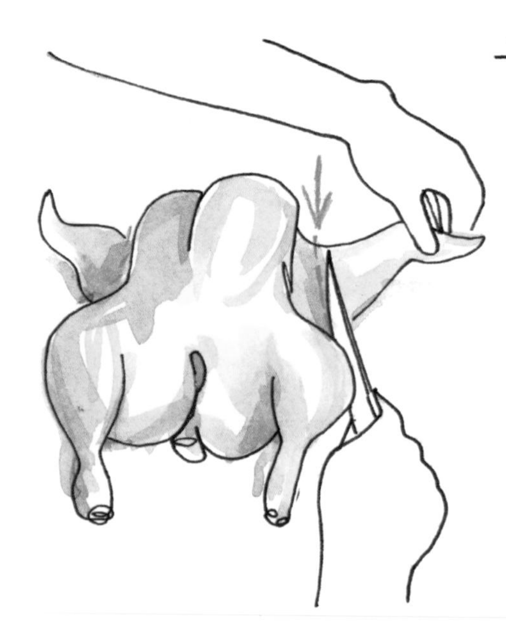

1. FIRST, CUT OFF BOTH WINGS and SET THEM ASIDE for STOCK.

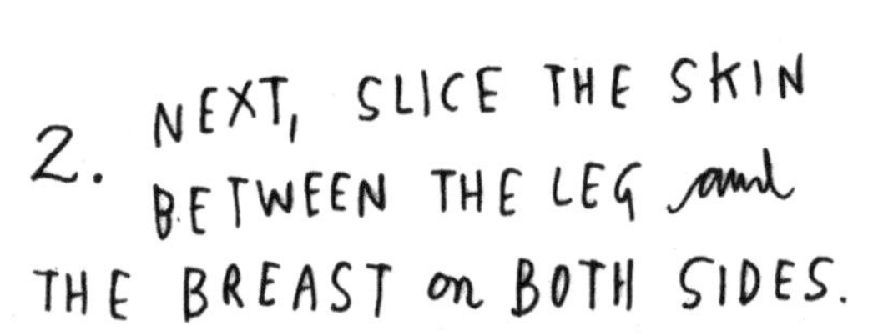

2. NEXT, SLICE THE SKIN BETWEEN THE LEG and THE BREAST on BOTH SIDES.

3. THEN, STICK YOUR THUMBS in THE CUTS. GRAB THE BACK of THE LEGS and TURN YOUR HANDS OUTWARD, DISLOCATING THE LEGS from THE BODY.

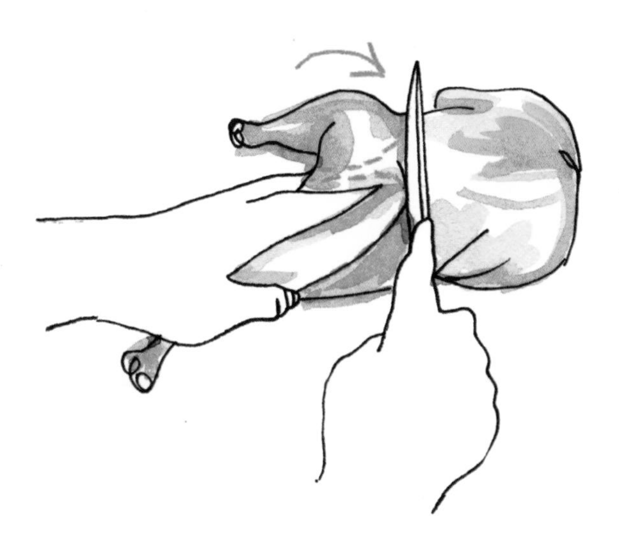

4. NEXT, FLIP THE BIRD OVER and CUT THROUGH THE JOINT to REMOVE THE RIGHT LEG. REPEAT ON OTHER SIDE.

5. TURN CHICKEN OVER AGAIN and SLICE ALONG EITHER SIDE of THE BREASTBONE.

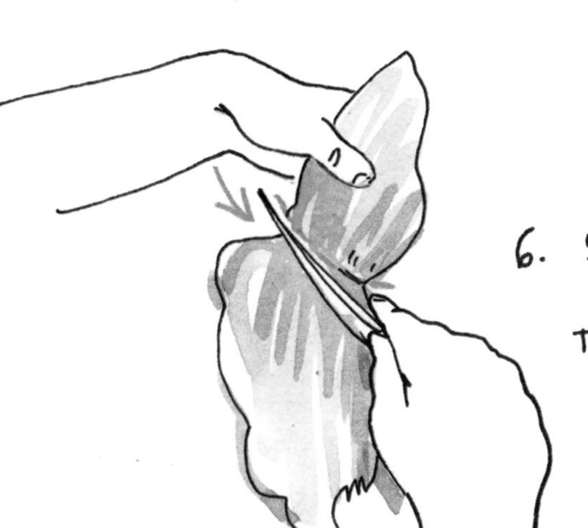

6. SLIDE your KNIFE DOWN and ALONG THE RIB CAGE, THEN CUT THROUGH THE WING JOINT to REMOVE EACH BREAST.

7. THIS LEAVES you with TWO BREASTS and TWO LEGS. CUT EACH of THOSE in HALF, ALONG THE LINES to THE RIGHT.

1 CHICKEN = 8 PIECES

Spicy Fried Chicken

serves 4 to 6

Gus's in Memphis makes the best fried chicken I've ever tasted. Once, on my way through town, I had lunch there alongside the after-church crowd. Spicy, crisp, and perfectly seasoned, this fried chicken was a revelation. Though I begged the cooks for any hints about how they got the crust so crisp and the chicken so tender, they didn't reveal anything, so I returned home and started to experiment. After cooking a whole lot of fried chicken, I found that cracking a couple of eggs into the buttermilk, as well as double-dredging, resulted in a crust that held up. And while I'm fairly certain the folks at Gus's don't use smoked paprika, I'm now addicted to brushing this sweet-and-smoky spice oil all over the chicken before serving it, so I'm not sure I'll ever be able to do it another way. Unless Gus's finally gives up their recipe.

1.8kg chicken, cut into 10 pieces, or 1.3kg bone-in, skin-on chicken thighs
Salt
2 large eggs
450ml buttermilk
1 tablespoon hot sauce (my favourite is Valentina!)
385g plain flour
1.3 to 1.8 litres grapeseed, peanut, or canola oil for frying, plus 55ml for the spicy oil
2 tablespoons cayenne pepper
1 tablespoon dark brown sugar
½ teaspoon smoked paprika
½ teaspoon toasted cumin, finely ground
1 garlic clove, finely grated or pounded with a pinch of salt

Prep the chicken in advance of cooking. If using a whole chicken, cut it into 10 pieces—follow the instructions on the previous page to get 8 pieces and then add in the wings for a total of 10 pieces. Save the carcass for your next batch of **Chicken Stock** (page 271). If using thighs, bone them out (refer to page 318 for instructions) and cut them in half. Season generously with salt on all sides. I prefer to season chicken the night before, but if you don't have that much time, try to give the salt at least an hour to diffuse throughout the meat before cooking. Refrigerate the chicken if seasoning more than an hour in advance; otherwise, leave it out on the worktop.

Whisk together the eggs, buttermilk, and hot sauce in a large bowl. Set aside. Whisk the flour and 2 generous pinches of salt together in another bowl. Set aside.

Place a wide, deep pan over medium heat. Add oil to a depth of 4cm, and heat to 180°C. Begin dredging the chicken, one or two pieces at a time. First, dredge in flour and shake off the excess, then dip into buttermilk, letting the excess drip back into the bowl, then return to the flour mixture and dredge a final time. Shake off the excess and place on a baking sheet.

Fry chicken in two or three rounds, letting the temperature of the oil drop to and hover around 160°C while the chicken cooks. Use metal tongs to turn the chicken occasionally, until the skin is a deep golden brown, about 12 minutes (closer to 16 minutes for large pieces, and 9 minutes for small pieces). If you are unsure that the meat is cooked through, poke through the crust with a paring knife and peek at the meat. It should be cooked all the way down to the bone, and any juice the meat gives off should run clear. If the meat is still raw or the juice has the slightest hint of pink, return the chicken to the oil and continue cooking until it's done.

Let cool on a wire rack set over a baking sheet.

Combine the cayenne pepper, brown sugar, paprika, cumin, and garlic in a small bowl, and add the 55ml oil. Brush the chicken with the spicy oil and serve immediately.

Variations

- For even more tender meat, marinate the seasoned chicken in the buttermilk overnight, as with **Buttermilk-Marinated Roast Chicken** (page 340).
- To make **Classic Fried Chicken**, omit the hot sauce and spicy oil. Add ½ teaspoon cayenne pepper and 1 teaspoon paprika to flour and prepare as above.
- To make **Indian-Spiced Fried Chicken**, omit the hot sauce and spicy oil. Season the chicken in advance with 4 teaspoons curry powder, 2 teaspoons ground cumin, and ½ teaspoon cayenne pepper in addition to salt. Add 1 tablespoon curry powder and 1 teaspoon paprika to the flour mixture and prepare as above. Make a glaze by heating 300g mango chutney with 3 tablespoons water, ¼ teaspoon cayenne pepper, and a pinch of salt. Brush onto the cooked chicken and serve immediately.

Chicken Pot Pie

Serves 6 to 8

I didn't grow up eating any classic American comfort foods. I think that's precisely why I've developed an obsession with pretty much all of them. Especially Chicken Pot Pie. With a creamy sauce, tender chicken, and flaky pastry, it's homey and sophisticated all at once. Early on in my cooking career, I decided I wanted to master all the nuances of Chicken Pot Pie. This recipe is the result.

For the filling

1.8kg chicken or 1.3kg bone-in, skin-on chicken thighs
Salt
Extra-virgin olive oil
3 tablespoons butter
2 medium onions, peeled and diced into 1cm pieces
2 large carrots, peeled and diced into 1cm pieces
2 large celery stalks, diced into 1cm pieces
225g fresh chestnut, button, or chanterelle mushrooms, trimmed and quartered
2 bay leaves
4 sprigs fresh thyme
Freshly ground black pepper
175ml dry white wine or dry sherry
125ml cream
675ml **Chicken Stock** (page 271) or water
65g flour
150g peas, fresh or frozen
10g finely chopped parsley leaves

For the crust

1 recipe **All-Butter Pie Dough** (page 386), but chill the dough in a single piece, or ½ recipe **Light and Flaky Buttermilk Biscuits** (page 392), or 1 package store-bought puff pastry
1 large egg, lightly whisked

Prep the chicken in advance of cooking. If using a whole chicken, follow the instructions on page 318 to quarter it, and save the carcass for your next batch of **Chicken Stock** (page 271). Season generously with salt. I prefer to season chicken the night before, but if you don't have that much time, try to give the salt at least an hour to diffuse throughout the meat before cooking. Refrigerate the chicken if seasoning more than an hour in advance; otherwise, leave it out on the worktop.

Set a large cast iron casserole or similar pot over medium-high heat. When the pan is hot, add enough olive oil to coat the bottom of the pot. When the oil shimmers, place half of the chicken pieces in the pan, skin side down, and brown evenly on all sides, about 4 minutes per side. Transfer to a plate and repeat with the remaining chicken.

Carefully discard the fat and return the pot to the stove over medium heat. Melt the butter and add the onion, carrots, celery, mushrooms, bay leaves, and thyme. Season lightly with salt and pepper. Cook, stirring occasionally, until the vegetables start to take on colour and soften, about 12 minutes. Pour in wine or sherry and deglaze the pan using a wooden spoon.

Nestle the browned chicken into the vegetables. Add the cream and chicken stock or water and increase the heat to high. Cover the pot and bring to a boil, then reduce to a simmer. Remove the breasts, if using, after 10 minutes of simmering, but cook dark meat for a total of 30 minutes. Turn off the heat, then transfer cooked chicken to a plate and allow the sauce to cool. Discard the bay leaves and thyme. After the sauce sits for a few minutes and the fat rises to the top, use a ladle or wide spoon to skim it into a liquid measuring cup or small bowl.

In a separate small bowl, use a fork to combine 125ml of the skimmed fat with the flour into a thick paste. When all the flour has been absorbed, stir in a ladleful of cooking liquid and combine. Return this thick liquid to the pot and bring the entire sauce back to a boil, then reduce to a simmer and cook until the sauce no longer tastes of raw flour, about 5 minutes. Taste and adjust seasoning with salt and freshly ground black pepper, then remove from heat.

Preheat the oven to 200°C. Set the oven rack to a centre-high position.

When the chicken is cool enough to handle, shred the meat and chop the skin finely. Save the bones for stock. Add the

shredded chicken and skin, peas, and parsley to the pot. Stir to combine, taste, and adjust seasoning as needed. Remove from the heat.

If using pie dough, roll out into a 38 by 28cm rectangle, about 3mm thick, and cut at least 4 2.5cm steam holes in the dough. If using biscuits, cut out 8 biscuits. If using puff pastry, gently defrost and unroll the dough, then cut at least 4 2.5cm steam vents in the dough.

Pour the filling into a 23 by 33cm glass or ceramic pan or shallow baking dish of similar size. Lay the prepared dough or puff pastry over the filling and trim the dough to leave a 1cm border around the lip of the pan. Tuck the dough back under itself and seal. If the dough won't stick to the pan on its own, use a little bit of the egg wash to encourage it to stick. If using biscuits, gently nestle them into the filling so that they're exposed about three-quarters of the way. Brush dough, puff pastry, or biscuits thoroughly and generously with egg wash.

Place on a baking sheet and bake for 30 to 35 minutes, until the dough or pastry is golden brown and the filling is bubbly. Serve hot.

Variations

- If you have a surplus of roasted or poached poultry on your hands, or just want to pick up a rotisserie chicken on the way home after work, cook the vegetables on their own. Add about 700g shredded, cooked chicken or turkey to the mixture and use butter to make the flour paste.

- For **Personal Pot Pies**, use the same recipe to make 6 individual pot pies in 450g ovenproof bowls or ramekins. Bake as directed above.

Conveyor Belt Chicken

2 thighs per serving

Though I've been cooking chicken this way for fifteen years, Conveyor Belt Chicken got its name one recent evening after I went surfing with my friend Tiffany. We were consumed with the unique brand of hunger that hits you only upon emerging from the ocean. She thought she had chicken thighs in the fridge, but I knew we didn't have time to roast or braise them—we'd gnaw our arms off before that could happen. We needed dinner, and quick.

As she drove us home, I told her we'd bone out the thighs and season them with salt. Then we'd cook them in a little olive oil, in a preheated cast iron pan over medium-low heat, skin side down, with another cast iron pan (or foil-wrapped can of tomatoes) weighing them down. Combining moderate heat with the weight encourages the fat to render, leaving behind crisp skin and tender meat. It's dark meat that cooks up as quickly and easily as white meat. After ten minutes or so, we'd flip the chicken, remove the weight, and let the meat cook through for two minutes more. Dinner would be ready in twelve minutes flat.

When we got home, we realised she had chicken breasts, not thighs, so we grilled them and made a salad that night. By the time we were eating dinner and my blood sugar levels had returned to normal, I'd completely forgotten about the thighs.

Tiffany didn't. The next night, she sent me a photo: she'd gone to the store, bought thighs, made the chicken according to the vague description I'd given in our hunger-addled state. With their brown, crisp skins and tender meat, they looked perfect, and apparently, they tasted perfect, too: after taking a bite, Tiffany's husband, Thomas, had declared he wanted to build a conveyor belt of this chicken straight to his mouth.

Thomas is one of my favourite people, so I do my best to make his dreams come true. When we eat together, I make Conveyor Belt Chicken every time, with cumin and hot pepper for chicken tacos, or with saffron and yoghurt for **Persian-ish Rice** (page 285), or just seasoned simply with salt and pepper, served with **Herb Salsa** (page 359) and whatever vegetables we can get our hands on to roast. I'm not so handy, so I'll leave the construction of the conveyor belt to Thomas.

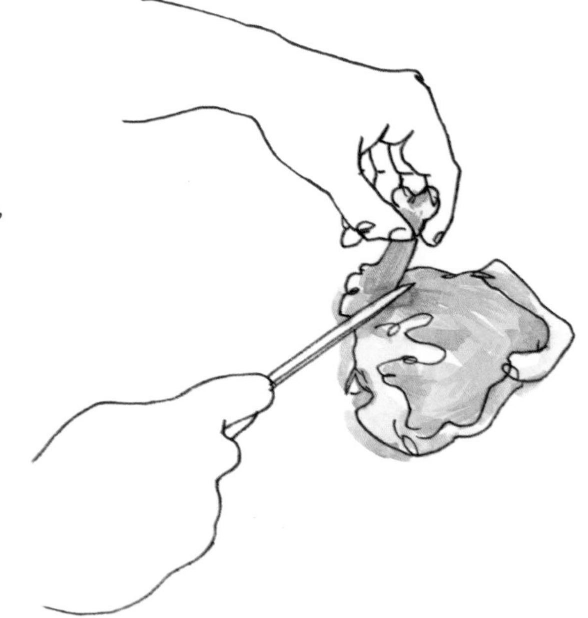

Chicken Confit

serves 4

Take a page out of the French farmwife's handbook and keep confit on hand to save you from dinnertime desperation. Easy enough to make while you watch a movie or do the Sunday crossword, there's no reason not to try this recipe. I make a big batch once or twice each winter. I just stick it in the fridge, where it quickly makes its way to the back of the bottom shelf, a spot I rarely think to look. But I inevitably find it just when I need it most—when an unexpected friend shows up for dinner, or I just can't muster the energy to cook. And, every time, I give silent thanks to that thoughtful, industrious earlier version of myself. You will, too.

If you can't find or make duck fat, pure olive oil will work just fine. But if you do make the effort to find or render your own duck fat, you'll be rewarded in flavour. (There aren't many other uses for duck fat in the kitchen, but for roasting or frying potatoes, the excess fat from confit is an unforgettable one.) Serve the chicken and potatoes with a pile of rocket or chicories dressed in a bright, **Honey-Mustard Vinaigrette** (page 240) and spoonfuls of **Herb Salsa** (page 359) for a welcome acidic contrast.

4 chicken legs, with thighs attached
Salt
Freshly ground black pepper
4 sprigs fresh thyme
4 cloves
2 bay leaves
3 garlic cloves, halved
About 900ml duck or chicken fat or olive oil

Prep the chicken a day in advance. Use a sharp knife to slit the skin at the base around each drumstick, just above the ankle joint. Cut all the way around, down to the bone, making sure to sever the tendons. Season with salt and pepper. Layer in a dish with the thyme, cloves, bay leaves, and garlic. Cover and refrigerate overnight.

To prepare, remove the aromatics and lay the legs into a large cast iron casserole or pot in a single layer. If using duck or chicken fat, warm gently in a medium saucepan just until it liquefies. Pour enough fat into the casserole or pot to submerge the meat, and then heat over a medium flame until the first bubbles emerge from the chicken. Reduce the heat so that the fat never surpasses the slightest simmer. Cook until the meat is tender at the bone, about 2 hours.

(Alternatively, cook the whole thing in the oven, at about 95°C. Use the same cues to guide you as in stovetop simmering.)

When the meat is cooked, turn off the heat and let it cool in the fat for a little while. Using metal tongs, carefully remove the chicken from the fat. Grab the bone at the ankle end to avoid tearing the skin.

Let the meat and fat cool, then place the chicken into a glass or ceramic dish, and strain the fat over it, ensuring it's completely submerged. Cover with a lid. Store in the fridge for up to 6 months.

To serve, remove the chicken from the fat, scraping off excess. Heat a cast iron pan over a medium flame, and place chicken, skin-side down, into the pan. As with **Conveyor Belt Chicken**, use the weight of a second, foil-wrapped cast iron pan to help render the fat and crisp the skin. Place the pan on top of the chicken and heat gently to crisp the skin at the same rate the meat reheats. As you start to hear crackles, rather than sizzles, pay closer attention to the meat so it doesn't burn. Once the skin is browned, flip the chicken and continue reheating the leg on the second side without a weight. The whole process will take about 15 minutes.

Serve immediately.

Variations

- For **Duck Confit**, cook 2½ to 3 hours, until the meat is tender and falling off the bone.
- For **Turkey Confit**, increase duck fat to 2 litres and cook 3 to 3½ hours, until the meat is tender and falling off the bone.
- For **Pork Confit**, season 225g pieces of pork shoulder as above and replace the duck fat with lard or olive oil.

Finger-Lickin' Pan-Fried Chicken

Makes 6 breasts and 6 tenders

I grew up eating pan-fried chicken *schnitzel* at least once a week, but cooking a hundred golden-brown, finger-lickin' chicken breasts one night downstairs at Chez Panisse really solidified my love for this classic dish. Cooking something a hundred times in a single night with total focus will increase your understanding of it a thousandfold. The most important thing I learned that night? Pan-fried chicken is all about the clarified butter in which it's cooked, which lends a well-rounded richness that you just can't get from olive oil. Clarifying butter is simple: just melt unsalted butter gently over sustained low heat. The whey solids will rise to the top of the clear, yellow fat, and the milk proteins will fall to the bottom. Skim the solids off the top with a fine strainer without agitating the proteins at the bottom. Carefully strain the remaining butter through cheesecloth or a tea strainer.

Another little tip: if you don't have time to make your own bread crumbs, use panko, the Japanese-style bread crumbs, and pulse them a few times in a food processor to get a finer texture.

6 boneless, skinless chicken breasts

100g fine white bread crumbs, preferably homemade, or panko

20g Parmesan, finely grated

130g, seasoned with a large pinch of salt and a pinch of cayenne

3 large eggs, beaten with a pinch of salt

400ml **clarified butter**, made from 450g butter (see page 68 for complete method)

Line one baking sheet with parchment paper, and another with paper towels.

If the tenders are still attached to the breasts, remove them. Use a sharp knife to remove the bit of silver skin, or connective tissue, at the top of the underside of each breast.

Place one chicken breast with the underside facing up on the cutting board. Lightly rub one side of a plastic bag with olive oil and place it, oil side down, on top of the breast. Pound the underside of the breast with a kitchen mallet (or, lacking that, use an empty glass jar) until it's evenly about 1cm thick. Repeat with the remaining breasts.

Season the breasts and tenders lightly with salt, and then set up a breading station. Set up three large, shallow bowls or roasting dishes, one each with the seasoned flour, the beaten eggs, and the bread crumbs. Mix the Parmesan into the bread crumbs.

Working like Henry Ford, coat all the breasts and tenders first in flour, then shake off the excess. Then dip and coat them all in egg, and shake off the excess. Finally, coat the pieces in bread crumbs and set them on the parchment-lined baking sheet.

Set a 25 or 30cm cast iron pan (or other frying pan) over medium-high heat and add enough clarified butter to come 5mm up the sides of the pan. When the fat shimmers, add a few bread crumbs to test the temperature of the fat. As soon as they sizzle readily, place as many chicken breasts as you can fit into the pan in a single layer. There should be space between each breast, and the fat should come at least halfway up the sides of the chicken to ensure that the breading cooks evenly.

Cook the breasts over medium-high heat until golden brown, 3 to 4 minutes, then rotate and flip. Cook until the second side is evenly brown, remove from the pan, and drain on the sheet lined with paper towels. (If you're unsure that the meat is cooked through, poke through the breading with a paring knife and check. Return to the pan and cook longer if you see any pink flesh.) Add more clarified butter to the pan as necessary and cook the remaining breasts and tenders in the same way. Sprinkle lightly with salt, and serve immediately.

Variations

- For **Pork Schnitzel**, thinly pound pork loin cutlets, bread them, and continue as above. Reduce cooking time to 2 to 3 minutes per side to prevent overcooking.

- For **Breaded Fish or Prawns**, don't salt either in advance. Instead, season immediately before breading and omit the cheese from the bread crumbs. Use the same breading method for prawns or any white flaky fish, including halibut, cod, or flounder. Increase heat and pan-fry prawns for 1 to 2 minutes per side and fish for 2 to 3 minutes per side to avoid overcooking. Or you can deep-fry as described on page 174. Serve with an acidic slaw or salad and **Tartar Sauce** (page 378).

- For a ***Fritto Misto***, omit the cheese and use the same breading method for olives or slices of Meyer lemon, blanched fennel, blanched artichokes, mushrooms, aubergines, or courgettes. Pan-fry as above, or deep-fry as described on page 174.

Sage- and Honey-Smoked Chicken

Serves 4

As a restaurant cook, I managed to avoid learning how to smoke meat. Somehow, I was never in the kitchen on the days we smoked fish or duck at Chez Panisse. At Eccolo, we asked a nearby smokehouse to smoke our sausages and meats for us. And since I never learned the skill, it remained a mystery. But when I started cooking with Michael Pollan, I was moved by his fascination with the technique. For a short, flavourful period of time, every time I had dinner with Michael and his family, something at the table was smoked. Michael still doesn't know it, but I learned to smoke by watching him. While he prefers smoking pork, I've grown to love using the technique to cook chicken. This recipe is all about the way the subtle aromas of sage and garlic mingle with the delicate applewood smoke and the sweetness of the honey glaze.

370g honey
1 bunch sage
1 head garlic, halved crosswise
120g kosher salt or 60g fine sea salt
1 tablespoon black peppercorns
1.8kg chicken
2–3 handfuls applewood chips

The day before you want to cook the chicken, make the brine. In a large pot, bring 1.2 litres of water to a boil with 275g honey, the sage, garlic, salt, and peppercorns. Add 1.2 litres of cold water. Allow the brine to cool to room temperature. Submerge the chicken in the brine, breast side down, and refrigerate overnight.

To cook the chicken, remove it from the brine and pat dry. Strain the brine through a sieve and stuff the cavity of the chicken with the brined garlic and sage. Fold the wingtips up and over the back of the bird. Tie the chicken legs together. Allow the bird to come up to room temperature.

Soak the wood chips in water for 1 hour, then drain. Prepare for grilling over **indirect heat**. (To learn more about cooking over indirect heat, see page 178.)

To smoke over a charcoal grill, light the charcoal in a chimney starter. When the coals glow red and are coated with grey ash, carefully dump them in two piles on opposite sides of the grill. Place a disposable aluminium pan in the centre of the grill. Toss about 50g wood chips on each pile of coals to create smoke. Place the grate on the grill and set the chicken, breast side up, over the drip pan.

Cover the grill with the air vents positioned over the meat. Open the vents halfway. Use a digital thermometer to help you maintain a temperature of 95° to 110°C, replenishing charcoal and wood as needed. When an instant-read thermometer inserted into the centre of the leg registers 55°C, brush the remaining 95g of honey all over the skin. Replace the lid of the grill and continue cooking until the thermometer registers 70°C when inserted into the centre of the leg, about 35 minutes more. Remove the chicken from the grill and allow to rest 10 minutes before carving.

To crisp the skin before serving, stoke the coals until they are very hot, or light burners on one side of grill to very high. Return the chicken to the indirect heat zone and cover the grill. Cook for 5 to 10 minutes until crisp.

To smoke over a gas grill, fill the smoker box with wood chips and light the burner closest to it on high until you see smoke. If your grill doesn't have a smoker box, place the chips in heavy-duty foil and fold into a pouch. Poke a few holes into the pouch and place under the grate over one of the burners. Heat over high heat until you see smoke. Once the chips are smoking, reduce the flame, lower the cover, and preheat the grill to 120°C. Maintain this temperature throughout cooking.

Place the chicken, breast side up, over unlit burners—this is the **indirect heat zone**—and cook 2 to 2½ hours. When an instant-read thermometer inserted into the centre of the leg registers 55°C, brush the remaining 95g of honey all over the skin. Replace the lid of the grill and continue cooking until the thermometer registers 70°C when inserted into the centre of the leg, about 35 minutes more. Remove the chicken from the grill and allow to rest 10 minutes before carving.

To crisp the skin before serving, stoke the coals until they are very hot, or light burners on one side of grill to very high. Return the chicken to the indirect heat zone and cover the grill. Cook for 5 to 10 minutes until crisp.

To serve, cut the chicken into quarters—it pairs really well with **Fried Sage Salsa Verde** (page 361)—or shred the meat to make pulled chicken for sandwiches.

Chicken and Garlic Soup

Makes 3.4 litres (serves 6 to 8)

This soup is so satisfying that I had to include it with the chicken—and not the soup—recipes. Made with a whole chicken, it yields a satisfying dinner for four (or two, with leftovers!). Cooking the chicken in homemade chicken stock gives this soup an extra layer of flavour. If you don't have any stock on hand, get some from the butcher instead of using canned or boxed stock—it'll make all the difference!

1.8kg chicken, quartered; or 4 large chicken legs and thighs
Salt
Freshly ground pepper
Extra-virgin olive oil
2 medium onions, diced
3 large carrots, peeled and diced
3 large celery stalks, diced
2 bay leaves
2.25 litres **Chicken Stock** (page 271)
20 garlic cloves, thinly sliced
Optional: Parmesan rind

Prep the chicken in advance of cooking. If using a whole bird, follow the instructions on page 318 to quarter it, and save the carcass for your next batch of **Chicken Stock** (page 271). Season generously with salt and freshly ground black pepper. I prefer to season chicken the night before, but if you don't have that much time, try to give the salt at least an hour to diffuse throughout the meat before cooking. Refrigerate the chicken if seasoning more than an hour in advance; otherwise, leave it out on the worktop.

Preheat a 9.5 litre cast iron casserole or similar pot over high heat. Add enough olive oil to coat the bottom of the pot. When the oil shimmers, add half the chicken pieces and brown thoroughly, about 4 minutes per side. Remove and set aside. Repeat with the remaining chicken.

Carefully tip most of the fat out of the pan. Return the pan to the stove and reduce the heat to medium-low. Add the onions, carrots, celery, and bay leaves and cook until soft and golden brown, about 12 minutes. Return the chicken to the pot and add 2.25 litres stock or water, salt, pepper, and Parmesan rind, if using. Bring to a boil, then reduce to a simmer.

Heat a small frying pan over medium heat and add enough olive oil to coat the bottom, then add the garlic. Gently sizzle the garlic for about 20 seconds, until it gives off an aroma, but don't let it take on any colour. Add it to the soup and continue to simmer.

If using breasts, remove them from the pot after 12 minutes and continue to simmer legs and thighs until they are tender, about 50 minutes total. Turn off the heat and skim the fat from the surface of the broth. Remove all the chicken from the soup. When the chicken is cool enough to handle, remove the meat from the bone and shred. Discard the skin if you prefer to (though I love to chop it finely and use it, too), and return the meat to the broth. Taste the soup and adjust the salt as needed. Serve hot.

Refrigerate, covered, for up to 5 days, or freeze for up to 2 months.

Variations

- For a delicate **Spring Garlic Soup**, omit garlic cloves. Instead, stew 6 stalks thinly sliced green garlic with the onion, carrot, celery, and bay leaves.
- To add some heartiness, add cooked rice, pasta, rice noodles, beans, barley, or farro to the soup.
- To turn the soup into a main course, ladle it into bowls over coarsely chopped baby spinach, and then add a poached egg to each bowl before serving.
- To make ***Pho Gà*** (Vietnamese chicken soup), omit the onion, carrot, celery, bay leaves, black pepper, and garlic. Instead, char 2 peeled onions and a 10cm piece of ginger directly over a gas burner for about 5 minutes or under the grill (the charred skins are full of flavour!) and add to the broth with 55ml fish sauce, 1 star anise, and 2 tablespoons brown sugar. Cook the chicken in this broth as directed above, for 50 minutes. Discard the onion and ginger and continue to prepare soup as above, shredding the chicken and adding it back to the pot. Pour over rice noodles, and top with fresh basil and bean sprouts.

Adas Polo o Morgh
Chicken with Lentil Rice

Serves 6 generously

Growing up, whenever Maman asked me what I wanted for dinner, I asked for *adas polo*. Though it might seem virtuous for a small child to request rice with lentils, I was really after the raisins and dates that Maman would sauté in butter right before serving the dish. I always looked forward to their sweetness, combined with the earthy flavour of the lentils. When served with some spiced chicken and topped with a big dollop of **Persian Herb and Cucumber Yoghurt** (page 371), the dish was peerless in my opinion. I've adapted and simplified the recipe a bit to turn it into a one-pot meal, a Persian version of Chicken with Rice, that universal comfort food.

1.8kg chicken; or 8 bone-in, skin-on thighs
Salt
1 teaspoon plus 1 tablespoon ground cumin
Extra-virgin olive oil
3 tablespoons unsalted butter
2 medium onions, thinly sliced
2 bay leaves
Small pinch saffron threads
500g basmati rice, unrinsed
1 cup black or golden raisins
6 Medjool dates, pitted and quartered
1 litre **Chicken Stock** (page 271) or water
200g cooked, drained brown or green lentils

Prep the chicken in advance of cooking. If using a whole bird, follow the instructions on page 318 to quarter it, and save the carcass for your next batch of **Chicken Stock** (page 271). Season generously with salt and 1 teaspoon cumin on all sides. I prefer to season chicken the night before, but if you don't have that much time, try to give the salt at least an hour to diffuse throughout the meat before cooking. Refrigerate the chicken if seasoning more than an hour in advance; otherwise, leave it out on the worktop.

Wrap the lid of a large cast iron casserole or similar pot with a tea towel secured to the handle with a rubber band. This will absorb steam and prevent it from condensing and dripping back onto the chicken, which would make the skin soggy.

Set the casserole over medium-high heat, and add olive oil to coat the bottom of the pan. Brown the chicken in two batches, so as not to crowd the pan. Begin with the skin side down, then turn and rotate the chicken around the pan to get even browning on both sides, about 4 minutes per side. Remove from pan and set aside. Carefully discard the fat.

Return the pan to medium-heat and melt the butter. Add the onions, cumin, bay leaves, saffron, and a pinch of salt and cook, stirring, until brown and tender, about 25 minutes.

Increase the heat to medium-high and add the rice to the pan and toast, stirring, until it turns a light golden colour. Add the raisins and dates and let them fry for a minute until they start to plump.

Pour in the stock and lentils, increase the heat to high, and bring to a boil. Season generously with salt and taste. In order to get the rice properly seasoned, make the liquid salty enough to make you slightly uncomfortable—it should be saltier than the saltiest soup you've ever tasted. Reduce the heat and nestle in the chicken, skin side up. Cover the pan and cook for 40 minutes over low heat.

After 40 minutes, turn off the heat and let the pan sit, covered, for 10 minutes to continue steaming. Remove lid and fluff rice with a fork. Serve immediately with **Persian Herb and Cucumber Yoghurt** (page 371).

Chicken with Vinegar

Serves 4 to 6

I cooked *Poulet au Vinaigre*, or Chicken with Vinegar, at the first dinner party I held after beginning my internship at Chez Panisse. I remember everyone—myself included—initially being confounded by the idea of cooking chicken with vinegar. We thought of heating the stuff for making pickles—and nearly being asphyxiated by the sharp fumes produced by hot vinegar. It hardly seemed appetising! But Chris Lee, my mentor, had suggested I practise cooking one of the classics, and being the ever-dutiful student, I set out to make it, and followed his instructions, word for word. As my friends sat down in my no-frills college apartment to a dinner of *poulet au vinaigre* and steamed white rice, we were rewarded for my diligence. The vinegar had tamed as it cooked, and was beautifully balanced by the richness of the crème fraîche and butter in the dish. It was a revelation, and it heightened my appreciation for what acid can do for a rich dish.

1.8kg chicken
Salt
Freshly ground black pepper
65g plain flour
Extra-virgin olive oil
3 tablespoons unsalted butter
2 medium onions, thinly sliced
175ml dry white wine
6 tablespoons white wine vinegar
2 tablespoons tarragon leaves, finely chopped
125ml double cream or crème fraîche (page 113)

Prep the chicken in advance of cooking. Follow the instructions on page 318 to cut the bird into 8 pieces, and save the carcass for your next batch of **Chicken Stock** (page 271). Season generously with salt and freshly ground black pepper. I prefer to season chicken the night before, but if you don't have that much time, try to give the salt at least an hour to diffuse throughout the meat before cooking. Refrigerate the chicken if seasoning more than an hour in advance; otherwise, leave it out on the worktop.

Place the flour in a shallow bowl or pie plate and season with a generous pinch of salt. Dredge the chicken pieces in flour, shake off the excess, and lay in a single layer on a wire rack or parchment-lined baking sheet.

Place a large frying pan or cast iron casserole over medium-high heat and add just enough olive oil to coat the pan. Brown the chicken in two batches, so as not to crowd the pan. Begin with the skin side down, then turn and rotate the chicken around the pan to get even browning on both sides, about 4 minutes per side. Place the browned chicken on a baking sheet, then carefully discard the fat and wipe out the pan.

Return the pan to medium heat and melt the butter. Add the onions, season with salt, and stir. Cook the onions, stirring occasionally, until they are tender and brown, about 25 minutes.

Increase the flame to high, add the wine and vinegar, and scrape the pan with a wooden spoon to deglaze. Add half of the tarragon and stir. Return the chicken, skin side up, to the pan, and lower the heat to a simmer. Set a lid ajar on the pan and continue to simmer. Remove the breasts when they are cooked, after about 12 minutes, but let the dark meat continue to cook until it's tender at the bone, 35 to 40 minutes total.

Transfer the chicken to a platter, increase the heat, and add the cream or crème fraîche. Let the sauce come to a simmer and thicken. Taste and adjust the seasoning with salt, pepper, and a little more vinegar if needed to perk up the sauce. Add remaining tarragon and spoon over the chicken to serve.

Glazed Five-Spice Chicken

Serves 4

David Tanis was the chef the first night I helped out in the kitchen at Chez Panisse. When I feared that my knife skills were inadequate, he had me dice cucumbers into minuscule pieces for hours. It showed me that with enough practice, I could learn to do anything in the kitchen. A few years later, David left Chez Panisse and now he writes one of my favourite columns, "City Kitchen" for *The New York Times* Food section. I love the column because every week he focuses on a single simple dish, to which he lends his elegant style.

One of my favourite recipes from "City Kitchen" described spicy lacquered chicken wings with Chinese five-spice. The recipe David shares is so simple and tasty that I've made it dozens of times over the years, adapting it to different cuts of meat and fish. I've found it works especially well with thighs served over **Steamed Jasmine Rice** (page 282) with **Vietnamese Cucumber Salad** (page 226); the leftovers make for a great rice bowl at lunch.

1.8kg chicken or 8 bone-in, skin-on chicken thighs
Salt
55ml soy sauce
55g dark brown sugar
55ml mirin (rice wine)
1 teaspoon toasted sesame oil
1 tablespoon finely grated ginger
4 garlic cloves, finely grated or pounded with a pinch of salt
½ teaspoon Chinese five-spice powder
¼ teaspoon cayenne pepper
10g coarsely chopped coriander leaves and tender stems
4 spring onions, green and white parts slivered

Prep the chicken the day before you want to cook. If using a whole chicken, follow the instructions on page 318 to cut the bird into 8 pieces, and save the carcass for your next batch of **Chicken Stock** (page 271). Season the chicken lightly with salt and let it sit for 30 minutes. Keep in mind that the marinade consists mostly of soy sauce, which is salty, so use only about half as much salt as you otherwise would.

In the meantime, whisk together the soy sauce, brown sugar, mirin, sesame oil, ginger, garlic, five-spice, and cayenne. Place the chicken in a resealable plastic bag and pour in the marinade. Seal the bag and squish the marinade around so all the chicken is evenly coated. Refrigerate overnight.

A few hours before you want to cook the chicken, pull it out of the fridge to come up to room temperature. Preheat the oven to 200°C.

To cook, place chicken skin side up in a shallow 20 by 33cm roasting dish, then pour the marinade over the meat. The marinade should generously cover the bottom of the pan. If it doesn't, add 2 tablespoons of water to ensure even coverage and prevent burning. Slide into the oven and rotate the pan every 10 to 12 minutes.

Remove the breasts, if using, after 20 minutes of cooking, to prevent overcooking. Continue cooking dark meat for another 20 to 25 minutes, until it's tender at the bone, or a total of 45 minutes.

When the dark meat is cooked, return the breasts to the pan and crank the oven to 220°C to let the sauce reduce and the skin to get dark brown and crisp, about 12 minutes. Brush the chicken with the marinade from the pan every 3 to 4 minutes to glaze them.

Serve warm, garnished with coriander and slivered spring onions.

Cover and refrigerate leftovers for up to 3 days.

Buttermilk-Marinated Roast Chicken

Serves 4

Once I grew comfortable working the spit at Eccolo, I never tired of roasting chicken over the wood fire each night. Eventually, I came up with the idea to marinate the birds in buttermilk overnight, like southern grandmothers do. Years later, I was cooking a dozen of these chickens for a special event when a friend who was hosting Jacques Pépin that very same day called in a panic to ask if I could prepare a picnic basket for the legendary chef. I wrapped up a bird, a green salad, and some crusty bread and sent it on its way before I could overthink it. Later that night, I received a message from Mr. Pépin saying that everything was classically perfect and entirely delicious. I can't think of a better endorsement for this recipe.

The buttermilk and salt work like a brine, tenderising the meat on multiple levels: the water it contains increases moisture, and the salt and acid it contains disables proteins, preventing them from squeezing liquid from the meat as the bird cooks (see pages 31 and 113). As an added bonus, the sugars in the buttermilk will caramelise, contributing to an exquisitely browned skin. While the beauty of roast chicken is that you can serve it anytime, anywhere, my favourite thing to serve alongside it is ***Panzanella*** (page 231), which plays the role of starch, salad, and sauce!

1.6 to 1.8kg chicken

Salt

450ml buttermilk

The day before you want to cook the chicken, remove the wingtips by cutting through the first wing joint with poultry shears or a sharp knife. Reserve for stock. Season it generously with salt and let it sit for 30 minutes.

Stir 2 tablespoons of kosher salt or 4 teaspoons fine sea salt into the buttermilk to dissolve. Place the chicken in a gallon-size resealable plastic bag and pour in the buttermilk. If the chicken won't fit in a gallon-size bag, double up two plastic produce bags to prevent leakage and tie the bag with a piece of twine.

Seal it, squish the buttermilk all around the chicken, place on a rimmed plate, and refrigerate. If you're so inclined, over the next 24 hours you can turn the bag so every part of the chicken gets marinated, but that's not essential.

Pull the chicken from the fridge an hour before you plan to cook it. Preheat the oven to 220°C, with a rack set in the centre position.

Remove the chicken from the plastic bag and scrape off as much buttermilk as you can without being obsessive. Tightly tie together the legs of the chicken with a piece of butcher's twine. Place the chicken in a 25cm cast iron ovenproof frying pan or shallow roasting pan.

Slide the pan all the way to the back of the oven on the centre rack. Rotate the pan so that the legs are pointing towards the rear left corner and the breast is pointing towards the centre of the oven (the back corners tend to be the hottest spots in the oven, so this orientation protects the breast from overcooking before the legs are done). Pretty quickly you should hear the chicken sizzling.

After about 20 minutes, when the chicken starts to brown, reduce the heat to 200°C and continue roasting for 10 minutes and then move the pan so the legs are facing the back right corner of the oven.

Continue cooking for another 30 minutes or so, until the chicken is brown all over and the juices run clear when you insert a knife down to the bone between the leg and the thigh.

When the chicken's done, remove it to a platter and let it rest for 10 minutes before carving and serving.

Variations

- If you don't have buttermilk on hand, substitute plain yoghurt or ***crème fraîche*** (page 113).

- For **Persian Roast Chicken**, omit the buttermilk. Make saffron tea as directed on page 287 and add to 300g plain yoghurt along with 1 tablespoon kosher salt or 2 teaspoons fine sea salt and 2 teaspoons finely grated lemon zest. Place the seasoned chicken in a resealable plastic bag and use your hands to coat it with the yoghurt mixture, inside and out. Continue as above.

Sicilian Chicken Salad

Makes about 900g

As we served spit-roasted chicken every night at Eccolo, we had to get creative and figure out all sorts of ways to use up the leftover cooked birds. Chicken pot pie, chicken soup, and chicken *ragù* all made it onto the menu regularly, but this salad quickly became our favourite way to use up all that chicken. Teeming with pine nuts, currants, fennel, and celery, it's a lovely Mediterranean play on traditional chicken salad. (And if you're short on time, pick up a rotisserie chicken from the store and use a good-quality store-bought mayonnaise spiked with a clove or two of pounded or finely grated garlic to speed things up.)

½ medium red onion, diced
55ml red wine vinegar
65g currants
750g shredded roasted or poached chicken meat (from about 1 roast chicken)
225ml stiff **Aïoli** (page 376)
1 teaspoon finely grated lemon zest
2 tablespoons lemon juice
3 tablespoons finely chopped parsley leaves
65g pine nuts, lightly toasted
2 small celery stalks, diced
½ medium fennel bulb, diced
2 teaspoons ground fennel seed
Salt

Combine the onion and vinegar in a small bowl and let sit for 15 minutes to macerate (see page 118).

In a separate small bowl, submerge the currants in boiling water. Let them sit for 15 minutes to rehydrate and plump up. Drain and place in a large bowl.

Add the chicken, aïoli, lemon zest, lemon juice, parsley, pine nuts, celery, fennel bulb, fennel seed, and two generous pinches of salt to the currants and stir to combine. Stir in the macerated onions (but not their vinegar) and taste. Adjust salt and add vinegar as needed.

Serve on toasted slices of crusty bread, or wrapped in leaves of romaine or Little Gem lettuces.

Variations

- For **Curried Chicken Salad**, omit pine nuts, lemon zest, and fennel bulb and seed. Substitute coriander for the parsley and season the mixture with 3 tablespoons yellow curry powder, ¼ teaspoon ground cayenne, 55g lightly toasted sliced almonds, and 1 tart apple, diced.
- To lend a little smokiness to the salad, use leftover **Sage- and Honey-Smoked Chicken** (page 330), instead of roasted or poached chicken.

MEAT

When you're standing at the butcher's counter trying to decide which cut to get for dinner, remember: time really is money, at least when it comes to meat. That is to say, more expensive cuts of meat—the ones that are already tender—cook quickly, while more economical, tougher cuts, will need to be tended to carefully over time. More expensive, tender cuts will benefit from **intense heat**; less expensive, tougher cuts appreciate **gentle heat**. For more about gentle and intense heat cooking methods, look back to page 156.

Here's another proverb for you. Ever heard the term *high on the hog*? Used to denote wealth, it's derived directly from butcher's terminology. From Dario Cecchini, the butcher who took me under his wing in Italy, I learned that until well into the twentieth century, entire Italian families would live off just a handful of hogs for the whole year. A travelling butcher called a *norcino* would come by each winter to slaughter animals and break them down into prime cuts. Then the legs would be turned to prosciutto, the bellies into pancetta, the scraps into salami. The lard would be rendered, and the loins—the highest cuts off a hog's back—would be saved for special occasions.

A few months after I returned to California, I happened upon a copy of *The Taste of Country Cooking* by the great southern chef Edna Lewis, where, she carefully recalls her family's annual hog harvest. She and her siblings looked forward to the visit of the itinerant butcher who'd help process the hogs on their family farm each December. The kids watched as the men carefully smoked the hams, bellies, and loins to preserve them for the coming months. They'd help the women render the leaf lard for pie, make liver pudding, and turn the scraps into sausages. As in Italy, so in the American South. I love how this story illustrates the universality of economical cooking.

Every time I make a decision at the butcher's counter, a diagram of a flying pig flashes through my mind. As a cut's distance from an animal's hoof or horn increases, so does its innate tenderness—and its price. Steaks and loins are cut from the least active parts of the animal, and they are the most tender. On the other hand, meat from legs and shoulders—cuts such as shanks, brisket, short ribs, or chuck—will always be tougher and less expensive. They are also often more flavourful.

The grand exception to this rule is minced meat. While butchers generally mince tougher stewing cuts, the mincing process gives these cuts a head start on the way to tenderness by breaking down their long, tough fibres. So burgers, meatballs, sausages, and kebabs exist at the intersection of economy and speed, making them ideal for weeknight dinners.

Speaking of weeknight dinners: use these recipes as basic guides. First, master the techniques, and then start experimenting with the flavour combinations and the cuts of meat. Except where noted, season your meat as early as possible. Remember, overnight is best, but any time sitting with salt is better than none. And for more evenly cooked meat, bring it up to room temperature before cooking.

Spicy Brined Turkey Breast

Serves 6, with plentiful leftovers for sandwiches

For months after groundbreaking American rancher Bill Niman started raising turkeys, he'd bring a couple of birds to us each week at Eccolo. He wanted feedback about which of his half dozen heritage breeds produced the most flavourful and tender meat. While it's got great flavour, heritage turkey meat can be really tough and dry. And after cooking scores of turkeys, I figured out my favourite methods for cooking them: braising the legs for a *ragù*, and brining and spit-roasting the breasts to slice for succulent sandwiches. After ordering a sandwich, one customer told us she realised she'd never before associated turkey sandwiches with turkey flavour! Even all of these years later, I often brine and roast a turkey breast on the weekend, and my lunch sandwiches are the envy of all the other writers in my office!

I formulated this brine for turkey meant for sandwiches, but if you'd like to use it for turkey—or any meat—to serve warm as a main dish, reduce the salt to 90g kosher salt or 7 tablespoons fine sea salt.

110g kosher salt or 125g fine sea salt
65g sugar
1 garlic head, halved crosswise
1 teaspoon black peppercorns
2 tablespoons red pepper flakes
½ teaspoon ground cayenne pepper
1 lemon
6 bay leaves
1 boneless skin-on turkey half-breast, about 1.6kg
Extra-virgin olive oil

Place the salt, sugar, garlic, peppercorns, pepper flakes, and cayenne in a large pot with 900ml of water. Use a vegetable peeler to remove the lemon zest, then halve the lemon. Squeeze the juice into the pot, then add the lemon halves and zest. Bring to a boil, then reduce to a simmer, stirring from time to time. When the salt and sugar have dissolved, remove from the heat and add 1.8 litres cold water. Allow the brine to cool to room temperature. If the turkey tender—the long strip of white meat on the underside of the breast—is still attached, remove it by pulling it off. Submerge the turkey breast and tender in the brine and refrigerate overnight, or up to 24 hours.

Two hours before cooking, remove the breast and tender, if using, from the brine and let sit at room temperature.

Preheat the oven to 220°C. Set a large cast iron pan or other ovenproof pan on the stove over high heat. Once it's hot, add a tablespoon of olive oil, then place the breast in the pan, skin side down. Reduce the flame to medium-high and brown the breast for 4 to 5 minutes, until the skin starts to take on some colour. Use tongs to flip the breast so it's skin side up, place the tender in the pan beside the breast, and slip the pan into the oven, pushing it as far back as it will go. This is the hottest spot in the oven, and that initial blast of heat will ensure the turkey browns beautifully.

Remove the tender from the pan when it reads 65°C on an instant-read thermometer at its thickest point, about 12 minutes. Check the temperature of the breast in a few different spots at this time, too, just to have a sense of where it is. Continue cooking the breast another 12 to 18 minutes, until it registers 65°C at its thickest point. (The internal temperature will start climbing rapidly once it hits 55°C, so don't wander too far away from the oven, and check the breast every few minutes.) Remove it from the oven and the pan, and allow to rest at least 10 minutes before slicing.

To serve, slice against the grain (crosswise) on the bias.

Variations

- For a little extra insurance against dryness, **bard**, or wrap, the brined turkey breast with strips of bacon or pancetta before roasting. If necessary, tie a few pieces of butcher's twine around the breast to keep the barding from falling off.

- Use the same brine for a 1.8 Kg **Boneless Pork Loin**. Brown it on all sides, then roast for 30 to 35 minutes to 55°C (for rare-medium-rare) or 57°C (for true medium-rare)—it'll rest out to 61-63°C. Allow to rest for 15 minutes before slicing.

- For a moist, flavourful **Spatchcocked Thanksgiving Turkey**, use the full 110g of salt. Add 2 sprigs thyme, 1 large sprig rosemary, and 12 sage leaves to the pot, but reduce the red pepper flakes to 1 teaspoon and skip the cayenne. Add 1 onion and carrot, peeled and sliced, and 1 stalk of celery, sliced. Bring everything to a boil. Increase amount of cold water added to 7.2 litres. Spatchcock the turkey (see page 316) and leave it in chilled brine for 48 hours for fullest flavour. Roast at 200°C until a thermometer inserted into the hip joint of the turkey registers 70°C. Allow to rest 25 minutes before carving.

Pork Braised with Chillies

Serves 6 to 8

This is the single most versatile recipe in this book. I've prepared pork according to this method for diplomats at the US Embassy in Beijing and to distinguished guests at a thousand-year-old castle in northern Italy. But I especially love cooking it with my students at the end of every Heat class. We shred the meat and make tacos that we pile high with **Simmered Beans** (page 280), **Bright Cabbage Slaw** (page 224), and **Mexican-ish Herb Salsa** (page 363). The best part? I get to take the leftovers home and enjoy all week long.

1.8kg boneless pork shoulder
Salt
1 garlic head
Neutral-tasting oil
2 medium onions, sliced
400g crushed tomatoes in their juice, fresh or canned
2 tablespoons cumin seed (or 1 tablespoon ground cumin)
2 bay leaves
8 dried chillies, such as Guajillo, New Mexico, Anaheim, or ancho, stemmed, seeded, and rinsed
Optional: For a touch of smokiness add 1 tablespoon smoked paprika
or 2 smoked peppers such as chipotle to the braise
450–675ml lager or pilsner beer
15g coarsely chopped coriander for garnish

The day before you plan to cook, season the pork generously with salt. Cover and refrigerate.

When you're ready to cook, preheat the oven to 160°C. Remove any roots from the head of garlic, then slice it in half crosswise. (Don't worry about adding the skins to the braise—they'll get strained out at the end. If you don't trust me, go ahead and peel the whole head of garlic—I'm just trying to save you some time and effort.)

Set a large, cast iron casserole or similar ovenproof pot over medium-high heat. When it's warm, add 1 tablespoon oil. When the oil shimmers, place the pork in the pot. Brown it evenly on all sides, about 3 to 4 minutes per side.

When the meat is brown, remove it and set it aside. Carefully tip out as much of the fat from the pot as you can, then return it to the stove. Reduce the heat to medium, and add 1 tablespoon neutral oil. Add the onions and garlic and cook, stirring from time to time, until the onions are tender and lightly browned, about 15 minutes.

Add the tomatoes and juice, cumin, bay leaves, dried chillies, and smoked paprika or peppers, if using, into the pot and stir. Nestle pork atop the aromatic base, and add enough beer to come 4cm up the sides of the meat. Make sure the peppers and bay leaves are mostly immersed in the juices so that they do not burn.

Increase the heat and bring to a boil on the stove, then slip the pot, uncovered, into the oven. After 30 minutes, check to make sure the liquid is just barely simmering. About every 30 minutes, turn the pork over and check the level of the liquid. Add more beer as needed to maintain the liquid at a depth of 4cm. Cook until the meat is tender and falls apart at the touch of a fork, 3½ to 4 hours.

Remove the cooked pork from the oven and carefully remove it from the pan. Discard the bay leaves, but don't worry about fishing out the garlic since the sieve will catch the skins. Using a food mill, blender, or food processor, purée the aromatics, and strain them through a sieve. Discard the solids.

Skim the fat from the sauce and then taste, adjusting salt as needed.

At this point, you can either shred the meat and combine it with the sauce to make pork tacos, or slice it and spoon the sauce over the pork to serve it as an entrée. Garnish with chopped coriander and serve with an acidic condiment such as Mexican crema, **Mexican-ish Herb Salsa** (page 363), or a simple squeeze of lime.

Cover and refrigerate leftovers for up to 5 days. Braised meat freezes exceptionally well. Simply submerge in cooking liquid, cover, and freeze for up to 2 months. To serve, return the braise to a boil on the stove with a splash of water.

Variations

- Any cut of meat from the list overleaf will make a fantastic braise or stew. Memorise the basics of the recipe above, and then apply the steps to any cut of dark, sinewy meat you'd like. Refer back to the Heat chapter, page 166, for a detailed step-by-step recipe of this braise, and a chart of average cooking times for various cuts of meat.

- When you're inspired to cook any of the classic braises and stews from around the world, do a little research. Compare a few different recipes for the same dish to see what ingredients or special steps are common to them all. Use the aromatics chart and the fat, acid, and spice wheels to guide you. The beauty of it all is, once you've got this braise in your pocket, you've got a hundred others in there, too.

Everything You Need to Know to Improvise a Braise

Best Braising Cuts

Pork

Spare Ribs
Shoulder
Shank
Sausages
Belly

Chicken, Duck, and Rabbit

Legs
Thighs
Wings (poultry only)

Beef

Oxtails
Short Ribs
Shank (*Osso buco*)
Chuck
Brisket
Round

Lamb and Goat

Shoulder
Neck
Shank

Classic Braises and Stews from Around the World

Adobo (Philippines)
Beef *Bourguignon* (France)
Beef *Daube* (France)
Beer-Braised Sausages (Germany)
Bigots (Poland)
Braised Pork Belly (All over!)
Cassoulet (France)
Chicken *Alla Cacciatora* (Italy)
Chilli Con Carne (US)
Coq au Vin (France)
Country-Style Ribs (US South)
Doro Wat (Ethiopia)
Fesenjan (Iran)
Ghormeh Sabzi (Iran)
Goat *Birria* (Mexico)
Goulash (Poland)
Lamb Tagine (Morocco)
Locro (Argentina)
Nikujaga (Japan)
Osso Buco (Italy)
Pork Cooked in Milk (Italy)
Pot au Feu (France)
Pot Roast (US)
Pozole (Mexico)
Ragù Bolognese (Italy)
Rogan Josh (Kashmir)
Roman Oxtail Stew (Italy)
Tas Kebap (Turkey)

Basic Braising Times

Chicken Breasts: 5 to 8 minutes if boneless, 15 to 18 minutes if on the bone. (If braising a whole chicken, split the breasts into quarters, cook them on the bone, and remove them from the pot when finished, about 15 to 18 minutes, allowing the legs to finish on their own.)

Chicken legs: 35 to 40 minutes

Duck legs: 1½ to 2 hours

Turkey legs: 2½ to 3 hours

Pork shoulder: 2½ to 3½ hours, longer if on the bone

Bony beef (short ribs, *osso buco*, oxtail): 3 to 3½ hours

Meaty beef (chuck, brisket, round): 3 to 3½ hours

Lamb shoulder on the bone: 2½ to 3 hours

Protein Shopping Guide

On average, 450g of each of the following will feed:

Fish fillet: 3 people

Shell-on shellfish (except for prawns): 1 person

Shell-on prawns: 3 people

Bone-in roast: 1.5 people

Steak: 3 people

Whole animals and meat on the bone: 1 person

Ground meat for burgers or sausages: 3 people

Ground meat for *ragù* or chilli: 4 people

AROMATIC FLAVOUR BASES of THE WORLD

FRANCE: Mirepoix

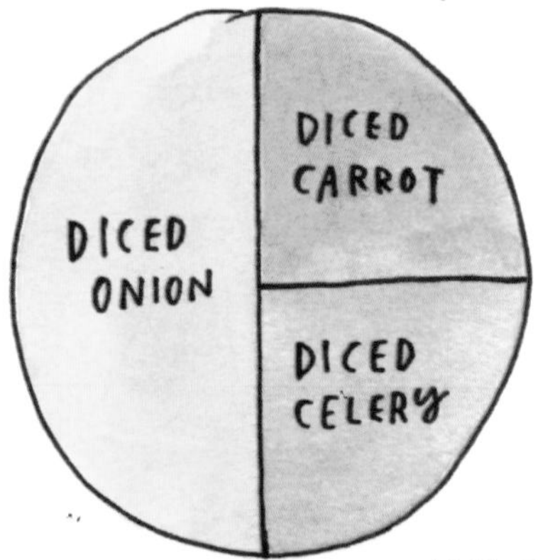

COOK in BUTTER or OLIVE OIL UNTIL SOFT WITHOUT BROWNING

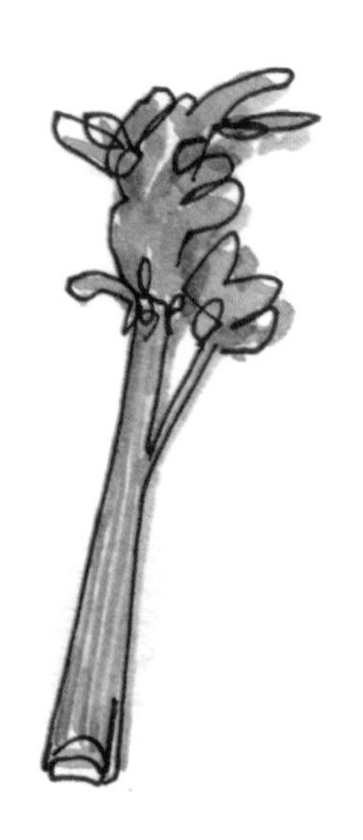

ITALY: Soffritto

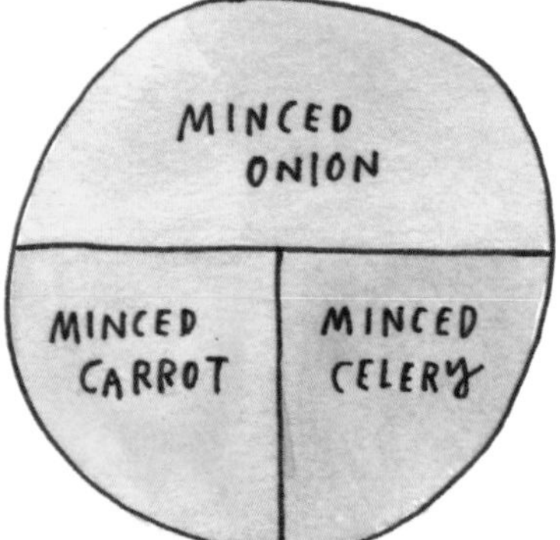

COOK in ABUNDANT OLIVE OIL UNTIL SOFT and BROWN

CATALONIA: Sofregit

CHOPPED ONION

CHOPPED TOMATO

(OPTIONAL: GARLIC and/or RED BELL PEPPERS)

COOK in ABUNDANT OLIVE OIL UNTIL SOFT and BROWN

INDIA:
Adu Lasan

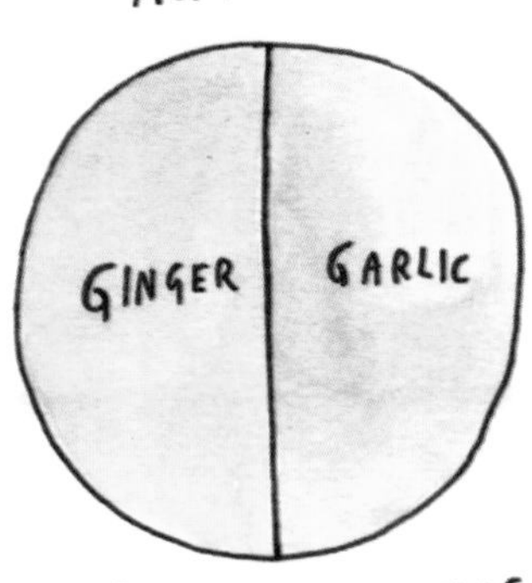

GRIND into A PASTE USING A MORTAR and PESTLE or FOOD PROCESSOR. RUB on MEAT or POULTRY BEFORE COOKING, or SIZZLE in OIL ALONG with SOFTENED ONIONS.

GUANGDONG, CHINA (CANTONESE COOKING):
Aromatics

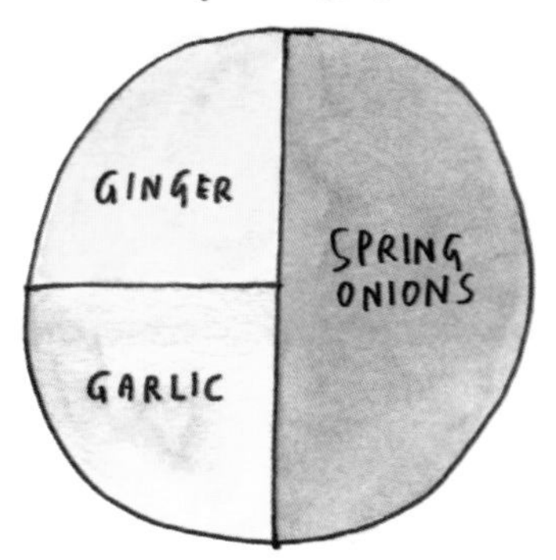

FOR MILD FLAVOUR, ADD in LARGE PIECES at THE START of COOKING. FOR STRONG FLAVOUR, MINCE and ADD at THE END of STIR-FRYING.

PUERTO RICO:
Recaíto

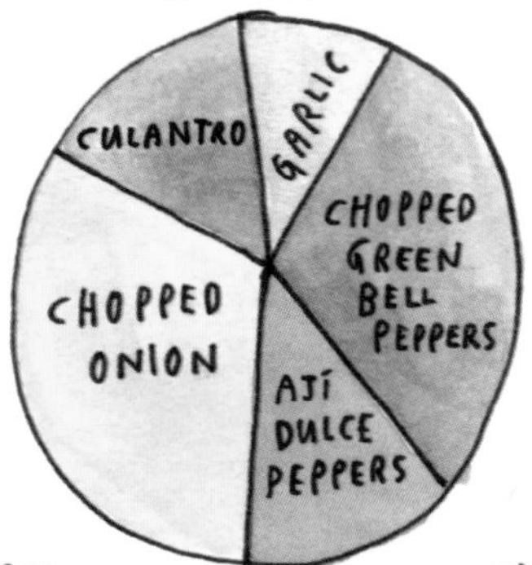

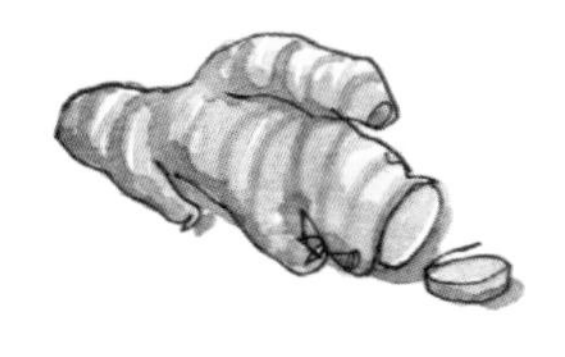

COOK in NEUTRAL OIL UNTIL SOFT and BEGINNING to BROWN

AMERICAN SOUTH:
The Holy Trinity

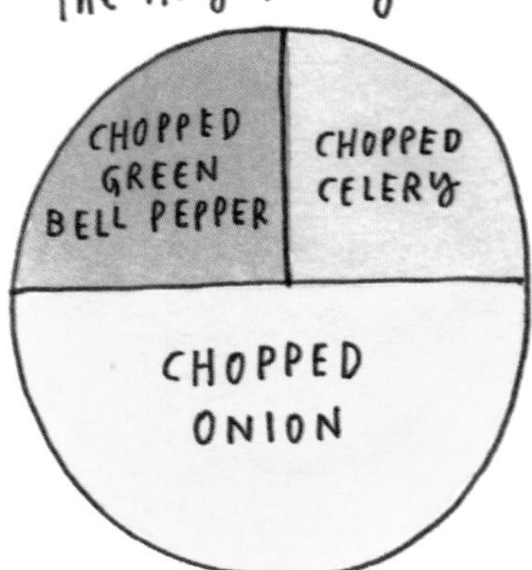

COOK in NEUTRAL OIL UNTIL SOFT

WEST AFRICA:
Ata Lilo

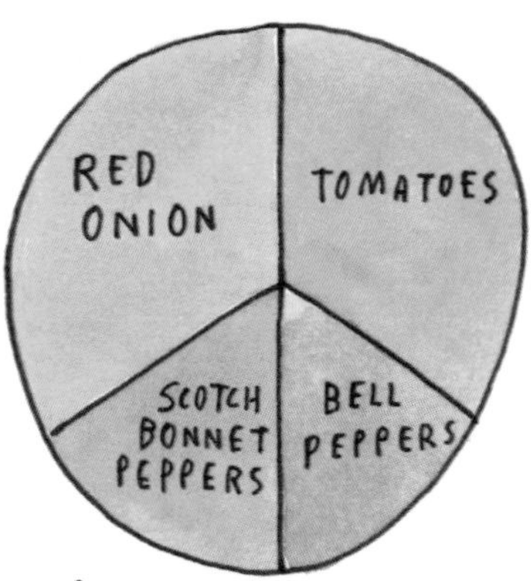

PURÉE EVERYTHING TOGETHER and REDUCE to A THICK PASTE

Steak

The key to cooking any steak perfectly is to sear the surface evenly on all sides while cooking the meat to your preferred doneness. But not all steaks are created equal: different cuts will cook differently depending on their fat content and the structure of the muscle fibres.

When cooking steak, a few rules apply no matter what cut you're using. First of all, trim silver skin, sinew, and excessive fat. Secondly, season any steak in advance to give salt the time it needs to perform its tenderising and flavour-enhancing feats. Bring any steak to room temperature for 30 to 60 minutes before cooking, whatever the method may be.

When grilling, always create various heat zones: glowing hot coals for direct heat, and a cooler, mostly coal-free spot for indirect heat. If using a gas grill, mimic the same effect with the burners. Don't leave grilling meat unattended—as it cooks, and its fat renders, it will drip down and cause flare-ups. When flames brush the surface of cooking meat, they leave behind awful, gaseous-tasting flavour compounds. So never, ever cook directly over flame.

If you don't have a grill, or the weather isn't conducive to grilling, simulate high-heat grilling by cooking steak in a blazing-hot cast iron frying pan. Preheat the pan in a 260°C oven for 20 minutes, and then carefully place it over a burner set to high heat. Cook as directed below, ensuring that you leave plenty of space between each steak in the pan to allow steam to escape. You might also want to open a window and disable your smoke alarm before you start. You can simulate indirect-heat cooking by simply preheating your cast iron pan on the stove and then cooking over a moderate flame.

My two favourite steaks are skirt and rib eye. Both are deeply flavourful. Reasonably priced, and simple to prepare, I think of skirt as a "weeknight" steak. Juicy and beautifully marbled, rib eye can get pricey, so I think of it as a "special occasion" steak.

Grill **skirt steak** over hot coals, or the **highest heat**, 2 to 3 minutes per side for rare/medium-rare.

Cook a **2.5cm thick rib eye**, about 225g, over **high heat**, about 4 minutes per side for rare, and about 5 minutes per side for medium.

In contrast, cook a **6cm thick bone-in rib eye**, about 900g 12 to 15 minutes per side for medium-rare, over **indirect heat** in order to allow a beautiful dark-brown crust to develop on every inch of its surface.

Press on any steak to judge its doneness. It'll be soft when rare, a little spongy when medium-rare, and firm when well-done. You can also always just cut into the steak and take a peek. Or use an instant-read meat thermometer: 46°C for rare, 51°C for medium-rare, 57°C for medium, 63°C for medium-well, and 68°C for well-done. Pull meat from the heat at these temperatures, then let it rest 5 to 10 minutes. It'll carry over another two or three degrees, to the perfect level of doneness.

And, however you cook a steak, always let it rest for 5 to 10 minutes, no matter how hungry you are! The resting time will give the proteins a chance to relax and allow the juices to distribute evenly throughout the meat. Then slice it against the grain, which will ensure tenderness in every bite.

Kufte Kebabs

Makes about 24 kebabs (serves 4 to 6)

Kufte, kofte, kefta—call it what you like. It's essentially a torpedo-shaped meatball, and every country in the Near and Middle East, as well as the Indian subcontinent, has its own variation. I cook this dish when friends request a Persian meal but I can't bear the thought of all the tinkering and chopping involved for ***Kuku Sabzi*** (page 306) or any of our other endlessly complicated dishes.

1 large pinch saffron
1 large onion, coarsely grated
675g minced lamb (preferably shoulder meat)
3 garlic cloves, finely grated or pounded with a pinch of salt
1½ teaspoons ground turmeric
6 tablespoons very finely chopped parsley, mint, and/or coriander in any combination
Freshly ground black pepper
Salt

Use the saffron to make **saffron tea** as directed on page 287. Push the onion through a sieve, press out as much liquid as possible, and discard the liquid.

Place the saffron tea, onion, lamb, garlic, turmeric, herbs, and a pinch of black pepper into a large bowl. Add three generous pinches of salt and use your hands to knead the mixture together. Your hands are valuable tools here; your body heat melts the fat a little bit, which helps the mixture stick together and yields less crumbly kebabs. Cook up a tiny piece of the mixture in a frying pan and taste for salt and other seasonings. Adjust as needed, and if necessary, cook a second piece and taste again.

Once the mixture is seasoned to your taste, moisten

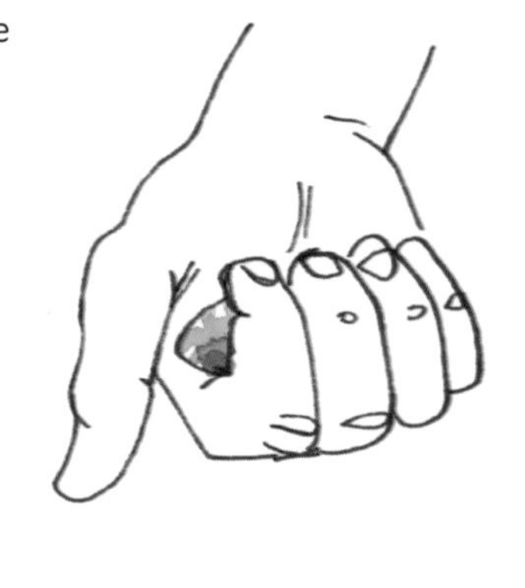

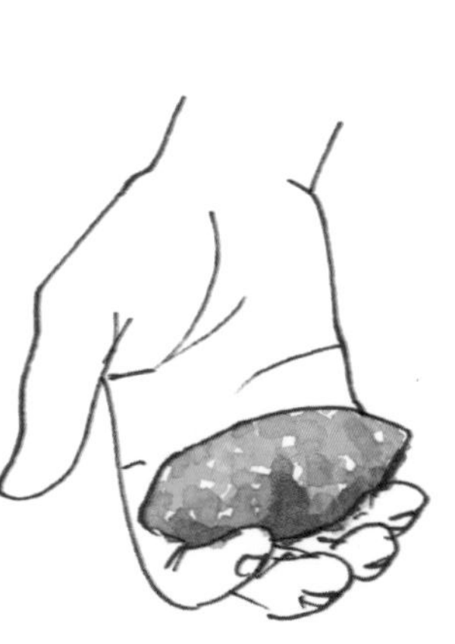

your hands and start forming oblong, three-sided meatballs by gently curling your fingers around 2 tablespoons of the mixture. Lay the little torpedoes onto a parchment-lined baking sheet.

To cook, grill the kebabs over hot coals until delightfully charred on the outside and just barely cooked through within, about 6 to 8 minutes. Rotate them often once they start to brown to give them an even crust. When done, the kebabs should be firm to the touch but give a little in the centre when squeezed. If you're not sure whether they're done, cut one open and check—if there's a dime-size diameter of pink surrounded by a ring of brown, it's done!

To cook indoors, set a cast iron frying pan over high heat, add just enough olive oil to coat the bottom of the pan, and cook for 6 to 8 minutes, flipping just once on each side.

Serve immediately or at room temperature, with **Persian-ish Rice** (page 285) and **Persian Herb Yoghurt** (page 371), or **Shaved Carrot Salad with Ginger and Lime** (page 227) and ***Charmoula*** (page 367).

Variations

- To make **Moroccan *Kofta***, omit the saffron and replace the mixed herbs with 10g finely chopped coriander. Reduce the turmeric to ½ teaspoon. Add 1 teaspoon ground cumin, ¾ teaspoon hot pepper flakes, ½ teaspoon finely grated ginger, and a small pinch of ground cinnamon. Continue as above.

- For **Turkish *Köfte***, use beef if desired. Omit the turmeric, saffron, and herbs and instead season with 1 tablespoon Turkish Aleppo pepper (or 1 teaspoon hot pepper flakes), ¼ cup finely chopped parsley, and 8 finely chopped mint leaves. Continue as above.

SAUCES

A good sauce can improve a delicious dish and save a less successful one. Learn to think of sauces as trusted sources of Salt, Fat, and Acid, which will always provide bright flavour. To get the best sense of how any sauce tastes, try it along with a bite of whatever you plan on serving it with to see how the flavours work together. Just before serving, adjust the salt, acid, and other flavourings.

SALSA MATHS

CHOPPED HERBS
+ SALT
+ OLIVE OIL to COVER
(USE MORE for A SAUCE to DRIZZLE, LESS for A THICKER SAUCE)
+ SHALLOTS MACERATED in ACID

HERB SALSA

Herb Salsa

Master herb salsa—it'll only take one attempt, that's how easy it is—and soon you'll find a hundred sauces up your sleeve. Get into the habit of buying a bunch of parsley or coriander every time you go to the store. Turn the herbs into salsa to spoon over beans, eggs, rice, meats, fish, or vegetables—really, anything you can imagine. It's a simple gesture that will improve almost any dish, from **Silky Sweet Corn Soup** (page 276) to **Tuna Confit** (page 314) to **Conveyor Belt Chicken** (page 325).

When using parsley, pick the leaves from the stems, which can be tough. Save the stems in your freezer for the next time you make **Chicken Stock** (page 271). Coriander stems, on the other hand, are the most flavourful part of the herb. They're also a lot less fibrous, so work the tender stems into your sauce.

I'm a salsa purist and recommend chopping everything by hand, but if that's simply out of the question for you, these recipes will absolutely work in a food processor—they'll just have a slightly thicker texture. Since different ingredients will break down at different rates in the machine, use it to chop everything individually and then stir it all together by hand in a separate bowl.

Basic Salsa Verde

Makes 175ml

3 tablespoons finely diced shallot (about 1 medium shallot)

3 tablespoons red wine vinegar

10g very finely chopped parsley leaves

55ml extra-virgin olive oil

Salt

In a small bowl, combine the shallot and vinegar and let sit for 15 minutes to macerate (see page 118).

In a separate small bowl, combine parsley, olive oil, and a generous pinch of salt.

Just before serving, use a slotted spoon to add the shallot (but not the vinegar, yet) to the parsley oil. Stir, taste, and add vinegar as needed. Taste and adjust salt. Serve immediately.

Cover and refrigerate leftovers for up to 3 days.

Serving suggestions: As a garnish for soup; with grilled, poached, roasted, or braised fish and meat; with grilled, roasted, or blanched vegetables. Try with **English Pea Soup**, **Slow-Roasted Salmon**, **Tuna Confit**, **Crispiest Spatchcocked Chicken**, **Finger-Lickin' Pan-Fried Chicken**, **Chicken Confit**, **Conveyor Belt Chicken**, **Spicy Brined Turkey Breast**, or ***Kufte* Kebabs**.

Variations

- For a crunchy **Bread Crumb Salsa**, stir in 3 tablespoons **Sprinkling Crumbs** (page 237) just before serving.
- To add some texture to the salsa, add 3 tablespoons finely chopped toasted almonds, walnuts, or hazelnuts to the parsley oil.
- For a spicy kick, add 1 teaspoon red pepper flakes or 1 teaspoon minced jalapeño pepper to the parsley oil.
- For an extra hint of freshness, add 1 tablespoon finely chopped celery to the parsley oil.
- For a little citrus touch, add ¼ teaspoon grated lemon zest to the parsley oil.
- For a little garlic fire, add 1 clove finely grated or pounded garlic.

- To make **Classic Italian Salsa Verde**, add 6 finely chopped anchovy fillets and 1 tablespoon capers, rinsed and coarsely chopped, to the parsley oil.
- To make **Mint Salsa Verde**, substitute 2 tablespoons finely chopped mint for half of the parsley.

Fried Sage Salsa Verde

Makes about 225ml

Basic Salsa Verde (page 360)
24 sage leaves
About 450ml neutral-tasting oil for frying

Follow the instructions on page 233 for frying sage.

Just before serving, crumble the sage into the salsa. Taste and adjust the salsa for salt and acid.

Cover and refrigerate leftovers for up to 3 days.

Serving suggestions: With Thanksgiving dinner; as a garnish for soup; with grilled, poached, roasted, or braised fish and meat; with grilled, roasted, or blanched vegetables; with **Simmered Beans**, **Crispiest Spatchcocked Chicken**, **Conveyor Belt Chicken**, **Spicy Brined Turkey Breast**, **Grilled Skirt Steak**, or **Rib Eye**.

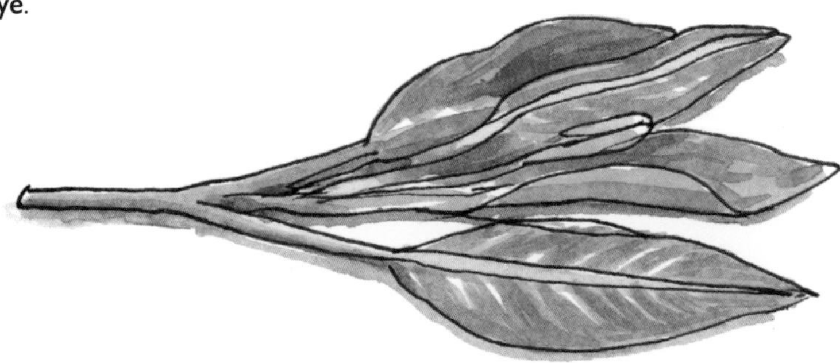

Classic French Herb Salsa

Makes 175ml

3 tablespoons finely diced shallot (about 1 medium shallot)

3 tablespoons white wine vinegar

2 tablespoons very finely chopped parsley leaves

1 tablespoon very finely chopped chervil

1 tablespoon very finely chopped chives

1 tablespoon very finely chopped basil

1 teaspoon very finely chopped tarragon

5 tablespoons extra-virgin olive oil

Salt

In a small bowl, combine the shallot and vinegar and let sit for 15 minutes to macerate (see page 118).

In a separate small bowl, combine parsley, chervil, chives, basil, tarragon, olive oil, and a generous pinch of salt.

Just before serving, use a slotted spoon to add the shallot (but not the vinegar, yet) to the herb oil. Stir, taste, and add vinegar as needed. Taste and adjust salt.

Cover and refrigerate leftovers for up to 3 days.

Serving suggestions: As a garnish for soup; with grilled, poached, roasted, or braised fish and meat; with grilled, roasted, or blanched vegetables; with **Simmered Beans**, **Slow-Roasted Salmon**, **Tuna Confit**, **Finger-Lickin' Pan-Fried Chicken**, **Chicken Confit**.

Variations

- For a pickly pucker, add 1 tablespoon finely chopped cornichons.
- To lighten and brighten the salsa, substitute the vinegar for lemon juice and add ½ teaspoon finely grated lemon zest.

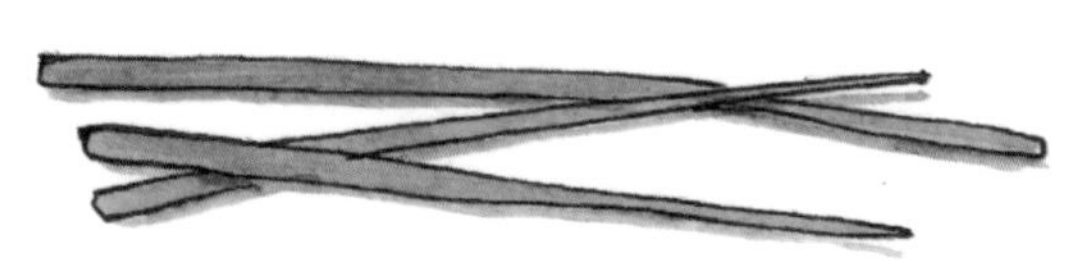

Mexican-ish Herb Salsa

Makes about 225ml

3 tablespoons finely diced shallot (about 1 medium shallot)

3 tablespoons lime juice

10g very finely chopped coriander leaves and tender stems

1 tablespoon minced jalapeño pepper

2 tablespoons very finely chopped spring onions (green and white parts)

55ml neutral-tasting oil

Salt

In a small bowl, combine the shallot and lime juice and let sit for 15 minutes to macerate (see page 118).

In a separate small bowl, combine the coriander, jalapeño, spring onions, oil, and a generous pinch of salt.

Just before serving, use a slotted spoon to add the shallot (but not the lime juice, yet) to the herb oil. Stir, taste, and add lime juice as needed. Taste and adjust salt.

Cover and refrigerate leftovers for up to 3 days.

Serving suggestions: As a garnish for soup; with grilled, poached, roasted, or braised fish and meat; with grilled, roasted, or blanched vegetables; with **Silky Sweet Corn Soup**, **Simmered Beans**, **Slow-Roasted Salmon**, fish tacos made with **Beer Battered Fish**, **Tuna Confit**, **Crispiest Spatchcocked Chicken**, **Conveyor Belt Chicken**, **Pork Braised with Chillies**.

Variations

- For a little crunch, add 3 tablespoons pomegranate seeds, or finely diced cucumber, cabbage, or jicama.
- For a little sweetness, add 3 tablespoons finely diced mango or kumquats.
- For a little creaminess, add 3 tablespoons finely diced ripe avocado.
- To make **Pumpkin Seed Salsa**, add 3 tablespoons chopped, toasted pumpkin seeds.

Southeast Asian-ish Herb Salsa

Makes about 275ml

3 tablespoons finely diced shallot (about 1 medium shallot)

3 tablespoons lime juice

10g very finely chopped coriander leaves and tender stems

1 tablespoon minced jalapeño pepper

2 tablespoons very finely chopped spring onions (green and white parts)

2 teaspoons finely grated ginger

5 tablespoons neutral-tasting oil

Salt

In a small bowl, combine the shallot and lime juice and let sit for 15 minutes to macerate (see page 118).

In a separate small bowl, combine the coriander, jalapeño, spring onions, ginger, oil, and a generous pinch of salt.

Just before serving, use a slotted spoon to add the shallot (but not the lime juice, yet) to the herb oil. Stir, taste, and add lime juice as needed. Taste and adjust salt.

Cover and refrigerate leftovers for up to 3 days.

Serving suggestions: As a garnish for soup or a marinade for meats; with grilled, poached, roasted, or braised fish and meat; with grilled, roasted, or blanched vegetables; with **Slow-Roasted Salmon**, **Tuna Confit**, **Crispiest Spatchcocked Chicken**, **Conveyor Belt Chicken**, **Glazed Five-Spice Chicken**, **Spicy Brined Pork Loin**, **Grilled Skirt** or **Rib Eye Steak**.

Japanese-ish Herb Salsa

Makes about 225ml

2 tablespoons very finely chopped parsley leaves

2 tablespoons very finely chopped coriander leaves and tender stems

2 tablespoons very finely chopped spring onions (green and white parts)

1 teaspoon finely grated ginger

55ml neutral-tasting oil

1 tablespoon soy sauce

3 tablespoons seasoned rice wine vinegar

Salt

In a small bowl, combine the parsley, coriander, spring onions, ginger, oil, and soy sauce. Just before serving, add the vinegar. Stir, taste, and adjust salt and acid as needed.

Cover and refrigerate leftovers for up to 3 days.

Serving suggestions: As a garnish for soup; with grilled, poached, roasted, or braised fish and meat; with grilled, roasted, or blanched vegetables; with **Slow-Roasted Salmon**, **Tuna Confit**, **Crispiest Spatchcocked Chicken**, **Conveyor Belt Chicken**, **Glazed Five-Spice Chicken**, **Spicy Brined Pork Loin**, **Grilled Skirt** or **Rib Eye Steak**.

Meyer Lemon Salsa

Makes about 275ml

1 small Meyer lemon

3 tablespoons finely diced shallot (about 1 medium shallot)

3 tablespoons white wine vinegar

10g very finely chopped parsley leaves

55ml extra-virgin olive oil

Salt

Quarter the lemon lengthwise, then remove the central membrane and the seeds. Finely dice the cleaned lemon, including the pith and peel. In a small bowl, combine the lemon bits and any juice you can manage to save with the shallot and vinegar. Let sit for 15 minutes to macerate (see page 118).

In a separate small bowl, combine the parsley, olive oil, and a generous pinch of salt.

To serve, use a slotted spoon to add the Meyer lemon and shallot mixture (but not the vinegar, yet) to the herb oil. Taste and adjust for salt and acid as needed.

Refrigerate, covered, for up to 3 days.

Serving suggestions: As a garnish for soup; with grilled, poached, roasted, or braised fish and meat; with grilled, roasted, or blanched vegetables. With **Simmered Beans**, **Slow-Roasted Salmon**, **Tuna Confit**, **Crispiest Spatchcocked Chicken**, **Chicken Confit**, or **Conveyor Belt Chicken**.

Variations

- To make a **Meyer Lemon and Olive Relish**, reduce the salt and add 3 tablespoons chopped, pitted green olives.
- To make a **Meyer Lemon and Feta Relish**, reduce the salt and add 3 tablespoons crumbled sheep's milk feta cheese.

North African *Charmoula*

Makes about 225ml

½ teaspoon cumin seed

125ml extra-virgin olive oil

40g coarsely chopped coriander leaves and tender stems

1 garlic clove

2.5cm knob of ginger, peeled and sliced

½ small jalapeño pepper, stemmed

4 teaspoons lime juice

Salt

Place the cumin seeds in a small, dry frying pan and set over medium heat. Swirl the pan constantly to ensure even toasting. Toast until the first few seeds begin to pop and emit a savoury aroma, about 3 minutes. Remove from the heat. Immediately dump the seeds into the bowl of a mortar or a spice grinder. Grind finely with a pinch of salt.

Place the oil, toasted cumin, coriander, garlic, ginger, jalapeño, lime juice, and 2 generous pinches of salt in a blender or food processor. Blend until no chunks or whole leaves remain. Taste and adjust salt and acid. Add water as needed to thin to desired consistency. Cover and refrigerate until serving.

Cover and refrigerate leftovers for up to 3 days.

Serving suggestions: Stir into **Basic Mayonnaise** (page 375) for a perfect condiment for turkey sandwiches; reduce the oil to 55ml and use as a marinade for fish or chicken; serve with rice, chickpeas, or couscous, braised lamb or chicken, grilled meats or fish. Drizzle onto an **Avocado Salad** or **Carrot Soup**; serve with **Persian-ish Rice**, **Slow-Roasted Salmon**, **Tuna Confit**, **Crispiest Spatchcocked Chicken**, **Conveyor Belt Chicken**, ***Kufte* Kebabs**.

Indian Coconut-Coriander Chutney

Makes about 225ml

1 teaspoon cumin seed

2 tablespoons lime juice

35g fresh or frozen grated coconut

1 to 2 garlic cloves

40g coriander leaves and tender stems (from about 1 bunch)

12 fresh mint leaves

½ jalapeño pepper, stemmed

¾ teaspoon sugar

Salt

Place the cumin seeds in a small, dry frying pan and set over medium heat. Swirl the pan constantly to ensure even toasting. Toast until the first few seeds begin to pop and emit a savoury aroma, about 3 minutes. Remove from the heat. Immediately dump the seeds into the bowl of a mortar or a spice grinder. Grind finely with a pinch of salt.

Pulse the lime juice, coconut, and garlic together in a blender or food processor for 2 minutes until no large chunks remain. Add the toasted cumin, coriander, mint leaves, jalapeño, sugar, and a generous pinch of salt and continue blending for another 2 to 3 minutes, until no chunks or whole leaves remain. Taste and adjust salt and acid. Add water if needed to thin to a drizzle-able consistency. Cover and refrigerate until serving.

Cover and refrigerate leftovers for up to 3 days.

Serving suggestions: Simmered lentils, or as a marinade for fish or chicken. With **Indian-Spiced Salmon**, **Tuna Confit**, **Crispiest Spatchcocked Chicken**, **Indian-Spiced Fried Chicken**, **Conveyor Belt Chicken**, **Spicy Brined Turkey Breast**, ***Kufte* Kebabs**.

Variation

- If you can't find fresh or frozen coconut, pour 225ml of boiling water over 30g dried coconut and let sit for 15 minutes to rehydrate. Drain and continue as above.

Salmoriglio
Sicilian Oregano Sauce

Makes about 125ml

- 10g very finely chopped parsley
- 2 tablespoons very finely chopped fresh oregano or marjoram or 1 tablespoon dried oregano
- 1 garlic clove, finely grated or pounded with a pinch of salt
- 55ml extra-virgin olive oil
- 2 tablespoons lemon juice
- Salt

Combine the parsley, oregano, garlic, and olive oil in a small bowl with a generous pinch of salt. Just before serving, add the lemon juice. Stir, taste, and adjust for salt and acid. Serve immediately. Refrigerate, covered, for up to 3 days.

Serving suggestions: With grilled or roasted fish or meat; with grilled, roasted, or blanched vegetables; with **Slow-Roasted Salmon**, **Tuna Confit**, **Crispiest Spatchcocked Chicken**.

Variation

- To make **Argentinian Chimichurri** sauce for spooning over grilled meats, add 1 teaspoon red pepper flakes and 1 to 2 tablespoons red wine vinegar to taste.

Yoghurt Sauce

I grew up spooning yoghurt on everything—including, embarrassingly, pasta!—not so much for its flavour, but because it was a handy way to cool down the steaming-hot food I usually couldn't wait to eat. Eventually, I grew to love yoghurt for its creaminess and acidity, and the way it complements rich and dry dishes equally well.

Serve these yoghurt sauces alongside **Indian-Spiced Salmon**, ***Adas Polo***, **Grilled Artichokes**, **Persian Roast Chicken**, or **Persian-ish Rice**. Or, bring them to the table as dips for crunchy raw vegetables or warm flatbread. I prefer to start with thick, drained yoghurt such as *lebne* or Greek yoghurt, but any plain yoghurt will work.

Herbed Yoghurt

Makes about 325ml

- 295ml plain yoghurt
- 1 garlic clove, finely grated or pounded with a pinch of salt
- 2 tablespoons finely chopped parsley
- 2 tablespoons finely chopped coriander leaves and tender stems
- 8 mint leaves, finely chopped
- 2 tablespoons extra-virgin olive oil
- Salt

In a medium bowl, combine the yoghurt, garlic, parsley, coriander, mint leaves, and olive oil with a generous pinch of salt. Stir, taste, and adjust seasoning with salt as needed. Cover and chill until serving.

Cover and refrigerate leftovers for up to 3 days.

Variations

- To make **Indian Carrot *Raita***, omit the olive oil. Add 65g coarsely grated carrot and 2 teaspoons finely grated fresh ginger to the yoghurt. Melt 2 tablespoons ghee or neutral-tasting oil in a small frying pan over medium-high heat. Sizzle 1 teaspoon cumin seed, 1 teaspoon black mustard seed, and 1 teaspoon coriander seed for about 30 seconds, or until the first seeds begin to pop. Pour immediately into the yoghurt mixture and stir to combine. Taste and adjust for salt. Cover and chill until serving.

Persian Herb and Cucumber Yoghurt

Makes 450ml

75g black or golden raisins

295ml plain yoghurt

1 Persian cucumber, peeled and finely diced

10g any combination finely chopped fresh mint leaves, dill, parsley, and coriander

1 garlic clove, finely grated or pounded with a pinch of salt

35g toasted walnuts, coarsely chopped

2 tablespoons extra-virgin olive oil

A generous pinch of salt

Optional: Dried rose petals for garnish

In a small bowl, submerge the raisins in boiling water. Let them sit for 15 minutes to rehydrate and plump up. Drain and place in a medium bowl. Add the yoghurt, cucumber, herbs, garlic, walnuts, olive oil, and salt. Stir to combine, taste, and adjust salt as needed. Chill until serving. If desired, garnish with crumbled rose petals before serving.

Cover and refrigerate leftovers for up to 3 days.

Borani Esfenaj
Persian Spinach Yoghurt

Makes 450ml

- 4 tablespoons extra-virgin olive oil
- 2 bunches spinach, trimmed and washed, or 675g baby spinach, washed
- 10g finely chopped coriander leaves and tender stems
- 1 to 2 garlic cloves, finely grated or pounded with a pinch of salt
- 295ml plain yoghurt
- Salt
- ½ teaspoon lemon juice

Heat a large frying pan over high heat, add 2 tablespoons olive oil, and when shimmering, add the spinach and sauté until just wilted, about 2 minutes. Depending on the size of the pan, you may have to do it in two batches. Immediately remove the cooked spinach from pan and place in a single layer on a baking sheet lined with parchment paper. This prevents the spinach from overcooking and discolouring.

When the spinach is cool enough to handle, squeeze all the water out with your hands, then chop it finely.

In a medium bowl, combine the spinach, coriander, garlic, yoghurt, and the remaining 2 tablespoons olive oil. Season with salt and lemon juice. Stir, taste, and adjust salt and acid as needed. Chill until serving.

Cover and refrigerate leftovers for up to 3 days.

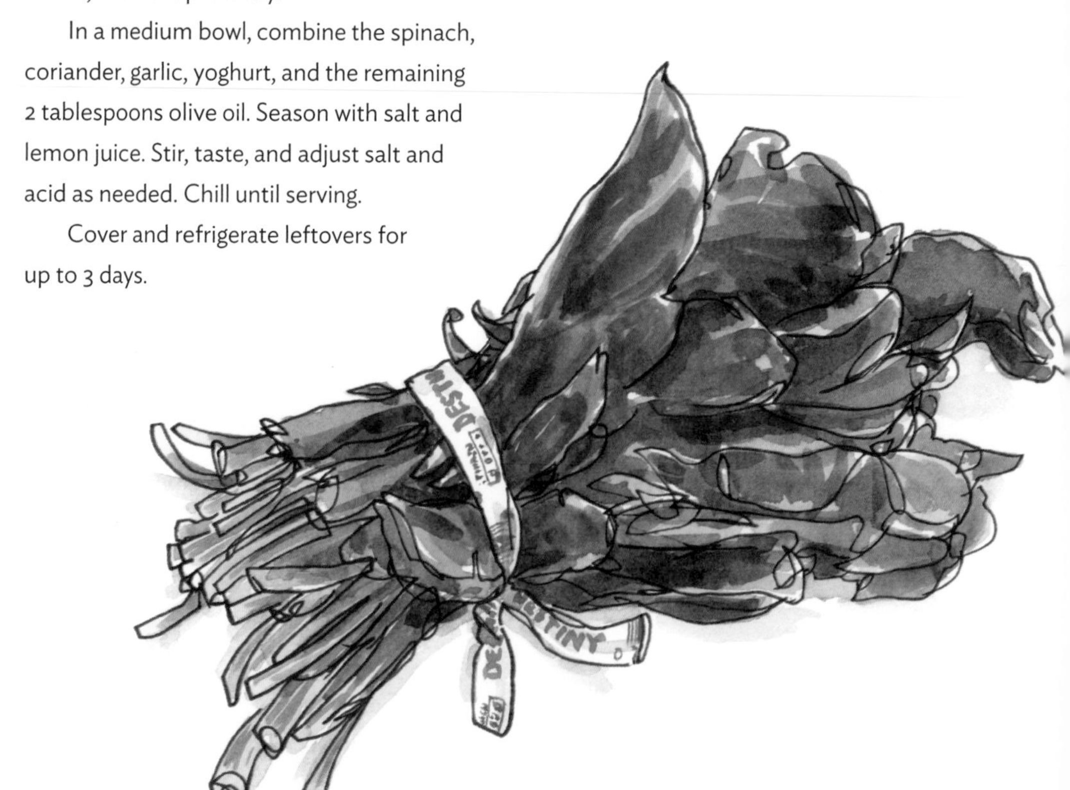

Mast-o-Laboo
Persian Beetroot Yoghurt

Makes 450ml

3 to 4 medium red or golden beetroots, trimmed

295ml plain yoghurt

2 tablespoons finely chopped fresh mint

Optional: 1 teaspoon finely chopped fresh tarragon

2 tablespoons extra-virgin olive oil

Salt

1 to 2 teaspoons red wine vinegar

Optional: Nigella (black cumin) seeds for garnish

Roast and peel the beetroots as directed on page 218. Allow to cool.

Coarsely grate the beetroots and stir into the yoghurt. Add the mint, tarragon, if using, olive oil, salt, and 1 teaspoon red wine vinegar. Stir and taste. Adjust salt and acid as needed. Chill until serving. If desired, garnish with nigella seeds before serving.

Cover and refrigerate leftovers for up to 3 days.

Mayonnaise

There might not be a sauce more polarising than mayonnaise, but I fall firmly in the camp of the devoted. And, as a teacher, I don't think there's a better way to illustrate the power of a little kitchen science than by making, breaking, and fixing a mayonnaise with my students. It's like a little miracle, every time. Refer back to the step-by-step recipe on page 86 for a refresher on all of the nuances of making and fixing a mayonnaise.

When making mayonnaise as the base for a sauce, such as **Tartar** or **Caesar Dressing**, leave it unsalted and make it as stiff as possible to account for all the other ingredients you'll be adding that will season and thin it out. On the other hand, to season a plain mayonnaise for spreading, dissolve the salt in a few tablespoons of water or whatever form of acid you plan to add, whether it's lemon juice or vinegar. If you add salt without dissolving it first, you'll have to wait a while for the mayonnaise to completely absorb it before you get an accurate idea of how it tastes. If you choose this route, add salt gradually, stopping to taste and adjust along the way.

To lend a Mediterranean flavour to **Aïoli**, **Herb Mayonnaise**, or ***Rouille*** you plan to serve with Italian, French, or Spanish food, use olive oil. To make an American-style base to use in **Classic Sandwich Mayo** or **Tartar Sauce**, use a neutral-tasting oil such as grapeseed.

Basic Mayonnaise

Makes about 175ml

1 egg yolk at room temperature

175ml oil (refer to page 374 to help you decide what type of oil to use)

Place the egg yolk in a deep, medium metal or ceramic bowl. Dampen a tea towel and roll it up into a long log, then form it into a ring on the worktop. Place the bowl inside the ring—this will hold the bowl in place while you whisk. (And if whisking by hand is simply out of the question, feel free to use a blender, stand mixer, or food processor.)

Use a ladle or bottle with a nozzle to drip in the oil a drop at a time, while whisking the oil into the yolk. Go. Really. Slowly. And don't stop whisking. Once you've added about half of the oil, you can start adding a little more oil at once. If the mayonnaise thickens so much that it's impossible to whisk, add a teaspoon or so water—or whichever acid you're planning on adding later on—to help thin it out.

If the mayonnaise breaks, refer to page 86 for tips on how to fix it.

Cover and refrigerate leftovers for up to 3 days.

Classic Sandwich Mayo

Makes about 175ml

1½ teaspoons apple cider vinegar

1 teaspoon lemon juice

¾ teaspoon yellow mustard powder

½ teaspoon sugar

Salt

175ml stiff **Basic Mayonnaise**

In a small bowl, mix the vinegar and lemon juice and stir to dissolve the mustard powder, sugar, and a generous pinch of salt. Stir the mixture into the mayonnaise. Taste and adjust salt and acid as needed. Cover and chill until serving.

Cover and refrigerate leftovers for up to 3 days.

Serving Suggestions: On a BLT or club sandwich, or in **Classic Southern Slaw** or on sandwiches made with **Spicy Brined Turkey Breast**.

Aïoli
Garlic Mayonnaise

Makes about 175ml

Salt

4 teaspoons lemon juice

175ml stiff **Basic Mayonnaise**

1 garlic clove, finely grated or pounded with a pinch of salt

Dissolve a generous pinch of salt in the lemon juice. Stir into the mayonnaise, and add garlic. Taste and adjust salt and acid as needed. Cover and chill until serving.

Cover and refrigerate leftovers for up to 3 days.

Serving suggestions: With boiled, grilled, or roasted vegetables, especially little potatoes, asparagus, or artichokes; with grilled fish or meats; with **Grilled Artichokes**, **Slow-Roasted Salmon**, **Beer-Battered Fish**, ***Fritto Misto***, **Tuna Confit**, **Finger-Lickin' Pan-Fried Chicken**, sandwiches made with **Spicy Brined Turkey Breast**, **Grilled Skirt**, or **Rib Eye Steak**.

Herb Mayonnaise

Makes about 225ml

Salt

175ml stiff **Basic Mayonnaise**

1 tablespoon lemon juice

4 tablespoons any combination very finely chopped parsley, chives, chervil, basil, and tarragon

1 garlic clove, finely grated or pounded with a pinch of salt

Dissolve a generous pinch of salt in the lemon juice. Stir into the mayonnaise, and add herbs and garlic. Taste and adjust salt and acid as needed. Cover and chill until serving.

Cover and refrigerate leftovers for up to 3 days.

Serving Suggestions: With boiled, grilled, or roasted vegetables, especially little potatoes, asparagus, or artichokes; with grilled fish or meats. With **Grilled Artichokes**, **Slow-Roasted Salmon**, **Beer-Battered Fish**, ***Fritto Misto***, **Tuna Confit**, **Finger-Lickin' Pan-Fried Chicken**, sandwiches made with **Spicy Brined Turkey Breast**, **Grilled Skirt**, or **Rib Eye Steak**.

Rouille
Pepper Mayonnaise

Makes about 225ml

Salt

3 to 4 teaspoons red wine vinegar

175ml stiff **Basic Mayonnaise**

65g **Basic Pepper Paste** (page 379)

1 garlic clove, finely grated or pounded with a pinch of salt

Dissolve a generous pinch of salt in the vinegar. Stir into the mayonnaise, along with the pepper paste and garlic. The pepper paste and vinegar will seem to thin out the mayonnaise at first, but the sauce will thicken with a few hours of refrigeration. Cover and chill until serving.

Variation

- To make **Chipotle Mayonnaise**, substitute 65g puréed canned chipotle peppers for the pepper paste.

Cover and refrigerate leftovers for up to 3 days.

Serve with boiled, grilled, or roasted vegetables, especially little potatoes, asparagus, or artichokes; with grilled fish or meats; with **Grilled Artichokes**, fish tacos made with **Beer-Battered Fish**, **Tuna Confit**, sandwiches made with **Spicy Brined Turkey Breast**, **Grilled Skirt**, or **Rib Eye Steak**.

Tartar Sauce

Makes 275ml

2 teaspoons finely diced shallot

1 tablespoon lemon juice

125ml stiff **Basic Mayonnaise** (page 375)

3 tablespoons chopped cornichons

1 tablespoon salted capers, soaked, rinsed, and chopped

2 teaspoons finely chopped parsley

2 teaspoons finely chopped chervil

1 teaspoon finely chopped chives

1 teaspoon finely chopped tarragon

1 **Ten-Minute Egg** (page 304), coarsely chopped or grated

½ teaspoon white wine vinegar

Salt

In a small bowl, let the shallot sit in the lemon juice for at least 15 minutes to macerate.

In a medium bowl, combine the mayonnaise, cornichons, capers, parsley, chervil, chives, tarragon, egg, and vinegar. Season with salt. Add the diced shallot, but not the lemon juice. Stir to combine, then taste. Add lemon juice as needed, then taste and adjust for salt and acid. Cover and chill until serving.

Cover and refrigerate leftovers for up to 3 days.

Serve alongside **Beer-Battered Fish** or **Prawns**, ***Fritto Misto***.

Pepper Sauce

Pepper sauces make for great condiments, dips, and sandwich spreads. Many, but not all, cuisines of the world, feature condiments that start with a base of pepper paste. And they aren't always unbearably spicy. Stir pepper paste into pots of beans, rice, soup, or stew to elevate flavour. Rub it onto meat before roasting or grilling, or add some into a braise. Add some pepper paste to mayonnaise and you've got French ***Rouille***, which is perfect for a sandwich made with **Tuna Confit** (page 314). Serve ***Harissa***, the North African pepper sauce, alongside ***Kufte* Kebabs** (page 356), grilled fish, meat, or vegetables, and poached eggs. Thick ***Romesco***, the Catalan pepper and nut sauce, makes a great dip for vegetables and crackers. Thin it out with a little water for an ideal condiment for roasted or grilled vegetables, fish, and meats. Serve ***Muhammara***, a pomegranate-laced walnut-and-pepper spread from Lebanon, with warm flatbreads and raw vegetables.

Basic Pepper Paste

Makes about 225g

85g dried chillies, such as Guajillo, New Mexico, Anaheim, or ancho
900ml boiling water
200ml extra-virgin olive oil
Salt

If you have very sensitive skin, put on rubber gloves to protect your fingers. Stem and seed the chillies by removing the stem and then tearing open each pepper lengthwise. Shake out the seeds and discard. Rinse the peppers, then cover them with boiling water in a heatproof bowl, and set a plate atop the peppers to submerge them. Let sit for 30 to 60 minutes to rehydrate, then drain them, reserving 55ml of the water.

Place the peppers, oil, and salt in a blender or food processor and blend for at least 3 minutes, until completely smooth. If the mixture is too thick for the blender to process, add just enough of the reserved water to thin out the paste. Taste and adjust seasoning as needed. If your paste is still not completely smooth after 5 minutes of blending, pass it through a fine-mesh sieve with a rubber spatula to remove the remaining pepper skins.

Cover with oil, wrap tightly, and refrigerate for up to 10 days. Freeze for up to 3 months.

Harissa
North African Pepper Sauce

Makes about 225g

1 teaspoon cumin seeds

½ teaspoon coriander seeds

½ teaspoon caraway seeds

225g **Basic Pepper Paste** (page 379)

30g sun-dried tomatoes, coarsely chopped

1 garlic clove

Salt

Place the cumin, coriander, and caraway seeds in a small, dry frying pan and set over medium heat. Swirl the pan constantly to ensure even toasting. Toast until the first few seeds begin to pop and emit a savoury aroma, about 3 minutes. Remove from the heat. Immediately dump the seeds into the bowl of a mortar or a spice grinder. Grind finely with a pinch of salt.

Blend the pepper paste, tomatoes, and garlic together in a food processor or blender until smooth. Add the toasted cumin, coriander, and caraway. Season with salt. Taste and adjust as needed.

Cover and refrigerate leftovers for up to 5 days.

Variation

- To make the Catalan pepper sauce called ***Romesco***, omit the cumin, coriander, and caraway. Instead, finely grind 55g toasted almonds and 55g toasted hazelnuts in a food processor, or pound together in a mortar and pestle. Set the nut paste aside in a medium bowl and purée the pepper paste, tomatoes, and garlic as directed above. Add to the nuts, then stir in 2 tablespoons red wine vinegar, 75g toasted **Sprinkling Crumbs** (page 237), and salt. Stir to combine, then taste and adjust salt and acid as needed. The sauce will be thick, so thin it out with water to your desired consistency.

Muhammara
Lebanese Pepper and Walnut Spread

Makes about 600g

1 teaspoon cumin

200g walnuts

225g **Basic Pepper Paste** (page 379)

1 garlic clove

75g toasted **Sprinkling Crumbs** (page 237)

2 tablespoons plus 1 teaspoon pomegranate molasses

2 tablespoons plus 1 teaspoon lemon juice

Salt

Preheat the oven to 180°C.

Place the cumin seeds in a small, dry frying pan and set over medium heat. Swirl the pan constantly to ensure even toasting. Toast until the first few seeds begin to pop and emit a savoury aroma, about 3 minutes. Remove from the heat. Immediately dump the seeds into the bowl of a mortar or a spice grinder. Grind finely with a pinch of salt.

Spread the walnuts out in a single layer on a baking sheet and place in the oven. Set a timer for 4 minutes and check on the nuts when it goes off, stirring them around to ensure even browning. Continue toasting another 2 to 4 minutes, until they are lightly browned on the outside and toasty when bitten into. Remove from the oven and the baking sheet and allow to cool.

Place the pepper paste, cooled walnuts, and garlic in a food processor and blend until smooth.

Add the pomegranate molasses, lemon juice, and cumin and pulse until combined. Taste and adjust for salt and acid.

Cover and refrigerate leftovers for up to 5 days.

Pesto

I once worked for a chef who had a marble mortar and pestle the size (and weight) of a small child. Even though it was horribly inconvenient and entirely messy to use, he insisted that we do so to pound all of the ingredients every time we made pesto, "to better connect with our culinary ancestors." (And in Italian, the word *pesto* just means "pounded.") While I'll let you imagine the countless eye rolls that comment generated, I will say we all took turns distracting him so we could just get the job done in a blender.

But as much as I hate to admit it, the pounded pestos always tasted better than the blended ones. Nowadays, in the interest of time and sanity, I use a hybrid method and pound the nuts and garlic separately to fine pastes in a mortar and pestle, then blend the basil in a blender and combine everything by hand in a big bowl.

For the tastiest pesto, don't skimp on the nuts and cheese. To use as a pasta sauce, spoon the pesto into a large bowl and add just cooked, drained pasta. Thin out with pasta water as needed, and garnish with (you guessed it) more Parmesan. Pesto is the rare pasta sauce that isn't heated, all for the sake of keeping it green.

In Liguria, where basil pesto originates, boiled little potatoes, green beans, halved cherry tomatoes, or wedges of sweet red tomatoes are often tossed into *pasta al pesto* at the last minute. Balance more bitter pesto made with *cima di rapa* or kale by adding a few dollops of fresh ricotta cheese after saucing the pasta.

Pesto is versatile, which is why I've included it here, among the sauces, rather than confining it to the pasta category. Some ideas to get you started: stuff pesto under the skin of **Crispiest Spatchcocked Chicken** before roasting, thin it with a little water and drizzle it over grilled or roasted fish or vegetables, or whip it into the ricotta for **Ricotta and Tomato Salad Toasts**.

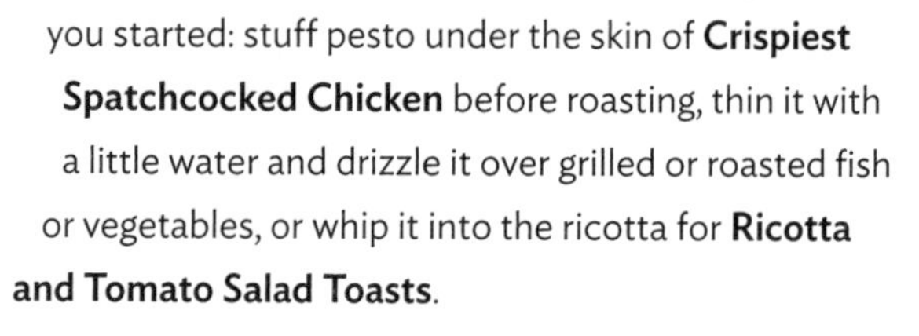

Basil Pesto

Makes 400g

175ml extra-virgin olive oil

60g (about 2 big bunches) fresh basil leaves

1 to 2 garlic cloves, finely grated or pounded with a pinch of salt

65g pine nuts, lightly toasted and pounded

100g Parmesan, finely grated, plus more for serving

Salt

The key to blending basil in a machine is to avoid overdoing it, because the heat the motor generates, along with oxidation that can occur from overchopping, will cause the basil to turn brown. So, give yourself a head start here, and run a knife through the basil first. Also pour half of the olive oil into the bottom of the blender or processor bowl, to encourage the basil to break down into a liquid as quickly as possible. Then pulse, stopping to push down the leaves with a rubber spatula a couple of times a minute, until the basil oil becomes a fragrant, emerald-green whirlpool.

To prevent overblending the basil, finish the pesto in a bowl. Pour the basil oil out into a medium bowl, and add some of the garlic, pine nuts, and Parmesan. Stir to combine, then taste. Does it need more garlic? More salt? More cheese? Is it too thick? If so, add a little more oil, or plan to add some pasta water. Tinker and taste again, keeping in mind that as the pesto sits for a little while, the flavours will come together, the garlic will become more pronounced, and the salt will dissolve.

Let it sit for a few minutes, then taste and adjust again. Add enough olive oil to cover the sauce to prevent oxidation.

Refrigerate, covered, for up to 3 days, or freeze for up to 3 months.

Variations

- Pesto lends itself particularly well to substitutions. Stick to the ratios in the recipe above, but change the greens, nuts, and cheese depending on what you'd like to eat for dinner, and what you have on hand:

Change the Greens

Cooked greens: *cima di rapa*, kale, wild nettles, chard

Raw, tender greens: rocket, pea shoots, spinach, baby chard

Herb pesto: parsley, sage, marjoram, mint

Cruciferous pesto: broccoli, cauliflower, Romanesco

Change the Nuts

Nuts, from most traditional to least. Use them raw, or lightly toasted:

- Pine nuts
- Walnuts
- Hazelnuts
- Almonds
- Pistachios
- Pecans
- Macadamia nuts

Change the Cheese

Change up your cheese, which is a great source of salt, fat, and acid in pesto. In the most traditional basil pestos, it's actually the only source of acid! Pretty much any hard grating cheese will work. The traditional cheeses are Parmesan and pecorino Romano, though Asiago, grana Padano, or even an aged Manchego will work fine.

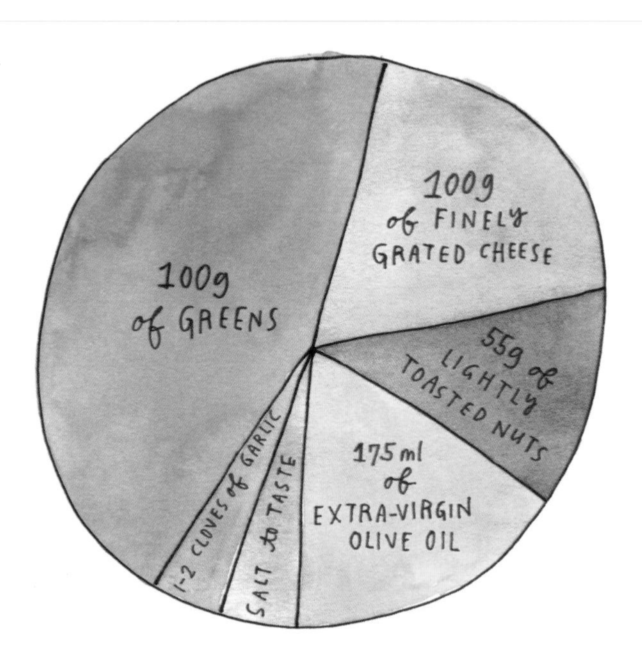

BUTTER-AND-FLOUR DOUGHS

Baking is one kitchen endeavour where precision matters. Everything in a baking recipe is there for a reason, from the temperatures to the carefully measured amounts to the chemical reactions set off by particular ingredients. Instead of changing the crucial particulars of a baked good, put your own spin on things by using different spices, herbs, or flavours.

This is the time to follow directions as closely as possible. And while I'm not generally one for kitchen gadgets, I urge you to invest in a digital kitchen scale to help here. Start baking with weights rather than volume, and you'll notice an immediate change in the quality and consistency of your baking.

Measurements matter in baking—and so do temperatures. If you're wondering why it's so important to keep everything chilled when making these butter-and-flour doughs, think of the chilly-minded pastry chef I worked with who made the most ethereal pastries I've ever tasted (or flip back to page 88 for a refresher). She knew that for flaky textures, it's imperative to discourage the formation of excess gluten, and that if butter is allowed to melt, the water it contains will combine with flour to make gluten, leading to tough, chewy pastries. But really, the proof is in the pudding pie.

All-Butter Pie Dough

Makes two 280g balls of dough, enough for two single-crust 23cm pies, one double-crust 23cm pie, or 1 Chicken Pot Pie

Use this dough to make the pie of your dreams, whether it's **Classic Apple Pie** or chess pie, **Chicken Pot Pie** or **Chocolate Pudding Pie**. Since it's made entirely with butter, this preparation requires a little forethought and care—chill everything thoroughly, work quickly, be extra careful not to add too much of it and extra attentive to prevent overworking the dough. Butter may be tricky to work with, but the result is a crust unparalleled in flavour.

One note: if you don't have a stand mixer, you can make this dough in a food processor or by hand with a pastry blender. Just make sure to freeze all of your tools, no matter which ones you use.

350g plain flour

1 generous tablespoon sugar

Large pinch of salt

225g chilled unsalted butter, cut into 1cm cubes

About 125ml ice water

1 teaspoon white vinegar

Place the flour, sugar, and salt in bowl of a stand mixer with the paddle attachment, then freeze the whole thing for 20 minutes (if you can't fit the bowl in your freezer, then just freeze the ingredients). Freeze the butter and ice water as well.

Fit the bowl on the mixer and turn to the lowest speed. Add the cubed butter, a few pieces at a time, and mix until the butter looks like broken walnut pieces. Distinct bits of butter lead to beautiful flakes in the dough, so avoid overmixing.

Add the vinegar in a thin stream. Add just enough water and mix as little as possible until the dough barely holds together—you'll probably need close to the entire 125ml. Some shaggy bits are fine. If you're not sure whether or not the dough needs more water, stop the mixer and take a handful of dough in your palm. Squeeze it hard, then gently try to break it apart. If it crumbles apart very easily and feels very dry, add more water. If it holds together or breaks into a few chunks, you're done.

On the worktop, pull out a long piece of cling film from the roll but do not cut it. In a quick, fearless motion, flip the bowl over onto the cling film. Remove the bowl, and avoid touching the dough. Cut the film from the roll and, lifting both ends, use it to encourage all the dough into a ball. Don't worry if there are a few dry bits—the flour will evenly absorb the moisture with time. Twist the film tightly around the dough to form a ball. Use a sharp knife to cut the ball in half through the film, wrap each half again tightly with film, and press each half into a disc. Chill for at least 2 hours or overnight.

To freeze unwrapped, prepared dough for up to 2 months, double-wrap it in cling film and then wrap it in aluminium foil to prevent freezer burn. Allow the dough to defrost in the refrigerator overnight before using.

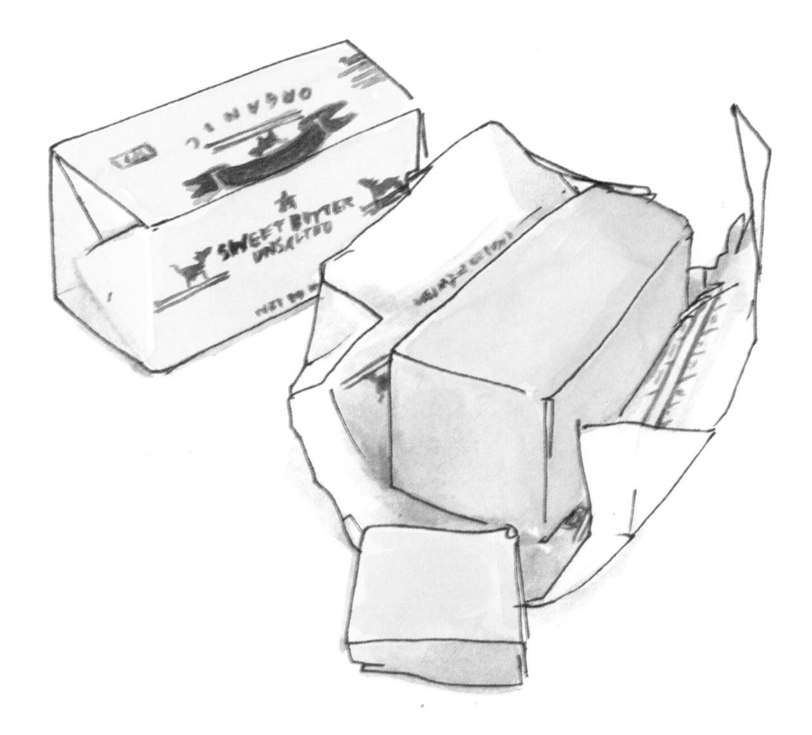

Classic Apple Pie

Makes one 23cm pie

1 recipe (2 discs) chilled **All-Butter Pie Dough** (page 386)

1.2kg tart apples, such as Honeycrisp, Fuji, or Sierra Beauty (about 5 large apples)

½ teaspoon ground cinnamon

¼ teaspoon ground allspice

½ teaspoon kosher salt or ¼ teaspoon fine sea salt

125g dark brown sugar

3 tablespoons plain flour, plus more for rolling

1 tablespoon apple cider vinegar

2 tablespoons double cream

Granulated or demerara sugar for sprinkling

Preheat the oven to 220°C and set a rack to the centre position.

Roll out one disc of chilled dough on a well-floured board until it's about 3mm thick and 30cm in diameter. Wind it around a lightly floured rolling pin and pick it up. Place the dough over a 23cm pie tin and unroll, gently pressing it into the corners of the tin. Trim any excess dough with a pair of scissors, leaving an overhang of about 2.5cm, and freeze for 10 minutes. Save and chill the trimmed bits as well. Roll out the second disc of dough to the same dimensions, cut a steam hole out of the centre, and chill in the fridge.

In the meantime, peel, core, and cut the apples into 2cm slices. Place the apples, cinnamon, allspice, salt, sugar, flour, and vinegar in a large bowl and toss to combine. Place the filling into the prepared pie tin. Use a rolling pin, as you did with the first round of dough, to pick up and gently unroll the second round over the pie filling. Use scissors to trim both crusts at the same time, leaving a 1cm overhang.

Tuck 5mm of the border underneath itself so you have a rolled cylinder that sits on the rim of the pie tin. Work with one hand inside the edge of the crust and the other on the outside. Use the index finger of the inside hand to push the dough between the thumb and forefinger of your outside hand, forming a V shape. Continue all around the crust, spacing the Vs about 2.5cm apart. As you crimp, pull the dough out just past the edge of the tin. It'll shrink back as it bakes. Patch any holes with dough trimmings.

Freeze the entire pie for 20 minutes. After removing it from the freezer, place the pie on a baking sheet lined with parchment paper. Brush the top crust generously with double cream, then sprinkle with sugar. Bake on the centre rack at 220°C for 15 minutes, then reduce heat to 200°C and bake another 15 to 20 minutes until lightly golden. Reduce heat to 180°C and bake until done, another 45 minutes. Allow pie to cool on a wire rack for 2 hours before slicing. Serve with **Vanilla**, **Cinnamon**, or **Caramel Cream** (pages 423 to 425).

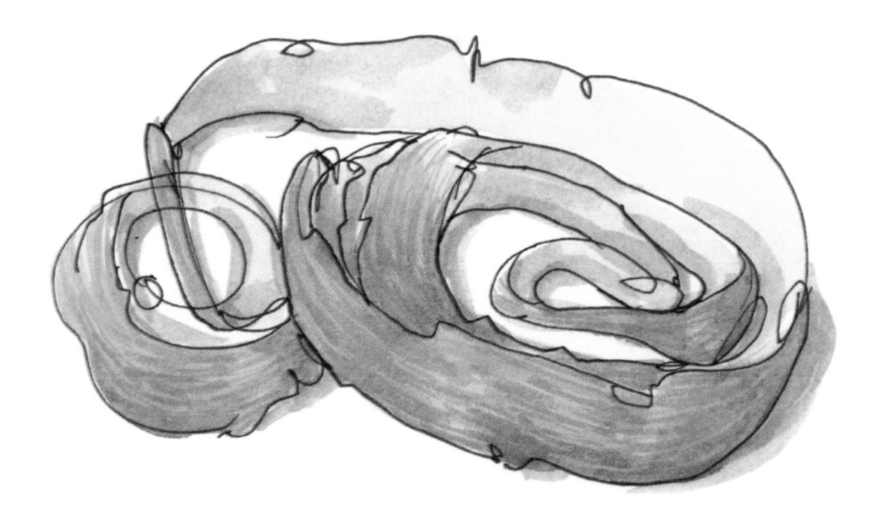

Classic Pumpkin Pie

Makes one 23cm pie

½ recipe (1 disc) chilled **All-Butter Pie Dough** (page 386)

Flour for rolling

2 large eggs

350ml double cream

425g pumpkin purée

145g sugar

1 teaspoon kosher salt or ½ teaspoon fine sea salt

1½ teaspoons ground cinnamon

1 teaspoon ground ginger

½ teaspoon ground cloves

Preheat the oven to 220°C and set a rack to the centre position.

Roll out the chilled dough on a well-floured board until it's about 3mm thick and 30cm in diameter. Wind it around a lightly floured rolling pin and pick it up. Place the dough over a 23cm pie tin and unroll, gently pressing it into the corners of the tin. Trim any excess dough with a pair of scissors, leaving an overhang of about 2cm. Save the trimmings.

Crimp the dough by rolling under itself so you have a rolled cylinder that sits on the rim of the pie tin. Work with one hand inside the edge of the crust and the other on the outside. Use the index finger of the inside hand to push the dough between the thumb and forefinger of your outside hand, forming a V shape. Continue all around the crust, spacing the Vs about 2.5cm apart. As you crimp, pull the dough out just past the edge of the tin. It'll shrink back as it bakes. Patch any holes with dough trimmings. Prick the dough all over with a fork, then freeze for 15 minutes.

Crack the eggs into a medium bowl and break them up with a whisk. Add the cream, pumpkin purée, sugar, salt, and spices to the bowl and whisk thoroughly to combine. Pour the custard mixture into the frozen shell.

Bake at 220°C for 15 minutes, then reduce heat to 160°C and bake until the centre is just barely set, about 40 minutes more. Allow to cool on a wire rack for an hour before slicing. Serve with **Tangy Whipped Vanilla**, **Cinnamon**, or **Caramel Cream** (pages 423 to 425).

Variation

- To make a **Chocolate Pudding Pie**, roll, crimp, and freeze a 23cm pie shell as directed on the previous page. Blind bake the shell: line the dough with parchment paper and fill with pie weights or dried beans. Bake at 220°C for 15 minutes, then reduce heat to 200°C and bake until lightly golden, another 10 to 15 minutes.

  Remove the crust from the oven, remove the pie weights or beans and parchment paper, and reduce the heat to 190°C. Return the crust to the oven and continue baking until the bottom of the crust is lightly golden and the outer crust is just starting to brown, another 5 to 10 minutes. Watch the crust closely on this final bake, as baking times will vary depending on the oven.

  Let the crust cool, then melt 55g of bittersweet chocolate and brush it all over the crust. Let it harden.

  Make 1 recipe **Bittersweet Chocolate Pudding** (page 416), but increase the cornflour to 40g. Press cling film onto the top of the pudding to prevent a skin from forming and cool the pudding to room temperature. Spoon the cooled pudding into the prepared crust, cover with cling film, and chill the pie overnight. To serve, top with billowy **Vanilla**, **Chocolate**, **Coffee**, or **Caramel Cream** (pages 423 to 425).

Light and Flaky Buttermilk Biscuits

Makes 16 biscuits (this recipe halves beautifully)

I learned this unconventional method from Tom Purtill, a young baker at one of my favourite diners in Oakland. The first time I tasted one of his biscuits, I begged him to come out of the kitchen and talk me through his process. And I'm so glad that I did, because every word he said was completely at odds with everything I knew about making biscuits. I'd always thought the key was to work the dough as little as possible, but he told me how he completely incorporated half of the butter into the dough to make it tender, and then rolled and folded the finished dough a few times to create flaky layers. It was so counterintuitive, in fact, that if the moistest, flakiest biscuit I'd ever seen weren't sitting right in front of me, I wouldn't have believed him.

But I did, and went straight home to try it out. I treated every word he'd said like gospel, and it worked! The key, just as he said, is to keep everything ice-cold so that the butter doesn't melt and combine with the flour to form gluten, which will make the biscuits tough. If you don't have a stand mixer, you can use a food processor. Or mix everything by hand using a metal pastry cutter—it'll just take a little while longer.

520g plain flour

4 teaspoons baking powder

1 teaspoon kosher salt or ½ teaspoon fine sea salt

225g unsalted butter, cut into 1cm cubes and chilled

225ml buttermilk, chilled

225ml double cream, chilled, plus 55ml more for brushing biscuits

Preheat the oven to 230°C. Line two baking sheets with parchment paper.

Freeze the cubed butter and the buttermilk for 15 minutes.

Place the flour, baking powder, and salt in the bowl of a stand mixer fitted with the paddle attachment and mix at low speed until combined, about 30 seconds.

Add in half of the butter, a few pieces at a time, and continue mixing at low speed until the mixture looks sandy and no distinct pieces of butter are visible, about 8 minutes.

Add the rest of the butter and continue mixing until the butter pieces are the size of large peas, about 4 minutes.

Transfer the mixture to a large, wide bowl and very briefly use your fingers to flatten the largest butter pieces: get some flour on your hands and run your thumb from the tip of your pinky to the tip of your index finger along your fingertips like you're making the "Cha-ching! Cash money!" motion.

Create a well in the centre of the mixture. Pour the buttermilk and 225ml cream into the well. Mix with a rubber spatula with broad, circular strokes until the dough comes roughly together. The dough may still appear shaggy, which is fine.

Lightly flour the worktop and turn the dough out of the bowl. Gently pat the dough out into a 2cm thick rectangle, about 23cm by 33cm. Fold the dough in half, then fold it again, then fold it a third time, then use a rolling pin to gently roll the dough back out to a 2cm thick rectangle, about 23cm by 33cm. If the top of the dough isn't yet smooth, gently repeat this rolling and folding one or two more times until it is.

Lightly flour the worktop and roll the dough to a height of about 3cm. Cut straight down with a 6cm biscuit cutter, wiping and flouring the cutter between each cut. This will ensure the biscuits rise straight up, instead of sloping over. Reroll the scraps once and cut remaining dough into biscuits.

Place the biscuits about 1cm apart on the prepared baking sheets and brush the tops generously with cream. Bake at 230°C for 8 minutes, then rotate pans and switch their oven positions. Continue baking another 8 to 10 minutes, until the biscuits are golden brown and feel light when picked up.

Transfer biscuits to a wire rack and cool for 5 minutes. Serve warm.

To freeze the biscuits for up to 6 weeks, freeze cut biscuits in a single layer on a baking sheet until solid, then transfer to plastic freezer bags and freeze. To bake, do not defrost. Brush frozen biscuits with cream and bake for 10 minutes at 230°C and 10 to 12 minutes at 190°C.

Variations

- For **Shortcakes**, add 100g sugar to the dry ingredients. After cutting the biscuits, brush with double cream and sprinkle with sugar. After baking, allow to cool for 5 minutes, then place each shortcake on a plate. Split in half and spoon in **Vanilla Cream** (page 423) and **Strawberry Compote** (page 407).

- For **Fruit Cobbler**, preheat the oven to 200°C. Prepare a half-recipe of shortcakes and chill in the fridge after cutting. Combine 1.2kg of fresh pitted cherries, sliced peaches or nectarines, or 1.2kg blackberries, boysenberries, or raspberries, with 150g of sugar, 25g cornflour, 1 teaspoon finely grated lemon zest, 3 tablespoons lemon juice, and a big pinch of salt in a large bowl. (For frozen fruit, increase cornflour to 40g.)

Pour fruit mixture into a 23cm by 23cm baking dish. Arrange the chilled shortcakes on top of the fruit. Place the baking dish on a baking sheet to catch any juices that bubble over. Brush shortcakes with double cream and sprinkle generously with sugar, then bake for 40 to 45 minutes, until the biscuits are cooked through and turning golden. Allow to cool slightly before serving, with vanilla ice cream if desired.

Aaron's Tart Dough

Makes 450g tart dough, enough for a 30cm tart

I used to be terrified of tart making, until my dear friend Aaron, who's as obsessive about flavour as I am, came up with this recipe after years of experimentation. Both versatile and forgiving, it works for any fruit or savoury tart. Once you can make a delicious tart, practise making a beautiful one. Lay out toppings with an eye toward aesthetics. Alternate different coloured plums, apples, tomatoes, or peppers for a striped pattern, or simply dot an asparagus tart with dollops of seasoned ricotta for contrast. The more senses to which your food appeals, the more delight it'll bring you.

One note: if you don't have a stand mixer, you can make this dough in a food processor or by hand with a pastry blender. Just make sure to freeze all your tools, no matter which ones you use.

235g plain flour
25 sugar
¼ teaspoon baking powder
1 teaspoon kosher salt or ½ teaspoon fine sea salt
115g unsalted butter cut into 1cm cubes, chilled
85ml **crème fraîche** (page 113) or double cream, chilled
2 to 4 tablespoons ice water

Whisk together the flour, sugar, baking powder, and salt in the bowl of a stand mixer. Freeze, along with the butter and the paddle attachment, for 20 minutes. Chill the crème fraîche and cream in the fridge.

Put the bowl of dry ingredients on the stand mixer and fit with the paddle attachment. Turn the speed to low, and slowly add the butter cubes. Once the butter is added, you can increase the speed to medium-low.

Work in the butter until it looks like broken-walnut-size pieces (don't overmix—bits of butter are *good*!). This will take about 1 to 2 minutes in the stand mixer, a little longer by hand.

Add the crème fraîche. In some cases, this will be enough to bind the dough with a bit of mixing. In other cases, you might need to add a spoonful or two of ice water. Resist the urge to add so much water, or mix for so long, that the dough comes completely together.

Some shaggy bits are fine. If you're not sure whether or not the dough needs more water, stop the mixer and take a handful of dough in your palm. Squeeze it hard, then gently try to break it apart. If it crumbles apart very easily and feels very dry, add more water. If it holds together or breaks into a few chunks, you're done.

On the worktop, pull out a long piece of cling film from the roll but do not cut it. In a quick, fearless motion, flip the bowl over onto the cling film. Remove the bowl, and avoid touching the dough. Cut the film from the roll and, lifting both ends, use it to encourage all of the dough into a ball. Don't worry if there are some dry bits—the flour will evenly absorb the moisture with time. Just twist the film tightly around the dough, press the ball into a disc, and chill for at least 2 hours or overnight.

To freeze the dough for up to 2 months, double-wrap it in cling film and then wrap it in aluminium foil to prevent freezer burn. Allow the dough to defrost in the refrigerator overnight before using.

THE HERRINGBONE TART
(to END ALL TARTS)

Apple and Frangipane Tart

Makes one 35cm tart

For the Frangipane

115g almonds, toasted

3 tablespoons sugar

25g marzipan

55g unsalted butter at room temperature

1 large egg

1 teaspoon kosher salt or ½ teaspoon fine sea salt

½ teaspoon vanilla extract

½ teaspoon almond extract

For the Tart

1 recipe **Aaron's Tart Dough** (page 395), chilled

Flour for rolling

6 tart, crunchy apples such as Honeycrisp, Sierra Beauty, or Pink Lady

Double cream

Sugar for sprinkling

To make the frangipane, place the almonds and sugar in a food processor and grind until very fine. Add the marzipan, butter, egg, salt, vanilla, and almond extract and mix until you have a smooth paste.

Flip a rimmed baking sheet upside down and place a piece of parchment paper on top (it'll be easier to shape and fold the tart without the rim of the tin getting in the way). Set aside.

Before unwrapping the dough, roll the disc on its edge on the worktop to form it into a uniform circle. Unwrap the dough and sprinkle the worktop, the rolling pin, and the dough with flour to prevent sticking. Working quickly, roll the dough out into a 35cm circle, to a thickness of about 3mm.

To roll the dough into a circle more easily, turn the dough a quarter turn with every roll. If the dough does begin to stick, lift it carefully from the worktop and use more flour as needed.

Roll the dough onto the rolling pin, and gingerly pick it up off the worktop. Carefully unroll it onto the upside-down, parchment-lined baking sheet. Refrigerate for 20 minutes.

In the meantime, work on the fruit. Peel, core, and cut the apples into 5mm slices. Taste a slice. If the apples are really tart, place them in a large bowl, sprinkle them with 1 to 2 tablespoons of sugar, and toss to coat.

Use a rubber or offset spatula to spread a 3mm thick layer of frangipane all over the surface of the chilled dough, leaving the outer 5cm uncovered.

Layer the apples onto the frangipane, making sure there is plenty of overlap. As the fruit cooks it will shrink and you don't want to end up with any naked parts on your tart. To make a herringbone design, lay two rows of apple slices at a 45-degree angle (make sure they are all pointing the same way), then reverse the angle of the next two rows to 135 degrees. Continue the pattern until the dough is covered in fruit. Use two different colours of fruits for a particularly visually striking tart. Green and purple plums, poached quince, or pears poached in red or white wine can also offer beautiful colours for you to work with. (If using more than one colour, the pattern becomes 45 degrees colour A, 45 degrees colour B, 135 degrees colour B, 135 degrees colour A to achieve stripes.)

To create a pleated crust, fold the outer dough up and over itself at 4cm-ish intervals while rotating the tart. With each pleat, crimp the dough tightly and push it up against the outer circle of fruit. For a more rustic look, simply fold the dough over the fruit at regular intervals. Leaving it on the parchment paper, return the tart to the baking sheet, now on the top side, and refrigerate for 20 minutes.

Preheat the oven to 220°C, and set a rack to the middle position of the oven. Just before baking, brush the crust generously with double cream and sprinkle generously with sugar. Sprinkle some sugar onto the fruit as well. (Brush savoury tarts with a lightly whisked egg and omit the sugar. When working with very juicy fruits, such as rhubarb or apricots, bake the tart for 15 minutes before sprinkling the fruit with sugar, which will encourage osmosis and cause it to weep. Give the crust a head start so it can stand up to the fruit.)

Bake on the middle rack of the oven at 220°C for 20 minutes. Then reduce the heat to 200°C for another 15 to 20 minutes. Then reduce the heat to 180 to 190°C (based on how dark the crust is) and cook until done, about another 20 minutes. Rotate the tart as it bakes to ensure even browning. If the crust browns too quickly, loosely place a piece of parchment paper over the tart and continue baking.

The tart will be done when the fruit is tender, the crust is a deep, golden brown, and you can stick a paring knife under the tart and lift it off the pan with ease. The underside should also be golden-hued.

Remove from the oven and allow to cool on a wire rack for 45 minutes before slicing. Serve warm or cooled, with ice cream, **Scented Cream** (page 422), or **crème fraîche** (page 113).

Cover and refrigerate unused frangipane for up to 1 week. Keep any uneaten tart wrapped at room temperature, for up to 1 day.

Variations

- When working with really juicy fruits, such as apricots, rhubarb, berries, peaches, or plums, sprinkle a little **Magic Dust** over the frangipane to help absorb the juices and prevent a soggy crust. To make the Magic Dust, simply combine 2 tablespoons each toasted almonds, sugar, and flour in a food processor and grind into a fine dust. Use 4 to 6 tablespoons Magic Dust per juicy tart.

- For savoury tarts, sprinkle about 2 tablespoons flour onto the rolled dough, and then spread on drained, cooled **Caramelised Onions** (page 254), or Parmesan, or both, to create a similar protective layer.

- For tarts made with precooked ingredients, such as roasted potatoes, radicchio, or butternut squash, adjust the baking time to 20 minutes at 220°C, plus 15 minutes at 200°C. Then check the tart for doneness, and continue baking at 180°C if necessary until the crust is golden brown and you can stick a paring knife under the tart and lift it off the pan with ease.

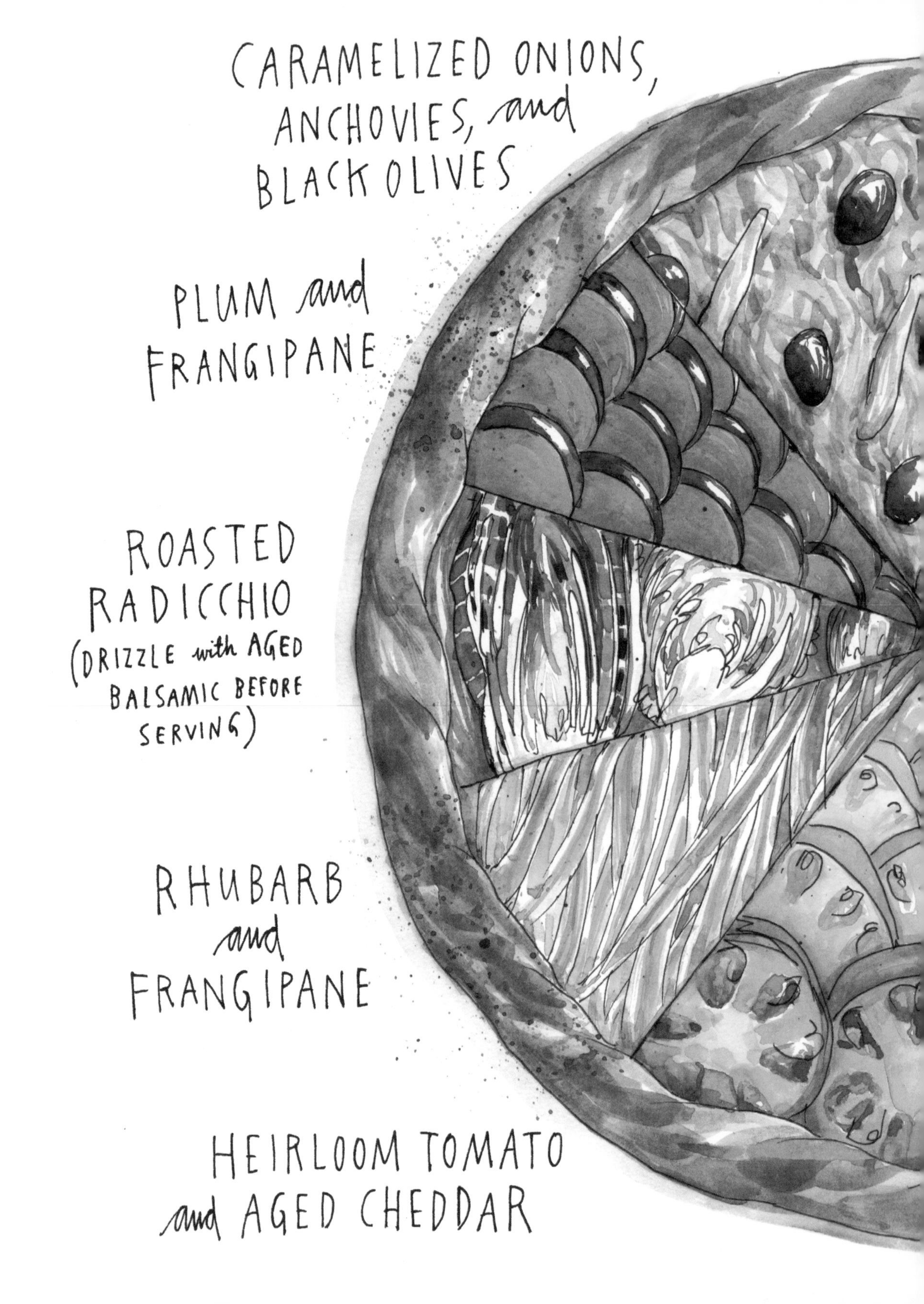
CARAMELIZED ONIONS, ANCHOVIES, and BLACK OLIVES
PLUM and FRANGIPANE
ROASTED RADICCHIO (DRIZZLE with AGED BALSAMIC BEFORE SERVING)
RHUBARB and FRANGIPANE
HEIRLOOM TOMATO and AGED CHEDDAR

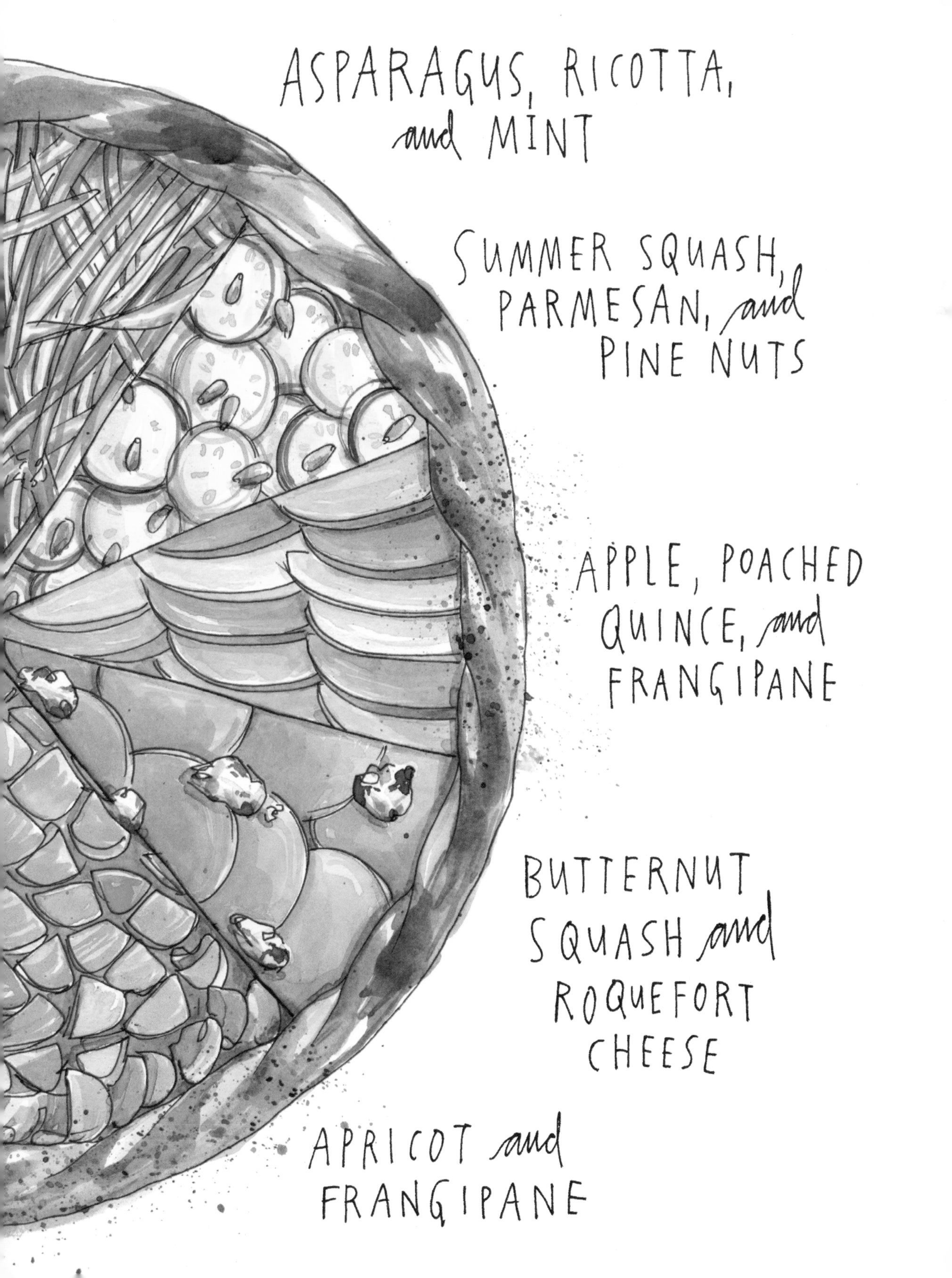
ASPARAGUS, RICOTTA, and MINT
SUMMER SQUASH, PARMESAN, and PINE NUTS
APPLE, POACHED QUINCE, and FRANGIPANE
BUTTERNUT SQUASH and ROQUEFORT CHEESE
APRICOT and FRANGIPANE

SWEETS

Nekisia's Olive Oil and Sea Salt Granola

Makes about 900g

Until recently, I'd never been one to voluntarily eat granola for breakfast. Too honey sweet, too bland, or simply not toasted enough, there always seemed to be something wrong with it. But then a friend sent me a bag of Nekisia Davis's Early Bird Granola and told me it'd change my life. As soon as I tore open the bag and tasted this nutty, darkly toasted, perfectly salted cereal, my opinion of granola changed forever.

I had to know how it was made, so I tracked down Nekisia and begged her to share the recipe. The answer: Salt, Fat, Acid, and Heat, of course. First, salt. She didn't have to explain to me what a generous dose of flaky salt would do for the cereal. Next, by replacing the neutral-tasting oils used in most granola with extra-virgin olive oil, Nekisia worked powerful flavour into the ingredient list. She gave the granola's sweetness a nice acid balance by using dark and robust grade A maple syrup, which is usually made at the end of sugaring season and is imbued with a light acidity. The slow, dark toast that comes with careful tending at low heat also offers another acidic counterpoint, as well as all the other complex flavours of caramelisation and the Maillard reaction.

Stir in a little dried fruit after baking, or sprinkle a handful of this granola over a bowl of yoghurt, for an extra hit of acid. Breakfast will never be the same.

300g old-fashioned rolled oats

125g hulled pumpkin seeds

150g hulled sunflower seeds

60g unsweetened coconut chips

140g halved pecans

150ml pure maple syrup, preferably dark and robust Grade A

125ml extra-virgin olive oil

75g brown sugar

Sel gris or Maldon sea salt

Optional: 150g dried sour cherries or quartered dried apricots

Preheat the oven to 150°C. Line a rimmed baking sheet with parchment paper. Set aside.

Place the oats, pumpkin seeds, sunflower seeds, coconut, pecans, maple syrup, olive oil, brown sugar, and 1 teaspoon salt in a large bowl and mix until well combined. Spread granola mixture in an even layer on prepared baking sheet.

Slide into the oven and bake, stirring with a metal spatula every 10 to 15 minutes, until granola is toasted and very crisp, about 45 to 50 minutes.

Remove granola from oven and season with more salt to taste.

Let cool completely. Stir in dried cherries or apricots if desired.

Store in an airtight container for up to 1 month.

Four Things to Do with Fruit

Most of the time, the best thing to do with fruit is to find a perfectly ripe piece of it and enjoy it out of hand. The copious stains running down the front of practically every shirt I own attest to the fact that I put this view into practice all summer long with berries, nectarines, peaches, plums, melons, and anything else I can get my hands on. As kitchen scientist Harold McGee says, "all cooked food aspires to the condition of fruit." Since I don't think there's much you can do to improve upon fruit, I suggest the next best thing, which is to do as little as possible to it. In addition to tarts and pies, these are my four go-to methods for showing off the glory of ripe fruit.

Precisely because these recipes are so simple, they do require that you start with the tastiest fruit you can get. Use ripe fruit at the height of its season (or, for the *Granita*, frozen fruit, which is frozen at its peak). You won't regret the extra effort.

Juice It and Make *Granita*

Granita is Sicilian shaved ice, one of my favourite refreshing desserts, in part because it's so simple to make. Since it's frozen with intermittent rather than constant stirring, the ice crystals that form are much larger and flakier than those you find in ice cream or gelato. They half melt, half crunch away on the tongue.

Squeeze your own citrus juice (or for a shortcut, buy freshly squeezed juice). Or juice any ripe or frozen fruit (my favourites are cherry, strawberry, raspberry, and melon) by blending it with a little water in a food processor or blender, and then straining out the solids. Make sure to squeeze every last bit of liquid out by pressing hard with a rubber spatula or the back of a ladle. Almond milk, coconut milk, root beer, coffee, espresso, or red wine will also make delicious *Granita* when you don't have fruit on hand.

Once you've got the juice, sweeten it and balance the acid with lemon or lime juice—whichever is more appropriate. Keeping in mind that everything tastes less sweet when it's frozen, add a little more sugar than you think it needs.

To get you started, here are a couple of basic recipes. Both make enough *Granita* to serve 4 people.

Orange *Granita*

450ml orange juice

50g sugar

6 tablespoons lemon juice

Pinch of salt

Coffee *Granita*

450ml strongly brewed coffee

100g sugar

Pinch of salt

Pour either mixture above—or one of your own devising—into a nonreactive (i.e., stainless steel, glass, or ceramic) dish or bowl. The mixture should be at least 2.5cm deep in the dish. Place in the freezer. After about an hour, begin stirring every once in a while with a fork as time allows. When you stir, make sure to mix up the more frozen edges and top layer really well with the slushier centre. The more diligently you stir, the finer and more even in texture (less icy) the finished *Granita* will be. Freeze the *Granita* until frozen throughout, about 8 hours. Stir things up a minimum of three times throughout the freezing process, then give the *Granita* a thorough final scrape right before serving until it's the texture of shaved ice. Serve with ice cream or a dollop of **Scented Cream** (page 422), if desired. Store, covered, in the freezer for up to a week.

Poach It in Wine

Peel, halve, seed or pit, and poach peaches, nectarines, apricots, plums, apples, pears, or quince in wine until tender (resist combining different fruits in a single pot, as they'll cook at different rates). Use red or white wine, sweet or dry, as your menu and tastes guide you. For every 900g of fruit, combine 900ml of wine, 265g sugar, a 2.5 by 8cm strip of lemon zest, half a scraped vanilla bean and

its seeds, and a generous pinch of salt in a heavy, nonreactive pot. Bring to a boil, then turn down to a simmer. Cover the fruit with a round piece of parchment paper with a 5cm hole cut in the centre. Simmer until the fruit is tender when pricked with a paring knife—this can take as little as 3 minutes for apricots, and as much as 2½ hours for quince. When the fruit is tender, remove it from the liquid and let it cool on a plate. If the poaching liquid is watery, rather than syrupy, reduce it over high heat until it's the consistency of maple syrup. Cool the syrup to room temperature and return the fruit to it. Serve the fruit warm or at room temperature, drizzled with some of its syrup, alongside mascarpone, **crème fraîche** (page 113), lightly sweetened ricotta, Greek yoghurt, vanilla ice cream, or **Scented Cream** (page 422).

For a visually striking dessert, poach half of the pears or quince in red wine and the other half in white wine, and alternate slices of each on the plate. In the winter months, add half a cinnamon stick, two cloves, and a few zips of nutmeg to the wine for a kick of warm spices.

For more poaching cues, refer back to page 405.

Roast It on a Bed of Fig Leaves

Line a small ceramic or glass roasting dish with fig leaves, which will lend a heavenly nutty aroma to the fruit (alternatively, use a few bay leaves or sprigs of thyme). Fill the dish with a single layer of fist-size bunches of grapes on the stem, or halved apricots, nectarines, peaches, or plums, with the cut side up. Sprinkle generously with sugar. Roast in a 220°C oven until tender within, and golden brown on the surface, about 15 minutes for smaller fruit and 30 minutes for larger fruit. Serve warm or at room temperature, with **Scented Cream** (page 422) or vanilla ice cream, or alongside **Buttermilk Panna Cotta** (page 418).

Make Compote

Use fresh, ripe fruit to make compote, which is simply fruit tossed with a little bit of sugar and allowed to sit, or macerate. If necessary, balance out excess sweetness with a few drops of lemon juice, wine, or vinegar. If you're unsure of what adding sugar to taste might look like, start with a generous sprinkle, let it be absorbed, then taste and add more as needed.

For a simple dessert, serve compote with cookies, or alongside **Scented Cream** (page 422), vanilla ice cream, mascarpone, sweetened ricotta, Greek yoghurt or **crème fraîche** (page 113). Or use it as a garnish for other desserts such as **Buttermilk Panna Cotta** (page 418), **Lori's Chocolate Midnight Cake** (page 410), **Fresh Ginger and Molasses Cake** (page 412), **Almond and Cardamom Tea Cake** (page 414), or **Pavlova** (page 421).

Use any of the fruits from the list below, either on their own or in combination. Add sugar and fresh lemon juice to taste, then let sit for about 30 minutes to macerate:

Sliced strawberries
Apricot, nectarine, peach, or plum slices
Blueberries, raspberries, blackberries, or boysenberries
Mango slices
Pineapple slices
Pitted, halved cherries
Segmented oranges, mandarins, or grapefruit
Thinly sliced, seeded kumquats
Pomegranate seeds

Variations

- For **Peach and Vanilla Bean Compote**, add the scraped seeds of ½ of a vanilla bean along with the sugar for every 6 peaches. Balance with lemon juice.
- For **Apricot and Almond Compote**, add ½ teaspoon almond extract and 20g toasted sliced almonds along with the sugar to every 900g of apricots. Balance with lemon juice.
- For **Rose-Scented Berries**, add 2 teaspoons rosewater to each 350g of berries along with the sugar. Balance with lemon juice.

Fruit : HOW and WHEN

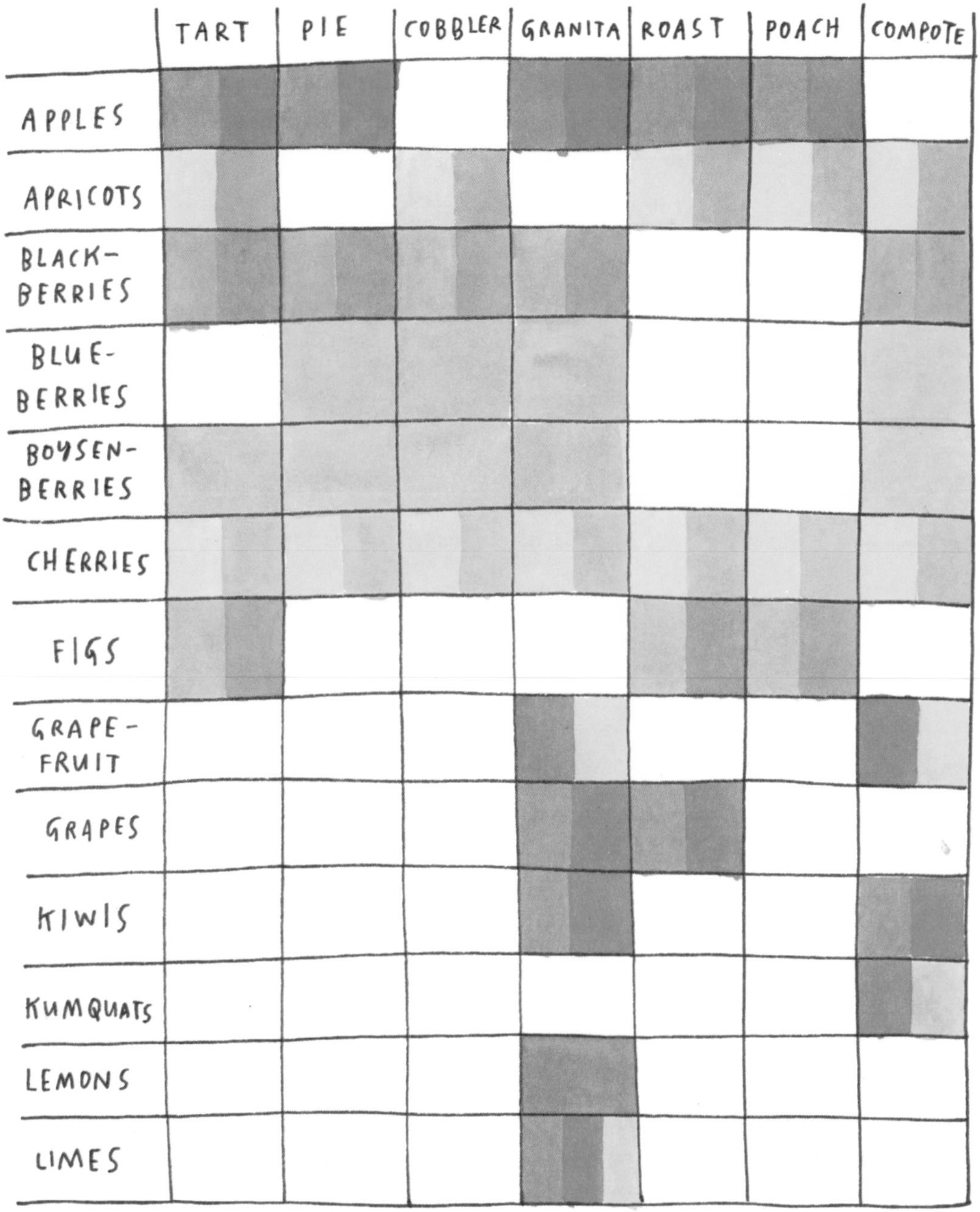

	TART	PIE	COBBLER	GRANITA	ROAST	POACH	COMPOTE
APPLES							
APRICOTS							
BLACKBERRIES							
BLUEBERRIES							
BOYSENBERRIES							
CHERRIES							
FIGS							
GRAPEFRUIT							
GRAPES							
KIWIS							
KUMQUATS							
LEMONS							
LIMES							

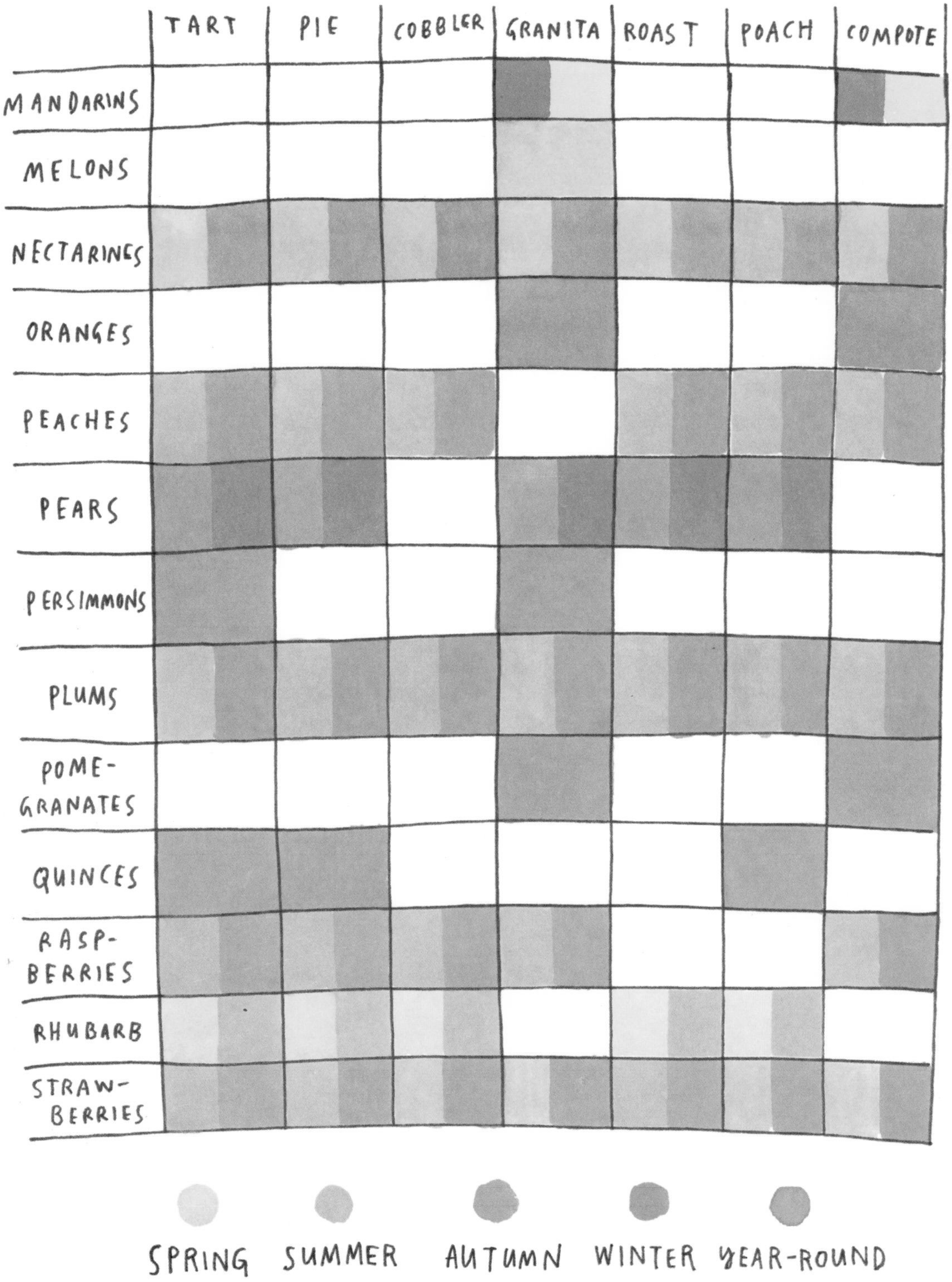

	TART	PIE	COBBLER	GRANITA	ROAST	POACH	COMPOTE
MANDARINS							
MELONS							
NECTARINES							
ORANGES							
PEACHES							
PEARS							
PERSIMMONS							
PLUMS							
POME-GRANATES							
QUINCES							
RASP-BERRIES							
RHUBARB							
STRAW-BERRIES							

SPRING SUMMER AUTUMN WINTER YEAR-ROUND

Two Favourite Oil Cakes

Lori's Chocolate Midnight Cake

Makes two 20cm cakes

Here's the recipe for the cake I mentioned in Fat—the one that changed everything for me. By age twenty, I'd given up on the idea that I'd ever encounter a chocolate cake recipe that yielded the flavourful bite I'd always dreamed of. After all, I came of age in the 1990s, the golden age of flourless chocolate cake. But all I'd ever wanted was a recipe for a cake that rivalled the moistness of cake mix cakes, yet offered that fancy-bakery flavour. A few months after I began waiting tables at Chez Panisse, my friend Lori Podraza brought in a Midnight Cake, topped with **Vanilla Cream**, to celebrate another cook's birthday. Though I'd given up on ever finding my ideal cake, I still took a slice. Who was I to turn down chocolate cake? One bite and I was sunk. I didn't know why it was so much better than any cake I'd ever tasted, nor did I care. Only months later did I realise that the cake is so moist because it's made with oil, rather than butter—just like the cake mix cakes I'd always loved!

55g Dutch-process cocoa powder, preferably Valrhona
300g sugar
2 teaspoons kosher salt or 1 teaspoon fine sea salt
255g plain flour
1 teaspoon bicarbonate of soda
2 teaspoons vanilla extract
125ml neutral-tasting oil
350ml boiling water or freshly brewed strong coffee
2 large eggs at room temperature, lightly whisked
450ml **Vanilla Cream** (page 423)

Preheat the oven to 180°C. Set a rack in the upper third of the oven.

Grease two 20cm cake tins, then line with parchment paper. Grease and sprinkle generously with flour, tap out the excess, and set aside.

In a medium bowl, whisk together the cocoa, sugar, salt, flour, and bicarbonate of soda, then sift into a large bowl.

In a medium bowl, stir the vanilla and oil together. Bring the water to a boil or brew the coffee. Add it to the oil-vanilla mixture.

Make a well in the centre of the dry ingredients and gradually whisk in the water-oil mixture until incorporated. Gradually whisk in the eggs and stir until smooth. The batter will be thin.

Divide the batter evenly between the prepared tins. Drop the tin onto the worktop from a height of 8cm a couple of times to release any air bubbles that may have formed.

Bake in the upper third of the oven for 25 to 30 minutes, until the cakes spring back from the touch and just pull away from the edges of the tin. An inserted toothpick should come out clean.

Cool the cakes completely on a wire rack before unmoulding them from the tin and peeling off the parchment paper. To serve, place one layer down on a cake plate. Spread 225ml **Vanilla Cream** in the centre of the cake and gently place the second layer atop it. Spread the remaining cream onto the centre of the top layer and chill for up to 2 hours before serving.

Alternatively, top with cream cheese frosting, serve with ice cream, or simply dust cakes with cocoa powder or powdered sugar. The batter also makes for fantastic cupcakes!

Tightly wrapped, this cake will keep for 4 days at room temperature, or for 2 months in the freezer.

Fresh Ginger and Molasses Cake

Makes two 23cm cakes

As *garde-manger* at Chez Panisse, I had to get to work at 6:00 a.m. I've never been an early riser. It took such an enormous effort for me to get myself to work on time that I always skipped breakfast. When the pastry cooks arrived at 8:00, they set out day-old cakes and cookies for everyone to snack on. By 8:15, any willpower I may have had to ignore these sweets had entirely evaporated. I'd snag a piece of ginger cake, make myself a huge glass of milky tea, slip on my wool beanie, and head back into the walk-in refrigerator. Between bites of the moist, spicy cake and steamy gulps of tea, I'd reorganise the meat and produce and prepare for the day's deliveries. Those quiet moments amid the utter busyness of the restaurant are among my favourite memories of working at Chez Panisse. I've adapted the original recipe to make it a little friendlier for home bakers. I couldn't resist making it a little saltier and spicier along the way, too. Enjoy it as I did, with a steamy cup of tea, at any time of day.

115g peeled, thinly sliced fresh ginger (about 150g unpeeled)
200g sugar
225ml neutral-tasting oil
225ml molasses
350g plain flour
1 teaspoon ground cinnamon
1 teaspoon ground ginger
½ teaspoon ground cloves
¼ teaspoon freshly ground black pepper
2 teaspoons kosher salt or 1 teaspoon fine sea salt
2 teaspoons bicarbonate of soda
225ml boiling water
2 large eggs at room temperature
450ml **Vanilla Cream** (page 423)

Preheat the oven to 180°C. Set a rack in the upper third of the oven. Grease two 23cm cake tins, then line with parchment paper. Grease and sprinkle generously with flour, tap out the excess, and set aside.

Purée the fresh ginger and sugar together in a food processor or blender until completely smooth, about 4 minutes. Pour the mixture into a medium bowl and add the oil and molasses. Whisk to combine and set aside.

In a medium bowl, whisk together the flour, cinnamon, ginger, cloves, pepper, salt, and bicarbonate of soda, then sift into a large bowl. Set aside.

Whisk the boiling water into the sugar-oil mixture until evenly combined.

Make a well in the centre of the dry ingredients and gradually whisk in the water-oil mixture until incorporated. Gradually whisk in the eggs and stir until smooth. The batter will be thin.

Divide the batter evenly between the prepared tins. Drop the tin onto the worktop from a height of 8cm a couple of times to release any air bubbles that may have formed.

Bake in the upper third of the oven for 38 to 40 minutes, until the cakes spring back from the touch and just pull away from the edges of the tin. An inserted toothpick should come out clean.

Cool the cakes completely on a wire rack before unmoulding them from the tin and peeling off the parchment paper.

To serve, place one layer down on a cake plate. Spread 225ml **Vanilla Cream** in the centre of the cake and gently place the second layer atop it. Spread the remaining cream onto the centre of the top layer and chill for up to 2 hours before serving.

Alternatively, top with cream cheese frosting, serve with ice cream, or simply dust cakes with powdered sugar. The batter also makes for fantastic cupcakes!

Tightly wrapped, this cake will keep for 4 days at room temperature, or for 2 months in the freezer.

Almond and Cardamom Tea Cake

Makes one 23cm cake

In contrast to moist, tender oil cakes, cakes made with butter should be rich in flavour and velvety in texture. The marzipan in this recipe ensures that this cake is both. With a sweet and salty, caramelised almond crust and a dense, flavourful crumb, this cake is an ideal companion for a steaming cup of afternoon tea.

For the almond topping

- 55g butter
- 3 tablespoons sugar
- 85g sliced almonds
- Pinch of flaky salt, such as Maldon

For the cake

- 145g plain flour
- 1 teaspoon baking powder
- 1 teaspoon kosher salt or ½ teaspoon fine sea salt
- 1 teaspoon vanilla extract
- 2½ teaspoons ground cardamom
- 4 large eggs at room temperature
- 255g marzipan at room temperature
- 200g sugar
- 225g butter at room temperature, cubed

Preheat the oven to 180°C. Set a rack in the upper third of the oven. Butter and flour a 23cm by 5cm round cake tin, then line with parchment paper.

Make the almond topping. In a small saucepan set over medium-high heat, cook the butter and sugar for about 3 minutes, until the sugar dissolves completely and the butter bubbles and froths. Remove from heat and stir in the sliced almonds and flaky salt. Pour this mixture into the cake tin and use a rubber spatula to distribute it evenly across the bottom of the tin.

For the cake, sift the flour, baking powder, and salt onto a piece of parchment paper to evenly combine and remove any lumps. Set aside.

In a small bowl, thoroughly whisk together the vanilla, cardamom, and eggs. Set aside.

Place the marzipan in the bowl of a food processor and pulse a few times to break it up. Add 200g sugar and process for 90 seconds, or until the mixture is as fine as sand. If you don't have a food processor, do this in your stand mixer—it'll just take a while longer, about 5 minutes.

Add the butter and continue processing until the mixture is very light and fluffy, at least 2 minutes. Stop and scrape down the sides of the bowl to ensure that everything is being combined evenly.

With the machine on, slowly start to add the egg mixture, spoonful by spoonful, as if making a mayonnaise (this is, indeed, an emulsion!). Let each addition of egg be absorbed, and the mixture regain its smooth, silky look, before adding more eggs. When all the eggs have been added, stop and scrape the sides of the bowl with a rubber spatula, then continue to mix until well combined. Scrape the batter into a large bowl.

Pick up the parchment paper and use it to sprinkle the flour atop the batter in three batches. Gently fold in the flour in between additions until just incorporated. Avoid overmixing, which will cause the cake to become tough.

Pour the batter into the prepared tin and bake on the prepared rack for 55 to 60 minutes, or until an inserted toothpick comes out clean. The cake will just pull away from the sides of the pan as it's done. Let the cake cool on a wire rack. Run a knife along the sides of the tin, then warm the bottom of the tin directly over the stovetop for a few seconds to encourage the cake to unmould. Remove the paper and set on a cake plate until ready to serve.

Serve this cake on its own, or with a berry or stone fruit **Compote** (page 407) and **Vanilla** or **Cardamom Cream** (page 423).

Tightly wrapped, this cake will keep for 4 days at room temperature, or for 2 months in the freezer.

Bittersweet Chocolate Pudding

Serves 6

For years now, I've cooked a regular dinner series together with the bakers at Tartine Bakery in San Francisco. We call it Tartine Afterhours—after the bakery closes, we push all of the tables together and cook all of our favourite foods and serve them to folks on big, beautiful family-style platters. It's not very fancy, but we pour everything we've got into it. Sometimes, around midnight, when we're in the middle of cleaning up, I'll realise I haven't eaten properly since breakfast. Looking around, I'm surrounded by pastries. As I'm invariably hot and sweaty after a long day's work, the only thing that ever looks good is a little bowl of chocolate pudding, calling out to me from the glass-doored fridge. I'll find a spoon, pull out a bowl of pudding, and taste a spoonful. Creamy and cool, it always hits the spot. One by one, the others will spot me and come over with their own spoons. Together, we'll silently finish the bowl and return to cleaning up. We always share just the one bowl. Somehow, this is one of my favourite parts of the night. Here is my slightly adapted version of the Tartine recipe—a little less sweet, and a little more salty. Like Tartine, though, I use Valrhona cocoa powder, which makes all the difference.

115g bittersweet chocolate, coarsely chopped

3 large eggs

675ml single cream

20g cornflour

150g sugar

15g cocoa powder

1¼ teaspoons kosher salt or heaped ½ teaspoon fine sea salt

Place the chocolate in a large, heatproof bowl and set a fine-mesh sieve over it. Set aside.

Crack the eggs into a medium bowl and whisk lightly. Set aside.

Pour the cream into a medium pan and set over low heat. Remove from the heat just as it starts to emit steam and come to a simmer. Don't let it boil—when dairy boils, its emulsion breaks and its proteins coagulate. The texture of a custard made with boiled dairy will never be completely smooth.

In a mixing bowl, whisk together the cornflour, sugar, cocoa powder, and salt. Whisk in the warm cream. Return the mixture to the pot and set over medium-low heat.

Cook, stirring constantly with a rubber spatula, for about 6 minutes, until the mixture visibly thickens. Remove from the heat. To test whether the mixture is thick enough, use your finger to make a line through the pudding on the back of the spoon. It should hold a line.

Slowly add about 400ml of the hot pudding mixture into the eggs while whisking continuously, then return it all back to the pot and set over low heat. Continue to stir constantly, cooking another minute or so until the mixture visibly thickens again or registers 97°C on a thermometer. Remove from the heat and pour through the sieve. Use a small ladle or rubber spatula to guide the pudding through the sieve.

Allow the residual heat to melt the chocolate. Use a blender (or stick blender, if you have one) to blend thoroughly until the mixture is satiny and smooth. Taste and adjust salt as needed.

Immediately pour into 6 individual cups. Gently tap the bottom of each cup on the worktop to pop air bubbles. Allow the pudding to cool. Serve at room temperature, garnished with **Scented Cream** (page 422).

Refrigerate, covered, for up to 4 days.

Variations

- To make **Mexican Chocolate Pudding**, add ¾ teaspoon ground cinnamon into the milk. Continue as above.

- To make **Chocolate-Cardamom Pudding**, add ½ teaspoon ground cardamom into the milk. Continue as above.

- To make **Chocolate Pudding Pie** (page 391), increase the cornflour to 35g and make pudding as directed. Refer to page 390 for complete instructions for assembling the pie.

Buttermilk Panna Cotta

Serves 6

This light custard has been an important part of the repertoire at Chez Panisse for decades. And I always assumed it was an original recipe. Years after I left the restaurant, a friend lent me his precious copy of *The Last Course,* the legendary, yet out-of-print, cookbook by Claudia Fleming, the legendary pastry chef. Right there on page 14 was Buttermilk Panna Cotta! The dessert had clearly migrated west from Claudia's menu at Gramercy Tavern in New York. Years later, I read a charming interview with Claudia where she said that nothing good is ever original and revealed that *she* had torn the recipe directly out of an issue of Australian *Vogue Living*! This recipe is such a classic, it's made its way around the world (more than once, I suspect).

Neutral-tasting oil
275ml double cream
85g sugar
½ teaspoon kosher salt or ¼ teaspoon fine sea salt
1½ teaspoons unflavoured powdered gelatin
½ vanilla bean, split lengthwise
400ml buttermilk

Using a pastry brush or your fingers, lightly coat the inside of six 175g ramekins, small bowls, or cups with oil.

Place the cream, sugar, and salt in a small saucepan. Scrape the seeds from the vanilla bean into the pan, and add the bean as well.

Place 1 tablespoon cold water in a small bowl, then gently sprinkle the gelatin atop. Let sit for 5 minutes to dissolve.

Heat the cream gently over a medium flame, stirring until the sugar dissolves and steam starts to rise from the cream, about 4 minutes (don't let the cream simmer—it'll deactivate the gelatin if it gets too hot). Reduce the heat to very low, add the gelatin, and stir to combine until all the gelatin dissolves, about 1 minute. Remove from the heat and add the buttermilk. Strain through a fine-mesh sieve into a measuring cup with a spout.

Pour the mixture into the prepared ramekins, cover with cling film, and refrigerate until set, at least 4 hours or overnight.

To unmould, dip the ramekins into a dish of hot water, and then invert the custards onto plates. Garnish with citrus, berry, or stone fruit **Compote** (page 407).

Can be prepared up to 2 days in advance.

Variations

- For **Cardamom Panna Cotta**, add ¾ teaspoon ground cardamom to the cream before heating. Continue on previous page.
- For a delicate **Citrus Panna Cotta**, add ½ teaspoon finely grated lemon or orange zest to the cream before heating. Continue on previous page.

Marshmallowy Meringues

Makes about 30 small meringues

My friend Siew-Chin is an egg white whisperer. From her I learned the importance of whipping egg whites for meringues slowly, in order to incorporate even-size bubbles, so that they will gain more volume and be more stable as they bake. The most important thing is to keep the egg whites clean and free of contamination. Any fat—whether from the yolks, your hands, or residue inside a bowl that's not perfectly clean—will prevent them from fulfilling their voluminous potential. I love this recipe because it yields particularly soft and chewy meringues, which are equally nice as little bites or when baked into larger cup sizes for individual **Pavlovas** (see variation on next page).

15g cornflour
300g sugar
175g (about 6 large) egg whites at room temperature
½ teaspoon cream of tartar
Pinch of salt
1½ teaspoons vanilla extract

Preheat the oven to 120°C. Line two baking sheets with parchment paper.

In a small bowl, whisk together the cornflour and sugar.

In the bowl of a stand mixer fitted with whisk attachment (if you don't have a stand mixer, you can use an electric hand mixer with the whisk attachment), whip the egg whites, cream of tartar, and salt. Starting on low, slowly increase to medium speed until trails start to become visible, and the egg white bubbles are very small and uniform, approximately 2 to 3 minutes. Take your time here.

Increase speed to medium-high, slowly and gradually sprinkling in the sugar-cornflour mixture. A few minutes after the sugar is added, slowly pour in the vanilla. Slightly increase speed and whip until the meringue is glossy, and stiff peaks form when the whisk is lifted, 3 to 4 minutes.

Spoon golf ball-size spoonfuls of meringue onto the parchment paper, using a second spoon to scrape it off the spoon. Flick your wrist to coax irregular peaks to form on top of each meringue.

Slip the baking sheets into the oven, and reduce the temperature to 110°C.

After 25 minutes, rotate the pans 180 degrees and switch their positions on the racks. If the meringues appear to be taking on colour or cracking, reduce the temperature to 95°C.

Continue baking for another 20 to 25 minutes, until the meringues easily lift off the paper, the outsides are crisp and dry to the touch on the outside and the centre is still marshmallowy. Just taste one to check!

Gently lift the meringues from the baking sheet and cool on a wire rack.

They'll keep in a tightly sealed container at room temperature, or individually wrapped, for up to a week if your house is not humid.

Variations

- Form the meringues into little **Pavlovas**. Spoon the meringues onto the parchment paper in 8 by 5cm ovals, then use the back of a spoon to gently create a divot in each meringue. Bake for about 65 minutes as directed above, cool completely, and then serve with **Scented Cream** (page 422) or ice cream topped with berry or citrus **fruit Compote** (page 407).

- For **Persian Pavlovas**, add ½ teaspoon ground cardamom and 1 tablespoon cooled saffron tea (see page 287) into the egg whites. Continue as above. Serve with **Rose-Scented Berries** (page 407), **Cardamom Cream** (page 423), toasted pistachios, and crumbled rose petals.

- For a **Meringue Fool**, layer crushed meringues into glasses with berry **Compote** (page 407) or lemon curd, and **Vanilla Cream** (page 423).

- To make a **Chocolate-Caramel Meringue Fool**, swirl 55g melted, cooled bittersweet chocolate into the meringue just before baking. Continue as above. Layer crushed meringues into glasses with chocolate ice cream, **Salted Caramel Sauce** (page 426), and **Caramel Cream** (page 425).

Scented Cream

Makes about 450ml

Both light and rich, whipped cream is a most delicious contradiction in terms. Cream has a unique ability to entrap air and change from its liquid form into a billowy solid (see page 423 for more).

When you're shopping, look for plain, unadulterated double cream—many brands have stabilisers added, such as carrageenan, or are put through extreme Ultra-High Temperature (UHT) pasteurization that affects how the cream will whip. For the most heavenly whipped cream, buy pure cream whenever possible.

Steep and spike it with any of the flavours listed below to customise it as you like. Pair caramel cream with apple pie, spoon bay leaf cream atop roasted peaches, and combine Toasted Coconut Cream with **Bittersweet Chocolate Pudding** (page 416). For frosting in a hurry, whip Scented Cream just past soft peaks to stiff, and spread it all over a baked, cooled cake. You'll see, there's not much that Scented Cream won't improve.

225ml double cream, chilled

1½ teaspoons granulated sugar

Any one of the flavour options on the next page

WHIP IT GOOD

Fig. 1

Fig. 2

Fig. 3

Chill a large, deep metal bowl (or the bowl of your standing mixer) and the whisk (or whisk attachment) in the freezer for at least 20 minutes before you begin. When the bowl is chilled, prepare the cream with your chosen flavouring as directed below, then add the sugar.

I prefer to whip cream by hand because it gives me more control, so I'm less likely to overwhip it and end up with butter. If you'd like to use a mixer, run it at a low speed. Whisk until the first soft peaks appear. If using a machine, switch to a handheld whisk and continue to whisk until all the liquid cream has been incorporated and the texture of the cream is uniformly soft and billowy. Taste and adjust sweetness and flavouring as desired. Keep chilled until serving.

Cover and refrigerate leftovers for up to 2 days. Use a whisk to bring deflated cream back to soft peaks as needed.

Flavour Options

Add into cream just before whipping:

- For **Spiced Cream**, add ¼ teaspoon ground cardamom, cinnamon, or nutmeg.
- For **Vanilla Cream**, add scraped seeds from ¼ vanilla bean or 1 teaspoon vanilla extract.
- For **Lemon Cream**, add ½ teaspoon finely grated lemon zest and 1 tablespoon Limoncello liqueur, if desired.
- For **Orange Cream**, add ½ teaspoon finely grated orange or mandarin zest and 1 tablespoon Grand Marnier, if desired.
- For **Rose Cream**, add 1 teaspoon rosewater.
- For **Orange-Flower Cream**, add ½ teaspoon orange flower water.
- For **Boozy Cream**, add 1 tablespoon Grand Marnier, amaretto, bourbon, framboise, Kahlúa, brandy, or rum.
- For **Almond Cream**, add ½ teaspoon almond extract.
- For **Coffee Cream**, add 1 tablespoon instant espresso powder and 1 tablespoon Kahlúa, if desired.

Bring half of the cream to a simmer (but no hotter) with any of the below. Steep for the indicated amount of time. Strain, chill, add remaining cream, and then whip as directed on the previous page.

- For **Peach Leaf Cream** (peach leaves have a heavenly almondlike flavour!), steep 12 gently torn peach leaves for 15 minutes.
- For **Earl Grey Cream**, steep 2 tablespoons Earl Grey tea leaves for 10 minutes.
- For **Bay Leaf Cream**, steep 6 gently torn bay leaves for 15 minutes.

Steep 2 hours to overnight in the chilled cream, then strain before whipping as directed on the previous page:

- For ***Noyau* (apricot kernel) Cream**, steep 12 apricot kernels, cracked and lightly toasted.
- For **Toasted Almond** or **Toasted Hazelnut Cream**, steep 35g coarsely chopped nuts.
- For **Toasted Coconut Cream**, steep 40g toasted shredded unsweetened coconut. The coconut will absorb some of the cream, so squeeze out as much cream as you can when straining.
- To make **Chocolate Cream**, scald 125ml of double cream with 1 tablespoon sugar in a small pan over medium-low heat until you start to see steam, then pour into a bowl over 55g finely chopped bittersweet chocolate. Stir to melt the chocolate and combine. Chill in the fridge until very cold, then combine with 125ml chilled double cream and whisk to soft peaks. Serve with **Lori's Chocolate Midnight Cake** (page 410), **Marshmallowy Meringues** (page 420), **Coffee *Granita*** (page 405), or vanilla ice cream.

- To make **Caramel Cream**, cook 50g sugar and 3 tablespoons water to a dark amber colour and stop with 125ml double cream (follow the method described on page 423). Add a pinch of salt. Chill in the fridge until very cold, then combine with 125ml chilled double cream and whip as directed above. Serve with **Apple and Frangipane Tart** (page 397), **Classic Apple Pie** (page 388), **Coffee *Granita*** (page 405), **Lori's Chocolate Midnight Cake** (page 410), or ice cream.

- To make **Tangy Whipped Cream**, combine 125ml chilled double cream with 3 tablespoons sugar and 55ml sour cream, Greek full-fat yoghurt, or **crème fraîche** (page 113) before whipping as directed above. Serve with **Apple and Frangipane Tart** (page 397), **Fresh Ginger and Molasses Cake** (page 412), or **Pumpkin Pie** (page 390).

- To make dairy-free **Coconut Cream**, scoop out the solid fat from two cans of coconut milk. Chill and whip as directed above. Save the coconut milk for cooking **Jasmine Rice** (page 282). Serve the cream with **Lori's Chocolate Midnight Cake** (page 410), **Bittersweet Chocolate Pudding** (page 416), **Chocolate Pudding Pie** (page 391), or ice cream.

Salted Caramel Sauce

Makes about 350ml

It's only fitting to end this book right where it began, with salt making all of the difference. And in caramel sauce, it does. By reducing its bitterness and creating a welcome contrast to its sweetness, a little salt will turn a caramel sauce from something tasty into something inexplicably, mouthwateringly delicious. The only way to know how much salt to add is to add it incrementally, allow it to dissolve, and to taste, again and again. If you get to a point where you can't tell if the sauce needs more salt or not, then simply remove a spoonful of the caramel from the entire batch, sprinkle a little salt on it, and taste that. If it's too salty, then you'll know you've reached the limit. If it tastes *even better*, then go for it and add a little more to the whole batch. You don't ever have to risk ruining the entire batch if you're unsure.

85g unsalted butter
145g sugar
125ml double cream
½ teaspoon vanilla extract
Salt

Melt the butter in a deep, heavy-duty saucepan over medium heat. Stir in the sugar and increase the heat to high. Don't worry if the mixture separates and looks broken. Keep the faith—it'll come back together. Stir until the mixture comes back to a boil, then stop stirring. As the caramel starts to take on colour, carefully swirl the pan to encourage even browning. Cook until the sugar is a deep golden brown (i.e., the "smoke alarm" stage illustrated on page 115) and it just barely starts to smoke, about 10 to 12 minutes.

Remove from the heat and immediately whisk in the cream. Take care, because the very hot mixture will bubble up furiously and may splatter. If any lumps of caramel remain, whisk the sauce gently over low heat until they dissolve.

Cool the caramel to lukewarm, then season it with the vanilla and a big pinch of salt. Stir, taste, and adjust the salt as needed. The caramel will thicken as it cools, and I like to serve it closer to room temperature rather than hot off the stove, as it sticks to ice cream and whatever else you want to serve it on better that way. But I can't lie—it's pretty darned tasty straight out of the fridge, too.

Cover and refrigerate leftovers for up to 2 weeks. Reheat gently in the microwave or by stirring in a saucepan over very low heat.

Serve alongside: **Classic Apple Pie**, **Classic Pumpkin Pie**, **Apple and Frangipane Tart**, **Lori's Chocolate Midnight Cake**, **Fresh Ginger and Molasses Cake**, in a **Chocolate-Caramel Meringue Fool**, or on top of ice cream.

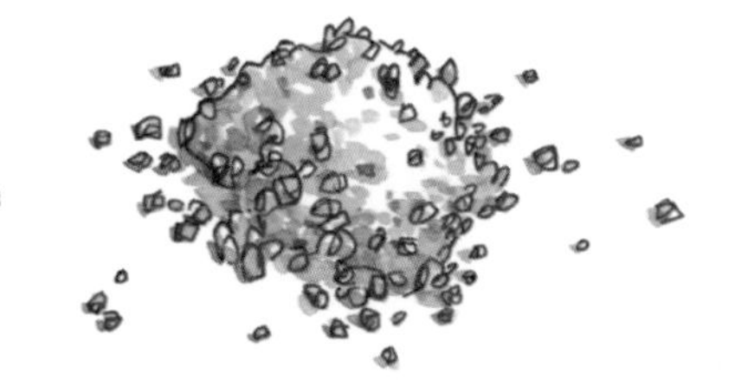

COOKING LESSONS

Now it's time to put the lessons of Salt, Fat, Acid, and Heat into daily practice. If you're not entirely sure where to start, choose a recipe that applies a specific lesson from **Part One** that intrigued you.

Salt Lessons

Seasoning from Within

Simmered Beans (page 280)
Any Pasta recipe (pages 288 to 302)
Sage- and Honey-Smoked Chicken (page 330)
Buttermilk-Marinated Roast Chicken (page 340)
Spicy Brined Turkey Breast (page 346)

Layering Salt

Greek Salad (page 230)
Caesar Dressing (page 247)
Pasta alla Puttanesca (page 294)
Pasta all'Amatriciana (page 294)
Glazed Five-Spice Chicken (page 338)

Fat Lessons

Emulsions

Tahini Dressing (page 251)

Pasta Cacio e Pepe (page 290)

Pasta Alfredo (page 291)

Chicken with Vinegar (page 336)

Mayonnaise and all of its wonderful variations (pages 374 to 378)

Almond and Cardamom Tea Cake (page 414)

Layering Fat

Blue Cheese Dressing (page 249)

Beer-Battered Fish with Tartar Sauce (pages 312 and 378)

Bittersweet Chocolate Pudding with Scented Cream (pages 391 and 422)

Acid Lessons

Layering Acid

Bright Cabbage Slaw (page 224)

Balsamic Vinaigrette (page 241)

Any-Other-Citrus Vinaigrette (page 244)

Caesar Dressing (page 247)

Blue Cheese Dressing (page 249)

Pasta alle Vongole (page 300)

Chicken with Vinegar (page 336)

Buttermilk Panna Cotta with Wine-Poached Fruit (pages 418 and 405)

Heat Lessons

Layering Heat

Grilled Artichokes (page 266)

Persian-ish Rice (page 285)

Chicken with Lentil Rice (page 334)

Roasted Butternut Squash and Brussels Sprouts in *Agrodolce* (page 262)

Browning

On the grill: Crispiest Spatchcocked Chicken, Thin or Thick Rib Eye Steak (pages 316 or 354)

On the stove: Finger-Lickin' Pan-Fried Chicken, Chicken with Lentil Rice, Pork Braised with Chillies (pages 328, 334, or 348)

In the oven: Roasted Butternut Squash and Brussels Sprouts in *Agrodolce*, Glazed Five-Spice Chicken (pages 262 and 338)

Preserving Tenderness

Scrambled Eggs (page 147)

Slow-Roasted Salmon (page 310)

Tuna Confit (page 314)

Finger-Lickin' Pan-Fried Chicken (page 328)

Turning Tough into Tender

Long-Cooked *Cima di Rapa* (page 264)

Simmered Beans (page 280)

Chicken Confit (page 326)

Pork Braised with Chillies (page 338)

A Few Other Lessons

Precise Timing

Boiled Eggs (page 304)
Scrambled Eggs (page 147)
Tuna Confit (page 314)
Skirt and Rib Eye Steaks (page 354)
Marshmallowy Meringues (page 420)
Salted Caramel Sauce (page 426)

Imprecise Timing

Caramelised Onions (page 254)
Chicken Stock (page 271)
Simmered Beans (page 280)
Pasta al Ragù (page 297)
Pork Braised with Chillies (page 348)

Knife Skills

Caramelised Onions—slicing (page 254)
Tuscan Bean and Kale Soup—slicing and dicing (page 274)
Sicilian Chicken Salad—dicing (page 342)
Kuku Sabzi—chopping greens and herbs (page 306)
Spatchcocked Chicken—basic butchery (page 316)
Conveyor Belt Chicken—basic butchery (page 325)
Herb Salsa—finely chopping herbs and fine dicing (page 359)

Improvising with Leftovers

Avocado Salad Matrix (page 217)
Blanched Greens with *Goma-Ae* Dressing (pages 251 and 258)
Pasta with Broccoli and Bread Crumbs Variations (page 295)
Kuku Sabzi (page 306)
Any Tart You Can Dream Up! (page 407)

SUGGESTED MENUS

A Light Persian Lunch:

Crumbled Feta, Sliced Cucumbers, and Warm Pitta Bread
Shaved Fennel and Radishes (page 228)
Kuku Sabzi (page 306) with Persian Beetroot Yoghurt (page 373)

Lunch on a Hot Summer Day:

Summer Tomato and Herb Salad (page 229)
Tuna Confit (page 314) with Simmered White Beans (page 280)

Classic Sandwich-and-Salad Situation:

Romaine Lettuce with Creamy Herb Dressing (page 248)
Sandwiches with Spicy Brined Turkey Breast (page 346) and Aïoli (page 376)

Conjuring Hanoi:

Vietnamese Cucumber Salad (page 226)
Pho Gà (page 333)

Pack-It-Ahead Picnic:

Kale Salad with Parmesan Vinaigrette (page 241)
Sicilian Chicken Salad Sandwiches (page 342)
Almond and Cardamom Tea Cake (page 414)

Even Better than Teriyaki:

Asian Slaw (page 225)
Glazed Five-Spice Chicken (page 338)
Steamed Jasmine Rice (page 282)

Hump Day Pick-Me-Up:

Little Gem Lettuce with Honey-Mustard Vinaigrette (page 240)
Chicken Pot Pie (page 322)
Garlicky Green Beans (page 261)

Warming Winter Dinner Party:

Winter *Panzanella* (page 234)
Brined Roasted Pork Loin (page 347)
Roasted Parsnips and Carrots (use roasting method on page 263)
Meyer Lemon Salsa (page 366)
Buttermilk Panna Cotta (page 418)
Wine-Poached Quince (page 405)

Not-Too-Indian:

Indian-Spiced Salmon (page 311)
Saffron Rice (page 287)
Indian Carrot *Raita* (page 370)
Indian Garlicky Green Beans (page 261)

Summer Supper:

Rocket with Lemon Vinaigrette (page 242)
Conveyor Belt Chicken (page 325)—try cooking it on the grill!
Cherry Tomato Confit (page 256)
Grilled Corn on the Cob (use grilling method on pages 266 and 267—parboiling is not necessary)
Strawberry Shortcakes (page 393)

Feeling French:

Garden Lettuces with Red Wine Vinaigrette (page 240)
Finger-Lickin' Pan-Fried Chicken (page 328)
Sautéed Asparagus (use sautéing method on page 260)
Classic French Herb Salsa (page 362)
Rhubarb and Frangipane Tart with Vanilla Cream (pages 400 and 423)

Flavourful Moroccan Feast:

Shaved Carrot Salad with Ginger and Lime (page 227)
Chickpeas Simmered with Moroccan Spices (page 280 and consult The World of Flavour on page 194)
Moroccan *Kofta* Kebabs (page 357)
Harissa, Charmoula and Herbed Yoghurt (pages 380, 367, and 370)

Kinda, Sorta, Izakaya:

Blanched Spinach (page 259) with *Goma-Ae* Dressing (page 251)
Crispiest Spatchcocked Chicken (page 316)
Japanese-ish Herb Salsa (page 365)

Winner, Winner, Chicken Dinner:

Bright Cabbage Slaw (page 224)
Spicy Fried Chicken (page 320)
Light and Flaky Buttermilk Biscuits (page 392)
Simmered Black-Eyed Peas (page 280)
Long-Cooked Collard Greens with Bacon (use long-cooking method on page 264)
Bittersweet Chocolate Pudding (page 416)

A Perfectly Balanced Thanksgiving:

Spatchcocked Thanksgiving Turkey (page 347)
Garlicky Green Beans (page 261)
Winter Chicories with Balsamic Vinaigrette (page 251)
Roasted Butternut Squash and Brussels Sprouts in *Agrodolce* (page 262)
Fried Sage Salsa Verde (page 361)
Apple and Frangipane Tart (page 397) with Salted Caramel Sauce (page 426)
Pumpkin Pie (page 390) with Tangy Whipped Cream (page 425)

Make-Your-Own-Taco Party:

Avocado and Citrus Salad with Macerated Onions and Coriander (page 217)
Pork Braised with Chillies (page 348) and Warm Tortillas
Mexican-ish Herb Salsa (page 363) and *crema*
Simmered Beans (page 280)

And Some Suggestions for Dessert . . .

- Apple and Frangipane Tart (page 397) with Whipped Crème Fraîche (page 113)
- Classic Pumpkin Pie (page 390) with Tangy Whipped Cream (page 425)
- Apple Pie (page 388) with Caramel Cream (page 425)
- Almond Milk *Granita* (page 404) with Toasted Almond Cream (page 424)
- Coffee *Granita* (page 405) with Chocolate Cream (page 424)
- Blood Orange *Granita* (page 404) with Earl Grey Cream (page 424)
- Roasted Apricots (page 406) with *Noyau* Cream (page 424)
- Poached Pears (page 405) with Salted Caramel Sauce (page 426)
- Peach Compote (page 407) with Peach Leaf Cream (page 424)
- Lori's Chocolate Midnight Cake (page 410) with Coffee Cream (page 423)
- Fresh Ginger and Molasses Cake (page 412) with Tangy Whipped Cream (page 425)
- Almond and Cardamom Tea Cake (page 414) with Nectarine Compote (page 407)
- Mexican Chocolate Pudding (page 417) with Spiced Cream (page 423)
- Buttermilk Panna Cotta (page 418) with Peach and Vanilla Bean Compote (page 407)
- Cardamom Panna Cotta (page 419) with Rose-Scented Berries (page 407)
- Citrus Panna Cotta (page 419) with Kumquat Compote (page 407)

TIPS FOR FURTHER READING

Once you become familiar with a writer or chef, and know that his or her recipes work, add her to your database of trusted sources. These are the chefs and writers I look to when searching for new recipes online or in books.

For dishes from around the world: Cecilia Chiang and Fuschia Dunlop (China), Julia Child and Richard Olney (France), Madhur Jaffrey and Niloufer Ichaporia King (Indian Subcontinent), Najmieh Batmanglij (Iran), Ada Boni and Marcella Hazan (Italy), Nancy Singleton Hachisu and Shizuo Tsuji (Japan), Yotam Ottolenghi, Claudia Roden, and Paula Wolfert (Mediterranean), Diana Kennedy and Maricel Presilla (Mexico), Andy Ricker and David Thompson (Thailand), Andrea Nguyen and Charles Phan (Vietnam).

For general cooking: James Beard, April Bloomfield, Marion Cunningham, Suzanne Goin, Edna Lewis, Deborah Madison, Cal Peternell, David Tanis, Alice Waters, The Canal House, and *The Joy of Cooking.*

For inspiring writing about food and cooking: Tamar Adler, Elizabeth David, MFK Fisher, Patience Gray, Jane Grigson, and Nigel Slater.

For baking: Josey Baker, Flo Braker, Dorie Greenspan, David Lebovitz, Alice Medrich, Elisabeth Prueitt, Claire Ptak, Chad Robertson, and Lindsey Shere.

For more on the science behind cooking: Shirley Corriher, Harold McGee, J. Kenji Lopez-Alt, Hervé This, and the folks at *Cook's Illustrated.*

ACKNOWLEDGEMENTS

This book is the culmination of fifteen years of cooking and thinking about cooking, and six years of research and writing. Along the way many people have made countless contributions, both large and small. I'd like to express deep gratitude to:

Alice Waters, for creating an immeasurably inspiring and educational community and welcoming me into it as a youngster. For instilling in me the aesthetic and sensual values that guide me in everything I do. For showing me just how much one determined woman with a vision can accomplish.

Michael Pollan and Judith Belzer, for friendship, guidance, and innumerable forms of support over the years, including the earliest encouragement to develop my harebrained ideas about cooking into a formal philosophy, and then a book.

Christopher Lee, for being the ultimate encyclopedic reference, for teaching me to respect my culinary ancestors, for showing me how to take my cooking to the edge, and for teaching me how to taste.

Lori Podraza and Mark Gordon, for patiently allowing me to test every single theory on you.

Thomas W. Dorman, for teaching me the difference between Quality and quality.

All of my teachers: Stephen Booth, Sylvan Brackett, Mary Canales, Dario Cecchini, Siew-Chin Chinn, Rayneil de Guzman, Amy Dencler, Samantha Greenwood, Charlie Hallowell, Robert Hass, Kelsie Kerr, Niloufer Ichaporia King, Charlene Nicholson, Cal Peternell, Dominica Rice, Cristina Roschi, Lindsey Shere, Alan Tangren, David Tanis, and Benedetta Vitali.

Sam Moghannam, Rosie Branson Gill, and Michelle McKenzie at 18 Reasons, and Alexis and Eric Koefoed at Soul Food Farm, for the earliest opportunities to teach and refine *Salt, Fat, Acid, Heat*. And Sasha Lopez, my first—and best—student.

My deeply supportive community of writers, including Chris Colin, Jack Hitt, Doug McGray, Caroline Paul, Kevin West, and everyone at the Notto, past and present: Roxy Bahar, Julie Caine, Novella Carpenter, Bridget Huber, Casey Miner, Sarah C. Rich, Mary Roach, Alec Scott, Gordy Slack, and Malia Wollan.

Sarah Adelman, Laurel Braitman, and Jenny Wapner for formative early input and unwavering friendship.

Twilight Greenaway, for the quinoa, and for being my sister. Justin Limoges, and Marlow Colt Greenaway-Limoges, for being my tummy triplets.

Aaron Hyman, for invariably following every thread of curiosity along with me, and for never letting me compromise.

Kristen Rasmussen for being my science and nutrition heroine. Harold McGee, for support with food science, and Guy Crosby, Michelle Harris, and Laura Katz for help with thorough fact-checking.

Annette Flores, Michelle Fuerst, Amy Hatwig, Carrie Lewis, Amalia Mariño, Lori Oyamada, Laurie Ellen Pellicano, Tom Purtill, Jill Santopietro, Gillian Shaw, and Jessica Washburn for recipe writing and testing support and advice.

The hundreds of home cooks who patiently, faithfully, and diligently tested recipes!

Thomas and Tiffany Campbell, Greta Caruso, Barbara Denton, Lex Denton, Philip Dwelle, and Alex Holey for your appetites, friendship, and for showing me how home cooks think.

Tamar Adler and Julia Turshen, for walking down the path of words and food alongside me.

David Riland, for steadfastness and compassion.

Sarah Ryhanen and Eric Famisan, for my writing room at the farm.

Peter, Kristin, Bodhi, and Bea Becker, for weaving me seamlessly into your fray every time I come to town.

Verlyn Klinkenborg, for *Several Short Sentences about Writing*.

The MacDowell Colony, The Headlands Center for the Arts, and Mesa Refuge for space, time, and invaluable creative support.

Alvaro Villanueva, for bringing endless patience, good humour, and creativity to the challenge of designing a book that breaks all the rules.

Emily Graff, whose keen eye for detail, organizational tendencies, and tireless support have improved this book immeasurably. Ann Cherry, Maureen Cole, Kayley Hoffman, Sarah Reidy, Marysue Rucci, Stacey Sakal, and Dana Trocker, whose work behind the curtain at Simon & Schuster has shaped this book and will give it a life of its own out in the world.

Jenny Lord, for saying just the right things at just the right time from half a world away.

Mike Szczerban, for wisdom and enthusiasm that help set this book on the right path, but more important, for a magical friendship built on a mutual love of books.

Wendy MacNaughton, for a brilliant sense of humour and adventure, a willingness to try anything, pep talks and come-to-Jesus moments, and of course, hard work. I don't know how I got so lucky as to have my favourite artist illustrate my book and become my dear friend along the way. You're unequivocally the best collaborator I could've wished for.

Kari Stuart, my dear friend and indefatigable champion in all things, without whom this book would have never seen the light of day. Amanda Urban, for giving me Kari. Patrick Morley, for being simply the best.

And finally, to my family, who taught me how to eat: Shahla, Pasha, and Bahador Nosrat; my aunts and uncles Leyla, Shahab, Shahram, Shahriar, and Ziba Khazai; and my grandmothers, Parvin Khazai and Parivash Nosrat. *Nooshe joonetan.*

– Samin

Thank you to my wonderful and ever-encouraging parents, Robin and Candy MacNaughton. (Mom, you're the original great chef in my life.)

Thank you to all the friends and family who enjoyed the spoils of one of the cooking/drawings fests, who bolstered us along the way, who gave us your thoughts, wisdom, support, and love. Your cheers were fuel.

A standing ovation for Trish Richman, my studio manager and personal air traffic controller. You are a crucial part of this project. Both the artwork and I would be a total mess without you.

Alvaro Villanueva! Your brilliant design, creative ideas, clear thinking, and patience are all astounding. You make landing hundreds of pieces of artwork look effortless. Thank you.

Thank you Kari Stuart for taking such good care of both Samin and me. You are a champion.

Charlotte Sheedy, my agent, my role model. A hundred cases of the best bourbon isn't enough to thank you for everything you do, which is always way beyond the call of duty in both your work and in the world.

Thank you Caroline Paul, my everything. You were there for every dinner, every clean up, every debrief, every discussion. There is nothing without you. Thank you for opening up our home and our life to this experience. I'm so happy I can cook for you now.

And Samin. When you first approached me to work with you I could barely scramble an egg. Only you—with your humour, patience, kindness, and genuine enthusiasm—could capture my attention like you did and show me how darn fun and fascinating cooking can be. You've changed my life. Thank you. It's an honor and a complete joy to work with you, to make art with you, to be your friend. This BLL's for you.

BIBLIOGRAPHY

Batali, Mario. Crispy Black Bass with Endive Marmellata and Saffron Vinaigrette, in *The Babbo Cookbook*. New York: Clarkson Potter, 2002.

Beard, James. *James Beard's Simple Foods*. New York: Macmillan, 1993.

———. *Theory and Practise of Good Cooking.*

Braker, Flo. *The Simple Art of Perfect Baking.* San Francisco: Chronicle Books, 2003.

Breslin, Paul A. S. "An Evolutionary Perspective on Food and Human Taste." *Current Biology,* Elsevier, May 6, 2013.

Corriher, Shirley. *BakeWise: The Hows and Whys of Successful Baking with Over 200 Magnificent Recipes.* New York: Scribner, 2008.

Crosby, Guy. *The Science of Good Cooking: Master 50 Simple Concepts to Enjoy a Lifetime of Success in the Kitchen.* Brookline, MA: America's Test Kitchen, 2012.

David, Elizabeth. *Spices, Salt and Aromatics in the English Kitchen.* Harmondsworth: Penguin, 1970.

Frankel, E. N., R. J. Mailer, C. F. Shoemaker, S. C. Wang, and J. D. Flynn. "Tests Indicate That Imported 'extra-Virgin' Olive Oil Often Fails International and USDA Standards." *UC Davis Olive Center.* UC Regents, June 2010.

Frankel, E. N., R. J. Mailer, S. C. Wang, C. F. Shoemaker, J. X. Guinard, J. D. Flynn, and N. D. Sturzenberger. "Evaluation of Extra-Virgin Olive Oil Sold in California." *UC Davis Olive Center*. UC Regents, April 2011.

Heaney, Seamus. *Death of a Naturalist*. London: Faber and Faber, 1969.

Holland, Mina. *The Edible Atlas: Around the World in Thirty-Nine Cuisines*. London: Canongate, 2014.

Hyde, Robert J., and Steven A. Witherly. "Dynamic Contrast: A Sensory Contribution to Palatability." *Appetite* 21.1 (1993): 1-16.

King, Niloufer Ichaporia. *My Bombay Kitchen: Traditional and Modern Parsi Home Cooking*. Berkeley: University of California, 2007.

Kurlansky, Mark. *Salt: A World History*. New York: Walker, 2002.

Lewis, Edna. *The Taste of Country Cooking*. New York: A. A. Knopf, 2006.

McGee, Harold. "Harold McGee on When to Put Oil in a Pan." *Diners Journal Harold McGee on When to Put Oil in a Pan Comments. New York Times*, August 6, 2008.

———. *Keys to Good Cooking: A Guide to Making the Best of Foods and Recipes*. New York: Penguin Press, 2010.

———. *On Food and Cooking: The Science and Lore of Cooking*. New York: Scribner, 1984; 2nd ed. 2004.

Mcguire, S. "Institute of Medicine. 2010. Strategies to Reduce Sodium Intake in the United States." Washington, DC: The National Academies Press. *Advances in Nutrition: An International Review Journal* 1.1 (2010): 49-50.

McLaghan, Jennifer. *Fat: An Appreciation of a Misunderstood Ingredient, with Recipes*. Berkeley: Ten Speed Press, 2008.

McPhee, John. *Oranges*. New York: Farrar, Straus and Giroux, 1967.

Montmayeur, Jean-Pierre, and Johannes Le Coutre. *Fat Detection: Taste, Texture, and Post Ingestive Effects*. Boca Raton: CRC/Taylor & Francis, 2010.

Page, Karen, and Andrew Dornenburg. *The Flavour Bible: The Essential Guide to Culinary Creativity, Based on the Wisdom of America's Most Imaginative Chefs*. New York: Little, Brown, 2008.

Pollan, Michael. *Cooked: A Natural History of Transformation*. New York: Penguin, 2014.

Powers of Ten—A Film Dealing with the Relative Size of Things in the Universe and the Effect of Adding Another Zero. By Charles Eames, Ray Eames, Elmer Bernstein, and Philip Morrison. Pyramid Films, 1978.

Rodgers, Judy. *The Zuni Cafe Cookbook*. New York: W. W. Norton, 2002.

Rozin, Elisabeth. *Ethnic Cuisine: The Flavour-Principle Cookbook*. Lexington, MA: S. Greene, 1985.

Ruhlman, Michael. *The Elements of Cooking: Translating the Chef's Craft for Every Kitchen*. New York: Scribner, 2007.

Segnit, Niki. *The Flavour Thesaurus: A Compendium of Pairings, Recipes, and Ideas for the Creative Cook*. New York: Bloomsbury, 2010.

"Smoke: Why We Love It, for Cooking and Eating." *Washington Post*, May 5, 2015.

Stevens, Wallace. *Harmonium*. New York: A. A. Knopf, 1947.

Strand, Mark. *Selected Poems*. New York: Knopf, 1990.

Stuckey, Barb. *Taste What You're Missing: The Passionate Eater's Guide to Why Good Food Tastes Good*. New York: Free, 2012.

Talavera, Karel, Keiko Yasumatsu, Thomas Voets, Guy Droogmans, Noriatsu Shigemura, Yuzo Ninomiya, Robert F. Margolskee, and Bernd Nilius. "Heat Activation of TRPM5 Underlies Thermal Sensitivity of Sweet Taste." *Nature*, 2005.

This, Hervé. *Kitchen Mysteries: Revealing the Science of Cooking=Les Secrets De La Casserole.* New York: Columbia UP, 2007.

———. *Molecular Gastronomy: Exploring the Science of Flavour.* New York: Columbia UP, 2006.

———. *The Science of the Oven.* New York: Columbia UP, 2009.

Waters, Alice, Alan Tangren, and Fritz Streiff. *Chez Panisse Fruit.* New York: HarperCollins, 2002.

Waters, Alice, Patricia Curtan, Kelsie Kerr, and Fritz Streiff. *The Art of Simple Food: Notes, Lessons, and Recipes from a Delicious Revolution.* New York: Clarkson Potter, 2007.

Witherly, Steven A. "Why Humans Like Junk Food." Bloomington: iUniverse Inc., 2007.

Wrangham, Richard W. *Catching Fire: How Cooking Made Us Human.* New York: Basic, 2009.

INDEX

✻ NOTES ✻

About Samin

Samin Nosrat is a writer, teacher, and chef. Called "a go-to resource for matching the correct techniques with the best ingredients" by *The New York Times*, and "the next Julia Child" by NPR's *All Things Considered*, she's been cooking professionally since 2000, when she first stumbled into the kitchen at Chez Panisse restaurant. Among other places, her writing has appeared in *Bon Appétit*, and *The San Francisco Chronicle*, and she has a column in *The New York Times*. She lives, cooks, and gardens in Berkeley, California. *Salt, Fat, Acid, Heat* is her first book. Samin's Netflix TV series of the same name launched in October 2018.

Photo by Grant Delin

About Wendy

Wendy MacNaughton is a *New York Times* bestselling illustrator and graphic journalist whose books include *Meanwhile in San Francisco* (Chronicle), *Knives & Ink* (Bloomsbury), *The Gutsy Girl* (Bloomsbury), *Lost Cat* (Bloomsbury), and *The Essential Scratch and Sniff Guide to Becoming a Wine Expert* (Houghton Mifflin Harcourt). She is a columnist for *The California Sunday Magazine*. She lives in San Francisco with her partner, several four legged animals, and a well used kitchen, thanks to Samin.

Photo by Leslie Sophia Lindell